MyWritingLab™ Online Course (access code required)

for *Writing for Life, Sentences and Paragraphs 3e,* by D. J. Henry

MyWritingLab is an online homework, tutorial, and assessment program that provides engaging experiences for today's instructors and students.

Writing Help for Varying Skill Levels

For students who enter the course at widely varying skill levels, MyWritingLab provides unique, targeted remediation through personalized and adaptive instruction. Starting with a pre-assessment known as the Path Builder, MyWritingLab diagnoses students' strengths and weaknesses on prerequisite writing skills. The results of the pre-assessment inform each student's Learning Path, a personalized pathway for students to work on requisite skills through multimodal activities. In doing so, students feel supported and ready to succeed in class.

Respond to Student Writing with Targeted Feedback and Remediation

MyWritingLab unites instructor comments and feedback with targeted remediation via rich multimedia activities, allowing students to learn from and through their own writing.

- When giving feedback on student writing, instructors can add links to activities that address issues and strategies needed for review. Instructors may link to multimedia resources in Pearson Writer, which include curated content from Purdue OWL.
- In the Writing Assignments, students can use instructor-created peer review rubrics to evaluate and comment on other students' writing.
- Paper review by specialized tutors through Tutor Services is available, as is plagiarism detection through TurnItIn.

Learning Tools for Student Engagement

Learning Catalytics

Generate class discussion, guide lectures, and promote peer-to-peer learning with real-time analytics. MyLab and Mastering with eText now provides Learning Catalytics—an interactive student response tool that uses students' smartphones, tablets, or laptops to engage them in more sophisticated tasks and thinking.

MediaShare

MediaShare allows students to post multimodal assignments easily—whether they are audio, video, or visual compositions—for peer review and instructor feedback. In both face-to-face and online course settings, MediaShare saves instructors valuable time and enriches the student learning experience by enabling contextual feedback to be provided quickly and easily.

Direct Access to MyLab

Users can link from any Learning Management System (LMS) to Pearson's MyWritingLab. Access MyLab assignments, rosters, and resources, and synchronize MyLab grades with the LMS gradebook. New direct, single sign-on provides access to all the personalized learning MyLab resources that make studying more efficient and effective.

Proven Results

No matter how MyWritingLab is used, instructors have access to powerful gradebook reports. These reports provide visual analytics that give insight to course performance at the student, section, or even program level.

Visit www.mywritinglab.com for more information.

THIRD EDITION

Writing for Life

Sentences and Paragraphs

D.J. Henry

Daytona State College

PEARSON

Boston   Columbus   Indianapolis   New York   San Francisco
Amsterdam   Cape Town   Dubai   London   Madrid   Milan   Munich   Paris   Montreal   Toronto
Delhi   Mexico City   São Paulo   Sydney   Hong Kong   Seoul   Singapore   Taipei   Tokyo

Executive Editor: Matthew Wright
Program Manager: Katharine Glynn
Development Editor: Erin Dye
Senior Product Marketing Manager: Jennifer Edwards
Executive Field Marketing Manager: Joyce Nilsen
Media Producer: Marisa Massaro
Content Specialist: Laura Olson
Media Editor: Kara Noonan
Project Manager: Donna Campion
Text Design, Project Coordination, and Electronic Page Makeup: Cenveo® Publisher Services

Program Design Lead: Heather Scott
Cover Designer: Studio Montage
Cover Illustration: Bangkok—nattanan726/ Shutterstock; Hand and Smart Phone—vvoe/ Shutterstock
Senior Manufacturing Buyer: Roy L. Pickering, Jr.
Printer/Binder: RR Donnelley/Roanoke
Cover Printer: Phoenix Color/Hagerstown

Acknowledgments of third-party content appear on pages 501–502, which constitute an extension of this copyright page.

Library of Congress Cataloging-in-Publication Data
Names: Henry, D. J. (Dorothy Jean) author.
Title: Writing for life : sentences and paragraphs / D.J. Henry.
Description: Third Edition. | Boston : Pearson, [2017] | Includes index.
Identifiers: LCCN 2015045205 | ISBN 9780134021706
Subjects: LCSH: English language--Rhetoric--Problems, exercises, etc. |
    Report writing--Problems, exercises, etc. | English
    language--Sentences--Problems, exercises, etc.
Classification: LCC PE1404 .H3976 2017 | DDC 808/.042076--dc23
LC record available at http://lccn.loc.gov/2015045205

10 9 8 7 6 5 4 3 2 1—V082—19 18 17 16

Student Edition ISBN 10: 0-13-402170-3
Student Edition ISBN 13: 978-0-13-402170-6
A la Carte Edition ISBN 10: 0-13-402011-1
A la Carte Edition ISBN 13: 978-0-13-402011-2

www.pearsonhighered.com

Brief Contents

Detailed Contents

PART 1 Getting Ready to Write

PART 4 Punctuation and Mechanics

PART 7 Reading Selections

APPENDIX
The Writing Portfolio MyWritingLab™

New to This Edition of *Writing for Life* . . .

Writing for Life, a two-book series consisting of both a sentences and paragraphs book and a paragraphs and essays book, answers the question students often ask about why they should learn to write well—"What's the point?" *Writing for Life* does more than motivate students; it teaches them to take charge of their own learning and helps them transfer the strategies they currently apply to reading visuals to the tasks of reading and writing text.

More Grammar Exercises

- The grammar chapters have been reorganized to move students from basic sentence-level concerns to issues of style. This new, more-natural progression makes content both easier to find and easier to assign in sequence.

New Readings

- Each reading, visual, and practice activity has been carefully evaluated to ensure that the topics are up-to-date and high-interest for today's students.

- Eight new readings have been added to Part 7, including "Getting Coffee Is Hard to Do" by Stanley Fish, "An American Slave: Written by Himself" by Frederick Douglass, "Gen X is Far From Mars, Gen Y Is Far From Venus: A Primer on How to Motivate A Millennial" By Rob Asghar, "All About Jazz, Uniquely American Music" by Moira E. McLaughlin, "Why War Is Never A Good Idea" by Alice Walker, "Lifetime Effects of Stress and What Causes It" by Rebecca J. Donatelle, "It's Time to Ban High School Football" by Ken Reed, and "The Benefits of Playing Sports Aren't Just Physical!" by the American Orthopaedic Society for Sports Medicine.

New Supporting Media and Deeper MyWritingLab Integration

- New videos on the writing process, the reading process, and creating portfolios help students with different learning styles understand these key concepts.

- Our two chapter-closing activities, "Writing Assignments" and "Academic Learning Logs," can now be completed in MyWritingLab and sent directly to instructors' gradebooks.

- Our unit-closing activities, "Unit Reviews" are available in MyWritingLab.

- The *Writing for Life* MyWritingLab etext course now contains an appendix on portfolio creation and use.

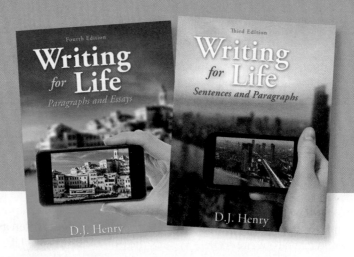

Features of *Writing for Life*

The focus of *Writing for Life* is apparent in the comprehensive and systematic approach to learning it provides by motivating and preparing students; engaging students with high-interest topics and meaningful visuals; establishing purpose and clear statements of learning objectives; offering relevant applications; and meeting today's students where they are.

How Does *Writing for Life* Effectively Motivate and Prepare Students for Success?

WHAT'S THE POINT? is a motivational teaching strategy that addresses the basic question on most students' minds: *Why do I need to know this?* The question and the instructional answer establish the student writer's purpose for studying the chapter. Sample student responses in think-aloud format model critical thinking.

OVERALL INSTRUCTIONAL VOICE establishes a clear, direct, respectful tone that honors adult learners.

EMPHASIS ON ACTIVE LEARNING motivates students to become active learners who assume responsibility for their learning, who reflect upon their progress, and who can and will improve their writing skills.

WRITING ASSIGNMENTS are presented in fully developed prompts that create realistic writing situations that direct students to consider audience and purpose as they employ the full writing process. Additional assignments provide topics and situations relevant to "Everyday Life," "College Life," and "Working Life." These Writing Assignments can also be completed online through MyWritingLab.com.

HIGH-INTEREST TOPICS such as tattoos, stress, obesity, eating disorders, pop culture icons, fashion, movies, music, relationships, natural disasters, heroes, and current events engage student interest and foster self-expression.

How Does *Writing for Life* Engage Students with Illustrations and Visuals?

HIGH-INTEREST VISUALS stimulate interest, clarify concepts, and facilitate student responses. Several visuals are brought to life with new animations accessible through the MyWritingLab/ etext course.

PHOTOGRAPHIC ORGANIZERS activate the thinking process, introduce and illustrate a pattern of organization, and stimulate prewriting activities. A set of photographs is arranged in a concept map that illustrates the structure of a particular pattern of organization.

VISUAL LEARNING ACTIVITIES introduce and facilitate writing assignments; concept maps, charts, graphs, and annotated examples enable students to "see" the concept clearly.

VISUAL INSTRUCTION offers annotated visuals with color-coded highlights that make key concepts jump off the page. Concepts and rules are further defined, explained, and illustrated with charts and graphs.

How Does *Writing for Life* Provide Students with Purpose and Core Learning Objectives (Outcomes)?

LEARNING OUTCOMES are statements that specify what learners will know or be able to do as a result of a learning activity.

PREPARING YOURSELF TO LEARN ABOUT WRITING in Chapter 1 teaches students to evaluate their attitudes, identify learning outcomes, generate a study plan, and create a portfolio that helps them "to track growth . . . organize work . . . and think about" their learning and their writing. Simple and easy-to-follow advice guides students to use checklists, reflective questions, and journal entries as they think about their writing and what they are learning.

SELF-ASSESSMENT TOOLS AND GUIDES include learning outcomes, reflective questions, behavior and attitude surveys, guidelines, checklists, scoring rubrics, and journal entries, complete with examples and explanations. For example, a paragraph scoring guide is introduced and explained and followed by a practice that asks students to score a set of paragraphs using the scoring guide. These activities transfer the responsibility of learning and assessment of learning to the student.

ACADEMIC LEARNING LOGS are end-of-chapter activities that test students' comprehension of the chapter's instruction. These activities can be completed online at MyWritingLab.com.

How Does *Writing for Life* Engage Students with the Writing Process?

EMPHASIS ON THE PROCESS is embedded in instruction throughout the textbook. The writing process is introduced and illustrated in Chapter 2 with a two-page spread of a four-color graphic with explanations of the entire writing process: Prewriting, Drafting, Revising, and Editing. Appropriate writing process icons appear throughout the textbook as signals to guide students through the writing process of particular assignments. Additionally, book-specific writing process videos can be found within the MyWritingLab/etext course.

WORKSHOP: WRITING A PARAGRAPH STEP BY STEP guides students one step at a time through the writing process from prewriting to editing, and each phase is highlighted with a writing process icon, so students know what they are doing at each point in the process, how they are to do it, and why it is important.

THE WRITING SITUATION is explained and illustrated in Chapter 2 in discussions and engaging activities about how the relationships among topic, audience, and purpose impact the creation of a piece of writing. Writing prompts are realistic writing situations based on everyday life, college life, and working life. These writing prompts stimulate role playing and critical thinking skills and illustrate the importance of *Writing for Life*.

DIRECT INSTRUCTION follows a logical order to best ensure comprehension and foster student ownership of the material. Each lesson moves systematically through three distinct phases: before learning activities, during learning activities, and after learning activities. Before, during, and after learning activities make excellent portfolio entries that foster student self-assessment.

TEXT STRUCTURE is covered extensively at every level, including word, sentence, paragraph, and essay levels. Lessons systematically guide students to consider the types and structures of words, phrases, and sentences; patterns of organization; levels of ideas; traits and function of a main idea; major supporting details; minor supporting details; parts of the paragraph; and parts of the essay. Writing prompts encourage students to adapt text structure to realistic writing situations.

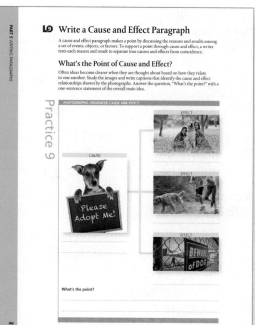

How Does *Writing for Life* Drive Grammar Instruction and Key Applications to Connect with Today's Student?

STUDENT MOTIVATION, always vital, seems to be even more crucial when it comes to mastering grammatical concepts. Unfortunately, too many times, grammar instruction is met with apathy and dread. Grammar has purpose. It's worth the effort to learn it. The purpose of instruction is to foster confidence and mastery. The core features of this text—designed to inspire and motivate—have been adapted to match the nature of instruction for grammatical concepts.

GRAMMATICAL CONCEPTS are comprehensively covered in an approach that combines an illustrated handbook with intensive practice. Examples are clearly annotated visuals with color-coded highlights that make key concepts jump off the page.

Reading Selections

We know that reading enhances our ability to write well. Therefore, the major emphasis within the in-book reader is the connection between reading and writing.

UNDERSTANDING THE CONNECTION BETWEEN READING AND WRITING This section opens with an attitude and behavior survey that asks students to reflect about their individual reading and writing experiences. Then, it explains the benefits a writer gains from reading, illustrates in a chart the similarities between reading and writing, and offers a practice that models the connection between reading and writing skills. Finally, the section closes by emphasizing the thinking processes students can use to make the connection between reading and writing. Students learn how to annotate a text, summarize a text, and read like a writer.

READING SELECTIONS include 18 high-interest essays, both contemporary and traditional, as models of effective writing. Topics cover a wide range of subjects including poverty, culture, careers, and race relations. All reading selections include word count, Grade Level, and Lexile score. The tone and purpose of these essays vary and include distinctive voices such as Amy Tan, Alice Walker, and Benjamin Franklin. In addition, a textbook excerpt of substantial length is included to offer students an opportunity to prepare to read and respond to academic assignments. Students are directed to annotate the text and maintain a vocabulary journal of new or difficult terms they encounter.

AFTER READING DISCUSSION QUESTIONS: MEANING, STRUCTURE, AND EXPRESSION focus student attention on four basic traits of an essay: Main Idea, Relevant Details, Logical Order, and Effective Expression. Many of the activities associated with each reading can be completed in the MyWritingLab/etext course.

THINKING PROMPTS TO MOVE FROM READING TO WRITING offer two fully developed writing situations based on the reading. These prompts ask students to consider audience and purpose as they form a response to what they have read.

Resources

Instructor's Manual for *Writing for Life: Sentences and Paragraphs*
(0-13-394894-3), by Steve Yarborough, is a practical supplement useful in any
classroom setting. The *Instructor's Manual* includes a summary of each chapter
as well as sample syllabi to assist with designing a course around *Writing for
Life: Sentences and Paragraphs*. There is also a complete discussion of how to use
each chapter in the classroom, including supplementary assignments and class
discussions.

Test Bank for *Writing for Life: Sentences and Paragraphs* (0-13-402007-3), by Steve
Yarborough, contains multiple-choice and true/false questions designed to test each
student's comprehension of every chapter.

See the Instructor's Manual for a complete listing of supplements available for
Writing for Life.

BREAKTHROUGH
To improving results

MyWritingLab™ Online Course (access code required)
for *Writing for Life, Sentences and Paragraphs 3e,* by D. J. Henry

MyWritingLab is an online practice, tutorial, and assessment program that provides engaging
experiences for teaching and learning.

MyWritingLab includes most of the writing assignments from your accompanying textbook.
Now, students can complete and submit assignments, and teachers can then track and respond to
submissions easily—right in MyWritingLab—making the response process easier for the instructor
and more engaging for the student.

Respond to Student Writing with Targeted Feedback and Remediation

MyWritingLab unites instructor comments and feedback with targeted remediation via rich
multimedia activities, allowing students to learn from and through their own writing.

Writing Help for Varying Skill Levels

For students who enter the course at widely varying skill levels, MyWritingLab provides unique,
targeted remediation through personalized and adaptive instruction, freeing up more class time for
actual writing.

NEW! Learning Tools for Student Engagement

Learning Catalytics

Generate class discussion, guide lectures, and promote peer-to-peer learning real-time analytics
using Learning Catalytics—an interactive student response tool that uses students' smartphones,
tablets, or laptops to engage them in more sophisticated tasks and thinking.

MediaShare

MediaShare allows students to post multimodal assignments easily—whether they are audio, video,
or visual compositions—for peer review and instructor feedback. In both face-to-face and online
course settings, MediaShare saves instructors valuable time and enriches the student learning
experience by enabling contextual feedback to be provided quickly and easily.

Direct Access to MyLab

Users can link from any Learning Management System (LMS) to Pearson's MyWritingLab.
Access MyLab assignments, rosters and resources, and synchronize MyLab grades with the LMS
gradebook. New direct, single sign-on provides access to all the personalized learning MyLab
resources that make studying more efficient and effective.

Visit www.mywritinglab.com for more information.

Acknowledgments

The publication of a text like this requires the effort and sacrifice of many people. I would like to begin with a heartfelt expression of appreciation for the Pearson English team. *Writing for Life* has afforded me the opportunity to work with and learn from a talented group of people. I thank the editorial team for giving me the opportunity to partner with Dorling Kindersley (DK), whose design so beautifully appeals to visual and verbal learners. I would like to specifically thank Richard Czapnik, Anthony Limerick, and Ian Midson from DK for their hard work on this project. Matt Wright, Executive Editor, is a wonderful partner to whom I am indebted and grateful for his enthusiastic support and active involvement throughout this process. It has been my pleasure and good fortune to work with Developmental Editor Erin Dye whose insights and diligence inspire and guide our through the production process. I also extend my deepest gratitude to Heather Brady, whose contributions to this series as writer and editor are of immeasurable value.

I would like to acknowledge the production team for *Writing for Life* beginning with Kathy Smith from Cenveo® Publisher Services, who served as copyeditor and project coordinator. I am also grateful to Ellen MacElree and Donna Campion, Production Managers. And I would like to acknowledge Dustin Weeks, Senior Professor of Library Sciences, Daytona State College, for his contributions of writing samples for student activities, and Steve Yarborough, Bellevue Community College, for composing the Instructor's Manual.

I would like to gratefully recognize the invaluable insights provided by the following colleagues and reviewers. I deeply appreciate their investment of time, energy, and wisdom. Terry Clark, *City Colleges of Chicago;* Nelda Contreras, *Brookhaven College;* Jay Lewenstein, *Imperial Valley College;* Tim Parrish, *Rockingham Community College;* Kimberly Pope, *South Mountain Community College;* Libby Stapleton, *Angelina College;* Vanessa G. Uriegas, *Southwest Texas Junior College;* Kelly Wilkes, *Columbus Technical College;* William M. Young, *Oglala Lakota College.* Finally, I wish to thank the following students for the honor of working with them; each demonstrated an eagerness to work and learn. I am so proud of their contributions to this edition: Hannah Davis, Joshua Hartzell, and Evan Praetorius.

1

Preparing to Learn about Writing

In countless situations in life, preparation is essential to success. Even a trip to the grocery store requires some planning in order to get all the items necessary to feed a family and run a household in the most economical way. A wise shopper thinks about the health and well-being of those who will consume the goods. She takes steps to buy the best products and foods at the cheapest prices. A careful shopper may create a menu, check the pantry and make a list of what is needed, read the ads for sale items, or clip coupons. In short, an effective shopper thinks about the outcome or goal of each shopping trip before she goes shopping.

Writing is an essential life skill, and learning to write well allows you to express yourself, influence others, succeed in college, and compete in the job market. By starting your academic career with this writing course, you are preparing for success. You are laying a sturdy foundation for writing for life. If you are like many others, you may have a few qualms about writing, but take heart! With the right attitude, a study plan, and clear goals, you can count on having good outcomes. You *can* learn to write well. So get ready to learn about writing!

Grocery List

Produce

Meat / deli
cooked chicken
...beef

zucchini
red onion
banannas
oranges

What's the Point of Preparing to Learn about Writing?

Like any other worthwhile endeavor, learning requires preparation. Preparation usually involves selecting a goal, adopting an attitude for success, setting aside time to accomplish the task, gathering tools or supplies, and planning a course of action.

PHOTOGRAPHIC ORGANIZER: PREPARING TO LEARN ABOUT WRITING

The following pictures represent one student's effort to prepare to learn about writing. Write a caption for each photograph that identifies her efforts to prepare to learn.

What is this?

....

....

....

What is this?

....

....

....

....

What is this?

....

....

....

....

What is this?

....

....

....

....

What's the point?

....

....

....

Practice 1

WRITING
FROM LIFE

One Student Writer's Response

The following paragraph records one student's efforts to prepare to learn about writing. As you read the paragraph, underline specific steps he took that you might use as well.

My Plan for Success

(1) I am very nervous about taking this English course! (2) Our professor Mrs. Hawkins gave the whole class advice about getting ready to learn about writing. (3) I am going to take her advice and create a study space and a study plan. (4) I have set up a study area in my bedroom with a table, chair, desk lamp, and computer. (5) On my desk are a dictionary, thesaurus, paper, pens, pencils, pencil sharpener, stapler, and hole-puncher. (6) The next step is to make a study schedule based on the list of assignments in the course syllabus. (7) I will study for this class every Monday, Tuesday, and Thursday evening from 5:00 p.m. until 7:00 p.m. (8) Also, I will study with Sherri, Jamal, and Anton every Wednesday for an hour after our class. (9) Our study group is going to be great! (10) If one of us has to miss class, we can get class notes and assignments from someone in the group. (11) I am also going to ask questions in class or see my teacher for help. (12) For example, Mrs. Hawkins makes notes on our papers about what needs more work. (13) I am going to make a list of the things I don't understand and ask her to explain them. (14) I am going to do my best.

As you prepare to learn about writing, take some time to evaluate yourself as a student writer. Think about your attitude, ways you can become an active learner, your relationship with your teacher, your study plan, and how you will track your growing writing abilities. The more you reflect and the more you prepare, the more likely you are to learn about writing and to become an effective writer.

L2 Adopt the Attitude of Learning

Use Positive Self-Talk

Many people have negative thoughts going through their minds that constantly repeat "I can't" phrases: "I can't write…. I can't spell." Often these attitudes are the result of a prior negative event. A basic step to success is changing that script in your head. Replace "I can't" thoughts with "I can." Then, take steps to prove that you can. For example, instead of believing "I just can't spell," think, "I can use a spell checker," or "I can make a list of words I often misspell and memorize their correct spellings." Success begins in your mind!

Be an Active Learner

Come to class. Be on time. Sit where you can see—and be seen. Take notes. Ask questions. Do your work—on time! Make connections between assignments and learning outcomes. Apply what you learn. Seek help. Find a study partner. Take responsibility for your own learning. The more you do, the more you learn!

Trust Your Teacher

One of the toughest tasks in a writing class is getting and accepting feedback on your writing. Many of us take the teacher's feedback as a personal rejection. Some of us become defensive. Think of feedback as a form of coaching from a personal trainer. A personal trainer assesses your strengths and needs, creates an exercise program, and corrects your form to ensure that you make progress. Likewise, your teacher is your writing coach who offers expert advice. So accept feedback as helpful advice. Take note of those errors, study the rules, and revise your work. Turn feedback into an opportunity to learn!

ADOPT THE ATTITUDE OF LEARNING

Read the following reflection written by a student that records how she feels about writing and why. On a separate sheet of paper, write a letter to her, giving her advice to help her overcome her anxiety.

I have some bad memories about writing. I will never forget one teacher; I call him "Mr. Gotcha." My papers were never good enough for him. At first, I spent a lot of time coming up with something to write about. It didn't matter how much time I spent, he always put red marks all over my papers, and he always gave me Ds. I never read his comments. I mean what was the point? I think he didn't like me because I was quiet and sat in the back of the class. On one day, I didn't hear the page number he told us to turn to, so I asked "where are we at?" And instead of answering my question, he said, "At? At? You are nowhere when you end a sentence with a preposition!" I had no idea what he was talking about. I still avoid writing as much as I can.

Practice 2

LO③ Create a Study Plan

A vital part of preparing to learn about writing is creating a study plan.

Gather Your Tools

Foster success by creating a place to study that is equipped with all the tools you will need: reference materials such as your textbook, a dictionary, and a thesaurus; pens (blue or black ink), pencils, and paper; a stapler and a 3-hole punch. Optional items include a computer and a printer. In addition, you will need a 3-ring binder to file the teacher's syllabus, handouts, assignments, class notes, textbook notes, and lab work. Be sure that you bring your textbook, binder, pens, and pencils to class every day.

Set Goals

Students who set goals reduce stress, improve concentration, and increase self-confidence. Use the following general guidelines to set effective goals. Aim high: Demand your best effort. Write goals down: Recording goals makes them clear and important. Be specific: Instead of writing, "Stop procrastinating," write, "Study English on Monday, Tuesday, and Wednesday evenings between 7 and 9 o'clock." Be positive: Instead of writing, "Don't make stupid errors," write, "Use commas properly." Set priorities: Rank goals based on need so you can pace your work. Set daily goals based on larger goals: Break a larger goal such as "Understand how to use semicolons" into a series of steps such as "Study the rule, take notes, and do the exercises; then proofread my paper for proper use of semicolons."

Take Action

Turn your goals into action steps by setting up a time schedule for your study. The following study plan is easy to use, flexible, and will help you set long-term, intermediate, and short-term goals.

SAMPLE STUDY PLAN	
Long-Term Schedule:	*Record ongoing weekly commitments such as job hours, class meetings, church, and so on, for the entire semester.*
Intermediate Schedule:	*Make a short list of the events taking place and the tasks to be completed in your class (or classes) this week. Make a fresh list each week, as these activities will change from week to week: Writing assignment Tuesday; Math quiz Tuesday; Chapter 3 in English by Wednesday.*
Short-Term Schedule:	*List your daily schedule. Be specific! Then, cross off each goal as you accomplish it. Monday: 9:00–9:30 Revise writing assignment; 12:00–12:30 Review math for quiz; 3:30 Return books to library.*

CREATE A STUDY PLAN

Complete the following chart to create your own study plan. Discuss your plan with your class or in a small group. How will your plan change throughout the semester?

SAMPLE STUDY PLAN

Long-Term Schedule:	
Intermediate Schedule:	
Short-Term Schedule:	

ADOPT THE ATTITUDE AND BEHAVIORS OF LEARNING

Complete the survey.

WRITING ATTITUDE AND BEHAVIOR SURVEY	Strongly Agree	Agree	Disagree	Strongly Disagree
1. I enjoy writing.				
2. Teacher feedback is discouraging.				
3. I enjoy sharing what I write with peers.				
4. I want to improve my writing.				
5. I have a quiet, well-equipped study place.				
6. I always come to class prepared.				
7. I complete assignments on time.				
8. I read and study to improve my writing.				
9. I manage my time wisely.				
10. I need to improve my writing attitude or behavior.				

L4 Monitor Your Mastery of Learning Outcomes

A **learning outcome** states what a student should know or be able to do as the result of a lesson or course of study. In *Writing for Life*, student writer outcomes are listed on the first page of each chapter. If you think about these learning outcomes as you study, your writing will improve more quickly. Notice the learning outcomes are stated as actions. Every assignment is an opportunity to prove mastery of one or more of these learning outcomes.

Practice 5

MONITOR YOUR MASTERY OF LEARNING OUTCOMES

To track your mastery of learning outcomes for student writers, answer the following questions.

1. What are the learning outcomes for this chapter?

2. Which of the chapter learning outcomes are also on your course syllabus?

3. Which outcomes have you already mastered? How could you prove mastery?

4. Which outcomes do you need to master? Write them in order from most important to know to least important to know.

5. How will you tie learning outcomes to the goals you set in your study plan?

Use the Reading Process to Strengthen Your Writing

Reading and writing are closely related thinking processes in two basic ways. First, both are ways of making meaning. When we read, we make meaning of a text composed by someone else. When we write, we make meaning by composing our own text. A reader receives a message; a writer sends a message. To understand a text or message, a reader thinks about the writer, the writer's background, and the writer's purpose for writing. Likewise, to send a text or message that is understandable, a writer thinks about the reader (audience), the reader's background, and the reader's purpose for reading. Thus, reading and writing rely on and strengthen each other. For example, reading benefits a writer in many ways. A writer gains the following by reading:

- New vocabulary
- Different opinions on a topic
- Details that support an opinion
- Additional facts about a topic

- Ways to apply writing skills:
  - How to punctuate
  - How to use fresh or creative expressions
  - How to vary sentences
  - How to organize ideas
  - How to create introductions and conclusions

Another way in which reading and writing are related is that they are both thinking processes best accomplished in specific stages. Careful thought before, during, and after reading a selection or writing a piece improves your ability to do both. The following chart shows the similarities between each stage of the reading and writing process.

The Thinking Process Connects Reading and Writing		
Thinking	**Reading**	**Writing**
Before	**Preread:** Ask questions and skim the text; note headings, words in bold or italics, or graphics; predict the author's audience, purpose, and point.	**Prewrite:** Ask questions and skim details to discover your audience, purpose, and point for writing; read for information to use in your writing.
During	**Read:** Comprehend the writer's purpose and point with the use of key words, main ideas, and supporting details. **Apply fix-up strategies:** Use context clues to understand new words; reread a few sentences or a paragraph; make a mental picture of the point.	**Draft:** Express your purpose and point through the use of key words, main ideas, and supporting details. **Revise:** Rephrase or reorganize ideas to clearly support your point; help readers to see your purpose and point; use details to create a mental picture for your reader.
After	**Reflect and Record:** Adjust your views based on new information gained through reading; write in response to what you have read; restate the writer's main points; agree or disagree with what you have read.	**Edit and Publish:** Create an error-free draft that expresses your new insights and skills as a writer.

Analyze the Reading Process to Strengthen Your Writing

Reading is a thinking process composed of a series of phases. The process is recursive; that is, the reader may loop or combine any of the stages at any point during the process. The following graphic illustrates the highly recommended **SQ3R** reading process

Watch the Video on mywritinglab.com

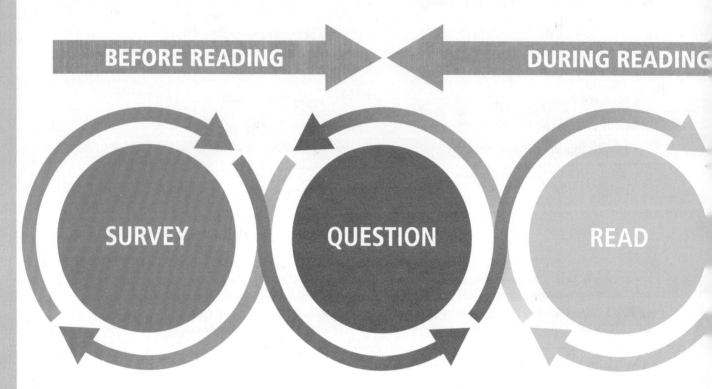

BEFORE READING

DURING READING

SURVEY

QUESTION

READ

Skim the selection to note the following: titles, subheadings, key terms in bold or italic type, graphics, pictures.

Ask the following: What is the topic? What do I already know? What is the author's purpose? How are the ideas organized? What is my purpose for reading?

Read to answer questions; adjust pace based on difficulty; reread to understand.

Practice 6

USE READING TO STRENGTHEN YOUR WRITING PROCESS

Reflect upon your own reading and writing processes by responding to the following.

1. Describe how you read. What method or process do you use to read?

2. Describe how you write. What steps do you take to write?

3. How are your thinking processes similar to or different from the ones described in the chart?

4. Predict how you can use reading to strengthen your writing.

AFTER READING

RECITE

REVIEW

Annotate the text; underline main ideas; circle key terms; record questions and short summaries in margins; restate ideas out loud.

Review questions based on headings; review new words; connect new ideas to prior knowledge; write a response.

USE THE READING PROCESS TO STRENGTHEN YOUR WRITING

Working with a peer or small group of classmates, answer the following questions:

1. How is each chapter in *Writing for Life* based on SQ3R?

2. How will using SQ3R to study this material help you improve as a writer?

3. Besides this material, what else can you, as a writer, read?

4. As a writer, how would you use SQ3R to get information from a magazine or newspaper?

5. How could you use SQ3R to edit a peer's paper?

Practice 7

Use the Flow of the Reading-Writing Interaction to Strengthen Your Writing

In this textbook, you will learn in depth about the writing process, and you will apply the writing process to your own writing. As you learn and apply the writing process, your writing will benefit if you use the flow of the interaction between reading and writing. At times, your professor may ask you to respond in writing to an assigned reading. At other times, you may choose to read independently to seek out ideas for your own writing. The following graphic and text suggest how to use the flow of the interaction between reading and writing. Also keep in mind that you can use the flow between reading and writing as a way to study this or any other textbook.

👁 Watch the Video on mywritinglab.com

PREREAD: SURVEY/ QUESTION

READ: QUESTION/ ANNOTATE

PREWRITE: RECITE/REVIEW/ BRAINSTORM

Preread: Survey/Question

- Create questions based on a survey of titles, headings, bold/italic terms, and visuals.

Ask:

- What is my prior knowledge of this topic?
- What is my purpose for reading?
- Who is the intended audience?

Read: Question/Annotate

- Continue to ask/record questions.
- Underline main ideas.
- Circle new or key words.
- Highlight key supporting details.
- Restate ideas out loud.

Ask:

- What prior knowledge can I use to make inferences about the text's meaning?
- What evidence allows me to make those inferences?

Prewrite: Recite/Review/Brainstorm

List, cluster, or outline topics based on your survey; leave room to fill in details during reading. Record predicted answers.

- Freewrite to analyze prior knowledge, purpose for reading, and audience.
- Freewrite a first response to the text.
- Take notes/Recite ideas: Record main ideas in your own words.
- Add supporting details from the reading to the list, cluster, or outline of key topics.
- Brainstorm/list topics from the reading to respond to in writing.
- Identify the intended audience of your writing.
- Compose an outline of ideas for your written response.

Draft

- Read your annotated text.
- Freewrite a response based on the completed list, cluster, or outline of key topics and details.
- Compose a thesis statement for your response.
- Compose an introduction, body, and conclusion of your response to the reading.

Review and Revise Your Draft

- Review your draft for clear use of wording, details, and organization.
- Annotate your draft with needed revisions.
- Rewrite your draft based on your review and annotations.

Proofread

- Reread your draft to identify/correct errors.
- Annotate your draft with needed corrections.
- Create and publish a polished draft.

USE READING TO STRENGTHEN YOUR WRITING

Work with a group of peers. Predict ways you can use the interaction between reading and writing to strengthen your writing.

Practice 8

Watch the Video on mywritinglab.com

L⑥ Create a Portfolio of Your Work

To ensure that you learn about writing and to develop writing skills, you need to track your strengths, your needs, and your growth. A portfolio enables you to organize your work and think about what you are learning.

What Is a Portfolio?

A portfolio is a collection of all the work you do as a writer organized in a notebook or in an electronic folder. Your portfolio shows how much time and effort you put into studying and practicing your writing. A portfolio allows you to assess your own strengths and needs, and to prove your learning outcomes. In your portfolio, you can show which learning outcomes you are working toward. You can also display the learning outcomes you have achieved. Your portfolio shows what you know and what you are able to do as a student writer.

What Should I Include in My Portfolio?

Your portfolio may include class notes and activities, textbook notes and exercises, grammar tests, lab activities, reflective journal entries, prewrites, drafts, revisions, edited drafts, and polished copies of your writing. By collecting and organizing your work, you are better able to reflect upon your strengths and needs. As a result, you are able to achieve the learning outcomes you need to as a writer. You should keep in your portfolio all the prewrites, drafts, and final copies of your writings. In addition, each of the lessons, practices, workshops, and learning logs in this textbook is tied to one or more learning outcomes. And the heading of each practice identifies its learning outcome. So the learning activities in *Writing for Life* are excellent entries for your portfolio.

What Is a Reflective Journal Entry?

A reflective journal entry is an informal piece of writing. When you reflect, you self-evaluate your work as a student writer. For example, you may write a journal entry that lists and responds to the feedback that your teacher gave on a piece of your writing. In this type of journal entry, you reflect upon both your "writing process" and your "writing progress."

Reflective Journals: Self-Evaluation

Critical Thinking Questions

To deepen your critical thinking about the feedback you have received, your reflective journal entry should answer the following questions:

☐ What steps did I take to write this piece? Did I prewrite, write, revise, and proofread? Do I need to spend more time on any one step?

☐ Which of my errors are proofreading errors? What steps will I take to catch these proofreading errors in my next piece of writing?

☐ Which of these errors results from the need to study a certain rule? Where can I find this rule? How much time do I need to learn this rule? How will I study this rule (take notes, complete exercises)?

What Is the Best Way to Set Up My Portfolio?

Many students purchase a 3-ring binder and tabbed dividers to section off different types of study and writing tasks. Be sure to date and label all work.

All work that is turned in for feedback should include the following information: At the top of the first page and flush with the left margin, place your name, your professor's name, the course name or number (include the section number if the course has multiple sections), and the date you're turning in the paper, each on a separate line with double-spacing throughout.

Iama Writer

Dr. Richards

ENC 001: Section 32

September 24, 2015

All independent work that is created for your notebook or portfolio should be labeled with the date and the type of work or learning outcome:

Oct. 9, 2015
Reflective Journal Entry for Narrative Paragraph

Oct. 10, 2015
Comma Splices, Chapter 7, pp. 118–133

Oct. 12, 2015
The Process Paragraph, Class notes

The point of labeling is to help you see and discuss your strengths and needs as they occur in real time.

Practice 9

Write an e-mail to a classmate who missed class. Explain the portfolio process. Explain how portfolio assessment will improve critical thinking.

L7 Learn the Elements of Language

Writing is the act of recording meaningful ideas using text as symbols to represent spoken sounds. When we write ideas, we often do so in units of meaningful thoughts, just as we do when we speak. You may already know something about these units of thoughts.

- A **word** is as a meaningful unit of language made up of one or more spoken sounds and their written symbols—letters.

- A **phrase** is a closely related unit of words that does not express a complete thought.

- A **sentence** is a closely related unit of words that expresses a complete thought as a statement, command, or question.

- A **paragraph** is a series of closely related sentences dealing with a specific point or idea.

- An **essay** is a series of closely related paragraphs dealing with a specific point or idea.

Words combine to form phrases. Phrases form sentences. Sentences form paragraphs. Paragraphs form essays. As you can see, words are the foundation of everything. Thus, words are sorted into classes or parts of speech based on their purpose and use. These parts of speech make up the *elements of language.* Effective writers study and apply these key elements of language to improve their writing.

Elements of Language: Parts of Speech	
Nouns	Words used to name ideas, objects, people, places, or animals
Pronouns	Words used instead of nouns
Verbs	Words used to assert an action or state of being
Adjectives	Words used to describe nouns
Adverbs	Words used to tell how, when, or where an action is performed
Prepositions	Words used before nouns and pronouns to connect them with other words
Conjunctions	Words used to connect other words and sentences
Interjections	Words used to imply emotion or feelings

Use the following mnemonic poem to cue you into the parts of speech and prepare you for further study and writing. You will learn more about each element in various parts of this textbook. Your teacher may give you feedback on your use of these elements in your writing.

> A noun's the name of anything,
> As: "school" or "garden," "toy," or "swing."
>
> A pronoun replaces any noun
> As: "it," "he," or "they" can be a clown
>
> Adjectives tell the kind of noun,
> As: "great," "small," "pretty," "white," or "brown."
>
> And like these three little words you often see—
> The articles: "a," "an," and "the."
>
> Verbs tell of something being done:
> "To read," "write," "count," "sing," "jump," or "run."
>
> Verbs may also speak of being in a state
> as: I "am," he "is," you "are," they "were" late.
>
> How things are done the adverbs tell,
> As: "slowly," "quickly," "badly," "well."
>
> Conjunctions join the words together,
> As: men "and" women, wind "or" weather.
>
> The preposition stands before
> A noun as: "in" or "through" a door.
>
> The interjection shows surprise
> As: "Oh, how pretty!" "Ah! How wise!"
>
> The whole are called the parts of speech,
> Which reading, writing, speaking teach.

> —Adapted from Tower David B. and Benjamin F. Tweed. *Tower's Elements: First Lessons in Language; or Elements of English Grammar.* Daniel Burgess & Co. NY: 1855. pp. 27–28.

Some students prefer to focus on mastering words, phrases, and sentences before learning how to compose paragraphs or essays. They then sharpen their use of the elements as they brainstorm, draft, and revise their writing. Make mastering the elements of language one of your ongoing learning goals.

LEARN THE ELEMENTS OF LANGUAGE: WHAT I KNOW—WHAT I NEED TO LEARN

Test what you already know about the elements of language. And to help you set study goals, complete this short self-assessment. On the line to the left, write the part of speech of the word in **bold.** To the right, substitute a different word for the word in **bold.** Write the answers to questions 9 and 10 in your portfolio.

1. _____ She walked to the **school**. _____

2. _____ A raccoon ran **into** the garage. _____

3. _____ He wanted cake **and** ice cream. _____

4. _____ He **walks** a mile everyday. _____

5. _____ The cat purred **softly.** _____

6. _____ **Our** team easily won the game. _____

1 PREPARING TO LEARN ABOUT WRITING

7. _____   Tomas bought an **expensive** car.   _____

8. _____   **Hey!** Slow down!   _____

9. What elements of language do you already know you have mastered? Explain.

10. What do you find most difficult or confusing about the elements of language? Explain.

Academic Learning Log: Chapter Review

QUESTIONS FOR PREPARING TO LEARN

To test and track your understanding of what you have studied, answer the following questions.

1. What are some of the materials and supplies needed by a writing student?

_____

_____

_____

2. What are the three attitudes of learning discussed in this chapter?

_____

_____

_____

3. What three general steps can you take to create a study plan?

_____

_____

_____

4. What is a learning outcome?

_____

_____

_____

5. What are the learning outcomes for this chapter?

6. How are the reading process and writing process similar?

7. How can reading improve writing?

8. What is a portfolio? What is included in a portfolio?

PORTFOLIO

9. What is a reflective journal entry?

10. What are the elements of language?

MyWritingLab™

Complete the Post-test for Chapter 1 in MyWritingLab.

2 Nouns and Pronouns

A noun names a person, animal, place, or thing. A pronoun stands in the place of a noun that has been clearly identified earlier in the text.

Thinking about a real-life situation helps us to understand the purpose of nouns and pronouns in our communication. The following photographs are from the movie *The Hunger Games: Catching Fire*. Study the pictures, complete the activity, and answer the question "What's the point of learning about nouns and pronouns?"

What's the Point of Nouns and Pronouns?

LO1

WRITING
FROM LIFE

PHOTOGRAPHIC ORGANIZER: NOUNS AND PRONOUNS

Read the following short review of *The Hunger Games: Catching Fire,* the science fiction-adventure film based on the book by Suzanne Collins. The film stars Jennifer Lawrence as the main character, Katniss Everdeen, who defies the corruption in the fictional nation of Panem. Work with a small group of your peers; fill in the blanks with the nouns and pronouns that have been omitted from each sentence. Answer the question "What's the point of learning about nouns and pronouns?"

_____ has become a widely popular _____. First, _____ was a best-selling _____ of three _____, written by _____. Then, _____ became a blockbuster _____ of _____. The main _____ is a young _____ named _____. _____ lives in a poor _____ of the _____ called _____. This popular and fast-paced _____ vividly depicts the age-old _____ between _____ and _____.

What's the point of learning about nouns and pronouns?

_____

_____

One Student Writer's Response

The following paragraph offers one writer's reaction to the activity based on "Review of *The Hunger Games: Catching Fire*"

> *This was a challenging activity, like putting together a puzzle with missing pieces. It was fun trying to figure it out with a group. We all came up with so many different ways to fill in each blank. We really had to study the words around each blank for clues. The activity taught me that we use nouns or pronouns in every statement we make, and without them, our ideas don't make sense.*

LO2 Identify Types and Uses of Nouns

Often, nouns are the first words we learn to speak as we hear the names of people and things that we want or need. The word "noun" comes from the Latin word *nomen*, which means "name." A **noun** names a person, animal, place, object, element, action, or concept.

One type of noun is the proper noun. A **proper noun** names an individual person, place, or thing. Proper nouns are always capitalized. The second type of noun is the common noun. A **common noun** is a general name for any member of a group or class. Common nouns are not capitalized.

Practice 2

IDENTIFY TYPES OF NOUNS

Complete the following chart. Use appropriate capitalization. Share your answers with a small group of peers or your class.

WHAT A NOUN NAMES	COMMON NOUNS	PROPER NOUNS
Person	politician	....
Animal	....	Lassie
Place	city	....
Object	vehicle	....
Element	....	none
Action	....	none
Concept	religion	....

A proper or common noun can function in a sentence as a subject, an object of a verb, an object of a preposition, or an appositive (which describes another noun).

Uses of a Noun

Function in Sentence   **Example**

PROPER NOUN AS SUBJECT

• Subject

Roberto has arrived.

VERB   *PROPER NOUN AS OBJECT OF VERB "ORDERED"*

• Object of a verb

Maria ordered a Coca-Cola.

PREPOSITION   *COMMON NOUN AS OBJECT OF THE PREPOSITION "AT"*

• Object of a preposition

We were at the theater.

SUBJECT (PROPER NOUN)   *COMMON NOUN AS APPOSITIVE DESCRIBING "CHRIS"*

• Appositive (describes another noun)

Chris is my hero.

IDENTIFY USES OF A NOUN

Locate the nouns in the following sentences. Then, identify the type and use of each noun by completing the charts below each sentence.

1. A superhero has superhuman powers and usually fights evil or crime.

NOUN	TYPE	FUNCTION

2. Superman, also known as Clark Kent, can fly, shoot beams of energy, move at supersonic speeds, and lift incredible amounts of weight.

NOUN	TYPE	FUNCTION

Practice 3

For more information on irregular spellings, see pages 242–259, "Improving Your Spelling."

L③ Recognize Count and Noncount Nouns

Count nouns name distinct individual units of a group or category. Count nouns usually refer to what we can see, hear, or touch. Count nouns are typically common nouns and can be singular or plural. Most plural count nouns are formed by adding *-s* or *-es*. However, many singular count nouns use irregular spellings in their plural form.

Examples of Count Nouns		
	Singular	**Plural**
Regular	character, story	characters, stories
Irregular	child, woman	children, women

Noncount nouns name a nonspecific member of a group or category. Noncount nouns, which are typically common nouns, do not have plural forms. Noncount nouns name things that cannot be divided into smaller parts. Often, noncount nouns represent a group of count nouns. The following chart illustrates the differences between noncount and count nouns.

Examples of Noncount and Corresponding Count Nouns	
Noncount Noun	**Count Noun**
money	pennies, nickels, dimes, coins, dollars, bills
time	days, weeks, months, years, eras

Practice 4

RECOGNIZE COUNT AND NONCOUNT NOUNS

Read the following sentences. Identify each **boldfaced** noun as a count or a noncount noun.

1. In *X-men*, the **series** of **movies,** Mystique is a dangerous **villain.**

2. She has scaly blue **skin** and yellow reptilian **eyes.**

3. She is a **shapeshifter** who can take on the **form** of other **humans** or **objects.**

4. She is also a **nudist** who loathes **clothing.**

5. Mystique's exact **age** remains unknown, but her own **words** indicate she is over 100 years old.

▲ *X-men: Days of Future Past*

Match Articles and Nouns

L0④

An **article** is an adjective that describes a noun as general or specific. An article indicates the noun's relationship to a larger group. The following graphic illustrates the general guidelines for use of an article before a noun.

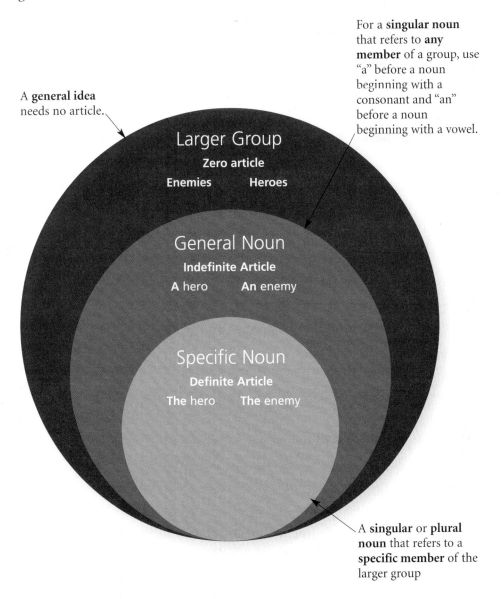

For a **singular noun** that refers to **any member** of a group, use "a" before a noun beginning with a consonant and "an" before a noun beginning with a vowel.

A **general idea** needs no article.

Larger Group
Zero article
Enemies   Heroes

General Noun
Indefinite Article
A hero   **An** enemy

Specific Noun
Definite Article
The hero   **The** enemy

A **singular** or **plural noun** that refers to a **specific member** of the larger group

---

MATCH NOUNS AND ARTICLES

Read the sentences below. Insert the correct article (*a*, *an*, or *the*) in the spaces in front of each noun. If no article is required, leave the space blank.

Of all (1) _____ types of movies, Justine loves (2) _____ action movies best. She enjoys (3) _____ special effects and (4) _____ action scenes. (5) _____ chase scene puts her on (6) _____ edge of her seat. (7) _____ example of (8) _____ good movie, according to her, (9) is _____ oldie-goldie, (10) _____ *Terminator*.

Practice 5

L5 Create Pronoun and Antecedent Agreement

Pronouns and antecedents work closely together to communicate an idea. A **pronoun** refers to or stands in the place of a noun that has been clearly identified earlier in the discussion. An **antecedent** is the noun to which a pronoun refers. Every pronoun should refer clearly and specifically to one particular antecedent.

ANTECEDENT OF PRONOUN "HE"   *PRONOUN "HE" REFERS TO ANTECEDENT "SUPERHERO"*

The modern superhero is a symbol of the culture from which he comes.

In the preceding example, the pronoun clearly refers to the antecedent.

For more information on using precision in drafting sentences, see pages 386–397, "Sentence Clarity: Point of View, Number, and Tense."

Make Pronouns and Antecedents Agree

A pronoun and its antecedent must agree with each other in three ways: person, number, and gender. The following chart presents pronouns based on these traits.

Pronouns: Person, Number, and Gender		
	Singular	**Plural**
First Person	I, me, my, mine	we, us, ours
Second Person	you, yours	you, yours
Third Person	he, him, his (**masculine**) she, her, hers (**feminine**) it, its (**neutral**)	they, their, theirs (**neutral**)

Pronoun agreement makes the relationship between a pronoun and its antecedent obvious and clear. **Faulty pronoun agreement** reflects vague wording and results in reader confusion. Remembering a few guidelines can help you establish pronoun agreement.

Guidelines for Clear Pronoun Agreement

- Pronoun choice establishes consistent use of the person of pronouns.
- Singular pronouns refer to or replace singular nouns.
- Plural pronouns refer to or replace plural nouns.
- Feminine pronouns refer to or replace feminine nouns.
- Masculine pronouns refer to or replace masculine nouns.
- Use gender-neutral plural pronouns and antecedents to make statements that could apply to women or men.

Practice 6

CREATE PRONOUN AND ANTECEDENT AGREEMENT

▲ Marlon Brando in *Superman*

Underline the antecedent of each pronoun in the following sentences. Then, fill in the blank with a pronoun that agrees with its antecedent. Refer to the chart on page 26.

1. The concept of the hero, along with .... distinct traits, is found in almost every culture.

2. In ancient stories, the hero is someone of noble birth; .... parents are divine or royal, wealthy, and highly respected.

3. Likewise, the modern superheroes Superman and Batman are of noble birth; .... both have powerful, wealthy, well-respected parents.

4. Superman is born to noble parents; .... is Kal-El, the son of Jor-El, a senior statesman of the planet Krypton.

5. Batman, also known as Bruce Wayne, is born to a family with a billion-dollar business; ..... is a vast and powerful company.

6. The classical hero is often separated from or abandoned by .... parents.

7. Jor-El foresees the destruction of .... home planet, so .... seals .... son in a

   space-basket and sends......... across the galaxy to Earth.

8. When .... is just a boy, Batman is also separated from .... parents; .... are

   murdered before .... eyes.

9. The modern superhero shares another trait with the classical hero; .... is the rescue or adoption of the hero by surrogate parents.

10. For example, the loyal butler Alfred of Bruce Wayne (Batman) becomes .... father figure, and the childless Kents find and adopt Kal-El (Superman) as ....son.

L6 Correct Faulty Pronoun Agreement

Faulty pronoun agreement usually occurs when the guidelines for clear agreement are ignored. Once you understand why faulty pronoun agreement occurs and how it can be corrected, you can avoid vague agreements in your writing; then, you can create pronoun agreement based on person, number, and gender.

Correct Faulty Pronoun Agreement due to Shift in Person

PROBLEM: When the person of the pronoun differs from the person of the antecedent, it is called a faulty **shift in person**. In the example below, the faulty shift is from third person to second person.

THIRD-PERSON ANTECEDENT "PERSON" DOES NOT AGREE WITH SECOND-PERSON PRONOUN "YOUR"

A person's thoughts lead to your actions.

CORRECTION #1: Correct the shift in person by changing the antecedent to agree with the pronoun.

REVISED SECOND-PERSON ANTECEDENT AGREES WITH SECOND-PERSON PRONOUN

Your thoughts lead to your actions.

CORRECTION #2: Correct by changing the pronoun to agree with the antecedent.

THIRD-PERSON ANTECEDENT AGREES WITH REVISED THIRD-PERSON PRONOUN

A person's thoughts lead to her actions.

Practice 7

CORRECT PRONOUN AGREEMENT BASED ON PERSON

Edit the following sentences for pronoun agreement based on person.

1. The behaviors we choose are influenced by your attitude about the behavior.

2. For example, if you don't like or value math, one is less likely to study the subject.

3. Our attitudes have two elements; one is your beliefs, and the other is your feelings.

4. If you believe you can do something, then most likely he can.

5. The strength of a person's belief in something or someone affects your attitude about the object of his belief.

6. A person can measure your feelings in three ways.

7. We can measure your feelings by evaluating how a person feels about a person, object, or event.

8. First, a person should evaluate your attitude as good or bad, positive or negative, accepting or unaccepting.

9. Often, when you change a person's behavior to get a reward or avoid punishment, your attitude also changes.

10. Sometimes an attitude changes when you try to be like someone he admires, so you adopt his or her attitude.

Correct Faulty Pronoun Agreement due to Shift in Number

PROBLEM: In a sentence with a faulty **shift in number,** the pronoun is a different number than the number of the antecedent. In the two examples below, the faulty shift is from singular to plural; the revised sentences show two different ways to correct the same problem.

SINGULAR ANTECEDENT DOES NOT AGREE WITH PLURAL PRONOUN

An individual is able to change their attitudes.

CORRECTION #1: Correct by making the antecedent the same number as the pronoun.

SINGULAR ANTECEDENT AGREES WITH SINGULAR PRONOUN

An individual is able to change her attitudes.

CORRECTION #2: Correct by making the pronoun the same number as the antecedent.

PLURAL ANTECEDENT AGREES WITH PLURAL PRONOUN

Individuals are able to change their attitudes.

VERB REVISED TO PLURAL TO AGREE WITH PLURAL SUBJECT "INDIVIDUALS"

Practice 8

▲ Michael Phelps swimming the 100m butterfly at the Fina World Aquatics Championship, 2009

Edit the following sentences for pronoun agreement based on number.

1. If a person thinks he can accomplish a task, then usually they do.

2. For example, athletes like Michael Phelps break records because he believes he can.

3. People who succeed possess certain traits that help him achieve his goals.

4. A person's level of commitment relates to their level of achievement.

5. Those who are determined to do whatever it takes usually achieve her goals.

6. A person's commitment is directly tied to their drive to accomplish their tasks.

7. Athletes, like Phelps, face hours of tedious training in his daily life to hone his skills.

8. A person who is willing to learn from others is also more likely to achieve their goals.

9. The traits of an individual affect their personal growth, development, and achievement.

10. People who are aware of his attitudes are better able to control his fortune.

Correct Faulty Pronoun Agreement due to Shift in Gender

PROBLEM: In a sentence with a faulty **shift in gender,** the pronoun is a different gender than the gender of the antecedent. Most often, gender agreement problems are due to using the masculine pronoun to refer to antecedents that could apply to either men or women.

SINGULAR ANTECEDENT IS NEUTRAL (COULD BE MASCULINE OR FEMININE)

A person expands his thoughts through reading.

MASCULINE PRONOUN DOES NOT AGREE WITH NEUTRAL ANTECEDENT

CORRECTION #1: Correct by rewording to make the pronoun the same gender as the antecedent.

NEUTRAL, SINGULAR ANTECEDENT AGREES WITH NEUTRAL, SINGULAR PRONOUN "HIS OR HER"

A person expands his or her thoughts through reading.

If you reword the sentence by making the pronoun and its antecedent (neutral and) plural, make sure all other parts of the sentence are plural as necessary.

NEUTRAL, PLURAL ANTECEDENT AGREES WITH NEUTRAL, PLURAL PRONOUN

People expand their thoughts through reading.

CORRECTION #2: Correct by rewording to make the antecedent the same gender as the pronoun. In the instance below, this requires adding a feminine proper noun ("Juanita") to match the feminine pronoun.

ADDED SINGULAR FEMININE ANTECEDENT TO AGREE WITH SINGULAR FEMININE PRONOUN

Juanita expands her mind through reading.

Practice 9

Edit the following two sentences for pronoun agreement based on gender.

1. In literature, a stock character represents a type usually based on his gender, a value, or a behavior.

2. An example of a stock character is the rebel who doesn't care what others think about her.

3. Another stock character is the dumb blonde who relies on her good looks, not her brains.

4. When a child is repeatedly exposed to stock characters in literature, they may stereotype real people in real life.

5. A person may be unaware of the stereotypes he encounters in books or in the media.

6. Reading can expand a person's view of his world.

7. More stories now offer nontraditional views of a hero and his quest.

8. A reader should think about what he reads and how it affects his view of the world.

9. Readers come into contact with ideas that differ from his or her own values.

10. For example, by reading stories about strong, independent women, a reader may begin to question his stereotypical beliefs about women.

Practice 10

Edit the following paragraph for pronoun agreement based on person, number, and gender.

When the hero of a story is a woman, their mission differs from the quest of a male hero. In addition, your typical heroine is quite different from the female hero. For example, a heroine exists as the object of a male's desire. In contrast, the female hero has their own journey. Female heroes often fight against what society expects of her. In contrast, the quest of a male hero gives them the chance to live up to what society expects of you. Male and female heroes reflect or challenge the values of your culture.

Use Pronoun Case Clearly

Pronoun case identifies the function of a pronoun in a sentence. The definitions and examples of the three cases of pronouns are shown in the following chart.

Pronoun Case						
	Subjective Case		Objective Case		Possessive Case	
	Singular	**Plural**	**Singular**	**Plural**	**Singular**	**Plural**
1st Person	I	we	me	us	my, mine	our, ours
2nd Person	you	you	you	you	your, yours	your, yours
3rd Person	he, she, it who whoever	they, those	him, her, it whom whomever	them	his, her, hers its, whose	their, theirs

    Subjective case pronouns act as subjects or predicate nouns. A **predicate noun** restates the subject, usually by completing a linking verb such as *is*.

SUBJECTIVE CASE PRONOUN

I admire Matthew McConaughey's performance in *The Dallas Buyer's Club.*

SUBJECT IS RENAMED BY SUBJECTIVE CASE PRONOUN

If anyone deserved an Oscar, it was he.

    Objective case pronouns act as an object of a verb or preposition. The **object** of a sentence is a noun or pronoun to which the action of a verb is directed or to which the verb's action is done.

VERB   OBJECT OF VERB

The movie held us spellbound.

PREPOSITION   OBJECT OF THE PREPOSITION

The movie ticket is for whom?

Possessive case pronouns show ownership.

POSSESSIVE CASE PRONOUN INDICATES OWNERSHIP OF "SEAT"

His seat had gum on it.

Practice 11

CORRECT PRONOUN CASE

Complete the following sentences with the proper case of each missing pronoun. Discuss your answers with a small group of your peers.

1. .... are looking for powerful moral figures .... are above .... and .... will come to rescue .... when .... need ....

2. People tend to read about heroes with .... can identify.

3. These powerful moral figures may be people in .... local communities.

4. .... may admire one of .... parents, one of .... teachers, or .... best friend.

5. Those .... we admire often become .... role models.

6. Colin is .... personal coach, and .... is a firefighter and paramedic .... devotes himself to others.

7. .... greatly admire Colin for .... kindness and patience with .... and others.

8. Because of Colin's influence in .... life, ... have begun reading about fitness and health issues.

9. A role model may also be someone .... is famous and unknown to .... personally.

10. President Obama is one .... many admire because of .... story and accomplishments.

Correct Faulty Use of Pronoun Case in Comparisons Using "as" or "than"

Pronouns in comparisons using "as" or "than" can be in the subjective, objective, or possessive case. Writers often confuse the subjective and objective cases because they think it sounds more formal.

PROBLEM: The objective case pronoun is being used as the subject of a clause.

INCORRECT USE OF OBJECTIVE CASE PRONOUN

Laura is as strong as him. ┄┄┄*DEPENDENT CLAUSE WITH IMPLIED VERB "IS"*

CORRECTION:

SUBJECTIVE CASE PRONOUN ACTS AS SUBJECT OF IMPLIED VERB "IS"

Laura is as strong as he [is].

PROBLEM: The subjective case pronoun is being used as the object of a verb.

INCORRECT USE OF SUBJECTIVE CASE PRONOUN

The movie affected Marion as much as I.

CORRECTION:

THE IMPLIED VERB "AFFECTED" REQUIRES THE OBJECTIVE CASE PRONOUN

The movie affected Marion as much as [it affected] me.

CORRECT PRONOUN CASE IN COMPARISONS

Complete the following sentences with the proper case of each missing pronoun. Discuss your answers with a small group of your peers.

1. Molly is a better athlete than .... even though Molly doesn't train as many

hours as ....

2. Injuries don't afflict Molly as much as ....

3. Molly is able to run faster than her sister Julie, so Molly has more trophies than

....

4. Mother is a better cook than ....

5. .... is more mature than ....

6. No one dislikes spinach more than ....

7. His hearing is worse than ....

8. Raul is more fluent in Spanish than ....

9. Mandy is as patient as ....

10. Sandy enjoyed the movie as much as ....

Practice 12

Correct Faulty Use of Case in Compound Constructions

In some instances, a pronoun is joined with a noun or another pronoun to form a **compound.**

- **Joseph and I** went to a concert together.

- The mailman delivered the letter to **Joseph and me**.

To decide whether the subjective or objective case should be used for a pronoun in a compound, use the same rules that apply to a pronoun that is not in a compound. Use the subjective case for pronouns that function as subjects and the objective case for pronouns that function as objects.

PROBLEM: The objective case pronoun is being used in a compound subject.

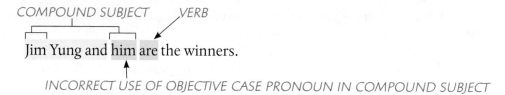

COMPOUND SUBJECT   VERB

Jim Yung and him are the winners.

INCORRECT USE OF OBJECTIVE CASE PRONOUN IN COMPOUND SUBJECT

CORRECTION: Replace the pronoun with the subjective case pronoun. To identify a pronoun as part of a compound subject, delete the other part of the compound so the pronoun stands alone, and see whether the sentence still makes sense.

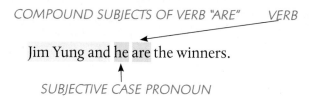

COMPOUND SUBJECTS OF VERB "ARE"   VERB

Jim Yung and he are the winners.

SUBJECTIVE CASE PRONOUN

PROBLEM: The subjective case pronoun is being used in a compound object.

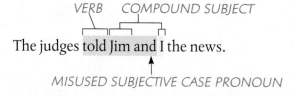

VERB   COMPOUND SUBJECT

The judges told Jim and I the news.

MISUSED SUBJECTIVE CASE PRONOUN

CORRECTION: Replace the pronoun with the objective case pronoun. To identify a pronoun as part of a compound object, delete the other part of the compound so the pronoun stands alone, and see whether the sentence still makes sense.

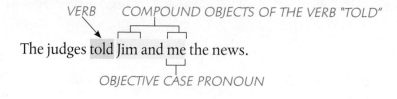

VERB   COMPOUND OBJECTS OF THE VERB "TOLD"

The judges told Jim and me the news.

OBJECTIVE CASE PRONOUN

CORRECT PRONOUN CASE IN COMPOUND CONSTRUCTIONS

Complete the following sentences with the proper case of each missing pronoun.

1. Jamal and .... are going to beat Justine and .... in the triathlon.

2. Two other teams and .... are trying to break the records held by last year's first place winners and ....

3. The coach told Jamal and .... that either Jamal or .... could win as individuals, too.

4. It will come down to Jamal and ...., the underdogs, against last year's winning team.

5. You and .... should enter the race, too.

6. Jamal said "You and .... make a strong team."

7. The coach also encouraged you and .... to compete.

8. The coach and .... agree that Joan and .... are strong competitors.

9. As much as Jamal and .... want to win, you and .... have the best chance of winning.

10. I can see it now, the 1st place medals being handed to you and ....

PRONOUN CASE REVIEW

Edit the following paragraph for proper pronoun case.

Many of us think of successful, modern athletes as heroes. Just as the classical hero embarks

on a challenging journey, so do them who are serious athletes. Hercules, Hector, and others like

they had to prove them stronger physically and mentally than a foe. Likewise a modern athlete

has to best a formidable opponent who him fears is stronger than him.

L8 Make Clear Pronoun References

Because a pronoun takes the place of a noun, careful writers make the relationship between a pronoun and its antecedent obvious and clear. Remembering a few guidelines can help you make clear pronoun references.

Guidelines for Clear Pronoun Reference
• A pronoun refers clearly and unmistakably to one antecedent.
• The antecedent of a pronoun is clearly stated.
• A pronoun appears near its antecedent.
• A pronoun does not make a broad or sweeping reference to an entire group of words.

Correct Faulty Pronoun References

Correct Faulty Pronoun Reference to More Than One Antecedent

PROBLEM: The pronoun does not unmistakably refer to one specific antecedent.

PRONOUN REFERS TO

After he twisted it, Jared put a bandage on his ankle.

CORRECTION: Correct by replacing the pronoun with a noun.

After he twisted his ankle, Jared put on a bandage.

ADDED NOUN REPLACES PRONOUN WITH NO CLEAR ANTECEDENT

Correct Faulty Pronoun Reference to Implied or Missing Antecedent

PROBLEM: The antecedent is not stated or is missing.

ANTECEDENT?   *PRONOUN REFERS TO ?*

The chocolate box is empty. Who ate it?

CORRECTION #1: Correct by replacing the pronoun with a noun.

ADDED NOUN REPLACES PRONOUN WITH NO CLEAR ANTECEDENT

The chocolate box is empty. Who ate the last piece?

CORRECTION #2: Correct by rewording to include a clear antecedent for the pronoun.

ANTECEDENT OF PRONOUN   *PRONOUN REFERS TO ANTECEDENT "PIECE"*

The last piece of chocolate is gone. Who ate it?

Correct Faulty Pronoun Reference due to Broad Pronoun References

PROBLEM: The pronoun refers to a group of words, such as an entire sentence.

ANTECEDENT OF PRONOUN?   *PRONOUN REFERS TO ?*

Joe gripes to Teesha about the music, which annoys Teesha.

CORRECTION: Correct by rewording to eliminate the pronoun.

Teesha is annoyed because Joe gripes to her about the music.

CREATE CLEAR PRONOUN REFERENCE

Edit the following sentences for clear pronoun reference. Share your answers with a small group of your peers.

1. Angela reads books and watches movies about heroic women because she enjoys it.

2. Angela told her mother that she was similar to her favorite female hero.

3. Angela and her mother like the dress she picked out for her party.

4. The repair person had to take the television off the stand to fix it.

5. The managers told the employees that they would receive pay raises.

6. The cookie jar is empty, and I want to know who ate it.

7. Mandy called Latisha's place all day, but she never answered.

8. When I parked my car next to your car, I noticed it had a flat tire.

9. My suitcase was in my car which is now gone.

10. Juan calls Julia constantly to ask her for advice he never takes, which amuses her.

NOUN AND PRONOUN CHAPTER REVIEW

Write a paragraph of three to five sentences that uses nouns and pronouns properly. Exchange your paragraph with a peer and edit each other's work. Suggested topic: A definition and example of a hero.

Editing Assignments

MyWritingLab™
Complete this Exercise
on mywritinglab.com

Editing for Everyday Life

Assume you are writing a thank you note for a gift you have received. Edit the note to ensure proper use of nouns, articles, and pronouns.

Dear Uncle Malcolm,

Matilda and me love the grill and cooking utensiles you gave us as the gifts. It was perfect, for us love to have people over and grill-out which is so much fun. Hopefully, you can join Matilda and I for one of them cookouts in near future. Thank you, again, it is unbelievable.

Sincerely,

Andre

Editing for College Life

Assume you are writing in response to an essay prompt for a college humanities class. Edit the introduction to the essay to ensure proper use of nouns, articles, and pronouns.

Essay Prompt: Discuss an important heroic figure in Western culture.

Student response: A important heroic figure in Western culture is Jesus whom is also known as The Christ. Even them whom do not believe Jesus is God in the flesh, admit that it is one of a most compelling storys. His life unfolds in the pattern similar to the classical heros. He bloodline can be traced to King David, and his claims to be the Son of God. He is separated from his father in heaven to fulfill the selfless, lethal mission on earth.After proving his spiritual power to overcome hatred and death, he is reunited with his father.

Editing for Working Life

Assume you are the chairperson of the United Way fundraising committee at your place of work. You have composed the following e-mail to call for donations. Edit the e-mail to ensure proper use of nouns, articles, and pronouns.

Dear Colleagues:

Your United Way contribution creates lasting changes right where you and me live. Local volunteers invest your contributions in an areas of education, income and health. Some of the funds support programes and services that help you with basic needs, such as childcare, emergency shelter and free health clinics. United Way also works to keep a people from needing them services in the first place. They work with a broad range of community partners. It focuses on prevention and community changes.

Academic Learning Log: Chapter Review

To test and track your understanding, answer the following questions.

1. A noun names a ...., animal, place, object, action, or concept.

2. A .... noun names an individual person, place, or thing; a .... noun is a general name for any member of a group or class.

3. A noun can function as a ...., object of a verb, object of a ...., or appositive.

4. .... nouns name distinct individual units of a group or category; noncount nouns name a nonspecific member of a group or category.

5. An .... article is used before a singular noun that refers to any member of a larger group.

6. The definite article .... is used before a singular or plural noun that refers to a specific member of a larger group.

7. A pronoun refers clearly and specifically to .... antecedent.

8. An antecedent is the .... to which a pronoun refers.

9. A pronoun and its antecedent must agree with each other in three ways: ...., ..., and ....

10. The three pronoun cases are .... case, ... case, and .... case.

11. **How will I use what I have learned about nouns and pronouns?**
    In your notebook, discuss how you will apply to your own writing what you have learned about nouns and pronouns.

12. **What do I still need to study about nouns and pronouns?**
    In your notebook, describe your ongoing study needs by describing what, when, and how you will continue studying pronouns and nouns.

MyWritingLab™

Complete the Post-test for Chapter 2 in MyWritingLab.

3

Adjectives and Adverbs

LEARNING OUTCOMES

After studying this chapter, you should be able to:

L① Answer the Question "What's the Point of Adjectives and Adverbs?"

L② Distinguish between Adjectives and Adverbs

L③ Use Participles as Adjectives

L④ Use Nouns and Verbs Formed as Adjectives

L⑤ Use Proper Placement of Adjectives

L⑥ Use Logical Order of Adjectives

L⑦ Use Adverbs with Purpose

An adjective describes a noun or a pronoun. An adverb describes a verb, an adjective, or another adverb.

Thinking about a real-life situation helps us to understand the purpose of adjectives and adverbs in our communication. The following photograph captures a particular fashion statement. Study the picture, complete the activity, and answer the question "What's the point of learning about adjectives and adverbs?"

What's the Point of Adjectives and Adverbs?

PHOTOGRAPHIC ORGANIZER: ADJECTIVES AND ADVERBS

Assume your college newspaper has called for students to submit articles about the types of fashion worn on campus. Study the photograph and fill in the blanks with adjectives and adverbs that best describe the woman's style of fashion. Work with a small group of your peers.

_____ fashion makes a _____

statement. Penciled eyebrows arch in a

_____, _____ line _____

above her _____ brow line. _____,

_____ eyeliner encircles her eyes and

sweeps _____ her temple like

_____ feathers. _____

chains, hooked from her _____

piercing to her _____

piercings, drape across her _____

cheek. _____ hair, _____ clothes,

and _____ lipstick complete the

_____ look.

▲ **Goth fashion**

✎
WRITING
FROM LIFE

What's the point of adjectives and adverbs?

_____

_____

One Student Writer's Response

The following paragraph offers one writer's reaction to the paragraph about goth fashion.

_This was so much fun. We all think so differently, so we came up with a
wide choice of words. I thought the woman looked great, but my friend
was freaked out by the piercings and the chain. So we really differed in the
words we chose. I learned that I can get my own point of view across based
on the kinds of adjectives and adverbs I choose._

L2 Distinguish between Adjectives and Adverbs

Adjectives and adverbs describe, modify, or limit the meaning of other words. Adjectives and adverbs have specific functions in a sentence and thus express precise meanings. Understanding the function and purpose of adjectives and adverbs allows a writer a thoughtful and effective expression of ideas.

An **adjective** modifies—in other words, it describes—a noun or a pronoun. It answers one or more of the following questions:

- What kind?
- Which one?
- How many?

ADJECTIVE "UNUSUAL" DESCRIBES NOUN "OUTFIT"

Maya wore an unusual outfit.

PRONOUN "SHE" DESCRIBED BY ADJECTIVE "BRAVE"

She is brave.

An **adverb** modifies, or describes, a verb, an adjective, or another adverb. It answers one or more of the following questions:

- How?
- Why?
- When?
- Where?
- To what extent?

VERB "DRESSES" DESCRIBED BY ADVERB "UNUSUALLY"

Maya dresses unusually.

NOUN "MAYA" DESCRIBED BY ADJECTIVE "UNUSUAL"

Maya is bravely unusual.

ADVERB "BRAVELY" DESCRIBES ADJECTIVE "UNUSUAL"

Identify the 20 **boldfaced** words in the following sentences as adjectives or adverbs. Write **adj** for *adjective* or **adv** for *adverb* above each boldfaced word.

1. Bikers **eagerly** pack a **crowded** Main Street in **beautiful** Daytona Beach, Florida.

2. Bike Week in Daytona Beach, widely **anticipated**, is an **annual**, **week-long**, **wild** party.

3. **Rowdy** bikers **loudly** gun their engines so a **deafening** roar fills the air.

4. **Many** bikers **proudly** wear **outlandish** outfits.

5. **Determined** partiers, bikers will **bravely** zoom through the **wet** streets on **rainy** days.

6. A **large** number of bikers display **colorful** tattoos such as **flaming** serpents.

Use Participles as Adjectives

L3

Many adjectives are formed by adding *-ed* or *-ing* to verbs. These **participle adjectives** serve two purposes: The *-ed* form describes a person's reaction or feeling; the *-ing* form describes the person or thing that causes the reaction.

-ED PARTICIPLE ADJECTIVE DESCRIBES HOW THE "AUDIENCE" REACTS

The amused audience laughed at the actor.

-ING PARTICIPLE ADJECTIVE DESCRIBES THE "ACTOR" CAUSING THE REACTION

The amusing actor made the audience laugh.

The following chart lists some of the most common participles used as adjectives.

Common Participles Used as Adjectives			
alarmed	alarming	exhausted	exhausting
amused	amusing	fascinated	fascinating
annoyed	annoying	frightened	frightening
bored	boring	horrified	horrifying
concerned	concerning	irritated	irritating
confused	confusing	pleased	pleasing
depressed	depressing	satisfied	satisfying
discouraged	discouraging	shocked	shocking
encouraged	encouraging	stimulated	stimulating
engaged	engaging	terrified	terrifying
excited	exciting	worried	worrying

USE PARTICIPLES AS ADJECTIVES

Complete the following ideas by filling in the blanks with the proper participle adjective.

1. Some .... parents protest the influence of pop stars.

2. .... youth often adopt the styles of their pop heroes.

3. Many of these .... stars wear .... outfits.

4. The .... trend of sexy clothing for preteens is one of their concerns.

5. Too many pop stars send .... messages to young people.

6. Other .... parents are more .... by peer pressure than the influence of stars.

7. A .... friend could lead a .... young person to take .... risks.

8. ...., Anna resented her boring routine and longed for a more .... life.

9. Although she had .... parents, she turned to Alexis, an .... friend, to have some fun.

10. That night, a .... Anna learned that Alexis took .... drugs and drove at .... rates of speed.

Use Nouns and Verbs Formed as Adjectives

L4

In addition to the *-ed* and *-ing* word endings or suffixes, many adjectives are formed by other types of word endings. Just as a suffix transforms a verb into a specific type of adjective or adverb, a suffix also can create adjectives out of nouns. Adjectives come in so many forms that using a few carefully chosen adjectives can add power and interest to your writing. For your reference, the following chart lists a few frequently used adjectives by some of their word endings.

Common Adjectives								
Word Endings	*-able* *-ible*	*-ful*	*-ic*	*-ish*	*-ive*	*-less*	*-ly* *-y*	*-ous*
Examples	acceptable	bashful	alcoholic	boorish	abusive	cheerless	antsy	ambiguous
	accessible	cheerful	aquatic	oafish	combative	jobless	cagy	auspicious
	capable	forgetful	dramatic	devilish	decisive	mindless	daffy	courageous
	honorable	graceful	erratic	elfish	instinctive	needless	earthy	glamorous
	laughable	joyful	gigantic	lavish	receptive	noiseless	lively	industrious
	obtainable	merciful	majestic	skittish	reflective	pointless	manly	malicious
	plausible	peaceful	melodic	snobbish	secretive	senseless	seemly	nervous
	tangible	rightful	organic	squeamish	selective	useless	smelly	righteous

---

USE NOUNS AND VERBS FORMED AS ADJECTIVES

Complete the following ideas by filling in the blanks with the proper adjective formed from a noun or verb in the chart "Common Adjectives." Work with a small group of your peers. Use a dictionary to look up unfamiliar words.

Practice 4

1. Fashion industry leaders are sometimes accused of .... practices.

2. Some say .... clothing is .... mostly because of the cheap labor of sweat shops.

3. Critics also think the use of animal skin for clothing is ....

4. Others say that most people in the fashion industry are .... and ....

5. And many would be .... if not for the fashion industry.

6. We need to be .... consumers and demand that goods be produced with respect for human rights.

7. A .... shopper buys from companies that pay their workers a living wage.

8. Although some may think that the action of one person is _____, actually decisive

   change often occurs with the action of one _____ person.

9. Write a sentence using an adjective formed from a verb from the charts "Common Adjectives" and "Common Participles Used as Adjectives." Suggested topic: Labor rights.

   ----

10. Write a sentence using an adjective formed from a noun from the chart "Common Adjectives." Suggested topic: Sweatshops.

L⑤ Use Proper Placement of Adjectives

A careful writer not only chooses the precise word for impact, but also arranges words in the most effective order for the greatest impact on the reader. As you work with adjectives, be aware that the placement of an adjective varies based on its relationship to other words.

Adjectives can appear before a noun.

ADJECTIVE DESCRIBES NOUN "FAN"

The bashful fan approached Rihanna.

Adjectives can appear after **linking verbs** such as *is, are, were, seems,* and *appears.*

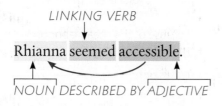

LINKING VERB

Rhianna seemed accessible.

NOUN DESCRIBED BY ADJECTIVE

Adjectives can appear after **sensory verbs**—those that describe physical senses—such as *look, smell, feel, taste,* and *sound.*

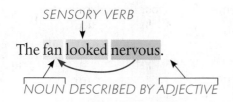

SENSORY VERB

The fan looked nervous.

NOUN DESCRIBED BY ADJECTIVE

USE PROPER PLACEMENT OF ADJECTIVES

Fill in the blanks by choosing the phrase that best completes the sentence's idea by appropriate placement of adjectives.

1. Isabel Allende is one of _____ from Latin America.

    a. the widely read most writers   **b.** the most writer widely read   **c.** the most widely read writers

2. Her writings create fascinating characters that must _____.

    a. face political and social issues   **b.** political and social issues face   **c.** issues political and social face

3. *House of Spirits*, her first novel, pays tribute to _____.

    a. women strong Latin American   **b.** strong Latin American women   **c.** women Latin American strong

4. Julia Alvarez has won _____ for her fiction.

    a. many prestigious awards   **b.** awards many prestigious   **c.** prestigious awards many

5. Alvarez _____ who explores immigration and women's issues.

    a. a gifted storyteller is   **b.** a storyteller gifted is   **c.** is a gifted storyteller

6. Carlos Santana remains one of _____ of all time.

    a. top the Hispanic rock stars   **b.** the top Hispanic rock stars   **c.** Hispanic rock stars the top

7. George Lopez _____ who examines Mexican American culture.

    a. a popular comedian is   **b.** a comedian is popular   **c.** is a popular comedian

8. Sonia Sotomayor is _____ of the Supreme Court of the United States.

    a. the first Hispanic justice   **b.** the Hispanic Justice first   **c.** first the Hispanic justice

9. Shakira is _____ who has sold more than 60 million albums worldwide.

    a. Colombian award-winning an singer   **b.** an award-winning Colombian singer   **c.** singer an award-winning Colombian

10. Geraldo Rivera _____ who knows how to make ratings soar.

    a. is journalist controversial a   **b.** a journalist is controversial   **c.** is a controversial journalist

L6 Use Logical Order of Adjectives

Adjectives that appear before a noun follow a particular order. Effective writers use adjectives sparingly. Rarely are more than two or three used in one sequence. The chart below outlines the preferred order of adjectives in English arranged by common types and includes three examples of expressions that follow that order. Notice that the order moves from the subjective description of *opinion* to objective descriptions such as *material* and *purpose*.

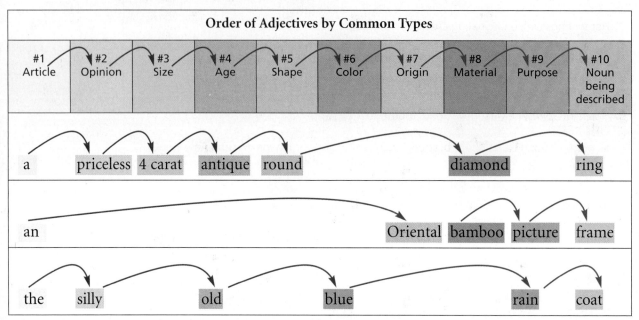

Order of Adjectives by Common Types

#1 Article	#2 Opinion	#3 Size	#4 Age	#5 Shape	#6 Color	#7 Origin	#8 Material	#9 Purpose	#10 Noun being described
a	priceless	4 carat	antique	round			diamond		ring
an						Oriental	bamboo	picture	frame
the	silly		old		blue			rain	coat

USE LOGICAL ORDER OF ADJECTIVES

A. Choose the option that best completes the idea by listing adjectives in the proper order.

1. .... cat sleeps all day.

   a. The sick, 16-year-old, black   **b.** The black, sick, 16-year-old   **c.** The 16-year-old, sick, black

2. For many, ... kitchen is a top priority.

   a. a modern, roomy, attractive   **b.** attractive, an, modern, roomy   **c.** an attractive, roomy, modern

3. .... actress, Julia Roberts is able to choose her roles.

   a. A beautiful, maturing   **b.** A maturing, beautiful   **c.** Maturing, beautiful a

4. Jamie fell to the ground in exhaustion after .... workout.

   a. the long, hard   **b.** long, hard the   **c.** the hard, long

5. A protestor threw red paint all over .... coat worn by the actress.

   a. the white, floor-length fur   **b.** the floor-length, white fur   **c.** the white fur floor-length

B. Describe each noun with a set of two or more adjectives. List adjectives in proper order.

1. _____ computer

2. _____ car

3. _____ song

4. _____ friend

5. _____ job

Use Adverbs with Purpose

L⑦

The most common use of adverbs is to describe verbs. In addition, adverbs modify other types of words such as adjectives and other adverbs. In purpose, adverbs answer the reporter's questions *When? Where?* and *How?*

Many adverbs are derived from adjectives, many adverbs end in *-ly*, and many adverbs are gradeable based on degree or quantity. The following chart lists some of the most frequently used adverbs based on the type of information they provide.

Common Adverbs				
Time, Frequency, or Sequence	**Place**	**Manner**	**Certainty or Negation**	**Degree or Quantity**
When?	**Where?**	**How?**	**How?**	**How much?**
after	everywhere	automatically	certainly	almost
always	here	badly	clearly	completely
consequently	inside	beautifully	maybe	enough
during	outside	cheerfully	never	fully
early	somewhere	fast	not	hardly
finally	there	happily	obviously	least
next		hard	perhaps	less
often		quickly	probably	not
sometimes		seriously	surely	really
then		slowly		too
while		well		very

Practice 7

Complete each sentence with the most appropriate adverb.

1. Every professional .... needs a charcoal gray suit.

   a. much   **b.** certainly   **c.** never

2. The white, long-sleeved oxford cloth shirt is .... a great accessory to any suit.

   a. always   **b.** hardly   **c.** almost

3. The professional can .... do without a pair of khaki pants.

   a. hardly   **b.** sometimes   **c.** almost

4. A pair of khaki pants .... goes well with a simple navy blazer and pair of penny loafers.

   a. really   **b.** seriously   **c.** sometimes

5. For those causal workdays, women may .... prefer to wear a causal shift with a cardigan and pumps.

   a. always   **b.** sometimes   **c.** never

6. A solid navy suit evokes power and gives a .... polished look.

   a. less   **b.** seriously   **c.** always

7. Most young professionals .... build a work wardrobe over time.

   a. quickly   **b.** cheerfully   **c.** slowly

8. A professional wardrobe doesn't .... lead to success, but it gives the right impression.

   a. automatically   **b.** really   **c.** finally

9. .... another necessity of a professional's wardrobe is the black dress shoe.

   a. Consequently   **b.** Obviously   **c.** Hardly

10. ...., a trench coat is a practical addition to the professional's wardrobe.

   a. First   **b.** Consequently   **c.** Finally

Comparative

The comparative degree compares and makes distinctions between two people or things, usually by using the adverbs *more* or *less* or adding the suffix *-er*.

COMPARATIVE ADJECTIVE "CUTER"
COMPARES "CAPRIS" WITH "CULOTTES"

Capris are cuter than culottes.

Superlative

The superlative degree makes distinctions among three or more people or things, usually by using the adverbs *most* or *least* or adding the suffix *-est*.

SUPERLATIVE ADJECTIVE "CUTEST" COMPARES NOUN
"OUTFIT" TO ALL THE OTHER OUTFITS

This is the cutest outfit of all.

Degrees of Adjectives and Adverbs			
Degree of Comparison	Absolute: One as _____ as	Comparative: Two *-er* _____than	Superlative: Three or More *-est* the _____
Adjectives	good	better	best
	bad	worse	worst
	much	more	most
Adverbs	busy	busier	busiest
	slowly	more slowly	most slowly

Practice 8

Complete the following sentences with the proper comparative or superlative.

1. Traditionally, men earn .... money than women for the same job and skills.

   a. much   **b.** more   **c.** most

2. Men earn on average 20% .... than women.

   a. much   **b.** more   **c.** most

3. Women are .... likely to work part time and less likely to negotiate their salaries.

   a. much   **b.** more   **c.** most

4. What is perhaps the .... factor in the wage gap between men and women?

   a. big   **b.** bigger   **c.** biggest

5. .... women choose lower-paying careers like social work, education, and non-profits.

   a. Much   **b.** More   **c.** Most

6. Men are .... likely to pursue high-paying careers like engineering, computer science, and finance.

   a. much   **b.** more   **c.** most

7. Male workers are not .... than women workers.

   a. busy   **b.** busier   **c.** busiest

8. Males are not .... workers than women.

   a. good   **b.** better   **c.** best

9. Experts agree that discrimination against women is the .... likely reason for this wage gap.

   a. much   **b.** more   **c.** most

10. The wage gap between men and women was .... in the past than it is now.

   a. bad   **b.** worse   **c.** worst

Spelling Guidelines
Comparative and Superlative Adjectives and Adverbs

NUMBER OF SYLLABLES	WORD ENDING	COMPARATIVE	SUPERLATIVE
One-syllable adjectives or adverbs	any kind	add -er	add -est
Examples	fast	faster	fastest
One-syllable adjectives	consonant-vowel-consonant	double last consonant add -er	double last consonant add -est
Examples	big	bigger	biggest
Two-syllable adjectives or adverbs	ending in -y	change -y to -i; add -er	change -y to -i; add -est
Examples	busy	busier	busiest
Two- or more syllable adjectives or adverbs	not ending in -y	no change in spelling; use *more*	no change in spelling; use *most*
Examples	thrilling	more thrilling	most thrilling

CORRECTLY SPELL COMPARATIVES AND SUPERLATIVES

Fill in the following chart with the correct spellings of each form of the comparatives and superlatives. Use *more* and *most* as needed.

	Comparative	Superlative		Comparative	Superlative
1. hard			**6.** simple		
2. exciting			**7.** pretty		
3. sad			**8.** clever		
4. cheap			**9.** happy		
5. dirty			**10.** careful		

Practice 9

Master *Good* and *Well*

Two of the most often-confused words in the English language are *good* and *well*. One reason these two words are so often confused is that *well* can be used as either an adverb or an adjective to discuss health issues.

• **Good** is an **adjective** that describes a noun or pronoun.

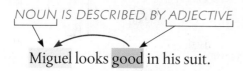

NOUN IS DESCRIBED BY ADJECTIVE

Miguel looks good in his suit.

• **Well** is an **adverb** that usually describes a **verb**.

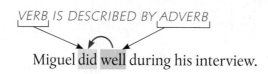

VERB IS DESCRIBED BY ADVERB

Miguel did well during his interview.

• Exception **Well** is an **adjective** when used to describe a person's health issues.

PRONOUN DESCRIBED BY ADJECTIVE

He feels well.

DISTINGUISH BETWEEN *GOOD* AND *WELL*

Fill in each blank with *good* or *well*.

1. Jermaine earns _____ grades.

2. Smoked ribs taste _____.

3. Whitney likes her steaks _____ done.

4. John is doing _____ at work.

5. The team played _____.

6. Marta is a _____ tennis player.

7. She does _____ under pressure.

8. Josh speaks _____ of you.

9. That's a _____ idea.

10. I don't feel _____.

Complete the following sentences by filling in the blanks with the appropriate form or order of the adjective or adverb in parentheses.

1. Beyoncé is a .... actress and singer. (fascinating/fascinated)

2. She performs .... in film and on stage. (good/well)

3. She is also .... known for her relationship with Jay Z. (good/well)

4. A ...., she began singing at age seven. (youth talented/ talented youth)

5. Beyoncé is .... woman. (a beautiful, young, African American/a young, African American, beautiful)

6. She is one of the .... working performers in the business. (hard/harder/hardest)

7. She .... has achieved .... success. (completely/certainly/finally; great/greater/greatest)

8. Earning $115 million, Beyoncé became the .... musician of 2014. (higher-paid female/highest-paid female/female higher-paid/female highest-paid)

9. Her .... work with several charities endears her to many. (good/well)

10. Many critics consider her to be today's .... talented singer of pop music. (most/more)

Editing Assignments

MyWritingLab™
Complete this Exercise
on mywritinglab.com

Editing for Everyday Life

Assume you are a parent writing to the principal of your child's school to protest the new policy about school uniforms. Edit to ensure proper use of adjectives and adverbs. Use your own paper, or complete the exercise on MyWritingLab.com.

I am writing to protest the new, unfair policy that requires students to wear uniforms.

School uniforms certain stifle self expression. Unfortunate, uniforms force children to find other ways to express who they are. The school has acted bad on this issue. We will do good to remember that children who wear school uniforms are more likely to use makeup early, and many resort alter their uniforms to be differently others. Wearing school uniforms may teach children that is better to conform to standard without thinking critical.

Editing for College Life

Assume you are writing a speech in favor of school uniforms for a college speech class. Edit to ensure proper use of adjectives and adverbs.

School uniforms are a smart move for parents, students, and educators. First, uniforms get rid of gang colors in schools. They also great decrease violence due to theft of clothing and shoes. Our khaki, standardized, attractive clothing will instill order and a sense of community among students. School uniforms also reduce the distractions of unsuitably or controversially clothing. Final, school uniforms help educators identify possibly intruders who don't belong on campus.

Editing for Working Life

Assume you are the principal of a school, and you have written a letter to send to parents and students about your school's new dress code. Edit to ensure proper use of adjectives and adverbs.

Forest High School has recent established the followed guidelines to aid parents and students in selecting the properly attire for the school. The student must be able to place his or her arms at his or her side and touch the bottom of his or her shorts or skirts with his or her longer finger. Clothing with bad chosen messages may not be worn in school. Shirts with reference to drugs, alcohol, gangs and weapons are not permitted in school. Clothing with sexual references is not suitably.

WHAT HAVE I LEARNED ABOUT ADJECTIVES AND ADVERBS?

To test and track your understanding, answer the following questions.

1. An adjective modifies a _____ or a _____.

2. An adverb modifies a _____, an _____, or another _____.

3. Participle adjectives are formed by adding _____ or _____ to verbs.

4. Adjectives often appear in the following order: _____, opinion, size, age, shape, _____, origin, material, purpose, noun being described.

5. Adverbs answer the questions _____, where, and _____.

6. Adjectives and adverbs take the form of two degrees: _____ and _____.

7. The _____ degree makes distinctions between two things, usually by using the adverbs *more* or *less* or by adding the suffix *-er*.

8. The _____ degree makes distinctions among three or more things, usually by using the adverbs *most* or *least* or by adding the suffix *-est*.

9. Good is an _____.

10. Most often, *well* is an _____.

11. **How will I use what I have learned about adjectives and adverbs?**
In your notebook, discuss how you will apply to your own writing what you have learned about adjectives and adverbs.

12. **What do I still need to study about adjectives and adverbs?**
In your notebook, describe your ongoing study needs by describing what, when, and how you will continue studying adjectives and adverbs.

PORTFOLIO

MyWritingLab™

Complete the Post-test for Chapter 3 in MyWritingLab.

4

Verbs

A verb is a word that states an action, the existence of a state of being, or a condition as it occurs in time.

Verbs vary in form to express the different times an action or state of being occurs relative to the speaker or writer. Thinking about a real-world situation helps us see the need for verbs to communicate. The following photographs capture the power of a tornado. Study the images, complete the activity, and answer the question "What's the point of verbs?"

What's the Point of Verbs?

PHOTOGRAPHIC ORGANIZER: VERBS

Assume you received a brochure from your city or town officials about tornadoes. The brochure began with this photo and paragraph. Predict the writer's meaning. First, read aloud the paragraph with all the verbs removed. Next, complete the paragraph by filling in the blanks with verbs you think best complete the idea. Then, draw on what you already know about verbs to answer the question "What's the point of verbs?"

✏️
WRITING
FROM LIFE

It's Up To YOU!

Each year, many people _____ or seriously _____ by tornadoes despite advance warning. Some _____ not _____ the warning. Others _____ the warning, but they _____ not _____ a tornado _____ actually _____ them. The preparedness information in this brochure, along with timely severe weather watches and warnings, _____ your life in the event a tornado _____ your area. After you _____ the warning or _____ threatening skies, YOU _____ the decision to seek shelter before the storm _____. It _____ the most important decision you _____ ever _____.

What's the point of verbs?

_____

_____

One Student Writer's Response

The following paragraph offers one writer's reaction to the brochure about tornados.

I could make sense of lots of the sentences, like the first one. But some of the others were hard to figure out, like sentences 2 and 3. The word "not" gave me a strong clue though. Basically, I thought that the author meant some did not listen to the warning and others did listen. All through school, I've heard about verbs in English class. I know a sentence has a subject and verb. But sometimes, I get confused about which kind of verb to use.

L2 Correctly Use the Present Tense

The **simple present tense** is used to describe an action or event in the present time, habitual actions, or general truth.

Past   Present   Future

An action or event in the present tense: I **love** spaghetti.

Habitual action: I **run** every morning.

A general truth: It **is** better to give than to receive.

Practice 2

CORRECTLY USE THE PRESENT TENSE

Complete each sentence with a present tense verb from the box.

drive	follows	is	offers	tries
fills	grabs	meets	puts	walks

1. Jena _____ to start her car.

2. Her car _____ out of gas.

3. She _____ a gas can from her trunk.

4. She _____ to the gas station.

5. A friend _____ her at the gas station.

6. Her friend _____ to drive her to her car.

7. Jena _____ up her gas can.

8. They _____ to her car.

9. Jena _____ the gas in her car.

10. Her friend _____ her back to the gas station.

Correctly Use the Past Tense of Regular and Irregular Verbs

The **simple past tense** is used to describe a completed action or event. The action or event might have taken place long ago or it might have happened recently, but either way, the past tense is used to indicate that it has already occurred. The simple past tense is also often used to tell a story. Frequently, the use of the past tense is signaled by particular expressions of time: *yesterday, last night, last week, last year, three years ago,* and so on. The following time line illustrates the sequence of tenses.

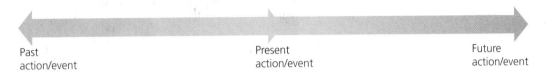

Past
action/event

Present
action/event

Future
action/event

The past tense takes on different forms for regular and irregular verbs.

Regular Verbs in the Past Tense

The following chart states the general rule for forming the past tense of regular verbs, the spelling rules for exceptions, and examples of each rule.

Rules for Forming Past Tense of Regular Verbs		
	Base Form	**Past Tense**
General Rule: Regular verbs form the past tense by adding **-ed** to the base form of the verb.	talk ⟶	talk**ed**
Spelling Exceptions: There are several exceptions to the way in which regular verbs form the past tense:		
1. When the base form of the verb ends in **-e,** only add **-d.**	share ⟶ escape	share**d** escape**d**
2. When the base form of the verb ends with a consonant and **-y,** delete the **-y** and add **-ied** in its place.	rely ⟶ marry	rel**ied** marr**ied**
3. When the base form of the verb ends with **-n, -p** or **-it,** double the last letter before adding the **-ed.**	ban ⟶ trap commit	ban**ned** tra**pped** commi**tted**

Practice 3

Fill in each blank with the past tense form of the regular verb in parentheses.

1. NFL quarterback Peyton Manning

_____ (train) to win.

2. Peyton _____ (improve) his game with a challenging training routine.

3. He _____ (plan) on increasing his core strength and flexibility.

4. The routine _____ (include) fire agility drills and old-fashioned iron pumping.

5. He never _____ (hurry);

▲ Peyton Manning works out

instead he _____ (use) proper form and _____ (resist) rushing.

6. Manning _____ (waste) no time and _____ (skip) nothing; he _____ (want) to be on top of his game.

7. Then, he _____ (suffer) a neck injury and _____ (miss) playing an entire season.

8. Eventually, doctors _____ (perform) a level one cervical fusion.

9. He _____ (play) for the Indianapolis Colts for fourteen years, before he was traded to the Denver Broncos.

10. Write a sentence with a regular verb in the past tense. Suggested topic: An admirable athlete.

_____

_____

Irregular Verbs in the Past Tense

Unlike regular verbs, irregular verbs do not use -ed to form the past tense. Nor does the past tense of irregular verbs conform to uniform spelling rules with clear exceptions. In fact, some of the most commonly used verbs are irregular, and most writers commit these words to memory so their proper use is automatic. The chart below lists the base form and past tense form of some commonly used irregular verbs. When in doubt about the correct form of a verb, consult a dictionary to check the spelling of the past tense of an irregular verb.

Some Common Irregular Verbs in the Past Tense			
Base Form	**Past Tense**	**Base Form**	**Past Tense**
become	became	lie (to recline)	lay
begin	began	light	lit
break	broke	lose	lost
bring	brought	make	made
buy	bought	mean	meant
choose	chose	meet	met
come	came	pay	paid
drink	drank	ride	rode
drive	drove	ring	rang
eat	ate	rise	rose
fall	fell	run	ran
feed	fed	say	said
feel	felt	sell	sold
fly	flew	send	sent
forget	forgot	shake	shook
forgive	forgave	sing	sang
freeze	froze	sit	sat
get	got	speak	spoke
go	went	spend	spent
grow	grew	swim	swam
hang	hung	take	took
have	had	teach	taught
hear	heard	tear	tore
hide	hid	think	thought
hold	held	throw	threw
keep	kept	understand	understood
know	knew	wake	woke (waked)
lay (to place)	laid	wear	wore
lead	led	win	won
leave	left	write	wrote

Practice 4

CORRECTLY USE IRREGULAR VERBS IN THE PAST TENSE

Fill in the blanks with the past tense form of the irregular verbs in the parentheses.

1. Written records of the Olympic Games .... (begin) in 776 BCE in Olympia, Greece.

2. For the next 1,200 years, the Olympic Games .... (take) place every four years.

3. The pentathlon .... (become) an Olympic sport in 708 BCE.

4. Running, jumping, discus throwing, wrestling, and boxing .... (make) up the pentathlon.

5. Olympic standards .... (fall) after Rome conquered Greece in the 100's BCE.

6. Earthquakes and flooding .... (send) Olympia beneath the earth, ending the games.

7. For centuries, most people .... (forget) about the Olympic games.

8. In 1896, Athens, Greece, ... (hold) the very first modern Olympic Games.

9. Thousands of athletes from all over the world .... (come) to the 2014 Olympic Games in Sochi, Russia.

10. Write a sentence using the past tense of an irregular verb. Suggested topic: A memorable moment in sports.

Key Verbs in the Past Tense: *To Have, To Do, To Be*

Three key verbs are used both as main verbs and as helping verbs to express a wide variety of meanings: *to have, to do,* and *to be*. These three verbs are irregular verbs, so it's essential to memorize their correct forms in the past tense.

To Have	**To Do**	**To Be**
had	did	was (singular)
		were (plural)

CORRECTLY USE IRREGULAR VERBS IN THE PAST TENSE

Fill in the blanks with the past tense form of the verbs *to have, to do,* or *to be*.

1. The winner .... the opportunity to overcome failure.

2. Three times, she .... not complete the task that .... before her.

3. Faith in her abilities and the courage to try again .... the keys to her final win.

4. She .... the determination to succeed.

5. Jonas also .... the determination to succeed.

6. He .... an injured veteran returning from war.

7. He .... to learn how to walk again.

8. He .... everything according to his doctors' and physical therapists' instructions.

9. His friends and family .... there to witness his first steps on his own.

10. Write a sentence using the past tense of *to have, to do,* or *to be*. Suggested topic: A past success.

....

....

....

....

LO ④ Correctly Use Helping Verbs
Can/Could/Would

Helping verbs are auxiliary verbs that team up with main verbs for precise expression of an action or state of being. Three helping verbs are often confused in usage: *can, could,* and *would.* These auxiliary verbs help express the meaning of ability, opportunity, possibility, permission, and intention. The following section provides definitions and examples for each of these three helping verbs.

Three Commonly Confused Helping Verbs: *Can, Could, Would*

• *Can* **expresses physical or mental ability in the present tense.**

"CAN" EXPRESSES A PHYSICAL ABILITY

I can walk for miles.

"CAN" EXPRESSES A MENTAL ABILITY

I can think clearly.

• *Could* **expresses physical or mental ability, opportunity, possibility, or permission in the past tense.**

"COULD" EXPRESSES A PHYSICAL OR MENTAL ABILITY

She could win a race.

"COULD" EXPRESSES A LOST OPPORTUNITY

You could have won the race.

"COULD" EXPRESSES POSSIBILITY

He could have been injured.

"COULD" EXPRESSES PERMISSION

He said that we could begin the competition.

- **Would** expresses past routine or intention in the past tense.

"WOULD" EXPRESSES PAST ROUTINE

He would practice every morning.

"WOULD" EXPRESSES PAST INTENTION

She said she would exercise later.

CORRECTLY USE *CAN*, *COULD*, AND *WOULD*

▲ E3 Media and Business Summit in Santa Monica

Complete each sentence with the helping verb that best completes the idea: *can, could,* or *would*.

1. Wii Fit .... change how you exercise.

2. By playing Wii Fit every day, you, your friends, and your family .... improve your personal health and fitness.

3. Before playing with Wii Fit, Beatrice .... not exercise for more than a few minutes without stopping.

4. Before she played with Wii Fit, she .... sit for hours and watch television.

5. You .... also personalize your workouts with Wii Fit Plus.

6. Wii Fit .... track your calories, create routines, and choose a trainer.

7. When I was getting back into shape last year, I loved that I .... choose my own routines.

8. Every day, I .... change up the trainer that talked me through my routines.

9. I .... not get bored because I had so many choices.

10. Write a sentence using *can, could,* or *would* as helping verbs. Suggested topic: Benefits of exercise.

....

....

L⑤ Correctly Use the Past Participle of Regular and Irregular Verbs

A **participle** is a verb form that can be used to establish tenses or voices, or it can be used as a modifier, which describes, restricts, or limits other words in a sentence. The **past participle** of a verb joins with helping verbs to form the present perfect and past perfect tenses and the passive voice. In addition, the past participle can act as an adjective that describes another word. Just as with the simple past tense, the past participle takes on different forms for regular and irregular verbs.

Past Participles of Regular Verbs

In general, regular verbs form the past participle by adding -*ed* to the base form of the verb. Just as with the simple past tense, there are several spelling exceptions for the past participle of regular verbs.

For more about the simple past tense, see pages 63, 65.

Base	Past Tense	Past Participle
share	share**d**	share**d**
rely	rel**ied**	rel**ied**
commit	commit**ted**	commit**ted**

Practice 7

CORRECTLY USE THE PAST PARTICIPLE OF REGULAR VERBS

Complete the following chart with the proper forms of the past tense and the past participle of each verb.

Base	Past Tense	Past Participle
1. allow		
2. ask		
3. believe		
4. blot		
5. change		
6. listen		
7. mug		
8. study		
9. try		
10. zip		

Past Participles of Irregular Verbs

As with the simple past tense, irregular verbs do not use *-ed* to form the past participle. Nor does the past participle of irregular verbs conform to uniform spelling rules with clear exceptions. In addition, the past participle forms of many irregular verbs vary from their past tense forms. Practice 8 and the chart that follows Practice 8 list the base form, past tense form, and past participle of the top 50 commonly used irregular verbs. These verbs appear in the order of the frequency of their use. As with the simple past forms of irregular verbs, when in doubt, careful writers consult a dictionary to find the form and spelling of the past participle of an irregular verb.

USE THE PAST PARTICIPLE OF IRREGULAR VERBS

The following chart contains the top ten irregular verbs listed by frequency of use. Supply the proper forms of the past tense and the past participle of each verb. Consult a dictionary as necessary.

Base		Past Tense	Past Participle
1.	say		
2.	make		
3.	go		
4.	take		
5.	come		
6.	see		
7.	know		
8.	get		
9.	give		
10.	find		

The 10 verbs listed in Practice 8 and the following chart of 40 words represents almost 90 percent of irregular verbs that are used most often in English. Master these verbs, and you will master the majority of the verbs you have to know. These are verbs you will likely be using as you read and write for everyday, college, and working life.

40 Irregular Verbs Ranked by Frequency of Use		
Base Form	**Past Tense**	**Past Participle**
think	thought	thought
tell	told	told
become	became	become
show	showed	shown/showed
leave	left	left
feel	felt	felt
put	put	put
bring	brought	brought
begin	began	begun
keep	kept	kept
hold	held	held
write	wrote	written
stand	stood	stood
hear	heard	heard
let	let	let
mean	meant	meant
set	set	set
meet	met	met
run	ran	run
pay	paid	paid
sit	sat	sat
speak	spoke	spoken
lie	lay	lain
lead	led	led
read	read	read
grow	grew	grown
lose	lost	lost
fall	fell	fallen
send	sent	sent
build	built	built
understand	understood	understood
draw	drew	drawn
break	broke	broken
spend	spent	spent
cut	cut	cut
rise	rose	risen
drive	drove	driven
buy	bought	bought
wear	wore	worn
choose	chose	chosen

Grabowski, E. & D. Mindt. 1995. A corpus-based learning list of irregular verbs in English. ICAME Journal 19: 5-22. [BUC, LOB]

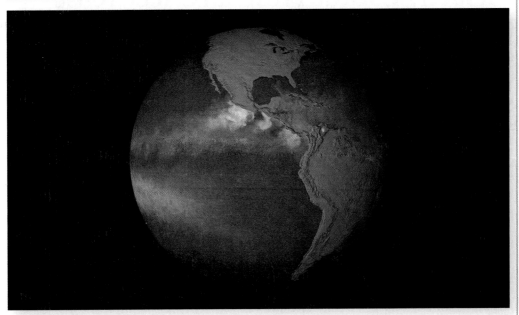

▲ Ocean temperatures

Test your current understanding of irregular verbs. Complete each sentence with an irregular verb from the chart "40 Irregular Verbs Ranked by Frequency of Use." Discuss your answers with a peer or your class.

1. Earth has .... warmer by 1°F over the past 100 years.

2. Scientists .... that human activity has .... to global warming.

3. Global warming is .... to be an average increase in the Earth's temperature,

   which in turn .... to changes in climate.

4. Experts and politicians, such as Al Gore, have .... about the impact of a warmer Earth.

5. Experts have .... a dire picture of changes in rainfall patterns, a rise in sea level, and a wide range of impacts on plants, wildlife, and humans.

6. Scientists .... that as Earth's temperature has .... warmer, glaciers have

   .... to melt and sea levels have ....

7. Since the Industrial Revolution, the need for energy to use machines has steadily .... higher and higher.

8. Before the Industrial Revolution, human activity .... very few gases into the atmosphere.

9. But our society is .... on burning fossil fuels, and we have .... a mixture of gases pollute the atmosphere.

10. The warning has been ....; most of us have .... idle in our vehicles for

    too long, but some of us have .... and .... against ....

    behaviors that have .... global warming.

L6 Correctly Use the Present Perfect Tense (*Has* or *Have* and the Past Participle)

The **present perfect tense** connects the past to the present. The present perfect tense states the relationship of a past action or situation to a current, ongoing action or situation. The present perfect tense is formed by joining the helping verbs **has** or **have** with a past participle.

CORRECTLY USE PAST PARTICIPLES

Complete the following chart with the appropriate past participle of the verbs in parentheses.

Subject	Helping Verb	Regular Past Participle	Irregular Past Participle
I	have	**1.** (accept)	**6.** (tell)
We	have	**2.** (allow)	**7.** (become)
You	have	**3.** (manage)	**8.** (keep)
He/She/It	has	**4.** (sip)	**9.** (spend)
They	have	**5.** (terrify)	**10.** (wore)

The purposes of the present perfect tense are:

• to express change from the past to the present.

PAST ACTION

PRESENT PERFECT "HAS CHANGED" STATES CHANGE FROM A PAST ACTION TO A PRESENT ONE

Theo was once a litter bug, but he has changed his ways.

• to express a situation or action that started in the past and continues to the present.

PRESENT PERFECT "HAVE VOLUNTEERED" STATES AN ONGOING ACTION, WHICH STARTED IN THE PAST AND IS CONTINUING NOW

Theo and Katie have volunteered with Adopt a Highway for several years.

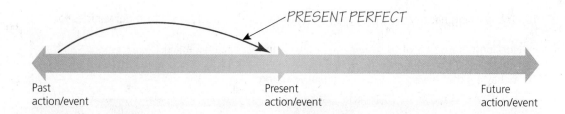

PRESENT PERFECT

Past
action/event

Present
action/event

Future
action/event

CORRECTLY USE THE PRESENT PERFECT TENSE

▲ Barge transporting garbage near the Statue of Liberty

Fill in the blanks with the present perfect tense of the verbs in parentheses. Verbs may be either regular or irregular. Use the helping verbs *has* or *have* to form the present perfect tense.

1. People .... (wrestle) with the trash problem ever since they settled in cities.

2. The government .... (collect) and .... (report) data on waste in the United States for more than 30 years.

3. Over the past 30 years, the waste produced in this country .... more than .... (double).

4. In recent years, Americans .... (generate) about 250 million tons of trash each year.

5. During this time, Americans .... (send) to landfills over 4 pounds of trash per person per day.

6. So far the average American .... not .... (cut) back on what he or she discards.

7. However, recycling .... (meet) with more approval as the amount of waste .... (rise).

8. Since the 1970s, burning trash to produce steam and electricity .... (show) to be another effective solution.

9. Write a sentence using the present perfect tense of a **regular** verb. Suggested topic: Littering. ....

....

10. Write a sentence using the present perfect tense of an **irregular** verb. Suggested topic: Litter clean-up. ....

....

L7 Correctly Use the Past Perfect Tense (*Had* and the Past Participle)

The **past perfect** connects two past actions or situations. The past perfect is formed by joining the helping verb *had* with a past participle.

CORRECTLY USE THE PAST PERFECT TENSE

Complete the following chart with the appropriate past participle of the verbs in parentheses.

Subject	Helping Verb	Regular Past Participle	Irregular Past Participle
I	had	**1.** (admit) _____	**6.** (leave) _____
We	had	**2.** (cheer) _____	**7.** (feel) _____
You	had	**3.** (object) _____	**8.** (bring) _____
He/She/It	had	**4.** (try) _____	**9.** (sit) _____
They	had	**5.** (zip) _____	**10.** (pay) _____

The purposes of the past perfect tense are:

• to connect a previous action or event with a later action or event.

PAST ACTION #2

PAST ACTION #1: THE PAST PERFECT "HAD LEFT" SHOWS THAT THIS ACTION OCCURRED BEFORE THE OTHER PAST ACTION "SAMUEL PUT…"

Samuel put out the trash, but the garbage truck had left.

• to express an action or event that happened before a certain past time.

PAST ACTION #2

PAST ACTION #1: THE PAST PERFECT "HAD SORTED" SHOWS THAT THIS ACTION OCCURRED BEFORE THE OTHER PAST ACTION "HE PUT…"

Before he put out the trash, he had sorted it for recycling.

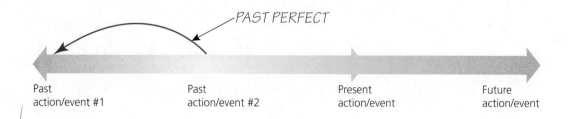

PAST PERFECT

| Past action/event #1 | Past action/event #2 | Present action/event | Future action/event |

▲ Waste manager

Fill in the blanks with the past perfect tense of the verbs in parentheses. The verbs may be regular or irregular. Use the helping verb *had* to form the past perfect tense.

1. In 1989, Chad Pregracke became a commercial clammer, and by 1996 he .... (crawl) all over the bottom of the Mississippi River and .... (live) on its shorelines.

2. Even before Chad worked as a commercial clammer, the accumulating garbage piles littering the river .... (horrify) him.

3. In 1997, Chad began cleaning up the garbage that government officials .... (ignore) in the Mississippi River.

4. By the time he finished his first season, Chad .... (remove) 45,000 pounds of refuse from the river.

5. Chad .... (begin) his nonprofit organization called Living Lands and Water by the time he was 23 years old.

6. Before I heard about Chad Pregracke, I .... (gave) money to various groups to clean up waterways.

7. I wish I .... (know) about Chad's work earlier.

8. I .... (think) only about giving money before Chad challenged us to give of our time, too.

9. Write a sentence using the past perfect tense of a **regular** verb. Suggested topic: Recycling.

....

....

10. Write a sentence using the past perfect tense of an **irregular** verb. Suggested topic: Littering.

....

....

L8 Correctly Use the Passive Voice (*To Be* and the Past Participle)

In English, verbs establish two types of voices: the active voice and the passive voice. So far, you have only worked with the active voice. Expressing what the subject of a sentence does, action verbs establish the **active voice.** When the subject of a sentence receives the action (or is acted upon), the sentence is in the **passive voice.** The passive voice is formed by joining *to be* with a past participle. In addition, the passive voice can be expressed in every tense.

The purpose of the passive voice is to tell the reader what is done to a subject.

Active Voice

SUBJECT "WASTE MANAGEMENT" PERFORMS THE ACTION

Waste Management serves 20 million customers.

Passive Voice

SUBJECT "CUSTOMERS" RECEIVES THE ACTION

Twenty million customers are served by Waste Management.

Examples of the tenses of the passive voice

Present Tense

SUBJECT   PRESENT TENSE OF "TO BE"   PAST PARTICIPLE OF "BREAK"

The compact fluorescent light bulb is broken.

Past Tense

SUBJECT   PAST TENSE OF "TO BE"   PAST PARTICIPLE OF "HURT"

Nobody was hurt.

Present Perfect Tense

SUBJECT   PRESENT PERFECT TENSE OF "TO BE"   PAST PARTICIPLE OF "PICK"

All the pieces have been picked up.

Past Perfect Tense

SUBJECT   PAST PERFECT TENSE OF "TO BE"   PAST PARTICIPLE OF "PUT"

The debris had been put in a sealed plastic bag.

Practice 14

▲ Plastic bag along a coral reef in Egypt

Fill in the blanks with the passive voice of the verbs in parentheses. The verbs may be regular or irregular. Use the verb *to be* to form the passive voice.

1. In recent years, inexpensive plastic bags .... (prefer) by most stores.

2. Plastic bags .... (price) under 2 cents a bag.

3. Last year, an estimated 500 billion to 1 trillion plastic bags .... (consume) worldwide.

4. Hundreds of thousands of sea turtles, whales, and other marine mammals .... (kill) by eating discarded plastic bags that they mistook for food.

5. Plastic bags .... (find) more often than other debris during coastal clean-ups.

6. Traditionally, plastic bags .... (see) as less harmful on the environment than paper bags.

7. Plastic bags .... (make) from natural gas or oil.

8. The choice to use reusable bags .... (make) before we went to the store.

9. Write a sentence using the passive voice of a **regular** verb. Suggested topic: Reusable cloth grocery bags.

....

....

10. Write a sentence using the passive voice of an **irregular** verb. Suggested topic: Benefits or dangers of paper bags to the environment.

....

....

LO 9 Correctly Use the Past Participle as an Adjective

For more information on participles as adjectives see pages 45–47.

The past participle is often used as an adjective that modifies a noun or pronoun. Both regular and irregular forms of the past participle are used as adjectives. The purposes of the past participle as an adjective are:

• to describe a noun or pronoun with a word or phrase.

PARTICIPLE "REUSED" DESCRIBES "WATER BOTTLES"

Reused water bottles are not safe.

PARTICIPLE PHRASE

Meant for single use, water bottles should not be reused.

• to describe the subject by completing a linking verb in the sentence.

LINKING VERB   *SUBJECT "CONTAINER" IS DESCRIBED BY PAST PARTICIPLE "WORN"*

The plastic container looks worn with use.

Practice 15

CORRECTLY USE THE PAST PARTICIPLE AS AN ADJECTIVE

Fill in the blanks with the past participle forms of the verbs in parentheses.

1. Plastic is the most widely .... (use) material in the United States.

2. .... (can) food and .... (bottle) water may contain a controversial chemical .... (call) bisphenol A (BPA).

3. Although .... (think) of as harmless by the plastics industry, BPA may affect the developing brains of children.

4. .... (educate) buyers avoid plastic products .... (imprint) with the number 7, which indicates the presence of BPA.

5. .... (create) by using petroleum, plastics can be toxic.

6. Consumers should buy food .... (store) in glass or metal containers.

7. .... (heat) plastic containers may leach chemicals into food.

8. .... , (obsess) Jena avoids all use of plastic.

9. She fears there still may be .... (hide) dangers.

10. Write a sentence using the past participle as an adjective. Suggested topic: A harmful product. ....

Editing Assignments

MyWritingLab™
Complete this Exercise
on mywritinglab.com

Editing for Everyday Life

Read the following blog. Edit to ensure proper usage of verbs.

Are you tire of seeing litter gum up our lakes and rivers? Are you ready to do something about it? For the past two years, our group has spend every Saturday cleaning up trash along our shores. Before we began, litter been a common sight. Since we began, we picked up broken glass, used needles, even soiled diapers. So you can imagine what it had look like before we took action. Because we have been so successful, we have been ask to expand our work. So come out and join us this Sunday for our first sweep of the East River. We need you!

Editing for College Life

Read the following paragraph written in response to a test question on a college biology exam. Edit to ensure proper usage of verbs.

Question: What is the human impact on tropical rain forests?

Student Answer: Sell for lumber or burn to clear land for ranching or farming, rain forests are being destroy at a rapid rate. Scientists has estimated that current rain forest destruction ranges from 22,000 square miles to 52,000 square miles per year. In many areas, only small fragments of forests are leave standing. These areas are too small to support many types of wildlife. At least 40% of the world's rain forests have been loss. Although the losses continue, some areas have been sit aside as protected preserves.

Editing for Working Life

Attention Sales Managers, Store:

Thank you for helping to keep our stores secure by taking part in our company's update security protocol. Last quarter's sales summary report an overall decrease in lost or stolen merchandise throughout the southeast region. Your store always been a prime example of excellence. Your associate team are well train and reflects our company values. All of the "secret sales reports" from last quarter shows how each of your team's associates could follow company policy. However, if any one member of your team can't assist a customer, there are always a manager on floor that could offer more thorough assistance. Last quarter, our stores in your region has made the most profit to date. Because of your store report the highest profitable earnings and lowest inventory lose, each of your store managers will receive a two hundred dollar bonus. In addition, each of your associates will receive a one hundred dollar bonus in your next paycheck.

Sincerely,

Deborah Haines
Regional Manager

PORTFOLIO

A. Review what you have learned throughout this chapter by completing the following activity. Read the following paragraph. Edit to ensure use of the appropriate forms of verbs.

Marine Debris

(1) Marine debris is define as any man-made, solid material that enters our waterways. (2) Debris can enter waterways directly as dump trash. (3) Or it can simply be wash out to sea by rivers, streams, or storm drains. (4) In addition to being unsightly, this litter pose a serious threat to everything with which it comes into contact. (5) Marine debris has prove to be life-threatening to marine organisms. (6) Entangle in marine debris, millions of seabirds, sea turtles, fish, and marine mammals have suffer or died. (7) As many as 30,000 northern fur seals per year get catch in abandon fishing nets and either drown or suffocate. (8) Whales mistook plastic bags for squid, and birds may confused plastic pellets for fish eggs. (9) Marine debris have already hurt coastal areas and the fishing industry, and the harm will continue unless we get involved.

B. To test and track your understanding, answer the following questions.

1. The _____ is used to describe an action or event in the present time, habitual actions, or general truths.

2. What is the general rule for forming the past tense of regular verbs? Give an example.

_____

_____

3. What are three exceptions to the way in which regular verbs form the past tense? Give examples.

a. _____

b. _____

_____

c. _____

_____

4. What are two traits of irregular verbs?

_____

5. What are the correct past tense forms of the following three irregular verbs: *to be, to have,* and *to do?*

....

6. List three often-confused helping verbs. ....

7. The present perfect tense is formed by joining the helping verbs .... or

.... with the past participle.

8. What are two purposes of the present perfect tense?

a. ....

b. ....

9. The past perfect tense is formed by joining the helping verb .... with the past participle.

10. What are two purposes of the past perfect tense?

a. ....

b. ....

11. The passive voice is formed by the combination of ....with a past participle.

12. What is the purpose of the passive voice? ....

13. What are two purposes of the past participle as an adjective?

a. ....

b. ....

14. How will I use what I have learned about verbs?
In your notebook, discuss how you will apply to your own writing what you have learned about verbs.

15. What do I still need to study about verbs?
In your notebook, describe your ongoing study needs by describing what, when, and how you will continue studying verbs.

PORTFOLIO

MyWritingLab™

Complete the Post-test for Chapter 4 in MyWritingLab.

5

Subjects, Verbs, and Simple Sentences

A simple sentence, also called an *independent clause*, includes a subject and a verb and expresses a complete thought.

Communicating about a real-life situation helps us to understand the purpose of subjects, verbs, and simple sentences. The photographs on these pages show one of the tallest buildings on earth. Read the statements given in Practice 1 about this sky scraper, and answer the question "What's the point of subjects, verbs, and simple sentences?"

What's the Point of Subjects, Verbs, and Simple Sentences?

Read the following set of statements. Circle the one that makes the most sense. Discuss why the statement you chose makes sense and why the other two do not.

WRITING
FROM LIFE

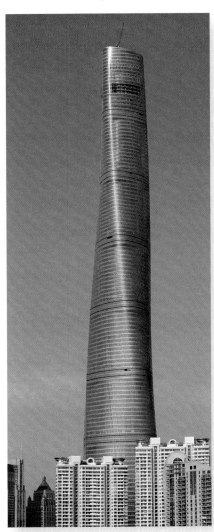

▲ *Shanghai Tower*

Shanghai Tower, the world's second-tallest building. Produces its own electricity through wind turbines.

Shanghai Tower, the world's second-tallest building, produces its own electricity through wind turbines.

What's the point of subjects, verbs, and simple sentences?

Subjects put people or places in.
verbs give active, simple sentace put all
together

One Student Writer's Response

The following paragraph offers one writer's reaction to the statements about Shanghai Tower and the importance of subjects, verbs, and simple sentences.

The last statement is the only one that made sense to me. The first statement gives a topic, and the second statement describes a topic and includes a verb "produces." Both statements sound like parts of an idea instead of complete thoughts.

A subject and a verb unite to state a focused and complete thought in a sentence.

L2 Recognize and State Subjects

A **subject** is the person, place, object, or topic about which a writer expresses a focused thought or makes an assertion. To identify a subject, ask: Who or what did this? Alternatively, ask: Who or what is this?

Types of Subjects

A subject is expressed in a variety of ways based on the focus of the writer's thought or point. Two common types of subjects include the **simple subject** and the **compound subject**.

Simple Subjects: Three Types

- **Simple Subject, Type 1:** A single person, place, object, or topic is the focus of thought.

  SUBJECT
  ↓

  Wind turbines produce renewable energy by converting wind power into electricity.

- **Simple Subject, Type 2:** A group of words expresses the focus of thought.

  SUBJECT
  ↓

  Using renewable energy reduces pollution.

- **Simple Subject, Type 3:** A suggestion, command, or order is the focus of thought.

  Support the use of renewable energy.
  ↑

  "YOU" IS UNDERSTOOD, BUT NOT STATED, AS THE SUBJECT OF THE SENTENCE, WHICH IS A COMMAND.

Compound Subject

- **Compound Subject:** Two or more people, places, objects, or topics are the subjects of a focused thought.

COMPOUND SUBJECTS

↓   ↓   ↓

The sun, wind, and biodiesel are also renewable energy sources.

COMPOUND SUBJECTS ARE OFTEN JOINED BY
THE COORDINATE CONJUNCTION "AND."

RECOGNIZE AND STATE SUBJECTS

Underline the subject once in each of the following sentences. Then, identify each subject by its type, writing *simple* or *compound* in the blanks. Share and discuss your responses in a small group or with your class.

.... **1.** Ferry boats and military crafts use wave-piercing technology.

.... **2.** Wave-piercers have a very narrow bow.

Simple **3.** Narrowing the bow reduces the up and down bounce of the boat's bow.

Simple **4.** The narrow hull pierces through the water rather than riding over the top.

Simple **5.** In 2008, the wave-piercer *Earthrace* proved that a boat powered by biodiesel—a form of renewable energy—could break records for racing around the world.

Com **6.** Waste cooking oil, soya oil, and canola oil are the biofuels that power *Earthrace*.

Com **7.** Monsoon conditions and large waves challenged the *Earthrace* crew during the last legs of their race around the world.

Com **8.** Captain Pete Bethune and his crew completed the trip in just over 60 days, breaking previous records.

9. Write a sentence using a simple subject. Suggested topic: A useful invention.

A useful invention is the wheel.

10. Write a sentence using a compound subject. Suggested topic: Energy sources.

Soler power is an energy source.

L3 Recognize and Use Verbs

A **verb** makes an assertion about a subject. A verb states an occurrence (*occur, happen*), a state of being (*is, seems*), or an action (*run, talk*) of the subject. Three basic types of verbs include **linking verbs, action verbs,** and **helping verbs**.

Linking Verbs

A **linking verb** connects the subject to a word that renames, describes, or defines the subject. Linking verbs often describe a state of being.

Commonly Used Linking Verbs

- *am, is, are, was, were, am being, has been*

SUBJECT LINKING VERB

Renewable power is natural power.

- *appear, become, look, seem, turn*

SUBJECT LINKING VERB

Water turns into energy or hydro power.

- *feel, smell, sound, taste*

SUBJECT LINKING VERB

The engine feels hot and smells like burning oil.

Fill in each blank with a linking verb that best completes the meaning of the sentence. Discuss your responses in a small group or with your class.

1. Energy _is_ the ability to do work.

2. We _use_ the warmth of the sun's energy.

3. Much of our energy _is_ from petroleum products.

4. The use of petroleum for energy _is_ to be a factor in global warming.

5. Alternative forms of energy _are_ ways to reduce our use of petroleum-based energy.

6. Solar, wind, and other renewable resources _are_ alternative forms of energy.

7. Solar panels _are turing_ the sun's energy into electrical power.

8. Wind power _is_ to be one of the most promising new energy sources.

9. A typical single wind turbine _are_ louder than a refrigerator but quieter than a blender.

10. State an idea using a linking verb. Suggested topic: Use of energy.

wind and the sun are good ways to go becase they are not going any were.

Action Verbs

An **action verb** shows the behavior of the subject.

SUBJECT   ACTION VERB

Sport utility vehicles guzzle gas.

Practice 4

Underline the action verb twice in each of the following sentences.

1. Shantel exercises to burn energy.

2. Michael jogs for an hour to burn around 700 calories.

3. Shantel jumps rope for 10 minutes every day.

4. She also climbs the 100 steps in the football stadium.

5. After jogging, Michael swims a half mile in the ocean.

6. Finally, he bikes for five miles.

7. Shantel and Michael win many physical fitness competitions.

8. They compete in Ironman triathlons.

9. They swim 2.4 miles, bike 115 miles, and run 26.2 miles in one day.

10. State an idea using an action verb. Suggested topic: Exercise. *I ran a mile a day.*

Helping Verbs

A **helping verb** is used with a main verb to create a verb phrase. Helping verbs are also used to form questions. The verbs *be*, *do*, and *have* can be used alone or as helping verbs.

```
┌─VERB PHRASE─┐
HELPING VERB  MAIN VERB
     ↓            ↓
```

I will begin a routine of regular exercise and healthful eating.

```
┌─VERB PHRASE─┐
HELPING VERB  MAIN VERB
     ↓            ↓
```

Have you lost weight?

Common Helping Verbs						
be	do	have	may	could	can	have to
being	does	had	might	should	shall	have got to
been	did	has	must	would	will	ought to
am						supposed to
are						used to
is						
was						
were						

RECOGNIZE AND USE VERBS: HELPING VERBS

Underline the <u>verb phrase</u> twice in each of the following sentences.

1. Hurricanes, ice storms, and tornadoes can <u>be</u> devastating natural disasters.

2. Due to lack of road access, emergency services may <u>be</u> delayed for up to 72 hours after a major disaster.

3. Citizens must <u>be</u> prepared before any major storm.

4. Lack of preparation can cause loss of property and even life.

5. One should <u>have</u> plenty of canned food, bottled water, and candles or oil lamps.

6. Buying a generator as an alternative power source would <u>be</u> wise.

7. Citizens <u>ought to</u> heed severe weather warnings.

8. Too many people <u>do</u> not heed severe weather warnings.

9. They may think they <u>will</u> have plenty of time to seek safety.

10. Most often, severe weather warnings <u>are</u> issued in plenty of time.

RECOGNIZE AND USE VERBS: HELPING VERBS

Underline the <u>subject</u> once and the <u>verb phrase</u> twice in each of the following sentences.

1. <u>Everyone</u> should <u>exercise</u> at least three times a week.

2. Most <u>people</u> <u>do</u> not get enough <u>exercise</u> in their daily routine.

3. Has <u>Eugene</u> lost <u>weight</u>?

4. <u>Lifting weights and walking</u> will <u>build</u> muscle and increase bone density.

5. <u>Fruits and vegetables</u> <u>taste</u> good and are good for you.

6. Poor eating <u>habits</u> are hard to change.

7. <u>To change</u> one must <u>be</u> determined.

8. <u>You</u> might <u>slide</u> back into old habits.

9. However, every <u>day</u> will <u>bring</u> a new opportunity to succeed.

10. State an idea using a helping verb. Suggested topic: A personal goal. *I want to own my own car dealership.*

▲ **Exercise class**

Practice 7

RECOGNIZE AND USE SUBJECTS AND VERBS

Follow the directions to create five sentences. Suggested topic for your sentences: Exercise: Barriers or benefits.

1. Write a sentence with a simple subject: Wind trubins are green.

2. Write a sentence with a compound subject: Devin whent to the store

3. Write a sentence using a linking verb: I tran the whele on my core

4. Write a sentence with an action verb: I run up a hill.

5. Write a sentence with a helping verb: I do not like this.

Compose the Simple Sentence

A **simple sentence** is a group of related words that includes a subject and a verb and expresses a complete thought. A simple sentence is also known as an **independent clause**. An idea that is missing a subject or a verb is a fragment or an incomplete thought.

For more information on correcting fragments, see pages 134–155.

Distinguishing Between a Fragment and the Simple Sentence

Fragment with missing subject:

VERB

Became the first female to win a major auto race.

Fragment with missing verb:

SUBJECT

Danica Patrick becoming the first female to win a major auto race.

Simple Sentence:

SUBJECT   VERB

Danica Patrick became the first female to win a major auto race.

COMPOSE SIMPLE SENTENCES

Create a simple sentence from each of the following fragments. From the box below, choose a subject or a verb that best completes each thought. Revise into simple sentences.

Verbs	Subjects
began	competitors
drives	Danica Patrick
increased	she
is	Patrick
made	
provide	
rates	

Danica Patrick at 2005 Indianapolis 500 race ▶

Practice 8

93

1. Danica Sue Patrick an American auto racing driver.

[handwritten: S S S V]

2. In 2008, became the first woman to win an Indy car race.

[handwritten: S V]

3. Indy racing as the most extreme form of auto racing.

[handwritten: S V V]

4. Losing the first 49 races in her Indy racing career her desire to win.

[handwritten: S V S V]

5. Determined, took the lead to win on the 198th lap of the 200-lap race.

[handwritten: S V]

6. Her were forced to pit for fuel in the final laps.

[handwritten: S V]

7. In 2010, racing in the NASCAR Nationwide series.

[handwritten: S V]

8. She the Number 10 Chevrolet SS for Stewart-Haas Racing.

[handwritten: S V S S V]

9. In 2014, finished in the top 10 in five NASCAR races.

[handwritten: S V]

10. Heroes like Danica Patrick hope to female competitors in sports and beyond.

[handwritten: S V]

L5 Locate Subjects and Verbs to Identify Complete Thoughts

To avoid fragments and to state ideas as complete thoughts, proofread to identify the subjects and verbs of each sentence. Identifying prepositional phrases as you proofread will help you locate the subject of the sentence.

Understand the Prepositional Phrase

A **preposition** is a word that has a noun or pronoun as its object and states a relationship between its object and another word. A prepositional phrase begins with a preposition and ends with the object of the preposition.

```
        ┌─PREPOSITIONAL PHRASE─┐
from the remains of plants and animals
    ↑                   ↑
PREPOSITION     OBJECTS OF THE PREPOSITION
```

The following chart lists a few common prepositions and examples of their objects.

Common Prepositions with Possible Objects			
Preposition	**Object**	**Preposition**	**Object**
about	the house	during	the storm
after	the movie	for	love
against	the current	from	the past
along	the street	in/into	a wallet
as/like	the parent	of	the boys
at	the moment	on	the chair
below	the surface	to	the college
by	evening	with	patience

Find the Prepositional Phrases

The object of the preposition can never be the subject or the verb of a sentence. Since subjects and verbs are often surrounded by prepositional phrases, you need to identify these phrases. Identifying prepositional phrases keeps you from confusing them with the subject of the sentence. And often, once these phrases are identified, the subject and the verb—or lack of either—becomes easier to recognize.

COMPOSE SIMPLE SENTENCES: IDENTIFY PREPOSITIONAL PHRASES

Place parentheses around all (prepositional phrases) in the following simple sentences.

1. The United States of America consumes about 882 million gallons of petroleum products each day.

2. After millions of years, some organic remains of animals and plants turn into crude oil.

3. The refining process of crude oil creates products like gasoline, diesel fuel, heating oil, and jet fuel.

4. The characteristics of gasoline depend on the type of crude oil.

5. The cost of crude oil acts as the main contributor to the record high gasoline prices of 2008.

6. The cost of crude oil accounts for 55% of the price of gasoline.

7. Distribution and taxes influence 45% of gasoline's price.

8. In 2012, concerns about military action against Iran caused high oil prices.

9. At the same time, some oil refineries in the U.S. were closing.

10. As a result, gas prices hit the high level of $3.50 in February of 2012.

Practice 9

The FIL Process

To identify subjects and verbs, follow these three simple steps:

1. **F**ind Prepositional Phrases: Place parentheses around (prepositional phrases).

2. **I**dentify the Verb: Underline the <u>verb</u> (action or linking) twice.

3. **L**ocate the Subject: Ask: Who or what did this or who or what is this? The answer is the subject. Underline the <u>subject</u> once.

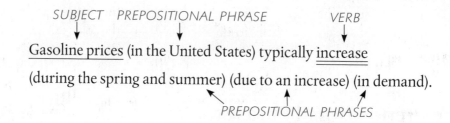

SUBJECT   PREPOSITIONAL PHRASE   VERB

Gasoline prices (in the United States) typically increase

(during the spring and summer) (due to an increase) (in demand).

PREPOSITIONAL PHRASES

COMPOSE SIMPLE SENTENCES: IDENTIFY SUBJECTS AND VERBS

Identify the subjects and verbs in the following simple sentences. Annotate each sentence: Place (prepositional phrases) in parentheses, underline the <u>verb</u> twice, underline the <u>subject</u> once.

1. Oil prices are set by commodities traders.

2. They make agreements to buy or sell oil at a specific date in the future at a specific price.

3. Like most goods, oil prices are affected by supply and demand.

4. Often predicting future oil prices as high, traders bid high for oil leading to high prices for oil in the future.

5. Thus, traders often cause higher prices by bidding high and passing the cost to the consumer.

6. Gas prices rise by an average of 10 cents per gallon due to summertime vacation driving.

7. We need to reduce our use of gasoline.

8. We must reduce our dependency upon fossil fuels.

9. One way of increasing fuel efficiency is to keep tires inflated.

10. The use of alternative energy is another option for us to consider.

Read the following paragraph written by a student. In each sentence, underline the <u>subject</u> once, underline the <u>verb</u> twice, and place parentheses around the (prepositional phrase). *Hint:* Some sentences use the understood subject *you*. Then, write three simple sentences of your own.

(1) For each gallon of gas used by driving, twenty pounds of carbon dioxide pollute the air.

(2) We, as residents in a large city, can take action to reduce our use of fuel. (3) First of all, our bus system runs on electronic and hybrid fuel and deserves our support. (4) Our use of mass transit will reduce pollution. (5) Obviously, a bus full of people, as opposed to the average car with one or two people, is a much more efficient use of fuel. (6) Secondly, many of us could carpool with our coworkers. (7) Think about it. (8) One car with four people, on the road is better than four people in four cars on the road. (9) Finally, we of able bodies should walk and bike more often. (10) Using our own energy for transportation causes no pollution at all.

(11) In addition to the benefits of less pollution, these changes in our behavior are going to save us money at the gas pump.

Write three simple sentences. Suggested topic: Transportation issues.

1. we need to carpool,

2. we need bettrings for gas

3. we need more glean.

Editing Assignments

MyWritingLab™
Complete this Exercise
on mywritinglab.com

Editing for Everyday Life

Read the following letter to the editor of a newspaper. In each sentence, underline the subject once, underline the verb twice, and place parentheses around the (prepositional phrase). Use your own paper, or complete this exercise on MyWritingLab.com.

Dear Editor:

An article about building solar power plants in our community appeared on Monday in the business section of your paper. Many of us in the area are excited about the benefits of solar energy. The uses for solar energy include heating water for domestic use and the space heating of buildings. The energy from one solar power plant will offer enough electricity to run hundreds of homes. The source of solar power is renewable. And the energy from the sun does not harm the quality of our air. The Chief Officer of The State Power and Light Company has earned our thanks.

Editing for College Life

Read the following paragraph written for a college economics class. In each sentence, underline the subject once, underline the verb twice, and place parentheses around the (prepositional phrase). Use your own paper, or complete this exercise on MyWritingLab.com.

The relationship between supply and demand sets the price in the market place. Demand is the purchase of specific quantities of a good or service at different prices in a given time. Supply is the creation and delivery of specific quantities of a good or service at different prices in a given time. For a demand to exist, someone must be willing to pay for the goods. Often, a product in high demand but short in supply will have a high price. In contrast, a product in low demand but high in supply will have a lower price.

Editing for Working Life

Read the following memo sent from a director to her staff. Identify subjects, verbs, and prepositional phrases. Underline subjects once, verbs twice, and place parentheses around (prepositional phrases). *Hint:* Some sentences use the understood subject *you.* Use your own paper, or complete this exercise on MyWritingLab.com.

TO: The Accounting Staff
FROM: Maya Berry, Director of Accounting
SUBJECT: Going Green

Dear Staff:

In compliance with our company's new energy policies, our department is making the following changes. All of the lights are to remain off in unoccupied rooms. On your way out of a room, remember to shut off the lights. Recycling bins for paper, aluminum, and plastic waste have been placed near each of your cubicles. Paper cups for coffee and water are no longer being provided in the break room. You must supply your own coffee mug or glass. I appreciate your cooperation in this matter.

Best Regards,
Maya Berry

Academic Learning Log: Chapter Review

WHAT HAVE I LEARNED?

To test and track your understanding, complete the following sentences. Use several sentences as needed for each response.

1. A subject is _the mane idea_

2. The two types of subjects are _simpole and compound_

3. A verb _is anachine word_

The three basic types of verbs are _linking, Helping, Acien_

4. A simple sentence is _swdject and a verld_

5. How will I use what I have learned?
In your notebook, discuss how you will apply to your own writing what you have learned about subjects and verbs. _idk_

6. What do I still need to study about subjects and verbs?
In your notebook, describe your ongoing study needs by describing what, when, and how you will continue studying subjects and verbs. _everything_

PORTFOLIO

MyWritingLab™
Complete the Post-test for Chapter 5 in MyWritingLab.

6

Compound and Complex Sentences

A compound sentence joins together two or more independent clauses. A complex sentence combines one independent or main clause and one or more dependent clauses.

Communicating about a real-life situation helps us to understand the purpose of compound and complex sentences. The photographs on these two pages illustrate the joy of adopting a child as a way to build a family. Read the statements given in Practice 1, complete the activities, and answer the question "What's the point of compound and complex sentences?"

What's the Point of Compound and Complex Sentences?

PHOTOGRAPHIC ORGANIZER: COMPOUND AND COMPLEX SENTENCES

The following ideas are stated using four types of sentences: (1) simple, (2) compound, (3) complex, and (4) compound-complex. Discuss with a small group of peers in what ways these sentences differ from each other.

1. Over 600,000 children in America lived in foster care in 2012.

2. A little over 50,000 of those children were adopted; another 102,000 were legally ready for adoption.

3. A birth mother often chooses to give up her child for adoption because she believes another family will be able to offer a more stable life for her child.

4. People adopt for a variety of reasons; for example, some people adopt to help a specific child or birth mother.

WRITING FROM LIFE

What's the point of compound and complex sentences?

One Student Writer's Response

The following paragraph offers one writer's thoughts about the differences among sentence types.

First, I found the subjects and verbs in each sentence. The first sentence is a simple sentence. In fact, all the sentences had a simple sentence in them. It's like different ways to put simple sentences together. I want to know why the commas and semicolons are used in sentences 2 and 4. The four types of sentences are four different ways to say something.

L2 Recognize Types of Clauses

A **clause** is a group of related words that includes a subject and a verb. Two types of clauses provide the basis of all sentences: the (1) **independent clause** and the (2) **dependent clause**.

1. The Independent Clause

A focused and complete thought expressed with a subject and a verb; also known as a *main clause* or **simple sentence**.

INDEPENDENT CLAUSE
(COMPLETE THOUGHT)

Adoptive family members can form strong bonds.

SUBJECT   VERB

2. The Dependent Clause

For more about subordinating conjunctions, see page. 107.

(1) An incomplete thought expressed with a subject and a verb marked by a subordinating conjunction such as *after, before,* or *when.*

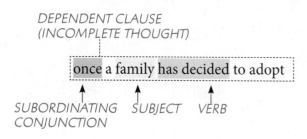

DEPENDENT CLAUSE
(INCOMPLETE THOUGHT)

once a family has decided to adopt

SUBORDINATING   SUBJECT   VERB
CONJUNCTION

(2) An incomplete thought marked by a relative pronoun, such as *who* or *which*, acting as the subject of the verb.

For more about relative pronouns, see page 108.

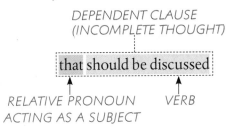

DEPENDENT CLAUSE
(INCOMPLETE THOUGHT)

that should be discussed

RELATIVE PRONOUN   VERB
ACTING AS A SUBJECT

Practice 2

RECOGNIZE TYPES OF CLAUSES

Identify each of the following clauses as **I** for independent or **D** for dependent. *Hint:* Circle subordinating conjunctions and relative pronouns.

I **1.** Other children in the adoptive family may feel left out.

_____ **2.** When an adopted child comes into the family.

D **3.** Children who live in adoptive families.

_____ **4.** If they can stay in contact with biological parents.

_____ **5.** Children of adoptive families can adjust and thrive.

D **6.** When they adopted a baby.

_____ **7.** Children need time to adjust.

I **8.** An adopted child leaves everything behind to start a new life.

_____ **9.** Which requires work and patience to ease the transition between the child's old and new lives.

_____ **10.** Parents who put their children first.

Compose Compound Sentences

L3

A compound sentence is made up of two or more independent clauses. A **compound sentence** links two or more independent clauses as **equally important** ideas through one of three methods.

Three Ways to Combine Independent Clauses into a Compound Sentence

1. A comma and a coordinating conjunction: The coordinating conjunction serves as a transition that shows the relationship of ideas within the sentence. Use the acronym FANBOYS to help you remember the seven coordinating conjunctions—*for, and, nor, but, or, yet,* or *so.*

[Independent clause,] and [independent clause.]

Coordinating Conjunctions (FANBOYS) and Meanings							
Coordinating Conjunction	For	And	Nor	But	Or	Yet	So
Meaning	Result	Addition	Negation	Contrast	Choice	Contrast	Result

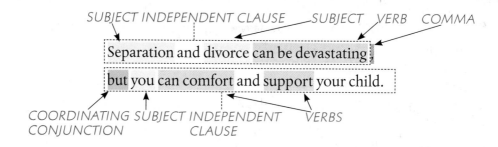

2. A semicolon, conjunctive adverb, and a comma: The conjunction shows the relationship of ideas within the sentence. In addition, the conjunctive adverb introduces the next clause. A comma follows the conjunctive adverb since it is an introductory element of the next clause:

[Independent clause;] therefore ,[independent clause.]

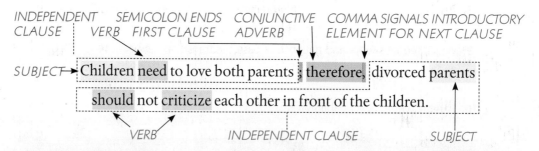

Common Conjunctive Adverbs and the Relationships They Express					
Addition	**Cause or Effect**	**Comparison or Contrast**	**Example**	**Emphasis**	**Time**
also	accordingly	however	for example	certainly	finally
besides	as a result	in comparison	for instance	indeed	meanwhile
further	consequently	in contrast		in fact	next
furthermore	hence	instead		still	then
in addition	therefore	likewise		undoubtedly	thereafter
incidentally	thus	nevertheless			
moreover		nonetheless			
		otherwise			
		similarly			

3. A semicolon: A semicolon joins two closely related independent clauses.

[Independent clause;] [independent clause.]

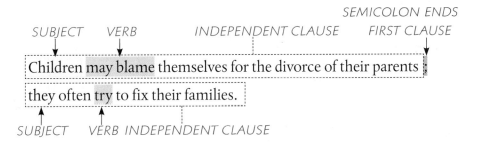

SUBJECT   VERB   INDEPENDENT CLAUSE   SEMICOLON ENDS FIRST CLAUSE

Children may blame themselves for the divorce of their parents ;
they often try to fix their families.

SUBJECT   VERB INDEPENDENT CLAUSE

COMPOSE COMPOUND SENTENCES

Insert the proper punctuation in each of the following compound sentences. **Hint:** Identify the subjects and verbs. Place parentheses around (prepositional phrases); underline the <u>subject</u> once; underline the <u>verb</u> twice.

1. A divorce creates a painful loss for everyone parents and children need time to mourn the loss of the family.

2. Parents should sit down together and talk with their children,′ so both parents can comfort them and promise to be there for them.

3. Eventually, a divorced parent will likely remarry as a result a new blended family faces several challenges.

4. Only the biological parent should discipline his or her children, and the same rules apply to all the children of the same age.

5. A blended family of biological and step children is a new start for everyone therefore the new family should create new family traditions such as a family movie night once a month.

6. Respect builds a strong family; respect of others reveals respect of self .

7. Boundaries are healthy, so a family should discuss expectations and define limits.

8. Healthy families are aware of their feelings, and they express them directly and honestly.

9. Members of a healthy family consider the viewpoints of others ; thus, they listen without interrupting.

10. Write a compound sentence. Suggested topic: Family traditions.

For more information on how to identify subjects, verbs, and prepositional phrases, see page 96.

Practice 4

Create compound sentences by combining the following sets of simple sentences. Vary the ways in which you join ideas. Use appropriate conjunctions and punctuation to show the relationship between ideas within each new sentence.

1. Positive thinking is a mental attitude. It focuses on thoughts, words, and images helpful to growth and success.

2. Positive thinking replaces negative thoughts. The positive thoughts "can" and "will" replace the negative thought "can't."

3. Positive thinking is contagious. You should surround yourself with positive people.

4. Gratitude increases happiness. Complaints increase discouragement.

5. A goal should become a vivid mental image. Jules imagines holding his diploma in his hand.

6. You don't give up. Failure often occurs before success.

7. Success requires planning. Goals offer motivation and direction.

8. Paul sees humor in everyday events. Paul feels little stress.

9. We should identify our negative thoughts about an issue, such as work. We should find ways to think positively about it.

10. Write a compound sentence. Suggested topic: An important personal goal.

Compose Complex Sentences

L④

A **complex sentence** contains one independent or main clause and one or more dependent clauses. A **dependent clause** expresses a **subordinate** or minor detail about an idea in the independent clause. A complex sentence joins independent and dependent clauses by placing a subordinating conjunction at the beginning of the dependent clause. **Subordinating conjunctions** state the relationship between the main clause and the subordinate clause.

Subordinating Conjunctions and the Relationships They Express				
Cause	**Contrast**	**Time**	**Place**	**Condition**
as	although	after	where	even if
because	as if	as	wherever	how
in order that	even though	as long as		if
now that	though	before		only if
since	whereas	once		that
so	while	since		unless
		until		what
		when		when
		whenever		whether or not
		while		

INDEPENDENT CLAUSE   DEPENDENT CLAUSE

Your role in society is set | before you are born.

SUBJECT   VERB   SUBORDINATING CONJUNCTION

COMPOSE COMPLEX SENTENCES

Practice 5

A. Underline the dependent clauses in each sentence. In the blank after each sentence, state the relationship between the dependent clause and the main clause.

1. Society was waiting to teach you how you are to act as a boy or a girl. _you_

2. Whether you were born rich, poor, or middle-class, your status also affects your role in society. _of_

3. Although you occupy a status or a position, you play a role. _of_

4. A father fulfills his role by providing food, shelter, and love because of his status as a parent. _and_

5. Often, the father assumes the role of provider while the mother assumes the role of care giver. _while_

B. Construct complex sentences by joining the independent clauses with a logical subordinating conjunction. Be sure to correctly punctuate your new complex sentence.

6. A father is involved with his child. His impact is powerful and positive.

....

7. A father treats his child's mother with respect. The child learns to treat women with respect.

....

8. A child with an involved father will do better in school. A father's attention increases a child's mental abilities.

....

....

9. Fathers often push independence. Mothers often stress nurturing.

....

10. Write a complex sentence using a subordinating conjunction. State the relationship between your dependent and main clauses. Suggested topic: Traits of a good father.

....

....

Practice 5

A special kind of subordinating conjunction is the relative pronoun. A **relative pronoun** connects the dependent clause to a noun in the main clause. The choice of a relative pronoun indicates whether the dependent clause is describing a person or thing.

Relative Pronouns and What They Indicate		
People	**Things**	**People or Things**
who	which	that
whom		
whose		

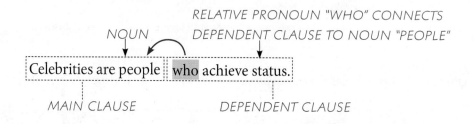

NOUN

RELATIVE PRONOUN "WHO" CONNECTS
DEPENDENT CLAUSE TO NOUN "PEOPLE"

Celebrities are people who achieve status.

MAIN CLAUSE   DEPENDENT CLAUSE

COMPOSE COMPLEX SENTENCES

Insert the relative pronoun that best completes each sentence. Circle the nouns described by the relative pronoun.

1. An ascribed status is something .... you are born into.

2. A female .... is born into a wealthy family did not choose the status of female or wealth.

3. An achieved status is a position .... you achieve or earn.

4. Both a college president and a bank robber are examples of those .... have achieved a status.

5. People .... are pleased with their social status often want others to recognize their special position.

6. A status symbol is a sign .... identifies the status of a person.

7. A wedding ring, ... is a status symbol, announces the status of a person as married.

8. One .... becomes a full time student may be assuming a master status which overrides all other statuses.

9. Each status is a guideline .... teaches us how to think and feel.

10. Write a complex sentence using a relative pronoun. Suggested topic: A status symbol.

Properly Place and Punctuate a Dependent Clause within a Complex Sentence

1. **Before the main clause:** A dependent clause at the beginning of a sentence acts as an introductory element and must be set off with a comma.

   Subordinating conjunction dependent clause, **main clause.**

   DEPENDENT CLAUSE   *MAIN CLAUSE*

   While a person sleeps | the body repairs itself.

   COMMA SIGNALS END OF DEPENDENT CLAUSE

2. **In the middle of the main clause:** The context of the clause controls the use of commas. Many dependent clauses in the middle of a sentence are **relative clauses.** Relative clauses are either essential or nonessential.

(a) If the dependent clause adds information **essential** to the meaning of the sentence, no commas are needed. Most often, essential information limits or restricts the meaning of a common noun such as *man* or *woman*.

Main *relative pronoun dependent clause* **clause**.

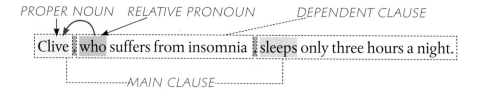

(b) If the dependent clause adds information that is **nonessential** to the meaning of the main clause, insert commas before and after the dependent clause. Usually a nonessential clause describes a proper noun.

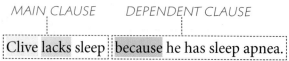

3. **After the main clause:** The context of the clause controls the use of commas in these instances:

(a) If the dependent clause begins with a **subordinating conjunction**, no comma is needed.

Main clause *subordinating conjunction dependent clause*.

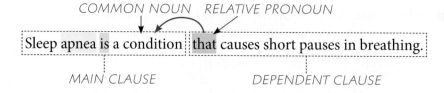

(b) If the dependent clause begins with a relative pronoun, determine if the information is essential or nonessential. An **essential** dependent clause does not need a comma.

Main clause *dependent clause*.

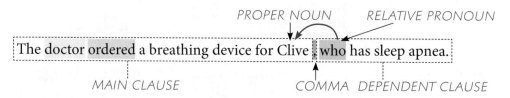

(c) Insert a comma before a dependent clause that is **nonessential**.

Main clause, *relative pronoun dependent clause*.

CORRECTLY PUNCTUATE COMPLEX SENTENCES

Edit each of the following complex sentences for proper punctuation.

1. Sleep is crucial to good health, because it improves the body's ability to function.

2. When you sleep your body regulates hormones and blood pressure.

3. People who get less than six hours of sleep a night, raise their risk of strokes.

4. Adequate sleep strengthens memories in a process called consolidation, which helps you perform a new skill better.

5. Dr. Somers who studies sleep and heart health says sleep prepares the body for the next day.

6. There is limited evidence, that short-term sleep deprivation harms those with heart problems.

7. Research also suggests, that lack of sleep could contribute to obesity and diabetes.

8. Rosie who is on a diet and is a short sleeper struggles to lose weight.

9. When people get enough sleep while dieting, fat accounts for a percentage of weight lost.

10. Write and correctly punctuate a complex sentence. Suggested topic: Your sleep habits.

COMPOSE COMPLEX SENTENCES

Create ten complex sentences by combining the following sets of simple sentences. Use appropriate subordinating conjunctions, relative pronouns, and punctuation to show the relationship between ideas within each new sentence.

1. Angelina Jolie and Brad Pitt use their status to help others. They have achieved world-wide stardom.

2. Pitt and Jolie are favorite targets of the press. They bring world attention to worthy causes.

3. They have founded the Jolie-Pitt Foundation. The Foundation was established in honor of their son Maddox.

4. The Jolie-Pitt Foundation gives millions of dollars to charities. These charities address poverty, health, and education worldwide.

----

5. Jolie raises public awareness of the plight of refugees around the world. She has worked as a UN Ambassador for Refugees since 2001.

----

6. Jolie has traveled to over 20 countries. She has worked with field staff, met with refugees, and offered aid.

----

7. Brad Pitt visited New Orleans' Lower 9th Ward shortly after Hurricane Katrina. He was shocked by the devastation.

----

8. Pitt started the Make It Right Foundation to build new homes in the area. The new homes are eco-friendly and sturdy.

----

9. The foundation has built 100 homes in the Lower 9th Ward. It is the largest, greenest community of single-family homes in the world.

----

10. They are committed to helping others in need. Pitt and Jolie donated more than $8 million to charity in a single year.

Practice 8

Compose Compound-Complex Sentences L⑤

A **compound-complex sentence** is two or more independent clauses and one or more dependent clauses. A compound-complex sentence joins coordinate and subordinate ideas into a single sentence. All the punctuation rules for both compound and complex sentences apply to the compound-complex sentence.

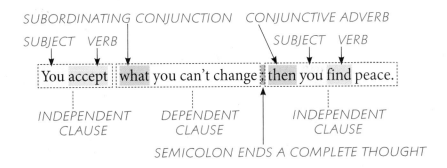

COMPOSE COMPOUND-COMPLEX SENTENCES

Create and properly punctuate four compound-complex sentences by combining the following simple sentences. Discuss your work with a classmate or with a small group of peers.

1. Deidra needs to understand. She can only change herself. She can't change other people.

_____

_____

2. Deidra doesn't like her job. She must be the one to make a change. She could look for another job or learn how to cope with conflict.

_____

_____

3. Deidra is afraid. She is afraid of failure and rejection. She doesn't take chances. She doesn't trust others easily.

_____

_____

4. Her distrust makes her seem unfriendly. Her attitude offends others. She has achieved the status of disgruntled employee.

_____

_____

Practice 10

Write and properly punctuate four different types of sentences. Suggested topic: Traits of an effective employee.

1. Simple

2. Compound

3. Complex

4. Compound-Complex

Editing Assignments

MyWritingLab™
Complete this Exercise
on mywritinglab.com

Editing for Everyday Life

In the following letter to her friend, a young woman shares her thoughts about meeting her future in-laws. Edit the paragraph for correct punctuation of sentence types. Use your own paper or complete the exercise on MyWritingLab.com.

Dear Billie Jean:

I just met my future in-laws. We are so different. You know. That I come from a single parent family. My mom was a career woman who made her own way and she taught me to do the same My mom and I are more like best friends than mother and daughter. Manuel's mother is different. She enjoys the status of a stay-at-home mom she loves cooking, cleaning, and controlling everyone. I hope she likes me. Because I like her.

Editing for College Life

Read the following paragraph about the term "social class" from the college textbook *Essentials of Sociology: A Down-to-Earth-Approach,* 7th ed. by James Henslin. Edit the paragraph for correct punctuation of sentence types.

To understand people, we must examine the social locations that they hold in life. Especially significant is social class which is based on income, education, and occupational prestige. Large numbers of people who have similar amounts of income and education and who work at jobs that are roughly equal in prestige make up a social class. Our social class affects our behavior it even affects our ideas and attitudes.

Editing for Working Life

Read the following memo written from a supervisor to an employee. Edit the paragraph for correct punctuation of sentence types.

To: Eugene Beltz
From: Amanda Ortiz, Manager
RE: Employee training

As I indicated in your yearly evaluation you are required to attend a series of training sessions. That will build your skills as a team member. Because you need to improve your public speaking skills you will join Toastmasters. You will also enroll in the workshop for conflict resolution it is scheduled for next month and it will last for six weeks. Once you have completed this training we will review your eligibility for promotion.

Academic Learning Log: Chapter Review

WHAT HAVE I LEARNED?

To test and track your understanding, answer the following questions.

1. What is a clause, and what are the two types of clauses? ....

....

2. What is a simple sentence? ....

....

3. What is a compound sentence? ....

....

4. What is a complex sentence? ....

....

5. What is a compound-complex sentence? ....

....

6. **How will I use what I have learned?**
   In your notebook, discuss how you will apply to your own writing what you have learned about sentence types. When will you apply this knowledge during the writing process?

7. **What do I still need to study about sentence types?**
   In your notebook, describe your ongoing study needs by describing what, when, and how you will continue studying sentence types.

MyWritingLab™

Complete the Post-test for Chapter 6 in MyWritingLab.

7

Run-ons: Comma Splices and Fused Sentences

A comma splice is an error that occurs when a comma is used by itself to join two sentences. A fused sentence is an error that occurs when two sentences are joined without any punctuation.

According to research, comma splices and fused sentences are two of the most common errors made by student writers. The photograph on the next page shows an exercise program. Read about this program and then answer the question "What's the point of learning about correcting comma splices and fused sentences?"

What's the Point of Correcting Run-ons—Comma Splices and Fused Sentences? **LO 1**

PHOTOGRAPHIC ORGANIZER: COMMA SPLICES AND FUSED SENTENCES

WRITING FROM LIFE

Read the following short description of CrossFit, a unique approach to physical fitness. The paragraph contains 2 comma splices and 4 fused sentences. How do these errors affect the reading of the paragraph?

CrossFit

CrossFit builds fitness through strength training, gymnastics, and sprinting. A trainee gains control, endurance, and flexibility CrossFit promotes a broad and general physical fitness program for everyone the workouts are based on functional movements they copy the natural actions carried out by the body in everyday life, for example, a squat is the action of standing from a seated position a dead-lift is the action of picking up an object off the ground, both are functional movements. A typical workout uses these kinds of movements in short, intense sessions.

What's the point of correcting comma splices and fused sentences?

....

....

....

One Student Writer's Response

The following paragraph offers one writer's response to the opening paragraph about CrossFit.

Reading this paragraph was kind of frustrating. There were no real pauses in the ideas, so it was hard to figure out where an idea ended or began. The paragraph needs punctuation (like periods) so the ideas are clear and easy to follow.

LO2 Recognize Comma Splices and Fused Sentences

Comma splices and fused sentences are punctuation errors that occur where independent clauses are improperly joined to form a compound sentence. To properly combine clauses into a compound sentence, the end of each independent clause must be signaled by appropriate punctuation, such as a semicolon, a comma followed by a coordinating conjunction, or a period at the end of the sentence.

Comma Splice

A **comma splice** occurs when a comma is used by itself (without a coordinating conjunction) to join two independent clauses.

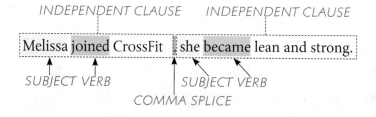

Fused Sentence

A **fused sentence** occurs when two independent clauses are joined without any punctuation.

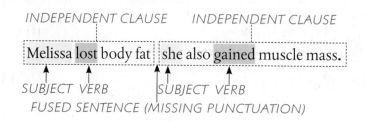

IDENTIFY COMMA SPLICES AND FUSED SENTENCES

Practice 2

Test your ability to identify comma splices, fused sentences, and properly combined clauses. In each blank, write **CS** for comma splice, **FS** for fused sentence, or **C** for correctly punctuated.

_____ **1.** I want to pass on to you my appreciation for your CrossFit workouts, your program really works.

CS **2.** I am an Army Major, I have been doing this for about three months, boy, I really saw the results today.

_____ **3.** We are required to pass a physical fitness test in the Army, today I achieved the highest results in all areas.

_____ **4.** I completed 77 push-ups in 2 minutes, 80 sit-ups in 2 minutes, and a 2 mile run in 13 minutes I got the perfect score of 300 points I credit all my success to CrossFit.

FS **5.** I am in the best shape of my life I am lighter, stronger, faster, and way healthier I no longer have joint pain.

_____ **6.** I look forward to these workouts, and my staff and I have made them a part of our daily physical training.

_____ **7.** CrossFit works for my wife, too, she was never active, but now she can do pull-ups, push-ups, sprints, and many other physically demanding exercises.

 8. My friends, family, and colleagues want to know more about CrossFit so I would appreciate some information to share with them.

C **9.** Scott, your kind remarks about CrossFit mean a lot to me, and I am pleased that you are seeing results from your hard work.

_____ **10.** CrossFit is a core strength and conditioning program this exercise program is not a specialized fitness program.

_____ **11.** CrossFit builds physical competence in each of ten recognized areas of fitness they are cardiovascular and respiratory endurance, stamina, strength, flexibility, power, speed, coordination, agility, balance, and accuracy.

C **12.** We train our clients in gymnastics from basic to advanced movements, so they gain the ability to control their bodies through strength and flexibility.

_____ **13.** We emphasize Olympic Weightlifting this sport has the unique ability to develop an athlete's explosive power, control of external objects, and mastery of key motor recruitment patterns.

_____ **14.** CrossFit improves the natural ability of the body to function, our exercises are based on natural movements.

_____ **15.** For example, the squat is essential to your well-being, the squat can both greatly improve your athleticism, the squat keeps your hips, back, and knees sound and functioning in your senior years.

CS **16.** The squat does not harm the knees, in fact, squats rehabilitate damaged or delicate knees.

_____ **17.** The squat, in the bottom position, is nature's intended sitting posture, and the rise from the bottom to a standing position is a natural movement.

 18. We encourage and assist our athletes to explore a variety of sports for they need to find ways to express and apply their fitness.

_____ **19.** This program can be adapted to everyone's level of fitness so no one should feel intimidated or afraid to try.

_____ **20.** CrossFit is not just for elite athletes anybody can succeed with CrossFit.

L3 Correct Comma Splices and Fused Sentences Five Ways

As a writer, you have the choice of several ways to correct or avoid comma splices and fused sentences. Each method creates a specific effect. Most experts recommend using a variety of these methods, rather than always relying on the same one.

1. Separate sentences using a period and capital letter.

Punctuating the independent clauses as separate sentences is a method often used to correct comma splices and fused sentences.

Incorrect:

INDEPENDENT CLAUSE   COMMA SPLICE

Many exercises use active shoulders active shoulders are shrugged up to the ears.

INDEPENDENT CLAUSE

Incorrect:

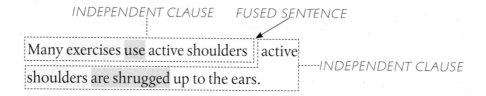

INDEPENDENT CLAUSE   FUSED SENTENCE

Many exercises use active shoulders active shoulders are shrugged up to the ears.

INDEPENDENT CLAUSE

Revised (Correct):

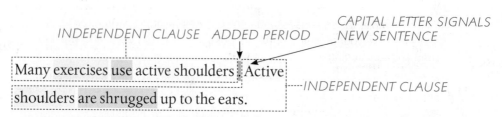

CAPITAL LETTER SIGNALS NEW SENTENCE

INDEPENDENT CLAUSE   ADDED PERIOD

Many exercises use active shoulders Active shoulders are shrugged up to the ears.

INDEPENDENT CLAUSE

▲ L-pull-up in lower position

▲ L-pull-up in top position

Edit the following sentences to eliminate comma splices and fused sentences. Separate clauses by inserting a period and capital letter as needed.

1. Robert hangs from the bar he flexes at the hips, his legs are parallel to the ground and at right angles to his body.

2. He keeps his legs parallel to the ground in addition, his legs are at right angles to his body.

3. He does not jerk his torso, instead he pulls until his head is over the bar.

4. He does as many repetitions as possible without dropping his feet below his bottom, throughout the entire set he maintains this L-shape.

5. Robert found the L-pull-up very challenging, at first, he had to keep his legs straight or tucked up under him.

6. Robert is able to complete 100 L-pull-ups at a time, he maintains perfect form.

7. Yesterday, Robert did 100 L-pull-ups, then he did 50 air squats.

8. His wife Chrissy is also an able athlete for example, she completed 250 wall balls, 90 jump rope double-unders, and 8 muscle ups in 12 minutes.

9. They work out daily, compete at opens, and coach others to own a gym is their ultimate goal.

10. Write a compound sentence. Suggested topic: The benefits of an L-pull-up.

2. Join sentences with a comma followed by a coordinating conjunction.

Sentences can be properly joined by inserting a comma followed by a coordinating conjunction between the independent clauses. The acronym FANBOYS stands for each of the coordinating conjunctions: *for, and, nor, but, or, yet, so.* This method of combining sentences states the relationship between ideas of equal importance.

Incorrect:

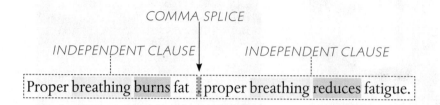

Incorrect:

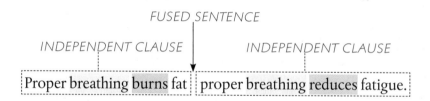

Revised (Correct):

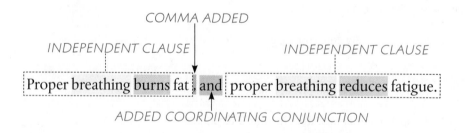

Woman Doing
Sit-ups ▶

Edit the
following
sentences to
eliminate comma
splices and fused
sentences. Join
independent
clauses with a
comma and a
coordinating
conjunction.

1. One should never hold one's breath during an exercise holding one's breath raises blood pressure.

2. Breath-holding deprives the body of oxygen, it reduces blood flow to the brain and increases the pressure in the chest.

3. Before exercising, Shawna practices proper breathing she sits straight in a firm chair with her fingertips gently resting on her stomach.

4. She inhales deeply through her nostrils; she feels her abdomen expand her diaphragm her chest rises as her lungs expand with air.

5. To exhale deeply, Shawna relaxes her chest and diaphragm she pulls her stomach toward her spine.

6. Shawna repeats this breathing pattern, she can notice how the air moves in and out of her body.

7. During exercise Shawna breathes deeply and fully, she inhales and exhales in a steady rhythm.

8. Shawna inhales during the exertion stage of the exercise she exhales during the recovery stage of the exercise.

9. Controlled breathing improves exercise it increases lung capacity.

10. Write a compound sentence using a comma and a coordinating conjunction. Suggested topic: Reducing stress through proper breathing.

3. Join sentences with a semicolon.

Use a semicolon to join independent clauses when no conjunction is present. A semicolon indicates that the two sentences of equal importance are so closely related that they can be stated as one sentence; however, a semicolon alone does not state the relationship between the two clauses. The relationship between clauses may be one of the following: *time, space, order of importance, general to specific, addition, cause, effect, comparison,* or *contrast.*

Incorrect:

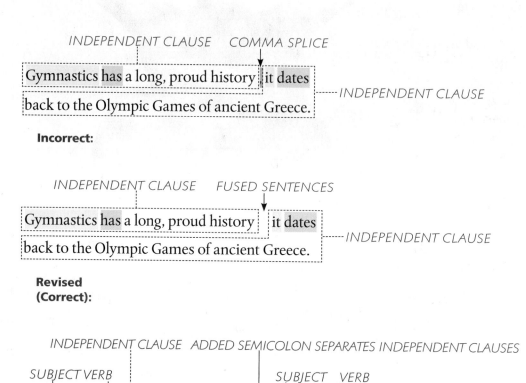

INDEPENDENT CLAUSE   *COMMA SPLICE*

Gymnastics has a long, proud history, it dates back to the Olympic Games of ancient Greece.

INDEPENDENT CLAUSE

Incorrect:

INDEPENDENT CLAUSE   *FUSED SENTENCES*

Gymnastics has a long, proud history it dates back to the Olympic Games of ancient Greece.

INDEPENDENT CLAUSE

Revised (Correct):

INDEPENDENT CLAUSE   *ADDED SEMICOLON SEPARATES INDEPENDENT CLAUSES*

SUBJECT VERB   *SUBJECT   VERB*

Gymnastics has a long, proud history; it dates back to the Olympic Games of ancient Greece.

INDEPENDENT CLAUSE

▲ Artistic Gymnastics

Edit the following sentences by inserting semicolons as needed to correct comma splices and fused sentences.

1. USA Gymnastics selects and trains teams for the annual World Championships and the Olympic Games, only the elite make the National Team.

2. The Senior Women's National Team may include up to 28 members, the Senior Team has included members as young as 16.

3. Senior Team member Alyssa Baumann became a 2014 World team gold medalist and a U.S. balance beam silver medalist she was only 17 years old.

4. Senior team member Simone Biles performs some of the hardest moves in competition, she dismounts from the balance beam with a full twisting double back flip.

5. Gabby Douglas won the 2012 Olympic all-around gold medal, she wants to repeat her win in the 2016 Olympics.

6. Another female star on the Senior Team is McKayla Maroney she is an expert in vaulting and floor exercises.

7. On vault Maroney performs the difficult Amanar vault this vault contains two and half twists in the backward salto or somersault.

8. The Senior Men's Team also has a depth of talent, the team won the bronze medal in the 2014 World Championship.

9. Senior Team member Danell Leyva claimed the parallel bars silver medal teammate Jake Dalton earned the bronze medal in the vault.

10. Write a compound sentence using a semicolon. Suggested topic: A well-known athlete.

For more information about joining ideas of equal importance, see pages 103–105, "Compound and Complex Sentences."

4. Join sentences with a semicolon followed by a conjunctive adverb.

Use a semicolon with a conjunctive adverb to join independent clauses. Conjunctive adverbs are transition words that state the relationships between ideas of equal importance. A few common examples include *also, consequently, for example, furthermore, however, then, meanwhile, therefore,* and *thus.*

Incorrect:

INDEPENDENT CLAUSE   *COMMA SPLICE*

In the overhead squat, an athlete holds a bar overhead she squats and stands.

INDEPENDENT CLAUSE

Incorrect:

INDEPENDENT CLAUSE   *FUSED SENTENCES*

In the overhead squat, an athlete holds a bar overhead she squats and stands.

INDEPENDENT CLAUSE

Revised (Correct):

INDEPENDENT CLAUSE   ADDED SEMICOLON SEPARATES INDEPENDENT CLAUSES

In the overhead squat, an athlete holds a bar overhead ; meanwhile , she squats and stands.

ADDED CONJUNCTIVE ADVERB WITH COMMA   INDEPENDENT CLAUSE

Not only do these transitions state the relationship between ideas, but also they introduce an independent clause and must be set off with a comma.

▲ Tara Nott of the United States

Edit and revise the following sentences to correct comma splices and fused sentences. Join independent clauses with a semicolon and one of the following transitions: *consequently, for example, furthermore, however, in addition, then, therefore,* or *thus.*

1. Tara Nott won an Olympic gold medal in weight lifting in 2000, she became the first U.S. athlete in 40 years to win an Olympic gold medal in weight lifting.

2. Tara Nott was 28 years old, 5 feet and 1 inch tall, and 105 pounds she was a tough and talented athlete.

3. Weightlifting was not her first choice as a sport, she is the only athlete to have ever trained in three Olympic sports.

4. She trained first as a gymnast she became an All-American soccer player.

5. She lifted 225 pounds, more than twice her body weight she won the gold medal.

6. Lifting depends more on technique than on bulk, a lifter relies on quickness and timing.

7. Nott paused to focus her mind, she took and held a big breath of air throughout the lift.

8. Tara Nott shattered the myth of massive, bulky lifters more women are now interested in weight lifting.

9. Her performance in the 2000 Olympics was inspirational it has been posted on YouTube.

10. Write a compound sentence using a semicolon and conjunctive adverb. Suggested topic: Going to the gym.

For more information on complex sentences, see pages 107–110, "Compound and Complex Sentences."

5. Join sentences using a subordinating conjunction.

Not all ideas are of equal importance. Frequently, writers choose to join ideas in a complex sentence made up of an independent clause and one or more dependent clauses. A subordinating conjunction signals the beginning of a dependent clause and states its subordinate relationship to the independent clause. Some examples of subordinating conjunctions include *although, as, because, if,* and *when.* Relative pronouns also connect a dependent clause to an independent clause. Examples of relative pronouns include *that, which,* and *who.*

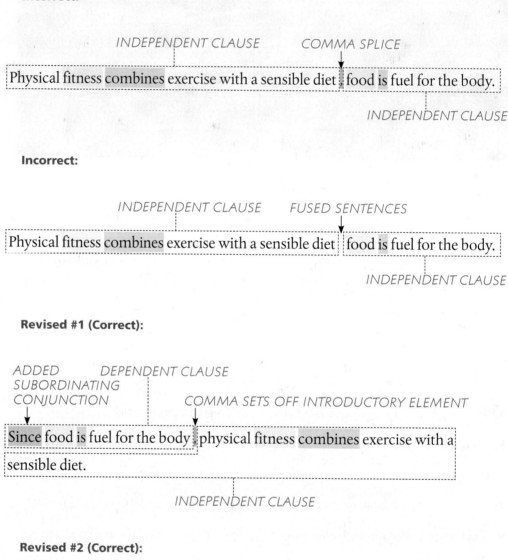

Incorrect:

INDEPENDENT CLAUSE   COMMA SPLICE

Physical fitness combines exercise with a sensible diet, food is fuel for the body.

INDEPENDENT CLAUSE

Incorrect:

INDEPENDENT CLAUSE   FUSED SENTENCES

Physical fitness combines exercise with a sensible diet food is fuel for the body.

INDEPENDENT CLAUSE

Revised #1 (Correct):

ADDED   DEPENDENT CLAUSE
SUBORDINATING
CONJUNCTION   COMMA SETS OFF INTRODUCTORY ELEMENT

Since food is fuel for the body, physical fitness combines exercise with a sensible diet.

INDEPENDENT CLAUSE

Revised #2 (Correct):

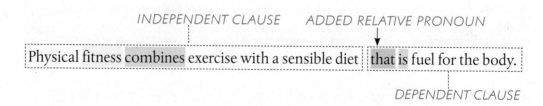

INDEPENDENT CLAUSE   ADDED RELATIVE PRONOUN

Physical fitness combines exercise with a sensible diet that is fuel for the body.

DEPENDENT CLAUSE

Bowl of beef stew
(Zone Diet) ▶

Revise the following compound sentences into complex sentences to correct comma splices and fused sentences. Use the following subordinating conjunctions: *although, because, that, which,* and *when.*

1. The Zone diet is an ideal diet, it reduces the risk of disease and improves athletic ability.

----

2. The Zone is more than a diet the Zone is a state of being refreshed, alert, and energized.

----

3. Your metabolism improves with this diet it is 30% protein, 30% fat, and 40% carbohydrates.

----

4. You adopt the Zone diet you reduce the causes and effects of heart disease, high blood pressure, and diabetes.

----

5. The Zone diet recommends a small amount of protein at every meal and for two snacks a day each serving of protein is around the size of your palm.

----

6. Compose a complex sentence using a subordinating conjunction. Suggested topic: Eating habits.

Practice 8

Edit the following sentences to correct comma splices and fused sentences.

1. Many people cannot tolerate gluten it is a protein in wheat, rye, and barley.

2. Celiac disease is a digestive disease it harms the small intestine and makes it hard for the body to digest food.

3. Many people have Celiac disease they cannot tolerate gluten.

4. Gluten is found mostly in foods but it can be found in medicines, vitamins, and lip balms.

5. People with Celiac disease eat foods or use products with gluten their immune system attacks their digestive system.

Editing Assignments

MyWritingLab™
Complete this Exercise
on mywritinglab.com

Editing for Everyday Life

Read the following e-mail appeal written to a friend. Edit to correct comma splices and fused sentences. Use your own paper or complete the exercise on MyWritingLab.com.

Dear Lara,

I am sending you this e-mail as a written plea to get you in the gym and working out I know we have talked a lot about your wanting to lose those growing inches and becoming healthier and stronger talk is only talk and will not help you become the person you envision it is very easy to keep putting off you will feel so much better after just one workout. You will not be worrying about your weight gain, you will be doing something about it. I am ready to go to the gym with you any time. —Heather

Editing for College Life

The following paragraph was written as an analysis of two popular diets for a health class. Edit to correct comma splices and fused sentences.

Two popular diets differ in several ways these diets are the Zone and Weight Watchers. The Zone focuses on wellness it recommends small portions of protein and fat and larger portions of fruits and vegetables in contrast Weight Watchers focuses on weight goals it recommends eating what you want you control portions. On the one hand, the Zone balances fat, protein, and carbohydrates for health on the other hand Weight Watchers focuses on calories in, calories out it includes exercise and social support. The Zone diet is debated by experts they say the diet's science is not proven. However, Weight Watchers has the support of most national organizations it is the most highly recommended diet.

Editing for Working Life

Read the following information which was written to future clients and posted on the home page of a local gym. Edit to correct comma splices and fused sentences.

Contact us and schedule your first session there is no charge for the first session it's on us. This first session will be used to determine your goals and establish your current fitness level you will then be put through a brief and intense workout. This will give you a taste of what we do and it will provide us with valuable information about you. The first session ends we will sit down and discuss what we learned about you and what you learned about us. You want to continue from there the next step is signing up for our Fundamentals Course.

WHAT HAVE I LEARNED ABOUT CORRECTING COMMA SPLICES AND FUSED SENTENCES?

To test and track your understanding, complete the following ideas. Use several sentences as needed for each response.

1. A comma splice is

2. A fused sentence is

3. What are the five ways to eliminate comma splices and fused sentences?

4. How will I use what I have learned about correcting comma splices and fused sentences?
In your notebook, discuss how you will apply to your own writing what you have learned about comma splices and fused sentences.

5. What do I still need to study about correcting comma splices and fused sentences?
In your notebook, describe your ongoing study needs by describing what, when, and how you will continue studying comma splices and fused sentences.

PORTFOLIO

Academic Learning Log: Chapter Review

MyWritingLab™

Complete the Post-test for Chapter 7 in MyWritingLab.

8

LEARNING OUTCOMES

After studying this chapter, you should be able to:

1 Answer the Question "What's the Point of Correcting Fragments?"

2 Identify Fragments

3 Recognize and Revise Seven Types of Fragments

Fragments

A fragment is an incomplete thought.

Thinking about a real-life situation helps us to understand the impact of fragments on our ability to communicate. The photo illustrates a couple talking about plans for home improvements. Read about the situation and answer the question "What's the point of learning about fragments?"

What's the Point of Correcting Fragments?

WRITING
FROM LIFE

PHOTOGRAPHIC ORGANIZER: FRAGMENTS

▲ **Kitchen under construction**

Suppose you are remodeling your kitchen. You ask two contractors the same questions. Below are their replies.

Contractor A:
"One month maybe…need a deposit…for materials…discounts at area dealers…guaranteeing work for five years…"

Contractor B:
"We can begin work on the kitchen in one month and finish in another month. Before we begin work, we need a deposit for materials. We have agreements with area dealers for discounts on your appliances. We guarantee our work for five years. Let's make an appointment to draw up plans and sign an agreement."

With which contractor will you be able to communicate easily and clearly if you hire one of them?

....

What's the point of learning about fragments?

....

....

....

....

....

One Student Writer's Response

The following paragraph offers one writer's reaction to the statements about the kitchen renovations given by the contractors.

Contractor A is hard to understand. Before he finishes one idea, he begins another one. It sounds like he has a hard time staying focused or paying attention. His ideas are all over the place. In contrast, contractor B makes his ideas clear and easy to follow. He finished his ideas and gave much more information.

The difference between contractor A and contractor B favors contractor B. He seems more professional and trustworthy. The contrast between these responses shows me that it is important to communicate in complete sentences. The way we express ourselves has an effect on our image and could even affect our ability to get a job.

L2 Identify Fragments

The ability to write ideas in complete thoughts or sentences is an important tool in building coherent paragraphs and essays. A sentence has two traits.

SENTENCE: Complete Thought—Complete Information

TRAIT ONE: A sentence states a complete and independent thought.

TRAIT TWO: A sentence contains a subject and a verb.

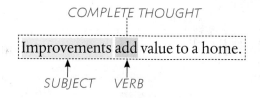

A **sentence** contains all the information needed to clearly express a complete thought. In contrast, a fragment is often recognized by what is missing from the thought. A **fragment** is an incomplete thought.

FRAGMENT: Incomplete Thought—Missing Information

A **fragment** is missing one of the following: a subject, a verb, or both subject and verb.

Missing Subject:	Happens before and after a paint job
Missing Verb:	Renee not using primer paint
Missing Subject and Verb:	To properly paint a wall

Even when a group of words includes both a subject and a verb, it still can be a fragment. A subordinating conjunction signals a fragment that has both a subject and a verb. These types of fragments are missing an independent clause.

Fragment (Missing an Independent Clause):

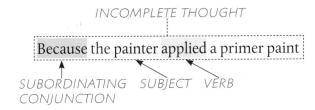

To identify a fragment, ask the following questions:

- Does the idea have a verb?
- What is the subject of the verb?
- Does the idea express a complete thought?

IDENTIFY FRAGMENTS

Identify fragments and sentences. Write **F** for *fragment* next to the incomplete thoughts. Write **S** for *sentence* next to the complete thoughts.

_____ **1.** Painting the interior is the low-cost way to improve a home.

_____ **2.** Selecting the type and color of the paint and using the proper tools.

_____ **3.** Save money by doing the painting yourself.

_____ **4.** Painting tools include masking tape, paint rollers, buckets, drop cloths, and sandpaper.

_____ **5.** A container that holds paint when using a paint roller.

_____ **6.** Another low-cost home improvement painting the front door.

_____ **7.** Two large planters of healthy plants spruce up the front entry.

_____ **8.** Accent lights that add atmosphere to a room.

_____ **9.** To make a room look instantly larger.

_____ **10.** You can transform your home with little money.

L3 Recognize and Revise Seven Types of Fragments

Sentences can be broken into smaller pieces or fragments. Often these fragments are either phrases or dependent clauses punctuated as if they are complete sentences. An effective writer understands fragments and how they are used to build complete sentences. The following examples illustrate the difference between a phrase, a dependent clause, and a sentence.

Phrase: Incomplete Thought

Moving into a new house

MISSING SUBJECT AND VERB

Dependent Clause: Incomplete Thought

which is a dream home

VERB

RELATIVE PRONOUN/SUBJECT

A Sentence: Complete Thought

We are moving into a new house which is a dream home.

▲ Couple moving home

This section discusses seven common types of fragments: (1) prepositional phrase, (2) appositive phrase, (3) infinitive phrase, (4) gerund phrase, (5) participle phrase, (6) dependent clause, and (7) relative clause, and techniques you can use to revise fragments into sentences. A writer may use two techniques to revise fragments into sentences:

- Combine existing ideas
- Add missing ideas

Phrase Fragments

A **phrase** is a group of words that acts as a single unit. A phrase is a fragment because it does not contain both a subject and a verb. To create a sentence, add information (such as a subject, a verb, or both) to the phrase, or join the phrase to an existing sentence.

1. Prepositional Phrase

A **prepositional phrase** begins with a preposition (such as *at, or, in, to, toward, for, since,* and *of*) and ends with the object of the preposition. A prepositional phrase adds information about direction, manner, space, and time such as *in the house* or *after the game.*

COMPLETE THOUGHT   PREPOSITIONAL PHRASE

Sue Ling was confident About remodeling a house .

SUBJECT VERB   PREPOSITION   OBJECT OF THE PREPOSITION

Revised to Combine Ideas:

COMPLETE THOUGHT

Sue Ling was confident about remodeling a house .

Revised to Add Ideas:

COMPLETE THOUGHT   COMPLETE THOUGHT

Sue Ling was confident She knew about remodeling a house .

ADDED SUBJECT ADDED VERB

REVISE PREPOSITIONAL PHRASE FRAGMENTS

Build two new sentences using each of the following prepositional phrases. First, combine the existing sentence with the prepositional phrase to create a new sentence. Then, create another new sentence by adding missing information to the prepositional phrase.

Prepositional phrase: for his family

Sentence: Cia Lin has been working to provide a home.

1. COMBINE IDEAS: ....

2. ADD IDEAS: ....

Prepositional phrase: at a tire factory

Sentence: He volunteers to work extra shifts.

3. COMBINE IDEAS: ....

4. ADD IDEAS: ....

Prepositional phrase: by working overtime

Sentence: He now has money to save.

5. COMBINE IDEAS: ....

6. ADD IDEAS: ....

Prepositional phrase: as a cost-saving step

Sentence: Cia Lin cancelled his land line phone.

7. COMBINE IDEAS: ....

8. ADD IDEAS: ....

Prepositional phrase: for a house

Sentence: He is saving his money.

9. COMBINE IDEAS: ....

10. ADD IDEAS: ....

Practice 3

2. Appositive Phrase

An **appositive phrase** contains a noun that renames or describes another noun in the same sentence. An appositive phrase combines with a complete thought to add detail. Place an appositive phrase next to the noun it renames.

APPOSITIVE PHRASE FRAGMENT   COMPLETE THOUGHT

A talented handy person   Jeri enjoys fixing up her home.

SUBJECT VERB

Revised to Combine Ideas:

COMPLETE THOUGHT

A talented handy person, Jeri enjoys fixing up her home.

INTRODUCTORY PHRASE SET OFF WITH A COMMA

Revised to Add Ideas:

COMPLETE THOUGHT

Jeri is a talented handy person who enjoys fixing up her home.

ADDED VERB   ADDED RELATIVE PRONOUN/SUBJECT OF NEW DEPENDENT CLAUSE

REVISE APPOSITIVE PHRASE FRAGMENTS

Build two new sentences using each of the following appositive phrases. First, combine the existing sentence with the appositive phrase to create a new sentence. Then, create another new sentence by adding missing information to the appositive phrase.

▲ Handy person

Appositive phrase: A low-cost, energy-saving step

Sentence: Fixing a leaky faucet lowers your water bill.

1. COMBINE IDEAS: ....

....

2. ADD IDEAS: ....

Appositive phrase: a mother of two

Sentence: Jaylin learned to fix things herself.

3 COMBINE IDEAS: ....

4. ADD IDEAS: ....

Appositive phrase: common household products

Sentence: Jaylin uses baking soda and vinegar to clear clogs.

5. COMBINE IDEAS: ....

6. ADD IDEAS: ....

Appositive phrase: bugs and rodents

Sentence: Mint repels pests in the home.

7. COMBINE IDEAS: ....

8. ADD IDEAS: ....

Appositive phrase: a cleaning agent

Sentence: Toothpaste can be used to shine faucets and remove grime from glass-top stoves.

9. COMBINE IDEAS: ....

....

10. ADD IDEAS: ....

3. Infinitive Phrase

An infinitive is a form of a verb, but it is not a verb. Combining *to* with a verb forms an *infinitive* as in the following: *to go, to talk,* and *to think.* An **infinitive phrase** is made up of an infinitive and the object of the infinitive such as *to quit smoking* or *to run a mile.* An infinitive phrase can act as a noun, adjective, or adverb.

COMPLETE THOUGHT   *INFINITIVE PHRASE*

Jeri crawled into her attic   To inspect the insulation .

SUBJECT   VERB

Revised to Combine Ideas:

COMPLETE THOUGHT

Jeri crawled into her attic to inspect the insulation .

Revised to Add Ideas:

COMPLETE THOUGHT   *COMPLETE THOUGHT*

Jeri crawled into her attic   She needed to inspect the insulation .

ADDED SUBJECT   ADDED VERB

REVISE INFINITIVE PHRASE FRAGMENTS

Build two new sentences using each of the following infinitive phrases. First, combine the existing sentence with the infinitive phrase to create a new sentence. Then, create another new sentence by adding missing information to the infinitive phrase.

Infinitive phrase: to install on your roof

Sentence: Solar water heaters are green and easy.

▲ Solar water heater

1. COMBINE IDEAS: ....

....

2. ADD IDEAS: ....

Infinitive phrase: to prevent roof leaks

Sentence: Solar panels need to be installed during the roofing process.

3. COMBINE IDEAS: ....

4. ADD IDEAS: ....

Infinitive phrase: to locate rafters

Sentence: It is easier for installation if there is no roof.

5. COMBINE IDEAS: ....

6. ADD IDEAS: ....

Infinitive phrase: to grow

Sentence: Solar savings begin the first day and continue over time.

7. COMBINE IDEAS: ....

8. ADD IDEAS: ....

Infinitive phrase: to go solar

Sentence: Now is the time.

9. COMBINE IDEAS: ....

10. ADD IDEAS: ....

Practice 5

-ing Phrases: Gerunds and Participles

An *-ing* phrase can function as either a noun or an adjective. An *-ing* phrase used as a **noun** is called a **gerund**. An *-ing* phrase used as an **adjective** is called a **participle**.

4. Gerund Phrase

A gerund is a form of a verb, but it is not a verb. A **gerund** is a **noun** that ends in *-ing*, such as *going*, *talking*, and *thinking*. A **gerund phrase** is made up of a gerund and the object of the gerund such as *quitting smoking* or *running three miles*. A gerund phrase functions as a **noun.** For example, a gerund phrase can be the subject of a sentence or an object of a verb or preposition.

COMPLETE THOUGHT   −ING PHRASE FRAGMENT (GERUND)

Jeri saved thousands of dollars   Doing her own home repairs .

Revised to Combine Ideas:

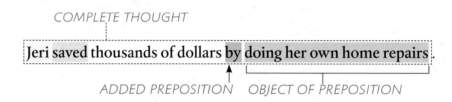

COMPLETE THOUGHT

Jeri saved thousands of dollars **by** doing her own home repairs .

ADDED PREPOSITION   OBJECT OF PREPOSITION

Revised to Add Ideas:

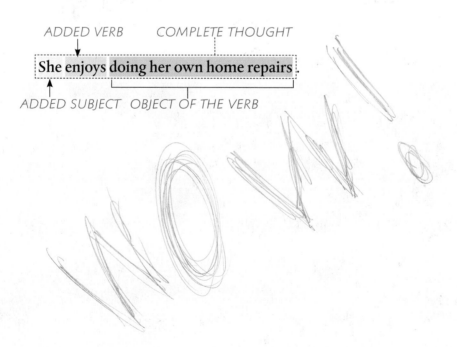

ADDED VERB   COMPLETE THOUGHT

She enjoys doing her own home repairs .

ADDED SUBJECT   OBJECT OF THE VERB

5. Participle Phrase

A participle is a form of a verb, but it is not a verb. A **participle** is an **adjective** that ends in *-ing*, such as *going, talking,* and *thinking.* A **participle phrase** is made up of a participle and the object of the participle such as *quitting gambling,* or *swimming a mile.* A participle phrase functions as an **adjective;** it describes nouns and other adjectives.

–ING PHRASE FRAGMENT (PARTICIPLE)   COMPLETE THOUGHT

Hammering a nail   Lou smashed his thumb.

SUBJECT   VERB

Revised to Combine Ideas:

COMPLETE THOUGHT

Hammering a nail, Lou smashed his thumb.

ADJECTIVE   COMMA

Revised to Add Ideas:

COMPLETE THOUGHT

Lou was hammering a nail when he smashed his thumb.

VERB   OBJECT OF VERB

Practice 6

Build two new sentences using each of the following *-ing* phrases. First, combine the existing sentence with the phrase to create a new sentence. Then, create another new sentence by adding missing words to the phrase.

Gerund phrase: Moving out of his parents' house.

Sentence: Keyshawn will be on his own for the first time.

1. COMBINE IDEAS: ....

....

2. ADD IDEAS: ....

....

Gerund phrase: renting an apartment

Sentence: Keyshawn has been thinking.

3. COMBINE IDEAS: ....

4. ADD IDEAS: ....

Gerund phrase: looking for months

Sentence: Keyshawn found a great apartment.

5. COMBINE IDEAS: ....

6. ADD IDEAS: ....

Participle phrase: sharing expenses

Sentence: Keyshawn has a roommate.

7. COMBINE IDEAS: ....

8. ADD IDEAS: ....

Clause Fragments

A **clause** is a set of words that contains a subject and a verb. An **independent clause** states a complete thought in a sentence that begins with a capital letter and ends with punctuation such as a period or a semicolon. In contrast, a **dependent clause** expresses an incomplete thought or fragment.

6. Dependent Clause

A **dependent clause**, also known as a **subordinate clause**, does not make sense on its own. A dependent clause is formed by placing a subordinating conjunction in front of a subject and a verb.

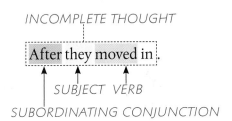

A **subordinating conjunction** states the relationship between two clauses.

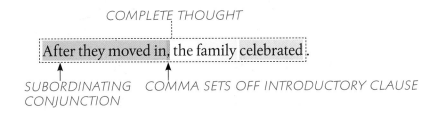

The following chart lists common subordinating conjunctions based on the relationships they express.

Subordinating Conjunctions and the Relationships They Express				
Cause	**Contrast**	**Time**	**Place**	**Condition**
as	although	after	where	even if
because	as if	as	wherever	if
in order that	even though	as long as		only if
now that	though	before		unless
since	whereas	once		when
so	while	since		whether or not
so that		until		
that		when		
		whenever		
		while		

To create a sentence, combine a dependent clause with an independent clause. Or revise the dependent clause into an independent clause by dropping the subordinating conjunction.

COMPLETE THOUGHT   *DEPENDENT CLAUSE FRAGMENT*

They hung the tire swing   Before they unpacked .

SUBJECT VERB   *SUBORDINATING CONJUNCTION*

Revised to Combine Ideas:

COMPLETE THOUGHT

They hung the tire swing before they unpacked .

INDEPENDENT CLAUSE   DEPENDENT CLAUSE

Revised to Add Ideas:

COMPLETE THOUGHT

They hung the tire swing; then they unpacked .

SEMICOLON JOINS TWO INDEPENDENT CLAUSES

Practice 7

REVISE DEPENDENT CLAUSE FRAGMENTS

Build two new sentences using each of the following dependent clause fragments. First, combine the existing sentence with the infinitive phrase to create a new sentence. Then, create another new sentence by adding missing information to the dependent clause.

Dependent clause: that even adults can enjoy

Sentence: A tire swing is an easy, thrifty, old-fashioned addition to the yard.

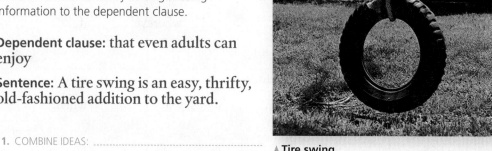
▲ Tire swing

1. COMBINE IDEAS: _____

2. ADD IDEAS: _____

Dependent clause: because she planned well
Sentence: Carla created the perfect yard.

3. COMBINE IDEAS: ....

4. ADD IDEAS: ....

Dependent clause: since she has three children
Sentence: She made a play arca.

5. COMBINE IDEAS: ....

6. ADD IDEAS: ....

Dependent clause: when she entertains outdoors
Sentence: Carla uses the gas grill and picnic table on her shady patio.

7. COMBINE IDEAS: ....

....

8. ADD IDEAS: ....

Dependent clause: where she relaxes
Sentence: Carla hung a hammock between two large shade trees.

9. COMBINE IDEAS: ....

10. ADD IDEAS: ....

Practice 7

7. Relative Clause

A **relative clause** describes a noun or pronoun in an independent clause. A **relative pronoun** introduces the relative clause and relates it to the noun or pronoun it describes.

Relative Pronouns				
who	whom	whose	which	that

Join the relative clause to the independent clause that contains the word it describes. Or revise the relative clause into an independent clause by replacing the relative pronoun with a noun.

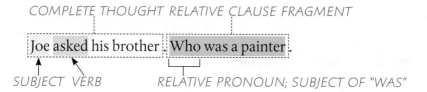

COMPLETE THOUGHT   RELATIVE CLAUSE FRAGMENT

Joe asked his brother   Who was a painter.

SUBJECT   VERB   RELATIVE PRONOUN; SUBJECT OF "WAS"

Revised to Combine Ideas:

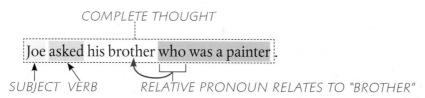

COMPLETE THOUGHT

Joe asked his brother who was a painter.

SUBJECT   VERB   RELATIVE PRONOUN RELATES TO "BROTHER"

Revised to Add Ideas:

COMPLETE THOUGHT

Dan was a painter.

NOUN REPLACES RELATIVE PRONOUN "WHO"

REVISE RELATIVE CLAUSE FRAGMENTS

With the following sets of ideas, build four new sentences using the relative clause. In each set, combine the existing sentence with the relative clause to create a new sentence. Then, create another new sentence by revising the relative clause into an independent clause.

Relative clause: that needed extensive repairs

Sentence: Heather bought an historic home.

1. COMBINE IDEAS: ....

2. ADD IDEAS: ....

Relative clause: who had prior experience in restoring historic homes

Sentence: Heather hired a contractor.

3. COMBINE IDEAS: ....

4. ADD IDEAS: ....

Relative clause: which proved the house was sound

Sentence: Heather paid for a home inspection.

5. COMBINE IDEAS: ....

6. ADD IDEAS: ....

Relative clause: that looked unsightly

Sentence: Some of the walls had huge cracks.

7. COMBINE IDEAS: ....

8. ADD IDEAS: ....

Relative clause: whose work she trusts

Sentence: Heather recommends her contractor to others.

9. COMBINE IDEAS: ....

10. ADD IDEAS: ....

Practice 9

A. Revise the ideas to eliminate fragments by combining or adding ideas.

1. After a storm hits. Homeowners can lessen the chance of further damage by taking a few simple steps.

   ....

   ....

2. Instead of waiting for insurance to kick in. Homeowners can help themselves with simple repairs to roofs and windows. That can prevent further water damage to their homes.

   ....

   ....

3. By putting up tarps. And boarding up broken windows with plywood. You can help prevent more serious repair work.

   ....

   ....

4. Getting a tarp over a hole in a leaky roof can prevent water from doing additional damage. To drywall, electrical systems, and flooring.

   ....

   ....

5. Homeowners have to use common sense. Not doing anything too risky and making sure the storm is over. Before going on the roof.

   ....

   ....

B. Proofread the following paragraph for fragments. Revise to eliminate fragments by combining or adding ideas.

▲ **A father and son prepare for a hurricane by putting plywood over the windows.**

Storm Shutters

(1) To protect a home from damage in wind storms, (2) Install impact-resistant shutters over all large windows and glass doors. (3) Not only do they protect doors and windows from wind-borne objects, but they can also reduce damage, (4) Caused by sudden pressure changes when a window or door is broken.

(5) Laminated windows (plastic bonded to glass) are another option, (6) And are a very good choice, (7) For either building a new home or adding to an old one.

(8) The easiest shutters to install are those that simply cover the opening with plywood. (9) In past hurricanes, many homeowners have seen their temporary plywood shutters blown off, (10) Because they were not properly fastened.

(11) If you have a wood-frame house, use strong fasteners to attach the panels over windows. (12) Have these temporary shutters stored and ready to use, (13) Since building supply stores often sell out of these materials quickly during a storm warning. (14) If your home is made with concrete blocks. (15) You will have to install anchors well in advance.

—Adapted from National Hurricane Center.
"Shutters." Hurricane Preparedness Week. Aug. 2008. <http://www.nhc.noaa.gov/HAW2/english/retrofit /shutters.shtml>.

Editing Assignments

MyWritingLab™
Complete this Exercise
on mywritinglab.com

Editing for Everyday Life

Assume you have been asked to give your feedback about a recent purchase you made. Edit to eliminate fragments. Use your own paper or complete the exercise on MyWritingLab.com.

To the Sales Manager at Best Buy:

Dusty Parrish assisted me today with purchasing a dishwasher. That I wanted at the best price offered in the area! Answering all of my questions about appliances and helping me in every way he can to make the best decisions. Happy to have bought my dishwasher from such a thoughtful person!

Sincerely,

Beth Agassi

Editing for College Life

Read the following paragraph written for a sociology class. Edit to eliminate fragments. Use your own paper or complete the exercise on MyWritingLab.com.

Social class is based on three areas. Property, prestige, and power. For example, property is one way to determine a person's standing in society. However, ownership is not the only important aspect of property For example, some powerful people control property. Such as managers of corporations. Although they do not own the property. If managers can control property for their own benefit. Awarding themselves big bonuses and large perks. It doesn't matter that they don't own the property. That they use for themselves.

Editing for Working Life

Read the following memo from an employee requesting a raise. Edit to eliminate fragments. Use your own paper or complete the exercise on MyWritingLab.com.

To: Serita Delgado
From: Latoya Williams
RE: Annual Evaluation

As you requested. I am writing to document my efforts. That qualify me for my yearly raise. Always willing to come in early or stay late. I have worked above expectations. When new team members are hired. I conduct their initial training. And follow up with them as a mentor. In addition, I have taken part in all available training sessions. Including those that are not required. Clients and coworkers writing me letters and emails of gratitude.

WHAT HAVE I LEARNED ABOUT CORRECTING FRAGMENTS?

To test and track your understanding of how to correct fragments, complete the following ideas. Use several sentences as needed for each response.

1. What are the two traits of a sentence?

2. A fragment is

3. A phrase is

4. A clause is

5. Two types of clauses are _____ and _____ clauses.

6. The five types of phrases discussed in this chapter include the _____, _____, _____, _____, and _____.

7. Two ways to eliminate fragments include _____ ideas or _____ ideas.

8. How will I use what I have learned?
In your notebook, discuss how you will apply to your own writing what you have learned about correcting fragments.

9. What do I still need to study about fragments?
In your notebook, describe your ongoing study needs by describing what, when, and how you will continue studying fragments.

PORTFOLIO

MyWritingLab™

Complete the Post-test for Chapter 8 in MyWritingLab.

9

Misplaced and Dangling Modifiers

A modifier is a word or phrase that describes, clarifies, or gives more information about another word in a sentence.

A misplaced modifier is a word or phrase illogically separated from the word it describes.

Modifiers are words that describe, restrict, or limit other words in a sentence. For example, modifiers help us communicate what we see or how we feel. The photo on the next page illustrates several people experiencing intense feelings.

What's the Point of Correcting Misplaced and Dangling Modifiers?

Practice 1

PHOTOGRAPHIC ORGANIZER: MISPLACED AND DANGLING MODIFIERS

Friends riding a roller coaster ▶

WRITING FROM LIFE

Read the sentence below that describes the roller coaster riders and answer the question.

Screaming with fear and joy, the roller coaster flew through the air.

What is the point of correcting misplaced and dangling modifiers?

One Student Writer's Response

The sentence made me laugh. Because of the wording, I thought of a cartoon roller coaster with a large mouth opened wide "screaming with fear and joy." Of course, the writer meant to describe the people riding the roller coaster. But the sentence doesn't include any information about the people. One way to clearly state the idea is to say, "The teenagers screamed with fear and joy as the roller coaster flew through the air."

Sentence clarity can be achieved through appropriately placed and clearly expressed modifiers. A **modifier** is a word or phrase that describes, clarifies, or gives more information about another word in a sentence. Confusion in meaning occurs when a modifier is misplaced in the sentence or when the word being modified is not stated in the sentence. To avoid confusion, place modifiers next to the word that is being described.

L2 Revise Misplaced Modifiers

A **misplaced modifier** is a word or phrase illogically separated from the word it describes. The following section offers a few examples and revisions of common types of misplaced modifiers.

Misplaced Modifiers

MISPLACED WORDS A misplaced word is separated from the word it limits or restricts.

WORD "ONLY" DESCRIBES?

Denise only refused to ride the tallest roller coaster.

Revision #1

WORD "ONLY" DESCRIBES "THE TALLEST ROLLER COASTER"

Denise refused to ride only the tallest roller coaster.

Revision #2

Only Denise refused to ride the tallest roller coaster.

WORD "ONLY" DESCRIBES "DENISE"

MISPLACED PHRASE A phrase that describes a noun is placed next to the wrong noun and separated from the noun it describes.

PHRASE "WITH A QUEASY STOMACH" DESCRIBES?

She got on the Ferris wheel with a queasy stomach.

Revision

PHRASE "WITH A QUEASY STOMACH" DESCRIBES "SHE"

With a queasy stomach, she got on the Ferris wheel.

MISPLACED CLAUSE A dependent clause that describes a particular word is placed next to the wrong word and is separated from the word the clause describes.

CLAUSE "WHO WAS TOO SHORT TO RIDE" DESCRIBES?

The little boy stood by his mother who was too short to ride.

Revision

CLAUSE "WHO WAS TOO SHORT TO RIDE" DESCRIBES "BOY"

The little boy who was too short to ride stood by his mother.

Practice 2

REVISE MISPLACED MODIFIERS

Coney Island
Amusement Park ►

Revise the following sentences to correct misplaced modifiers.

1. The Cyclone roller coaster thrills crowds at Coney Island which has an 85 foot drop at a 60 degree angle.

2. The 150 feet tall and 2000 pound Jeremy loves to ride Wonder Wheel at Coney Island.

3. Melissa only got sick at the top of the Astrotower, which is 275 feet tall.

4. Jeremy and Melissa exploding in the night sky watched the fireworks.

5. Coney Island is one of the last urban parks still open to tourists having survived since the late 1800s.

Practice 2

6. Smothered in ketchup, Janice loves Nathan's hot dogs.

7. Only Coney Island is open between Easter and Halloween.

8. Colin threw up on a woman who got sick from the ride.

9. Among his friends, Roberto rode only the Wonder Wheel.

10. Mindy had to leave before the park shut down completely exhausted.

L3 Revise Dangling Modifiers

A **dangling modifier** is a word, phrase, or clause that modifies a word not stated in the sentence. Therefore, the dangling modifier seems to describe the nearest word, yet it doesn't make sense. To revise dangling modifiers, you may need to add or rephrase ideas.

Dangling Modifiers: Two Revision Tips

A **dangling modifier** is a phrase that describes a word not stated in the sentence.

EXAMPLES What do the phrases in the following sentences describe?

Sentence #1

When smothered in chili and cheese, we can eat dozens.

Sentence #2

Hungry and thirsty, my hotdog and cola disappeared quickly.

Sentence #3

Eating 20 hotdogs and buns in 5 minutes, my stomach inflated like a balloon.

REVISION TIP #1 Change the dangling modifier into a logical clause with a subject and a verb.

Revised Sentence #1

ADDED SUBJECT AND VERB TO CREATE DEPENDENT CLAUSE

When hotdogs are smothered in chili and cheese, we can eat dozens.

Revised Sentence #2

ADDED SUBORDINATING CONJUNCTION, SUBJECT, AND VERB TO CREATE DEPENDENT CLAUSE

Because I was hungry and thirsty, my hotdog and cola disappeared quickly.

Revised Sentence #3

ADDED SUBJECT AND VERB TO CREATE INDEPENDENT CLAUSE

I ate 20 hotdogs and buns in 5 minutes, and my stomach inflated like a balloon.

REVISION TIP #2 Revise the main clause to include the word being modified.

Revised Sentence #1

PHRASE DESCRIBES ADDED NOUN "HOTDOGS"

We can eat dozens of hotdogs smothered in chili and cheese.

Revised Sentence #2

PHRASE DESCRIBES ADDED SUBJECT "I"

Hungry and thirsty, I made my hotdog and cola disappear quickly.

ADDED SUBJECT AND VERB

Revised Sentence #3

PHRASE DESCRIBES ADDED SUBJECT "I"

Eating 20 hotdogs and buns in 5 minutes, I inflated like a balloon.

Practice 3

REVISE DANGLING MODIFIERS

Revise the following sentences to eliminate dangling modifiers.

1. Gaudy with bright lights and tacky signs, you must go and have fun. _____

_____

2. Crushed by fans and media, Nathan's Famous Restaurant begins its historic hotdog-eating

contest. _____

_____

3. Since beginning in 1916, Joey has created the most excitement as a contestant. _____

_____

4. With cheeks like a chipmunk, the last five hotdogs vanished. _____

_____

5. As a champion Major League Eater, 59 hotdogs in 12 minutes broke a World Record.

_____

6. A competitive eating champion, Joey's nickname is The Gurgitator. _____

_____

7. Gulping in big bites, hotdogs quickly slide down his throat. _____

_____

8. Every year, Joey eats his Nathan's hotdogs in the same red shirt. _____

_____

9. To be a competitive eater, certain skills must be developed. _____

_____

10. At the age of twelve, Joey's mom brought him to Coney Island for the first time.

_____

REVISING MISPLACED AND DANGLING MODIFIERS REVIEW

Revise to correct misplaced and dangling modifiers. Move or add ideas as needed.

1. On a gold leash, a woman walked by leading a toy poodle with green and pink hair.

▲ Santa Monica Pier, Los Angeles

2. After getting the courage, the ride took off without Anthony.

3. We saw a stilt-walker on vacation roaming the boardwalk.

4. Laughing loudly, the gag amused the tourists.

5. While swimming in the ocean, something nibbled at my feet.

6. After surfing for hours, my body board lay on the beach.

7. Topped with chocolate and nuts, we enjoyed our ice cream cones.

8. Taking a vacation, my stress level dropped.

9. Working without vacations, our health may suffer.

10. To relax and have fun, an amusement park offers low-cost thrills.

▲ Family looking at an amusement park map

Editing Assignments

Editing for Everyday Life

Edit the following feedback from a guest to a resort hotel. Eliminate misplaced or dangling modifiers. Use your own paper or complete the exercise on MyWritingLab.com.

I am writing to register a complaint. Tripping over a tear, the hallway carpet made me fall. I was referred to a doctor suffering from a broken ankle. Missing work as a result, my paycheck is affected. Most distressing, however, is the way your staff treated me at the time. The manager on duty only took responsibility for the torn carpet. Clumsy and avoidable, she blamed my actions. I will never again stay at your hotel, nor will I recommend it to others.

Editing for College Life

Edit the following paragraph written for a college health class. Eliminate misplaced or dangling modifiers. Use your own paper or complete the exercise on MyWritingLab.com.

Laughter has a positive physical effect. For instance, abdomen muscles get the same work out as sit-ups while laughing hard for several minutes. Laughing stimulates the heart and many body systems. Also laughing, the immune system becomes stronger. Laughter has a positive mental effect. Less depressed and anxious, a good sense of humor helps a person. For example, many senior citizens have a sense of humor according to experts who overcome depression and suicidal thoughts. So joyfully, a vacation, a day at an amusement park, or even a roller coaster ride improves our well-being.

Editing for Working Life

Edit the following response from a resort hotel to the feedback given by a guest. Eliminate misplaced or dangling modifiers. Use your own paper or complete the exercise on MyWritingLab.com.

We appreciate your complaint writing us about your recent stay at the Beach Front Resort. Concerned about the unfortunate events you describe, this letter outlines our response. We are conducting a full investigation of the incident. Our Executive Manager is talking to our employees looking into the matter. Reporting the incident, our insurance agent will determine liability. If you have any further questions, you may contact Mr. Cyrus Smith of concern.

Academic Learning Log: Chapter Review

To test and track your understanding, answer the following questions.

1. What is a misplaced modifier? _____

_____

2. How is a misplaced modifier corrected? _____

_____

3. What is a dangling modifier? _____

_____

4. What are two ways to correct a dangling modifier? _____

_____

_____

5. **How will I use what I have learned about misplaced and dangling modifiers?**
   In your notebook, discuss how you will apply to your own writing what you have learned about misplaced and dangling modifiers. During the writing process when will you apply this knowledge?

6. **What do I still need to study about misplaced and dangling modifiers?**
   In your notebook, describe your ongoing study needs by describing what, when, and how you will continue to study about misplaced and dangling modifiers.

PORTFOLIO

MyWritingLab™

Complete the Post-test for Chapter 9 in MyWritingLab.

10

Subject-Verb Agreement: Present Tense

In the present tense, subjects and verbs must agree in number. Singular subjects must take singular verbs; plural subjects must take plural verbs.

Subject-verb agreement in the present tense ranks as one of the most common errors in written standard English. For many people, subject-verb agreement reflects regional speech or the informal way we speak in daily life. For example, many Southerners say "you was" instead of "you were." It is important to understand the difference between regional speech and standard English. Then, you can choose the language that will be the most effective for a given situation.

What's the Point of Subject-Verb Agreement?

Yearly review of an employee ▶

WRITING
FROM LIFE

Complete the following activity and answer the question "What's the point of subject-verb agreement?"

Assume you are a manager, and you are completing the yearly review of the employees in your unit. You have asked each employee to submit a self-evaluation. Read the following two drafts of a self-evaluation that will be submitted by a member of your unit. Is one draft more likely to be effective in securing a raise? Why or why not?

Draft A:
Making good decisions are one of my strengths. When I face a decision, I think about the different choices that is possible. Each of the choices provide its own good point, and each also provide its own downside. The key to effective decisions unlock the best options.

Draft B:
Making good decisions is one of my strengths. When I face a decision, I think about the different choices that are possible. Each of the choices provides its own good point, and each also provides its own downside. The key to effective decisions unlocks the best options.

What's the point of subject-verb agreement?

One Student Writer's Response

The following paragraph records one writer's thoughts about the point of subject-verb agreement in the self-evaluation example.

> *Draft B is more likely to help the employee get a raise. This draft used singular verbs with singular subjects and plural verbs with plural subjects. As a result, Draft B sounds polished and professional. In contrast, Draft A mixed singular subjects with plural verbs or plural subjects with singular verbs. As a result, Draft A doesn't seem clear or controlled. Our group made a chart to show the differences between the two drafts.*
>
> *Draft A:*
>
> | Subject | Verb |
> |---|---|
> | Making decisions | are |
> | Choices that | is |
> | Each | provide |
> | Key | unlock |
>
> *Draft B:*
>
> | Subject | Verb |
> |---|---|
> | Making decisions | is |
> | Choices that | are |
> | Each | provides |
> | Key | unlocks |
>
> *As our group talked, some of us were confused by the use of the letter "s" to make a word plural. The teacher explained that the "s" is used to make many subjects plural, but the "s" is also used to make some verbs singular. So, in most cases, if there is an "s" on the subject, I now look to see if I can drop the "s" on the verb.*

L2 Apply Basic Subject-Verb Agreement Rules

In the present tense, subjects and verbs must agree in number. A singular subject must have a singular verb; a plural subject must have a plural verb. The following chart uses the sample verb "sleep" to illustrate present tense agreement in number.

Present Tense Agreement		
	Singular **Subject** and **Verb**	Plural **Subject** and **Verb**
First Person	I sleep	We sleep
Second Person	You sleep	You sleep
Third Person	He She —— sleeps It	They sleep

For standard verbs, only the third-person singular verb is formed by adding -s or -es.

Third-person singular subject	→	present tense verb ends with -s or -es
He	→	watches
She	→	learns
It	→	lives

APPLY SUBJECT-VERB AGREEMENT RULES

Fill in the following charts with the correct form of each subject and verb. A few blanks are completed as examples.

1. To Work

	Subject	Verb
First Person (singular)	I	work
Second Person		
Third Person (singular)		

2. To Commute

	Subject	Verb
First Person (plural)		
Second Person		
Third Person (plural)	They	commute

3. To Reach

	Subject	Verb
First Person (singular)		
Second Person		
Third Person (singular)		

4. To Plan

	Subject	Verb
First Person (singular)		
Second Person		
Third Person (singular)		

5. To Agree

	Subject	Verb
First Person (plural)		
Second Person		
Third Person (singular)	He	

L3 Create Subject-Verb Agreement with Key Verbs in the Present Tense: *To Have, To Do, To Be*

Three key verbs are used both as main verbs and as helping verbs to express a wide variety of meanings: *to have, to do,* and *to be*. Memorize their present tense singular and plural forms to ensure subject-verb agreement.

To Have: Present Tense		
	Singular **Subject** and **Verb**	Plural **Subject** and **Verb**
First Person	I have	We have
Second Person	You have	You have
Third Person	He She It ⎱ has	They have

CREATE SUBJECT-VERB AGREEMENT: *TO HAVE*

Write the form of the verb *to have* that agrees with the subject in each of the following sentences.

1. Jerome .... worked various jobs in the food industry for several years.

2. He and his brother .... a plan to open their own pub.

3. Their passion for making craft beer and entertaining people .... fueled their dream of owning their own pub.

4. They .... saved enough money for a down payment on a building in a great location.

5. The location for the pub .... a spectacular view of the river.

6. Now the brothers .... to find investors for additional start-up funds.

7. Both .... excellent credit histories.

8. A smart investor .... to see this business as a good risk.

9. When you start a business, you .... challenges both expected and unexpected.

10. I .... mixed hard work with reality to make my dream come true.

To Do: Present Tense		
	Singular **Subject** and **Verb**	Plural **Subject** and **Verb**
First Person	I do	We do
Second Person	You do	You do
Third Person	He She —does It	They do

CREATE SUBJECT-VERB AGREEMENT: *TO DO*

Write the form of the verb *to do* that agrees with the subject in each of the following sentences.

1. Successful people enjoy the work they _____.

2. Eric _____ his best work when he enjoys what he is doing.

3. However, successful people _____ face unpleasant obstacles and tasks in their work.

4. Too often, lack of self-confidence _____ keep us in unfulfilling jobs.

5. Enjoyment _____ outrank money as the main goal of a satisfying career.

6. Many times, Lee _____ work over 40 hours a week to complete a project.

7. Her managers _____ take notice of her hard work.

8. She always _____ outstanding work.

9. I _____ make sacrifices to achieve success.

10. You _____ feel satisfied when you achieve a promotion or raise.

The verb **to do** is often used with the adverb "not" to express a negative thought, such as in the contractions *doesn't* and *don't*. Contractions combine the verb and the adverb into shorter words. The verb part of the contraction must still agree with its subject.

To Do and *Not*: Contraction Form		
	Singular **Subject** and **Verb**	Plural **Subject** and **Verb**
First Person	I don't agree	We don't agree
Second Person	You don't seem well	You don't seem well
Third Person	He She —doesn't care It	They don't care

Practice 5

Fill in the blank with the form of the verb *to do* that agrees with the subject of each of the following sentences. Use the contractions *doesn't* and *don't* as needed.

1. People whose only goal is to make money, usually .... not.

2. A national poll indicated that 80% of American workers .... not enjoy their jobs.

3. Usually, a person .... make a fortune in a job he or she hates.

4. Serena Williams .... not play tennis only for the money; she loves the game.

5. In your haste to make a living, ... forget to make a life.

6. An unemployed person .... often have the luxury of waiting for the perfect job.

7. When you are applying for a job, ... submit a resume or cover letter that contains typos.

8. I make sure that I .... talk poorly about former bosses during a job interview.

9. A job candidate in sloppy clothes .... not make a good impression.

10. No matter how discouraged you may get, ... not give up.

The ***to be*** verb is unusual because it uses three forms in the present tense: *am*, *is*, and *are*.

To Be: **Present Tense**		
	Singular **Subject** and **Verb**	Plural **Subject** and **Verb**
First Person	I am	We are
Second Person	You are	You are
Third Person	He She —is It	They are

CREATE SUBJECT-VERB AGREEMENT: *TO BE*

Steve Jobs with the
Apple iPhone▶

Write the form of
the verb *to be* that
agrees with the
subject of each
of the following
sentences.

1. In computer science class, I .... learning about the life of Steve Jobs. Jobs was working for a video gaming company when he and a computer-building friend, Steven Wozniak, started a computer business, Apple.

2. You .... probably familiar with many Apple products.

3. The iMac, the MacBook, the iPod, and the iPad .... his designs.

4. Steve Jobs said, "I .... convinced that the only thing that kept me going was that I loved what I did. You've got to find what you love."

5. The nation .... still seeing the creative genius of Jobs, who passed in 2011 from a rare type of pancreatic cancer.

6. What .... your favorite Apple products?

7. Apple's engineers .... working on new products.

8. The Apple Watch .... at the forefront of wearable computers.

9. Apple .... a prominent digital service company.

10. Jobs, worth billions, ... remembered as the picture of success.

CREATE SUBJECT-VERB AGREEMENT: *TO HAVE, TO DO, TO BE*

▲ Oprah Winfrey

Write the form of *to have*, *to do*, or *to be* that agrees with the subject of each of the following sentences. Then, follow the instructions to write three sentences of your own.

1. Oprah Winfrey's success .... not come easily, but .... the result of several factors.

2. Oprah, who .... goal oriented, says, "You are where you .... today in

your life based on everything you .... believed."

3. She .... the ability to recognize an opportunity, and she .... seize the moment.

4. Unlike Oprah, many people .... have the courage to follow their passion.

5. Difficulties throughout her life .... served as lessons and .... made her wiser.

6. Her dedication to others and her passion for excellence .... key aspects of her success.

7. Worth nearly $3 billion, Oprah .... have to work; she .... living her dream life.

8. Write a sentence using a form of the verb *to have*. Suggested topic: A dream or goal.

....

....

9. Write a sentence using a form of the verb *to do*. Suggested topic: A positive step toward a goal.

....

....

10. Write a sentence using a form of the verb *to be*. Suggested topic: A trait of success.

....

....

....

Create Subject-Verb Agreement with Subjects Separated from Verbs

LO 4

Subjects are often separated from their verbs by **prepositional phrases**. A **preposition** is a word that has a noun or pronoun as its object and states a relationship between its object and another word. A prepositional phrase begins with a preposition and ends with the object of the preposition. The object of the preposition can never be the subject of a sentence. Identifying prepositional phrases keeps you from confusing them with the subject of the sentence. The verb of a sentence agrees with the subject, not the object of the preposition.

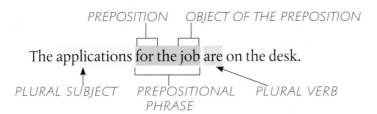

PREPOSITION   OBJECT OF THE PREPOSITION

The applications for the job are on the desk.

PLURAL SUBJECT   PREPOSITIONAL   PLURAL VERB
                  PHRASE

The following chart of prepositional phrases lists a few common prepositions and sample objects.

Common Prepositional Phrases			
Preposition	**Object**	**Preposition**	**Object**
at	work	of	concern
from	home	on	the desk
in	the office	with	experience

CREATE SUBJECT-VERB AGREEMENT

Choose the verb form that agrees with the subject of each of the following sentences. Cross out prepositional phrases. Underline the subject. Circle the appropriate verb.

1. Demand for goods and services (affects affect) the job market.

2. The opportunities for healthcare occupations (has have) surged because of the fast growth in demand for health services.

3. The need for healthcare and social assistance (is are) going to create 4 million new jobs from now until 2016.

4. As more women enter the labor force, demand for childcare services (is are) expected to grow.

5. The longer life spans of an aging population (has have) increased the need for jobs in healthcare.

6. The need of assisted living facilities for Alzheimer's patients (is are) only going to grow.

7. However, the number of nurses trained for Alzheimer's care (is are) alarmingly low.

8. Applicants with work experience in healthcare (has have) excellent job opportunities.

9. The structure and funding of healthcare (is are) changing rapidly.

10. Competition for jobs in management (has have) been keen.

Practice 8

L5 Create Subject-Verb Agreement with Singular or Plural Subjects

To establish subject-verb agreement, first identify a subject as plural or singular. Some subjects may seem singular or plural when actually they are not. The following section identifies and discusses several of these types of subjects and the rules of their agreement with verbs.

Indefinite Pronouns

Indefinite pronouns do not refer to specific nouns. Most indefinite pronouns are singular; a few are plural, and some can be either singular or plural. Consider the context of the indefinite pronoun to achieve subject-verb agreement.

• Singular indefinite pronouns agree with singular verbs.

> Each of the workers has a concern.

SINGULAR INDEFINITE PRONOUN

SINGULAR VERB "HAS" AGREES WITH SINGULAR INDEFINITE PRONOUN "EACH"

Singular Indefinite Pronouns					
anybody	each	everyone	neither	no one	somebody
anyone	either	everything	nobody	nothing	someone
anything	everybody	much	none	one	something

• Plural indefinite pronouns agree with plural verbs.

> Few of the workers have a concern.

PLURAL INDEFINITE PRONOUN

PLURAL VERB "HAVE" AGREES WITH PLURAL INDEFINITE PRONOUN "FEW"

Plural Indefinite Pronouns			
both	few	many	several

Singular or Plural Indefinite Pronouns Based on Context				
all	any	more	most	some

CREATE SUBJECT-VERB AGREEMENT: INDEFINITE PRONOUNS

Choose the verb form that agrees with the subject of each of the following sentences. Cross out prepositional phrases as needed. Underline the subject. Circle the appropriate verb.

1. Most of us (does do) want a fulfilling career.

2. Many (dreams dream) about starting businesses where they can enjoy a hobby all day.

3. Some of the experts (urges urge) job-seekers to "do what you love and the money will follow."

4. No one (wants want) to spend all day doing something he or she has no interest in.

5. However, few of us (realizes realize) that having to earn money at something often changes the way we feel about it.

6. Both of my sisters (has have) careers they love.

7. None of my friends (has have) found a job yet.

8. Everyone (desires desire) a fulfilling and good-paying job.

9. I've been looking for a job, and several in the paper (catches catch) my attention.

10. A few of them (seem seems) very promising.

Collective Nouns

Collective nouns name a collection of people, animals, or items as a unit. The agreement between a collective noun and a verb depends on the context of the sentence.

• **When a collective noun acts as one unit, use a singular verb.**

A board of directors makes the decision.

↑
SINGULAR COLLECTIVE NOUN   *SINGULAR VERB*

• **When a collective noun represents the individuals in a group, use a plural verb.**

PLURAL VERB
↓
The board have differing opinions.
↑
PLURAL COLLECTIVE NOUN

Common Collective Nouns				
audience	class	crowd	gang	staff
band	committee	faculty	group	team
cast	company	family	herd	troop
choir	crew	flock	jury	unit

Collective vote ▶

Practice 10

▲ The Rolling Stones – "A Bigger Bang Tour" – Shanghai

Choose the verb form that agrees with the subject of each of the following sentences. Cross out prepositional phrases as needed. Underline the subject. Circle the appropriate verb.

1. One mega-successful English band (is are) the Rolling Stones.

2. Formed in 1962, the group (is are) the longest-lived continuously active band in rock and roll history.

3. The crowd of fans always (screams scream) with one voice in appreciation.

4. In their personal lives, the band (has have) led wild lives in the past but (has have) become calmer in recent years.

5. A set of new songs (is are) included on their album *A Bigger Bang*.

6. The vast majority of successful musical groups (makes make) most of their money touring.

7. For example, The Rolling Stones band (has have) earned $92.5 million in one tour.

8. This cast of aging characters (is are) still going strong.

9. Their audience (does do) not agree on who is the most popular member of the Rolling Stones.

10. Write a sentence using a collective noun. Suggested topic: A successful performing group.

Either-or/Neither-Nor

Either or *neither* often signal a singular subject that requires a singular verb.

- To ensure subject-verb agreement, identify and cross out prepositional phrases.

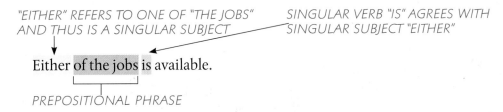

"EITHER" REFERS TO ONE OF "THE JOBS" AND THUS IS A SINGULAR SUBJECT

SINGULAR VERB "IS" AGREES WITH SINGULAR SUBJECT "EITHER"

Either of the jobs is available.

PREPOSITIONAL PHRASE

Either-or/neither-nor joins parts of a subject; the verb agrees with the nearer part of the subject.

- When all parts of the subject are singular, the verb is singular.

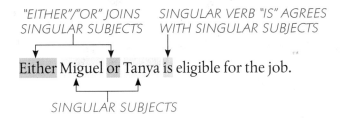

"EITHER"/"OR" JOINS SINGULAR SUBJECTS

SINGULAR VERB "IS" AGREES WITH SINGULAR SUBJECTS

Either Miguel or Tanya is eligible for the job.

SINGULAR SUBJECTS

- When all parts of the subject are plural, the verb is plural.

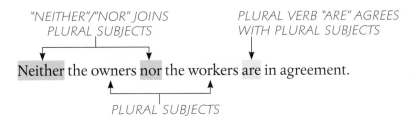

"NEITHER"/"NOR" JOINS PLURAL SUBJECTS

PLURAL VERB "ARE" AGREES WITH PLURAL SUBJECTS

Neither the owners nor the workers are in agreement.

PLURAL SUBJECTS

- When one part of the subject is singular and the other part is plural, the verb agrees with the nearer part. For smooth expression, place the plural part of the subject closer to the verb.

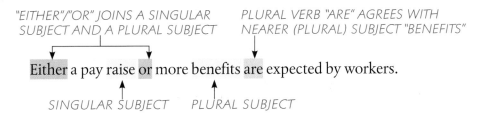

"EITHER"/"OR" JOINS A SINGULAR SUBJECT AND A PLURAL SUBJECT

PLURAL VERB "ARE" AGREES WITH NEARER (PLURAL) SUBJECT "BENEFITS"

Either a pay raise or more benefits are expected by workers.

SINGULAR SUBJECT   *PLURAL SUBJECT*

CREATE SUBJECT-VERB AGREEMENT: *EITHER-OR/NEITHER-NOR*

▲ Bus mechanics walk the picket line in Hollywood, CA

Choose the verb form that agrees with the subject of each of the following sentences. Cross out prepositional phrases as needed. Underline the subject. Circle the appropriate verb.

1. Neither family nor friends (is are) supposed to cross a picket line.

2. Neither the union leaders nor the company president (has have) given in on any point.

3. Either fringe benefits or a higher wage (is are) likely, but not both.

4. Either businesses or the market (has have) the right to set the minimum wage.

5. Neither government nor politicians (has have) the moral authority to set a worker's wage.

6. Neither the organizers of the strike nor the workers on strike (responds respond) to the jeers of bystanders.

7. Neither slander nor violence (is are) an acceptable way to negotiate working conditions.

8. Either Mr. Barnett or Ms. Hawkins (has have) to announce the result of the negotiations.

9. Either of the two offers (is are) acceptable.

10. Write a sentence using *either* or *neither*. Suggested topic: The ideal job.

- -

- -

Subjects after Verbs

In some instances, a writer may choose to place the subject after the verb. To ensure subject-verb agreement, identify the verb, identify (and cross out) prepositional phrases, and ask who or what completes the action or state of being stated by the verb.

There and **here** are never the subject of a sentence. Both of these words signal that the subject comes after the verb.

SIGNALS THAT THE SUBJECT   PLURAL VERB "ARE" AGREES WITH
APPEARS AFTER THE VERB ———— THE PLURAL SUBJECT "WEBSITES"

There are helpful websites for the job seeker.

PLURAL SUBJECT PREPOSITIONAL PHRASE

Agreement in Questions relies on understanding that the subject comes after the verb or between parts of the verb.

SINGULAR VERB "DOES HELP" AGREES WITH SINGULAR SUBJECT "INTERNET"

How does the Internet help a job seeker find a job?

SINGULAR SUBJECT

Writers having difficulty determining the subject in a question can identify it by reversing the word order into a statement as in the example below.

The Internet helps a job seeker find a job.

CREATE SUBJECT-VERB AGREEMENT: SUBJECTS AFTER VERBS

Choose the verb form that agrees with the subject of each of the following sentences. Cross out prepositional phrases. Underline the subject. Circle the appropriate verb.

1. There (is are) many different types of jobs described in the Occupational Outlook Handbook on the U.S. Department of Labor's website.

2. Here (is are) job search tips and information about the job market in each state.

3. There (is are) a search box on each page of the website to help find information about a specific occupation or topic.

4. (Is Are) you interested in learning about how to use the Internet as a job seeker?

5. (Has Have) you considered using social media in your job search?

6. There (is are) a way to use social media to network and find a job.

7. There (is are) those who use Facebook as a network to tap into for job prospects.

8. Here (is are) two more social media to use in a job search: LinkedIn and Twitter.

9. (Does Do) using social media to look for a job sound like a good idea?

10. Write a question. Suggested topic: Applying for a job.

....

....

Agreement with Relative Pronouns

Agreement with relative pronouns relies on identifying the relationship among a **relative pronoun** (a pronoun such as *that, which, who,* and *whom* that introduces a dependent clause), its **antecedent** (the word the pronoun refers to), and its verb. When a relative pronoun refers to a plural antecedent, it requires a plural verb. When a relative pronoun refers to a singular antecedent, it requires a singular verb. Note that relative pronouns signal a dependent clause. The antecedent for the relative pronoun is often found in the independent clause.

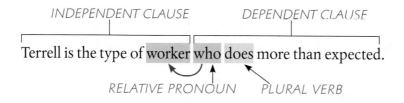

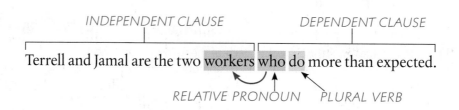

Relative Pronouns			
who	which	that	whoever

CREATE SUBJECT-VERB AGREEMENT: RELATIVE PRONOUNS

Choose the verb form that agrees with the relative pronoun in each of the following sentences. Underline the antecedent of the relative pronoun once. Underline the relative pronoun twice. Circle the appropriate verb.

1. Shantel has applied for the job that (is are) posted.

2. Shantel has applied for all of the jobs that (has have) been posted recently.

3. This position requires public speaking, which (is are) one of Shantel's strengths.

4. Shantel is one who (does do) well in the spotlight.

5. A person who (is are) a good problem solver makes an excellent manager.

6. Job skills that (is are) basic include being on time.

7. Employers want someone, like Shantel, who (handles handle) responsibility well.

8. Shantel is also strong in human relations, which (refers refer) to how well one (relates relate) to others.

9. Many employers are looking for an effective writer who (produces produce) quality memos, letters, and reports.

10. Write a sentence using a relative pronoun. Suggested topic: A workforce skill.

- -

- -

SUBJECT-VERB AGREEMENT REVIEW

Circle the verb form that agrees with its subject in each sentence.

1. Job Corps (is are) the nation's largest career technical training program for low-income students.

2. There (is are) 125 Job Corps centers located across the nation.

3. The program, which (is are) funded by Congress, has been training young adults for meaningful careers since 1964.

4. Youth who (participates participate) in Job Corps learn technical and academic skills.

5. A member of the staff (creates create) a personal career development plan for each participant.

6. When students successfully (gets get) jobs, they graduate from Job Corps.

7. Anybody who (is are) between the ages of 16 and 24 is eligible for Job Corps.

8. The mission of Job Corps (focuses focus) on attracting eligible young people, giving them skills, and placing them in jobs.

9. If you or your friends (has have) an interest in joining Job Corps, please call today.

10. (Is Are) anyone you know interested?

Editing Assignments

Editing for Everyday Life

Read the following e-mail a parent sent to a child's teacher. Edit the paragraph to ensure subject-verb agreement. Use your own paper or complete the exercise on MyWritingLab.com.

Dear Mr. Greer,

Troy's father and I thanks you for the support you has given Troy. Troy is one of the many children who has trouble learning. Being organized and staying focused is his biggest problems. However, since you has been working with him, he has improved. The thing that have helped most are your website. Either I or my older children checks your website every night to see what Troy needs to do. Thank you, Mr. Greer, for being one of the teachers who cares.

Editing for College Life

The following paragraph was written for a business communication class. Edit the paragraph to ensure subject-verb agreement. Use your own paper or complete the exercise on MyWritingLab.com.

THE EFFECTIVE HANDSHAKE

Business negotiations in America usually begins and ends with a handshake. Here is some hints for an effective handshake. Use a firm grip that show confidence, sincerity, and power. Too tight handshakes signals a power play. Fingertip handshakes or a loose grip comes across as weak or uncommitted. Use caution with people who has arthritis. An effective handshake don't yank the other person's hand. Positive words and a warm tone of voice reinforces the handshake.

Editing for Working Life

Read the following cover letter submitted with an application for the position of an office manager for a small business. Edit the paragraph to ensure subject-verb agreement. Use your own paper or complete the exercise on MyWritingLab.com.

Dear Ms. Samula:

I am applying for one of the openings that are posted on your website. There is several skills that I brings to the job. Organization and communication is necessary skills for an office manager. Both my former co-workers and my former boss has written recommendations which states my strengths in these two areas. If you needs more information, here is my home and evening phone numbers.

Sincerely,

Jordan Jackson

WHAT HAVE I LEARNED ABOUT SUBJECT-VERB AGREEMENT?

To test and track your understanding, answer the following questions.

1. What is the rule for subject-verb agreement? ....

....

2. How is the third-person singular verb formed?

The third-person singular verb is formed ....

3. What are the three forms of the present tense of the verb *to be*? ....

4. .... separate subjects from their verbs.

5. Indefinite and collective pronouns are singular or plural based on the .... of the sentence.

6. When *either-or* joins part of a subject, the verb agrees with the .... part of the subject.

7. .... and .... are never the subject of a sentence.

8. In a ...., the subject comes after the verb or between parts of the verb.

9. Agreement with relative pronouns relies on identifying the relationship among a relative

pronoun, its ...., and its verb.

10. How will I use what I have learned about subject-verb agreement?
In your notebook, discuss how you will apply to your own writing what you have learned about subject-verb agreement.

11. What do I still need to study about subject-verb agreement?
In your notebook, describe your ongoing study needs by describing what, when, and how you will continue studying subject-verb agreement.

PORTFOLIO

MyWritingLab™

Complete the Post-test for Chapter 10 in MyWritingLab.

11

The Comma

A comma is a valuable, useful punctuation device because it separates the structural elements of a sentence into manageable segments.

Misuse of the comma ranks as one of the most common errors in punctuation. The following photographs show two of the most popular pets owned by Americans. Complete the following activity about pets and answer the question "What's the point of commas?"

What's the Point of Commas?

LO 1

Practice 1

WRITING
FROM LIFE

PHOTOGRAPHIC ORGANIZER: COMMAS

▲ Kittens with a German Shepherd

Read the following paragraph that was written to post on a website about pets. This draft does not include any commas. Where are commas needed? Why?

> More of us own a dog than any other type of pet. However we do have more fish and cats than dogs. Americans by and large keep more than one fish. Also many of us own more than one cat yet usually we own only one dog. A recent National Pet Owners Survey by the American Pet Products Manufacturer's Association broke down pet ownership in the United States. Americans own 145 million freshwater fish 95.6 million cats 83.3 million dogs 20.6 million birds 18.1 million small animals 8.3 million horses 11.5 million reptiles and 13.6 million saltwater fish.

What's the point of commas?

_____

_____

One Student Writer's Response

The following paragraph offers one writer's reaction to the website posting about pets.

> *I had to reread parts of the paragraph about pets. The ideas kept running together, or a statement didn't make sense to me. One person in our group went comma crazy and wanted to put in a comma every time she paused to take a breath as she read out loud. There were only two places that I was sure about using commas. I put commas after "However" and between each animal in the list in the last sentence. I think that commas help the reader make sense of the ideas.*

The primary purpose of the **comma** is to make a sentence easy to read by indicating a brief pause between parts of the sentence that need to be separated.

L2 Use Commas with Items in a Series

Use commas to separate a **series of items** in a list. A series of items in a list can be **three** or more words, phrases, or clauses. In addition, a series of items can be made up of subjects, verbs, adjectives, participles, and so on. Items in a series are parallel and equal in importance.

Series of Words

COMMAS SET OFF SERIES OF WORDS (SUBJECTS AND VERBS)

Max, Misty, and Rocky fetch, bow, and shake.

Series of Phrases

COMMAS SET OFF SERIES OF PHRASES

Smokey loves to chase cars, to bark loudly, and to beg for food.

Series of Clauses

COMMAS SET OFF SERIES OF CLAUSES

Doug is a trainer who loves dogs, who uses praise, and who gets results.

Note: Journalists for newspapers and magazines often omit the comma before the coordinating conjunction that joins the last item in the series; however, in academic writing, this comma, which is called the **serial comma**, is usually included.

USE COMMAS FOR ITEMS IN A SERIES

Chocolate Lab puppy ▶

Edit the following sentences. Insert commas to separate a series of items in a list.

1. A Labrador Retriever is a dog that is gentle that gets along well with everyone and that is a good choice for a family.

2. The Labrador is medium sized and has an easy-to care-for, dense, weather-resistant coat.

3. The Lab has an even temperament is outgoing and enjoys other dogs and people.

4. This dog is large enthusiastic and bouncy; it thrives on vigorous exercise and athletic activities.

5. It is peaceful with other animals is eager to please and is very responsive to training.

6. Labradors can be found in guide and assistance dog programs, substance detection, efforts, and search and rescue work.

7. Labradors are also known for chewing objects mouthing human hands being rowdy and jumping excitedly.

8. Some Labrador Retrievers can be neurotic, hyperactive, dominant, or aggressive.

9. They can suffer serious health problems from joint and bone problems to eye diseases and heart disease to cancer.

10. Write a sentence that lists a series of items. Suggested topic: The traits of an ideal pet.

LO❸ Use Commas with Introductory Elements

Use commas to set off the introductory element of a sentence. **Introductory elements** are ideas that appear at the beginning of a sentence. Introductory elements come before a main clause. Introductory elements can be a word, phrase, or clause.

Introductory Word

COMMA SETS OFF INTRODUCTORY WORDS

Overall, living with pets provides certain health benefits.

Introductory Phrase

COMMA SETS OFF INTRODUCTORY PHRASE

In one study, pet ownership was linked to lower blood pressure.

Introductory Dependent Clause

COMMA SETS OFF INTRODUCTORY CLAUSE

Since Maria adopted a dog, she has walked every day.

Practice 3

USE COMMAS WITH INTRODUCTORY ELEMENTS

Edit the following sentences by inserting commas to set off introductory elements.

1. According to research owning a pet can help us fight heart disease and depression.

2. In one study it was found that heart patients who owned pets were more likely to be alive a year later than those who didn't own pets.

3. Additionally spending time with a pet causes the body to produce hormones that calm us down and make us feel pleasure.

4. Even if a pet is not a cuddly animal an owner still develops a strong emotional bond with it.

5. Because dogs need to be walked at least once a day owners are more likely to increase health and reduce stress through daily exercise.

6. Additionally pets offer love and companionship.

7. In fact research shows that nursing home residents reported less loneliness and stress when visited by dogs.

8. While owning a pet does require more work and responsibility the benefits are worthwhile.

9. Ultimately a loving bond between a human and an animal benefits both.

10. Write a sentence that uses an introductory element. Suggested topic: Disadvantages of owning a pet.

Use Commas to Join Independent Clauses L4

Use a comma with a coordinating conjunction to join two or more equally important and logically related independent clauses. An **independent clause** is a complete thought or sentence. When two or more independent clauses are joined together, they form a compound sentence. To join sentences with a coordinating conjunction, place the comma before the conjunction. The acronym **FANBOYS** identifies the seven coordinating conjunctions: *for, and, nor, but, or, yet,* and *so.* The following chart lists these conjunctions and the logical relationships they establish between ideas.

Coordinating Conjunctions and the Relationships They Establish: FANBOYS						
For	And	Nor	But	Or	Yet	So
reason, result	addition	negation	contrast	choice, condition, possibility	contrast	addition, result

Correct Use of a Comma to Join Independent Clauses

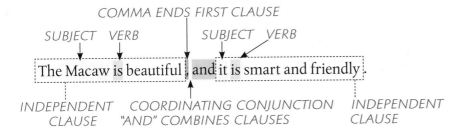

COMMA ENDS FIRST CLAUSE

SUBJECT VERB   SUBJECT VERB

The Macaw is beautiful, and it is smart and friendly.

INDEPENDENT   COORDINATING CONJUNCTION   INDEPENDENT
CLAUSE   "AND" COMBINES CLAUSES   CLAUSE

Practice 4

USE COMMAS TO JOIN INDEPENDENT CLAUSES

Hand feeding a Java Finch. ▶

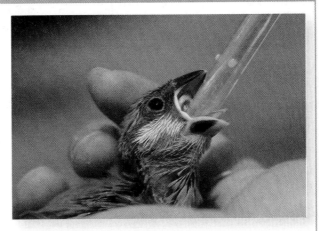

Edit the following sentences. Insert a comma and coordinating conjunction to properly join independent clauses.

1. A baby bird can be raised to be a healthy, trusting, well-behaved companion bird a baby bird can be raised to be insecure, fearful, unsociable, and a poor eater.

2. Hand feeding is the best way to raise a baby bird it introduces the baby to the taste of food.

3. Many owners use a syringe to feed a baby bird a syringe allows the flow of formula to match the rhythm of the baby's breathing pattern.

4. The syringe method also uses the natural feeding response it teaches the baby how to eat.

5. Newly hatched birds are called nestlings they need a small, warm nest to thrive.

6. A nest can be created by lining a small bowl or box with paper towels placed under a heat lamp or on a heating pad the nest needs to be kept between 85° to 90°F.

7. Excessive heat will kill a bird cold temperatures make the bird sluggish and unwilling to eat.

8. Young nestlings are fed every 15 to 20 minutes for at least twelve hours a day older ones are fed every 30 to 45 minutes.

9. Baby birds cannot have milk birds cannot digest milk it gives them diarrhea.

10. Write a sentence that contains two independent clauses. Properly join the clauses with a coordinating conjunction and a comma. Suggested topic: How to raise a baby animal.

LO❺ Use Commas with Parenthetical Ideas

Use commas to set off a parenthetical idea. A **parenthetical idea** interrupts a sentence with information that is **nonessential** to the meaning of the sentence. Such an idea could be enclosed in parentheses. However, more often, a comma comes before and after such an idea. These interruptions can be words, phrases, or clauses.

Parenthetical Word

COMMAS SET OFF PARENTHETICAL WORD

A tarantula, surprisingly, can be a fun pet.

Parenthetical Phrase

COMMAS SET OFF PARENTHETICAL PHRASE

A tarantula, despite its reputation, is not dangerous.

Parenthetical Clause

COMMAS SET OFF PARENTHETICAL CLAUSE

A tarantula, which is large and hairy, is beautiful.

Note: Two specific types of parenthetical ideas are the **nonessential appositive** (word or phrase) and the **nonessential clause.** The uses and misuses of commas with nonessential clauses are discussed in greater detail in the next section.

▲ Tarantula

Edit the following sentences by inserting commas to set off parenthetical ideas.

1. A tarantula generally is comfortable in a two-and-a-half- or five-gallon aquarium.

2. A diet of crickets along with other insects is fine for tarantulas.

3. A tarantula molts which is the shedding and replacing of its skin to grow larger.

4. Many tarantulas unfortunately are accidentally injured by their owners.

5. Tarantulas many of which are quite docile are noiseless pets.

6. Tarantulas enjoy a hiding area a half log or a small stone cave where they can spend their day.

7. Insects should be gut loaded or well fed before being fed to a tarantula.

8. The Mexican Red Knee Tarantula a popular pet will grow to a leg span of six inches and live up to thirty years.

9. The Cobalt Blue Tarantula which is one of the most aggressive species of tarantulas should not be handled.

10. Write a sentence that contains a parenthetical idea. Suggested topic: An unusual pet.

Use Commas with Nonessential Clauses

A parenthetical idea, the **nonessential clause** offers additional and unnecessary information that does not change the meaning of the sentence. Often nonessential information appears in a relative clause introduced by the relative pronouns *who* or *which*. A nonessential relative clause gives information about a nearby noun.

Use commas to set off a nonessential clause. Commas come before and after a nonessential clause that interrupts a sentence. A single comma sets off a nonessential clause at the end of a sentence.

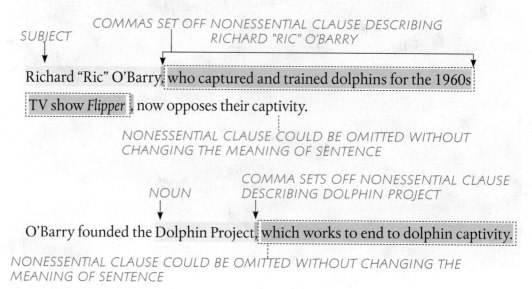

SUBJECT

COMMAS SET OFF NONESSENTIAL CLAUSE DESCRIBING RICHARD "RIC" O'BARRY

Richard "Ric" O'Barry, who captured and trained dolphins for the 1960s TV show *Flipper*, now opposes their captivity.

NONESSENTIAL CLAUSE COULD BE OMITTED WITHOUT CHANGING THE MEANING OF SENTENCE

NOUN

COMMA SETS OFF NONESSENTIAL CLAUSE DESCRIBING DOLPHIN PROJECT

O'Barry founded the Dolphin Project, which works to end to dolphin captivity.

NONESSENTIAL CLAUSE COULD BE OMITTED WITHOUT CHANGING THE MEANING OF SENTENCE

Practice 6

USE COMMAS WITH NONESSENTIAL CLAUSES

Edit the following sentences by inserting commas to set off nonessential clauses.

▲ Killer whale

1. SeaWorld which is a chain of marine mammal parks in the United States owns most of the captive killer whales in the world.

2. *Oricunus orca* which is better known as the killer whale is the largest species in the dolphin family.

3. Dr. Thomas White who is a marine expert and author opposes the captivity of whales and dolphins.

4. The 2013 film *Blackfish* which is a documentary focuses on SeaWorld's orca Tilkum.

5. Tilkum who was captured in 1983 killed his SeaWorld trainer Dawn Brancheau in 2010.

6. SeaWorld defends keeping and showing Tilkum who has been linked to the deaths of two other people.

7. The group PETA which stands for People for the Ethical Treatment of Animals asks the public to boycott SeaWorld.

8. Theme parks which are meant to be fun should never exploit animals.

9. SeaWorld which is also a respected zoo does rescue, rehabilitate, and release hundreds of wild animals.

10. Write a sentence that contains a nonessential clause. Suggested topic: An animal in need of protection.

Use Commas with Dates and Addresses L⑥

Use commas to set off information in dates and addresses. When a date or address is made up of two or more parts, a comma separates the parts. When the parts of a date are both words or are both numbers, a comma separates the parts. And a comma follows the last item unless it is the final detail of a list or sentence.

• Place commas after the day, date, and year of a date.

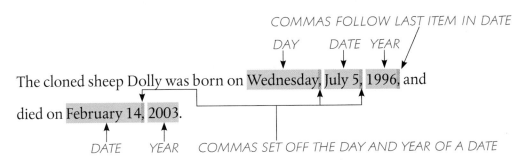

COMMAS FOLLOW LAST ITEM IN DATE
DAY   DATE   YEAR

The cloned sheep Dolly was born on Wednesday, July 5, 1996, and died on February 14, 2003.

DATE   YEAR   COMMAS SET OFF THE DAY AND YEAR OF A DATE

• Place commas after the street name, town or city, and state of an address.

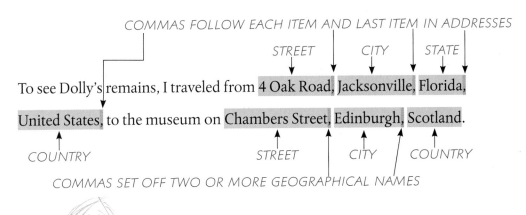

COMMAS FOLLOW EACH ITEM AND LAST ITEM IN ADDRESSES
STREET   CITY   STATE

To see Dolly's remains, I traveled from 4 Oak Road, Jacksonville, Florida, United States, to the museum on Chambers Street, Edinburgh, Scotland.

COUNTRY   STREET   CITY   COUNTRY
COMMAS SET OFF TWO OR MORE GEOGRAPHICAL NAMES

USE COMMAS FOR DATES AND ADDRESSES

Edit the following sentences by inserting commas to set off dates and addresses.

1. A tabby cat named CopyCat was born on December 22, 2001 and was the first cloned pet.
2. CopyCat gave birth the old-fashioned way to three kittens in September 2006 in College Station Texas.
3. Mira is the first cloned pet dog. She was born on December 5, 2007 and now lives in Mill Valley California.
4. The first Jersey calf cloned in the United States Millie was born at 400 West Main Avenue Knoxville Tennessee on August 28 2000 and died in June 2001.
5. The first cloned camel was born on April 8 2009 in Dubai United Arab Emirates.

▲ First cloned cat

Practice 7

195

6. Second Chance is a cloned Brahman bull; he was born on August 9 1999 at Texas A&M University in College Station Texas.

7. Replica Farm specializes in cloning horses; it is located at 442 U.S. Highway 202/206N Bedminster New Jersey.

8. On Friday May 1 2009 Replica Farms announced its prices for cloning a horse.

9. Replica Farm showcased the cloned colt Saphir of Olympic Gold jumper Sapphire on Friday September 17 2010.

10. Write a sentence that contains a date and address. Suggested topic: Your date and place of birth.

L❼ Apply Other Uses of the Comma

Commas are also used in two additional ways.

1. Use commas to separate consecutive **coordinate adjectives** of equal importance. **Coordinate adjectives** are a series of two or more adjectives that could be arranged in any order or could be strung together with the word *and*. They each modify the noun directly.

   • **Commas between consecutive coordinate adjectives:** Use two questions to determine whether adjectives are coordinate.

     A. Can the word *and* be smoothly placed between the adjectives?

     B. Can the order of the adjectives be reversed?

   If the answer is *yes* to either of these questions, then separate these coordinate adjectives with a comma.

Cloning may have harmful, irreversible effects.

COMMA SEPARATES COORDINATE ADJECTIVES DESCRIBING NOUN "EFFECTS"

2. Use commas to set off direct speech.

   • **Commas after a verb that introduces a quotation:** The comma is used to set off the "said" clause, called the **speech tag**, and the comma is placed before the quoted information.

COMMA SETS OFF SPEECH TAG FROM QUOTATION

Mr. Caplan said, "Pet cloning is a scam, not a service."

SPEECH TAG   QUOTATION MARKS ENCLOSE SPEAKER'S EXACT WORDS

APPLY OTHER USES OF THE COMMA

Edit the following sentences by inserting commas as needed to separate adjectives or to introduce a quotation.

1. Cloned animals can suffer unpredictable serious health issues.

2. Clear convincing evidence exists that cloning is dangerous.

3. Many thought that cloning would produce healthy strong offspring.

4. Instead, cloned offspring can be overly large short-lived animals.

5. According to Dr. Latish "Cloning is an unethical dangerous practice."

6. In contrast, Dr. Shay states "Cloning will lead to the end of diseases."

7. Randy Swizer, a biologist says "The genes of cloned animals reveal problems so the animals often appear abnormal and enlarged."

8. Instead of cloning animal lovers should adopt one of the thousands of unwanted abandoned animals in shelters.

9. Miguel Lopez said "I love my frisky friendly kitty I adopted from the Humane Society."

10. He also said he wanted to take home a shy skinny dog that had been abused.

COMMA REVIEW

Edit the following sentences by inserting commas as needed.

1. From the first moment I saw her I loved my small helpless puppy.

2. Peanut who was a mix between a Chihuahua and a poodle could fit in the palm of my hand.

3. She was born on August 28 1990 in Austin Texas.

4. Even though she was an old slow dog she loved to run bark and play.

5. Peanut's best friend was Kitty our large black cat.

6. Kitty also an old animal came to live with us on Monday January 15 1992.

7. We took them for their annual checkups to Dr. Parks who had been their veterinarian for years.

8. He often scolded us and said "You need to put these animals on diets for their weights put them at risk for all sorts of health problems."

9. Our two beloved pets Peanut and Kitty passed away within days of each other and we buried them under the oak tree at 36 Big Buck Trail Winter Beach California.

10. Now the only pet we have is Bella a cute skinny feline with tiger markings who is a frisky young troublemaker.

Editing Assignments

MyWritingLab™
Complete this Exercise
on mywritinglab.com

Editing for Everyday Life

Assume you breed and raise potbellied pigs, and you have posted the following information on your website. Edit to ensure proper use of commas. Insert commas as needed. Use your own paper or complete the exercise on MyWritingLab.com.

> I have raised Sheba who is a potbellied pig as a house pet. I wanted to make sure she had the care feeding housing and training necessary to produce a happy healthy pig. If you are interested in adopting Sheba, come see her at 25 Lexington Avenue New Haven California.

Editing for College Life

Assume you have been asked to write a short paper about cloning for a college science class. Edit to ensure proper use of commas. Insert commas as needed. Use your own paper or complete the exercise on MyWritingLab.com.

> *In recent years more and more animals such as sheep mice cattle goats cats rats horses and even a dog have been cloned. The first cloned dog was named Snuppy which is short for "Seoul National University puppy." Snuppy is practically identical to his cell-donor. Because cloned animals are identical to one another researchers can better study normal development reactions to drugs and the effects of pollution. Cloning might in addition keep certain species of animals from dying out. Ultimately owners may clone their beloved pets for emotional reasons.*

Editing for Working Life

Assume you are the office manager of a small business. You have composed the following memo. Edit to ensure proper use of commas. Insert commas as needed. Use your own paper or complete the exercise on MyWritingLab.com.

> **To: All Employees**
>
> Studies have shown that pets in the workplace boost employee morale output and even sales so our company is taking part in Take Your Dog To Work Day. Make sure your dog is bathed groomed and vaccinated. If you are constantly in and out of your office you may want to bring a portable kennel for your dog's comfort. Please remember to bring treats food a bowl a leash and a favorite toy for your dog. Submit your form to participate by May 2 2015 so you can bring your dog to work. As Jonathan Swift said "Every dog must have his day."

Academic Learning Log: Chapter Review

WHAT HAVE I LEARNED ABOUT COMMAS?

To test and track your understanding, answer the following questions.

1. Use commas to separate a series of items in a list; this list can include _3_ or more words, phrases, or clauses.

2. Use commas to set off the _intruduty_ elements, ideas that appear at the beginning of a sentence.

3. Use commas in union with a coordinating conjunction to create a _compound_ sentence, which is a sentence made up of two or more independent clauses.

4. Use a pair of commas to set off a _Prethenicol_ idea, which is an idea that interrupts a sentence.

5. Use commas to set off a nonessential clause; often nonessential information appears in a relative clause introduced by _who_ or _wicht_

6. When a date or address is made up of _2 or mor_ parts, use a comma to separate the parts.

7. Use commas between _coldinet_ adjectives.

8. Ask two questions to determine whether adjectives are coordinate:

   A. _and_

   B. _reveslsr_

9. Use a comma _after_ a verb that introduces a quotation.

10. **How will I use what I have learned about commas?**
    In your notebook, discuss how you will apply to your own writing what you have learned about commas.

11. **What do I still need to study about commas?**
    In your notebook, describe your ongoing study needs by describing what, when, and how you will continue studying commas.

PORTFOLIO

MyWritingLab™

Complete the Post-test for Chapter 11 in MyWritingLab.

12

The Apostrophe

The apostrophe is used to show ownership and to form contractions by replacing omitted letters or numbers.

Thinking about a real-life situation helps us to understand the purpose of the apostrophe in our writing. Complete the following activity and answer the question "What's the point of the apostrophe?"

What's the Point of the Apostrophe?

Practice 1

The signs depicted in these photographs illustrate two different uses of the apostrophe. Study the signs shown in the photographs on these pages and explain why an apostrophe was used in each one.

WRITING
FROM LIFE

What's the point of apostrophes?

New York City Law
"Don't Honk: $350 Penalty" ▶

One Student Writer's Response

The following paragraph offers one writer's reaction to the pictures that use apostrophes.

The two restaurant signs use apostrophes to show ownership. The apostrophe in the "Don't Honk" sign indicates that the letter "o" has been dropped to make "do not" into the contraction "don't."

L2 Use the Apostrophe for Ownership

The **possessive form** of a noun and some pronouns is created by using an apostrophe followed, at times, by an -s. The possessive tells the reader that someone or something owns or possesses the next stated thing.

OWNER   POSSESSION

Deborah's iPod

The following chart lists and illustrates the rules for using an apostrophe to show possession.

Using the Apostrophe for Ownership		
To Show Possession for	**Correct Use of Apostrophe**	**Example**
A singular noun	add 's	Joe's cup
A singular noun ending with -s	add 's	Tess's pen
A regular plural noun ending with -s	add '	girls' soccer team
An irregular plural noun	add 's	men's ties
Compound words	add 's	son-in-law's car
Joint ownership of an item	add 's to the last noun	Adam and Kate's children
Individual ownership	add 's to both nouns	Bush's and Obama's speeches
Pronouns ending with "one" or "body"	add 's	anybody's guess

Practice 2

USE APOSTROPHES FOR OWNERSHIP

Change the phrases below into possessives by adding an (') or an ('s).

1. the promises of a friend ....

2. the schedule of the bus ....

3. the outfit of Ross ....

4. the ice cream of Ben and Jerry ....

5. the house of his mother-in-law ....

6. the shoes of the children ....

7. the cars of Josh and Eli ....

Use the Apostrophe for Contractions

An apostrophe is used to indicate the omission of letters to form a **contraction.** Most often, a contraction is formed to join two words to make one shorter word such as *don't* for *do not*. However, sometimes an apostrophe is used to form a one-word contraction such as *ma'am* for *madam* and *gov't* for *government*. An apostrophe (') takes the place of the letter or letters that are dropped to form the contraction.

   The use of contractions gives a piece of writing an informal tone that records on paper the way we speak in general conversation. Writing for college courses usually requires a formal, academic tone. Thus, many instructors discourage the use of contractions. Check with your instructors about the required tone of your writing assignments. To ensure proper use of the apostrophe, the following chart illustrates how contracted verbs are formed.

Apostrophe Use in Common Contractions	
The apostrophe replaces omitted letters.	
'm APOSTROPHE REPLACES "A" IN "I AM" I am = I'm	's APOSTROPHE REPLACES "I" IN "IS" it is = it's
're APOSTROPHE REPLACES "A" IN "THEY ARE" they are = they're	've APOSTROPHE REPLACES "HA" IN "HAVE" I have = I've
n't APOSTROPHE REPLACES "O" IN "NOT" do not = don't	'll APOSTROPHE REPLACES "WI" IN "WILL" we will = we'll

USE APOSTROPHES IN CONTRACTIONS

Use apostrophes to form contractions for the following words.

1. I am ....

2. she is ....

3. would not ....

4. let us..

5. we are ....

6. will not ....

7. she has ....

8. it has ....

9. it will ....

10. we have ....

Practice 3

L4 Recognize and Correct Common Misuses of the Apostrophe

Quite often, the apostrophe is misused in several specific ways. The following chart lists and illustrates these common misuses of the apostrophe. Always base your use of an apostrophe on a specific rule. Proofread your writing for these common mistakes.

• Do not use an apostrophe to form a plural noun.

Correct Plural	Incorrect Plural
smiles	smile's

• Do not use an apostrophe to form a possessive pronoun.

Correct	Incorrect
his	his'
theirs	their's

• Do not omit the apostrophe to form the possessive indefinite pronoun.

Correct	Incorrect
somebody's	somebodys

• Do not confuse contractions with similar sounding words.

Contraction	Possessive Pronoun
it's (it is)	its
who's (who is)	whose
they're (they are)	their

Practice 4

RECOGNIZE AND CORRECT MISUSE OF THE APOSTROPHE

Underline the word that best completes each sentence.

1. Around 9 million Americans have (their / they're) identities stolen each year.

2. Identity theft occurs when (someones / someone's) using the personal identification of (other's / others) without (their / they're) permission.

3. (Your / You're / Your's) wise to protect (your / you're / yours) personal identification information, which is (your / you're / your's) name, Social Security number, or credit card number.

4. Identity thieves are crooks (who's / whose) goal is fraud, and (their / they're) hoping (your your's / you're) not paying attention.

5. Some victims of identity theft resolve (their / they're) problems quickly; others find (their / they're) required to spend hundreds of dollars and countless hours repairing the damage to (their / they're) credit rating.

6. An identity thief is a person (who's / whose) willing to dive in dumpsters to find (someone's / someones) personal information.

7. For a thief (its / it's) as easy as stealing a wallet or purse.

8. (Its / It's) difficult to predict how long the effects of identity theft may linger.

9. (There / Their / They're) are several steps to take to recover if (you're / your) a victim.

10. For example, Bob, (whose / who's) identity was stolen, placed an alert on (his' / his) credit reports.

REVIEW OF THE APOSTROPHE

▲ Identity theft

Edit the paragraph for correct use of the apostrophe.

(1) A person may ask that a fraud alert be placed on her's credit report. (2) Its an important step to take if she suspects shes been, or shes about to be, a victim of identity theft. (3) An alert is wise if her's wallets been stolen or if shes been taken in by a scam. (4) With a fraud alert, likely creditors must confirm hers identity before issuing credit in her name. (5) However, the creditors actions to verify ones identity may not always work. (6) When a fraud alert is placed on an individuals credit report, shes allowed to get one free credit report from each of the three nationwide consumer reporting companies. (7) And, by request, only the last four digits of a persons Social Security number will appear on her's credit reports.

Write a sentence that correctly uses the apostrophe. Suggested Topic: Identity theft.

Editing Assignments

Editing for Everyday Life

Assume you have been a victim of identity theft. You have written a letter to get information from businesses that dealt with the identity thief. Edit the body of the letter for correct use of apostrophes. Use your own paper or complete the exercise on MyWritingLab.com.

As we discussed on the phone, Im a victim of identity theft. The thief made an illegal purchase. In addition, a fake accounts been opened at your company. Based on federal law, Im requesting that you provide me, at no charge, copies of application and business records in youre control relating to the thiefs illegal transaction.

Editing for College Life

Assume you are writing a response to a short-answer exam question in a college business class. Edit the paragraph for correct use of apostrophes. Use your own paper or complete the exercise on MyWritingLab.com.

Exam Question: What is a credit freeze?

Student Response: Many states laws let consumers "freeze" their credit. A consumer restricts access to his' or her's credit report. A credit freezes effect is powerful. Potential creditors and other third parties will not be able to get access to the persons' credit report unless he or she temporarily lifts the freeze. This means that its unlikely that an identity thief would be able to open a new account in the victims name. In some states, anyones able to freeze they're credit file, while in other states, only identity theft victims can.

Editing for Working Life

Assume you own a small retail business, and you have detected an illegal transaction by an identity thief. You have written a letter to the customer who has had his identity stolen. Edit the body of the letter for correct use of apostrophes. Use your own paper or complete the exercise on MyWritingLab.com.

Were contacting you about a potential problem involving identity theft. Its recommended that you place a fraud alert on you're credit file. A fraud alert tells creditor's to contact you before their to open any new accounts or change your existing accounts. Call any one of the three major credit bureaus. As soon as one credit bureau confirms you're fraud alert, the others are notified to place fraud alerts. Theyll all send they're credit reports to you, free of charge, for your review.

WHAT HAVE I LEARNED ABOUT THE APOSTROPHE?

To test and track your understanding, answer the following questions.

1. What are two general purposes of an apostrophe?

    a. To show ....

    b. To form ....

2. What are four common misuses of the apostrophe to avoid?

    a. Using apostrophes to form ....

    b. Using apostrophes to form ....

    c. .... to form possessive indefinite pronouns

    d. Confusing contractions with ....

3. How will I use what I have learned about the apostrophe?
In your notebook, discuss how you will apply to your own writing what you have learned about the apostrophe.

4. What do I still need to study about the apostrophe?
In your notebook, describe your ongoing study needs by describing what, when, and how you will continue studying the apostrophe.

PORTFOLIO

MyWritingLab™
Complete the Post-test for Chapter 12 in MyWritingLab.

13

Quotation Marks

Quotation marks are used to set off exact words either written or spoken by other people or to set off titles of short works.

Quotation marks help us to record the ideas of other people. We have little trouble identifying who is saying what in our daily conversations. However, when we capture speech in writing, we face several challenges. The same can be said for the use of quotation marks for a title of a publication. Complete the following activity and answer the question "What's the point of quotation marks?"

What's the Point of Quotation Marks?

PHOTOGRAPHIC ORGANIZER: QUOTATION MARKS

Assume you are an avid fan of *The Simpsons*. You love the show so much that you have subscribed to a blog about it, and you read the following posting on the blog. As you read the paragraph, underline the ideas that you think should be in quotation marks.

WRITING
FROM LIFE

▲ An inflatable Homer Simpson dressed as Santa Claus

(1) *The Simpsons* may seem like a simple cartoon. (2) However, critics and educators see much more. (3) Ken Tucker of *Entertainment Weekly* said, The Simpsons are the American family at its most complicated. (4) Homer is a prime example. (5) *The Simpsons'* creator Matt Groening describes Homer as a a loveable oaf. (6) But some see this cartoon father as lazy, stupid, and a poor role model for fathers. (7) The show is also famous for making fun of almost every aspect of American life. (8) For example, the episode Dial N for Nerder deals with Homer's struggle to lose weight and the effects of childish pranks. (9) Across the country, colleges offer courses that study the significance of *The Simpsons*. (10) To that Bart says, Holy Cow, and Homer says, D'oh!

What's the point of quotation marks?

....

....

....

One Student Writer's Response

The following paragraph offers one writer's reaction to the paragraph about *The Simpsons.*

I have always had a hard time knowing when to use quotation marks and where to put them. For example, I put quotation marks around the title "The Simpsons." But someone in my group said that you aren't supposed to put quotation marks around the title of a show because it's not a short work like one episode is. So we underlined "Dial N for Nerder." We also underlined everything that came after the words "said" and "says." I need to know if periods and commas go inside or outside of quotation marks.

L2 Apply General Guidelines for Quotation Marks

Use **quotation marks (" ")** to set off **direct quotes**—the exact words spoken by someone or quoted from another source—and for titles of short works. Always use quotation marks in pairs. The first quotation mark **(")**, also called the **opening quotation mark**, indicates the beginning of the quoted material. The second quotation mark **(")**, also called the **closing quotation mark**, indicates the end of the quoted material. Four general rules guide the use of quotation marks with other pieces of punctuation.

General Guidelines for Using Quotation Marks

1. Place commas (,) and periods (.) inside the quotation marks (" ").

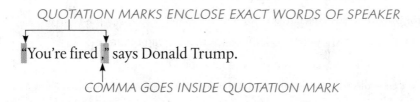

QUOTATION MARKS ENCLOSE EXACT WORDS OF SPEAKER

"You're fired," says Donald Trump.

COMMA GOES INSIDE QUOTATION MARK

2. Place semicolons (;) and colons (:) outside the quotation marks.

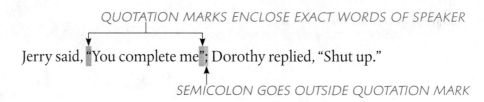

QUOTATION MARKS ENCLOSE EXACT WORDS OF SPEAKER

Jerry said, "You complete me"; Dorothy replied, "Shut up."

SEMICOLON GOES OUTSIDE QUOTATION MARK

3. Place a question mark (**?**) inside quotation marks when it is part of the quotation. Place a question mark outside quotation marks when the larger sentence is a question, but the quotation included in it is not.

QUOTATION MARKS ENCLOSE EXACT WORDS OF SPEAKER

Indiana Jones said, "Snakes. Why'd it hafta be snakes?"

QUESTION MARK GOES INSIDE QUOTATION MARK

QUOTATION MARKS ENCLOSE EXACT WORDS OF SPEAKER

Did he really say "I hate snakes"?

QUESTION MARK GOES OUTSIDE QUOTATION MARK BECAUSE THE SENTENCE ITSELF IS A QUESTION, BUT THE QUOTATION INCLUDED IN IT IS NOT

4. Use single quotation marks for quoted information—or titles of short works—that appear within direct quotation.

DOUBLE QUOTATION MARKS ENCLOSE THE WORDS POE WROTE

Edgar Allan Poe wrote, "Quoth the raven, 'Nevermore.'"

SINGLE QUOTATION MARKS ENCLOSE THE WORD STATED BY THE RAVEN

APPLY GENERAL GUIDELINES FOR QUOTATION MARKS

Insert quotation marks and other punctuation as needed.

1. A headline on Forbes.com states, Country Fireball: Inside the Rise of Florida Georgia Line.

2. Forbes.com reporter Zack O'Mally Greenburg writes, Tyler Hubbard, 27, and Brian Kelly, 29, of Florida Georgia Line embody what it means to be on the Forbes 30 Under 30 list in the music category.

3. The article reports, Over the past three years Florida Georgia Line and its boozy, genre-bending brand of country (Lynyrd Skynyrd meets late-90s hip-hop) has propelled it from utter anonymity to mainstream stardom.

4. Florida Georgia Line's smash single Cruise has become the most-downloaded country song of all times.

5. Greenburg also reports, Cruise moved 8 million units in barely two years, he continues, —and helped them earn $24 million last year.

6. In the article, Greenburg asks the duo, Florida Georgia Line—how'd it happen, and how did you get to where you are today

7. Can you believe that a part of the group's ritual before every concert is to, as Hubbard states, take a shot of Fireball

Practice 2

Practice 2

8. Kelly describes his work in three words, Fun. Authentic. Party Hubbard describes his work in two words, Fast, fun.

9. As a former neighbor who watched Brian Kelly grow up, I say, Well done, Tyler and Brian!

10. Write a quotation that records an idea stated by someone else. Suggested topic: An opinion about a singing star.

L❸ Use Correct Format and Punctuation for Direct Quotations

One part of a direct quotation is the **speech tag** or the credit given to the source, the person who spoke or wrote an idea. A speech tag is formed by a subject (the speaker) and a verb that indicates the subject is speaking. A speech tag can appear at the beginning, in the middle, or at the end of a quote.

Punctuating Direct Quotations

• Speech tag at the beginning of quote

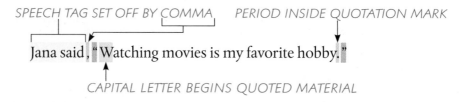

• Speech tag in the middle of quote

(1) Quotation is stated in one sentence:

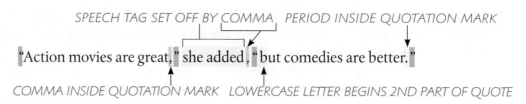

(2) Quotation is stated in two sentences:

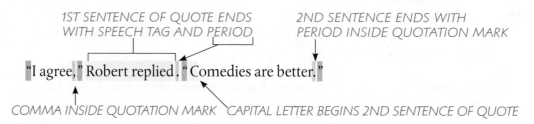

• **Speech tag at the end of quote**

QUESTION MARK INSIDE QUOTATION MARK   SPEECH TAG

"Do you want to go see a movie tonight?" Robert asked.

USE CORRECT FORMAT AND PUNCTUATION FOR DIRECT QUOTATIONS

Edit each sentence to ensure correct punctuation of direct quotes and titles. Insert quotation marks and other punctuation as needed. Discuss your answers with your classmates.

1. I am Jeff McIntyre, he said to the House of Representatives and am honored to be here to represent the American Psychological Association

2. He stated The repeated exposure to violence in mass media places children at risk

3. One of the risks he listed was increases in aggression

4. A report submitted to the Senate says James Q. Wilson, one of our foremost experts on crime, has observed Youngsters are shooting at people at a far higher rate than at any time in recent history

5. An expert in media literacy, Elizabeth Thoman says We can take responsibility for our role in allowing media violence

6. If children watch TV less she says they will see less violence

7. The best way to help children is to watch TV with them and talk to them about what they see Thoman states.

8. The American Psychiatric Association reports By the time they reach 18, American children will have seen 16,000 virtual murders and 200,000 acts of violence

9. Parents should carefully select TV programs the American Academy of Pediatrics claims in a recent report and avoid use of media as a baby-sitter

10. Write a direct quotation to record something someone else said. Suggested topic: Advice you have received.

LO4 Use Correct Format and Punctuation for Dialogue

Including dialogue in a piece of writing adds interest, details, and authenticity. Dialogue conveys action, time, place, and the traits and values of the speakers. Most often, dialogue is associated with creative writing, story telling, and journalism, but a well-crafted or carefully chosen piece of dialogue also can effectively support a point in an academic paper. The following chart offers a few basic tips for formatting and punctuating dialogue.

Tips for Formatting and Punctuating Dialogue
• Use quotation marks to indicate a speaker's exact words.
• Use speech tags to make sure the reader knows who is speaking.
• Vary the placement of speech tags.
• Begin a new paragraph to change speakers; record each person's turn at speaking, no matter how brief, in a separate paragraph.
• When a speaker's speech is longer than one paragraph: Begin the speech with a quotation mark.   Do not use a quotation mark at the end of the first paragraph or subsequent paragraphs.   Instead, begin each new paragraph in the speech with a quotation mark.   End the speech with a closing quotation mark at the end of the last paragraph.

Apply Appropriate Formatting

Note the ways in which Aesop's fable "The Hare and the Tortoise" applies a few of the appropriate formatting and punctuation rules for writing dialogue.

Comment:
New paragraphs signal changes in speaker

Comment:
Varied use of the speech tag

The Hare was once boasting of his speed before the other animals. "I have never yet been beaten," said he, "when I put forth my full speed. I challenge anyone here to race with me."

The Tortoise said quietly, "I accept your challenge."

"That is a good joke," said the Hare; "I could dance round you all the way."

"Keep your boasting till you've beaten," answered the Tortoise. "Shall we race?"

So a course was fixed and a start was made. The Hare darted almost out of sight at once, but soon stopped and, to show his contempt for the Tortoise, lay down to have a nap. The Tortoise plodded on and plodded on, and when the Hare awoke from his nap, he saw the Tortoise just near the winning-post and could not run up in time to save the race.

Then said the Tortoise, "Plodding wins the race."

—Æsop. *Fables*, retold by Joseph Jacobs. Vol. XVII, Part 1. The Harvard Classics. New York: P.F. Collier & Son, 1909–14; Bartleby.com, 2001. www.bartleby.com/17/1/.[10 Sept. 2008].

Practice 4

Write out the dialogue between Blondie and Dagwood in this cartoon strip. Use appropriate formatting and punctuation.

Blondie copyright © 2008 King Features Syndicate, Inc. World Rights reserved.

Use Direct and Indirect Quotations

L⑤

The spoken or printed words of other people are written in two ways: as a direct quotation or as an indirect quotation. So far, you have been learning about the **direct quotation**, which uses a pair of quotation marks to indicate someone else's exact words. In contrast, an **indirect quotation** rephrases or rewords what someone said or wrote. An indirect quotation is a **paraphrase** of someone else's words. Never use quotation marks with indirect quotations. To paraphrase a direct quotation into an indirect quotation, follow the steps shown in the chart.

How to Paraphrase a Direct Quote into an Indirect Quote
1. Remove quotation marks and internal capital letters.
2. Consider adding the word *that* to introduce the paraphrased idea.
3. Revise verbs into past tense, except for actions continuing in the present.
4. Revise verbs that command into their infinitive forms; revise speech tag for logical sense.
5. Revise pronouns and signal words as needed.

Original Direct Quotation:

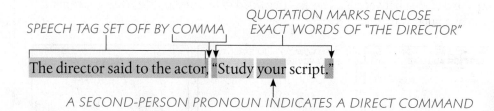

SPEECH TAG SET OFF BY COMMA

QUOTATION MARKS ENCLOSE EXACT WORDS OF "THE DIRECTOR"

The director said to the actor, "Study your script."

A SECOND-PERSON PRONOUN INDICATES A DIRECT COMMAND

Revised Indirect Quotation:

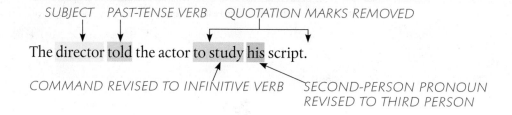

SUBJECT   *PAST-TENSE VERB*   *QUOTATION MARKS REMOVED*

The director told the actor to study his script.

COMMAND REVISED TO INFINITIVE VERB   *SECOND-PERSON PRONOUN REVISED TO THIRD PERSON*

Original Direct Quotation:

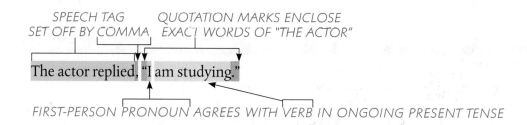

SPEECH TAG SET OFF BY COMMA   *QUOTATION MARKS ENCLOSE EXACT WORDS OF "THE ACTOR"*

The actor replied, "I am studying."

FIRST-PERSON PRONOUN AGREES WITH VERB IN ONGOING PRESENT TENSE

Revised Indirect Quotation:

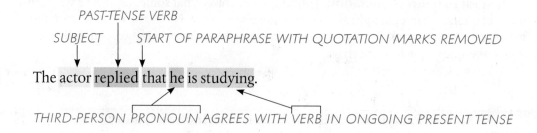

PAST-TENSE VERB

SUBJECT   *START OF PARAPHRASE WITH QUOTATION MARKS REMOVED*

The actor replied that he is studying.

THIRD-PERSON PRONOUN AGREES WITH VERB IN ONGOING PRESENT TENSE

USE DIRECT AND INDIRECT QUOTATIONS

Paraphrase the following direct quotes into indirect quotes. Work with a classmate or small group of peers.

1. Woody Allen said, "Eighty percent of success is showing up."

-----

2. "Piles of gold are not as good as stores of grain," warns a Chinese proverb.

-----

3. "Movies are a combination of art and mass medium," according to film critic Pauline Kael.

-----

4. "Advice is what we ask for," Erica Jong said, "when we already know the answer but wish we didn't."

-----

5. Actress Bridget Bardot said, "I have been very happy, very rich, very beautiful, much adulated, very famous and very unhappy."

-----

6. Local weather reports advise, "Conditions are favorable for severe thunderstorms and possible tornadoes."

-----

7. "Achievable goals are the first step to self-improvement," advises J. K. Rowling.

-----

8. Professor Robbins states in her course syllabus, "Students who exceed three unexcused absences may be dropped from the course."

....

....

9. "Learn to value yourself," Ayn Rand advises, "which means: to fight for your happiness."

....

....

10. My mother always said, "If you can't say something nice, don't say anything at all."

....

....

Practice 5

L6 Use Quotation Marks for Certain Types of Titles

Quotation marks are also used to set off the titles of short works such as essays, short stories, short poems, songs, articles in magazines, TV episodes, and chapter titles in books.

- Follow the general rules for using quotation marks.
- Do not use quotation marks to set off titles of larger publications such as magazines, newspapers, and books. These larger publications are set off with italics or underlining.

Poems

QUOTATION MARKS SET OFF POEM'S TITLE

Have you read the poem "Oranges" by Gary Soto?

Songs

QUOTATION MARKS SET OFF SONG'S TITLE

Taylor Swift had another hit song with "Shake It Off."

Television Shows

QUOTATION MARKS SET OFF THE TITLE OF THE EPISODE

My favorite episode of *The Simpsons* is "All about Lisa."

THE TITLE OF THE TV SHOW IS SET IN ITALICS

USE QUOTATION MARKS FOR CERTAIN TYPES OF TITLES

Edit each sentence to ensure correct punctuation of titles.

1. Cinderella is a classic folk tale about a young woman rising above unjust treatment and finding her true love.

2. The song Hey Cinderella by Suzy Bogguss is about a woman's disappointment with married life.

3. The web article Cinderella Is Dead says that the modern woman no longer needs to be rescued by a prince.

4. Shel Silverstein's poem In Search of Cinderella is a witty look at the story from the prince's point of view.

5. The song It's Midnight Cinderella by Garth Brooks tells the story of a man who makes a pass at a girl whose Prince Charming has left her.

6. The poem Cinderella by Anne Sexton mocks the idea that a woman needs a Prince to rescue her.

7. The newspaper article Who Is This Year's Cinderella Team? predicts the teams most likely to make it to the Super Bowl.

8. Susan submitted her thesis Cinderella: The Durable Myth to Professor Jordan.

9. Professor Jordan exclaimed, Susan, I am eager to read your interpretation of the Cinderella myth!

10. Write a sentence that includes a title. Punctuate the title correctly. Suggested topic: Your favorite poem, song, or television show.

REVIEW OF QUOTATION MARKS

Write a dialogue of four to six sentences based on a recent conversation you have had or that you have heard. Use appropriate format and punctuation. Work in pairs or with a small group of your classmates. Use your own paper.

Editing Assignments

MyWritingLab™
Complete this Exercise
on mywritinglab.com

Editing for Everyday Life

Assume your local community theater is hosting an "open microphone" night, and you have written a skit. Edit the following dialogue. Use the proper format; insert quotation marks and punctuation as needed.

Nick says look I don't care what you are doing. When our daughter calls you drop everything and answer her. Justine says What? Now I'm a bad mother? Is that what you think? Nick sighs and says I didn't say that. Justine snaps You didn't have to. It's in your eyes. Nick says Really? My eyes? Are you an expert on body language? Justine says Listen, since I am such a horrible mother, do you want a divorce? Nick sighs again No I do not want a divorce. Why do you always go there?

Editing for College Life

Assume you have written a personal response to an assigned poem for your English class. Edit the paragraph. Insert quotation marks and other punctuation as needed.

The poem Ulysses by Tennyson describes a hero returning home after a long journey and many battles. During his travels, he had become famous and honored for his deeds. However, once home, he becomes restless and unhappy. He describes his wife as aged, and he calls his subjects a savage race that hoard, and sleep, and feed and know not me. So he decides to return to a life of adventure and sets off on a new journey. His purpose is as he says, to strive, to seek, to find, and not to yield.

Editing for Working Life

Assume you are submitting a report to your manager about a conflict between an employee and a supervisor. Edit the paragraph. Insert quotation marks and other punctuation as needed.

On July 6 at 6:30 a.m., Jordan Michaels reported a conflict with Julie Towers, his floor supervisor. Mr. Michaels says that the two of them argued about his schedule. Mr. Michaels said, Julie Towers grabbed my arm and pushed me so hard I stumbled. Ms. Towers admits, I lost control, but he said you are a dumb broad. Jordan is often rude and belligerent. Both have agreed to read the article How to Avoid Conflict in the Workplace and to see a counselor for anger management.

Academic Learning Log: Chapter Review

WHAT HAVE I LEARNED ABOUT QUOTATION MARKS?

To test and track your understanding, answer the following questions.

1. Quotation marks are used in pairs to indicate _____ and

   _____ .

2. _____ and _____ go inside the quotation marks.

3. Semicolons and colons go _____ the quotation marks.

4. Use a pair of quotation marks to set off a _____, which records the exact words of another person.

5. A _____ is the credit given to the source of a quotation.

6. A speech tag can be placed _____, _____, or

   _____ .

7. **How will I use what I have learned about quotation marks?**
   In your notebook, discuss how you will apply to your own writing what you have learned about quotation marks.

8. **What do I still need to study about quotation marks?**
   In your notebook, describe your ongoing study needs by describing what, when, and how you will continue studying quotation marks.

PORTFOLIO

MyWritingLab™
Complete the Post-test for Chapter 13 in MyWritingLab.

14

End Punctuation: Period, Question Mark, and Exclamation Point

End punctuation marks the end of a complete thought.

In our everyday conversations, we signal the end of complete thoughts by our tone of voice. We pause more fully at the end of a complete thought. And our voices can go up in a question, come down in a warning, or explode with a strong feeling. Thinking about how we use our voice to express verbal ideas helps us to understand the purpose of end punctuation in our writing. Complete the following activity and answer the question "What's the point of end punctuation?"

What's the Point of End Punctuation?

PHOTOGRAPHIC ORGANIZER: END PUNCTUATION

Read the following transcript of a 911 call. In this draft there is no end punctuation or capital letters. Study this draft of the call. Then, insert the needed end punctuation and capitalization to show where one complete thought ends and another one begins. Use a question mark, an exclamation point, or a period. Answers may vary, so discuss your revisions with a peer.

WRITING
FROM LIFE

911

hello hello, 911 hello can you hear me I need help my
house is on fire what did you say this is Dorothea Gomez
oh oh my please come quickly Princess, Princess where
are you I can't find my cat

What's the point of end punctuation?

....

....

....

....

One Student Writer's Response

The following paragraph offers one writer's reaction to the paragraph "911."

This activity really helped me see the real purpose of end punctuation. First of all, it's pretty clear that ideas run together and get confusing without end punctuation. And end punctuation makes the meaning of the idea clear, too. For example, "Hello!" has a different meaning than "Hello?" Our group had fun coming up with a whole bunch of different ways to say the same words by changing the end punctuation.

A **sentence** is a complete thought that begins with a capital letter and ends with a specific type of end punctuation. The **punctuation marks** that indicate the end of a sentence (called **end punctuation**) are **the period**, **the question mark**, and **the exclamation point**. Each of these end punctuation marks indicates the purpose or type of a sentence. The following sections present a series of charts that show the relationships among end punctuation, the type of sentence, and the purpose of the sentence. Each section also explains common end punctuation misuses to avoid.

L2 Apply the Principles of the Period

End Punctuation	Type of Sentence	Purpose of Sentence
The Period (.)	Ends a declarative statement	To inform
	Ends a mild imperative statement	To command without urgency

SUBJECT   VERB   PERIOD

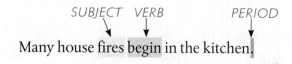

Many house fires begin in the kitchen.

"YOU" IS THE IMPLIED SUBJECT OF VERB

Turn off the stove.

PERIOD ENDS IMPERATIVE STATEMENT

Practice 2

APPLY THE PERIOD

Edit each sentence to ensure proper use of the period and capital letters.

1. the biggest fire hazard in most kitchens is a grease fire it also results in the most costly damage.

2. kitchen fires occur for two main reasons the grease is too hot the frying food is left unattended.

3. two foods are frequently linked to grease fires kitchen fires start most often when people are cooking fried chicken and French fries.

4. for a fire in a cooking pan, use an oven mitt to clap on the lid then the pan should be moved off the burner.

5. the stove should be immediately turned off the lack of oxygen will stop the flames in the pan or pot.

6. never use water to put out grease fires water repels grease and spreads the fire.

7. large amounts of baking soda or salt will smother a fire however, flour will explode or feed the fire.

8. swatting at a fire with a cloth is unwise the action fans the flames and spreads the fire.

9. to prevent a kitchen fire, follow these safety tips don't let the grease get too hot don't walk away from cooking food always keep a fire extinguisher nearby.

10. Write a sentence that ends with a period. Suggested topic: Another possible cause of house fires. ---------------------------------

----

Apply the Principles of the Question Mark L❸

End Punctuation	Type of Sentence	Purpose of Sentence
The Question Mark (?)	Ends an interrogative statement May begin with *what, who,* or *how*	To ask a direct question
	May invert order of subject and helping verb	To question
	Often uses a helping verb such as *do, can, will,* or *would*	To make a request

Direct Question

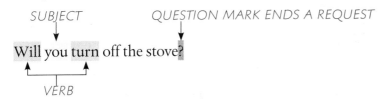

SUBJECT   QUESTION MARK ENDS A REQUEST

Will you turn off the stove?

VERB

Do not use a question mark at the end of an indirect question. An **indirect question** tells about or reports a question asked by someone by paraphrasing it rather than reporting the exact words used. An indirect question usually begins with phrases like *I wonder if* or *he asked*. Place a period at the end of an indirect question.

Indirect Question

PHRASE INDICATES INDIRECT QUESTION   PERIOD ENDS INDIRECT QUESTION

I wonder if I turned off the stove before I left this morning.

APPLY THE QUESTION MARK

Insert a period or a question mark as needed to appropriately end each idea.

1. Does my insurance policy cover the cost of repairing damage from a house fire

2. He asked his insurance agent if he had coverage for house fires

3. Will you please check our insurance policy to see if we are covered in case of a house fire

4. Did you know that fire insurance policies have four areas of coverage

5. Be sure to ask if your policy covers loss of use of your dwelling, other structures, personal property, and additional living expenses

6. Jermaine asked about the difference between replacement value and cash value of a loss

7. Will you ask the insurance adjuster if the water damage from the firefighters is covered

Practice 3

8. I wonder if I have to buy additional insurance to cover water damage

9. Write an indirect question. Suggested topic: Fire prevention.

....

10. Write a direct question. Suggested topic: Fire prevention.

....

L④ Apply the Principles of the Exclamation Point

End Punctuation	Type of Sentence	Purpose of Sentence
The Exclamation Point (!)	Ends an exclamatory statement	To express strong emotion
	Ends a strong imperative (command)	To express urgency, warning, or a forceful command
	Ends an interjection, a single word or phrase used as an exclamation that stands apart from the rest of a sentence	To cry out, to utter an emotion
	Used with interjections beginning with *how* or *what*	To emphasize an idea

SUBJECT   VERB   EXCLAMATION POINT ENDS EXCLAMATORY STATEMENT

The pan is on fire!

VERB   EXCLAMATION POINT ENDS STRONG IMPERATIVE STATEMENT

Put out the fire!

EXCLAMATION POINTS SET INTERJECTIONS APART FROM MAIN SENTENCE

Wow! What a disaster! The kitchen is destroyed.

SUBJECT   VERB

Practice 4

APPLY THE EXCLAMATION POINT

Insert a period or an exclamation point as needed to appropriately end each idea. Use capital letters as needed to make your point. Discuss your responses with your classmates.

1. Hey call the fire department now

2. I told you be careful you should never smoke in bed

3. Well now is not the time to point fingers. just call for help

4. Stop don't flail at the fire with that towel it's making the fire spread

5. Hello, 911 our home is on fire send help please

6. Oh no the roof is about to collapse

7. Ma'am, come this way we will get you out hurry

8. Your shirt is on fire drop and roll now

9. What a relief thanks for coming so quickly you saved our lives

10. Write a sentence of exclamation. Suggested topic: An emergency call.

Practice 5

END PUNCTUATION REVIEW

Insert the appropriate end punctuation for each sentence. Capitalize words as needed.

1. Be prepared take a course in fire safety

2. Do you want to protect your property and family by purchasing Sure Safe Insurance, you will

3. Act now before a fire occurs have an evacuation plan and practice it often

4. I wonder if you will buy a fire extinguisher you will good will you learn how to use it

5. Does your home have a smoke alarm in every room

6. Working smoke alarms greatly increase your chances for survival so install them now

7. What types of smoke alarms are available is one brand better than the others

8. Shawntel asked how much smoke alarms cost they vary between $6 and $40

9. It is crucial to maintain a smoke alarm test the alarm monthly replace batteries at least once a year replace the alarm every 8 to 10 years

Practice 5

10. Write a sentence with a purpose of your own choosing. Use appropriate end punctuation. Suggested topic: How to respond to a fire.

Smoke alarm being tested ▶

Editing Assignments

MyWritingLab™
Complete this Exercise
on mywritinglab.com

Editing for Everyday Life

Assume your house has been damaged by a fire. You are writing an e-mail to your insurance agent about your claim for your losses. Edit the paragraph to insert appropriate end punctuation. Capitalize words as needed. Use your own paper or complete this exercise on MyWritingLab.com.

I am very unhappy with the way in which my claim has been handled I have spoken to at least six different people no one gives me a clear answer what is holding up my claim is there any additional information you need from me please contact me as soon as possible I am ready to file an official complaint

Editing for College Life

Assume you are giving a speech about fire safety for a college speech class. Edit the paragraph to insert appropriate end punctuation. Capitalize words as needed. Use your own paper or complete this exercise on MyWritingLab.com.

Is your home fire proofed you can prevent injury from fires, such as burns, and take precautions to prevent fires from starting in the first place Follow these simple tips extinguish all cigarettes in ashtrays before you go to bed don't smoke and drink before bed don't smoke in bed anytime soak matches with water before discarding keep pads and cloths away from hot burners never spray combustible fluids in a barbeque grill keep a fire extinguisher on hand be ready be alert

Editing for Working Life

Assume you are an insurance agent, and you are responding to a dissatisfied client. Edit to insert appropriate end punctuation. Capitalize words as needed. Use your own paper or complete this exercise on MyWritingLab.com.

> Dear Ms. Jones:
>
> I am sorry to hear about your displeasure with our service I will contact our claims department and address your concerns you will hear from me as soon as possible I wonder if we have updated your contact information please check the attached form let me know of any changes or mistakes in the information hopefully we can resolve this problem to your satisfaction we appreciate your business

WHAT HAVE I LEARNED ABOUT END PUNCTUATION?

To test and track your understanding, answer the following questions.

1. The .... ends a declarative or a mild .... statement.

2. The purpose of a declarative sentence is to ....; the purpose of an imperative sentence is to ....

3. The question mark ends an ....; the purpose of this sentence type is to ....

4. A question mark is not used at the end of an .... question.

5. An exclamation point ends an .... statement, a strong ...., and an ....

6. The purpose of an exclamatory sentence is to express ...., urgency, ..., or a forceful ....

7. **How will I use what I have learned about end punctuation?**
   In your notebook, discuss how you will apply to your own writing what you have learned about end punctuation.

8. **What do I still need to study about end punctuation?**
   In your notebook, describe your ongoing study needs by describing what, when, and how you will continue studying end punctuation.

Academic Learning Log: Chapter Review

PORTFOLIO

MyWritingLab™

Complete the Post-test for Chapter 14 in MyWritingLab.

15

Capitalization

Capitalization clearly identifies the beginning of a new idea or the names of specific people, places, and things.

Digital media is having a clear impact on our use of letters. More and more often, e-mails, text messages, and websites use capital letters at random. By thinking about capitalization and digital media, we can better understand the purpose and rules in the use of capital letters. Complete the following activity and answer the question "What's the point of capitalization?"

Internet Safety and Spy Software Leader Since 1999

Software 4 Parents.com

Internet Filtering & Monitoring Software

As seen On
NBC's Today Show
Wall Street Journal
USAToday.Com

ABOUT US   LINKS   HOME   CONTACT US

...ftware can Secretly Record Email, Chat, IM...Even Passwo...

...how you feel about your child or how trusting you are that what's going on ..., check it, check it, and double check it...

What's the Point of Capitalization?

PHOTOGRAPHIC ORGANIZER: CAPITALIZATION

Study the photograph on the previous page and the following two examples of personal messages. All offer instances of the random use of capital letters in digital media. Work with a peer or small group of your classmates. Identify the edits you would make for proper use of capital letters. Discuss why the writers used capital letters as they did and give reasons for your edits.

Computer receipt from a car rental company:

Thank You for renting from Us. We appreciate Your Loyalty.

E-mail message:

whoa dude . . . WHAT HAPPENED last night After i left? Casey did WHAT?

What's the point of capitalization?

WRITING
FROM LIFE

One Student Writer's Response

The following paragraph offers one writer's reaction to the text message.

Our group actually debated about some of the letters. For example in the photo of the software, we argued about the phrase "As seen On." Some of us didn't think any of those words should be in caps. Others thought the phrase was a title, so the word "seen" should be in caps. In the personal messages, it seemed like the writers used caps to stress important ideas.

Apply the Seven Rules of Capitalization

L❷

Capitalization refers to writing letters (and sometimes words) in uppercase letters. Following seven basic rules will ensure proper use of capitalization in your writing.

RULE 1: Capitalize the first word of every sentence.

CAPITAL LETTERS INDICATE THE START OF A SENTENCE

People should not send text messages while driving. It is too dangerous.

Practice 2

Edit the following paragraph for proper use of capitalization.

text messaging requires the use of a person's eyes and hands. some drivers use their knees to steer the car to free up their hands to type or read a message. they may keep one hand on the steering wheel. still, they have to take their eyes off the road to type and send the message. sending or answering a text message while driving shows a lack of common sense. no one knows how many car crashes occur because of drivers distracted by texting. however, the evidence is mounting. an estimated 20 percent of drivers send or receive messages while behind the wheel, according to a Nationwide Insurance study. the practice is taking a deadly toll. many states have proposed banning the practice of texting while driving.

RULE 2:   **Capitalize the pronoun *I*.**

ALWAYS CAPITALIZE THE FIRST-PERSON SINGULAR PRONOUN "I"

I enjoy being online because I like chatting with friends and I like shopping.

Practice 3

Edit the following paragraph for proper use of capitalization.

i get so annoyed with Joe. He is a non-stop text messager. i never see him without his iPhone. i regret buying it for him. When i try to talk with him, he ignores me because he is typing out a message. i taught him better manners than this. i am ready to cut off his phone service just so i can talk to him.
　　Yesterday, i said to Joe, "i hope you aren't texting while you're driving!" He actually looked up from his phone and replied, "i never text and drive. i don't have a death wish." Well, at least i got a response from him, and i do believe him. i think he is a really good kid. i also think he doesn't believe i really will take away his phone. i just want him to be polite, and i want to be able to talk with him. Of course, i can be just as bad. Sometimes i don't respond to him if a good book has hooked my attention.

RULE 3: Capitalize the first letter of the first words in written greetings and salutations (for example, *Dear friends*, or *Best regards*).

CAPITALIZE THE FIRST LETTER OF THE FIRST WORDS OF GREETINGS OR CLOSINGS (IN LETTERS, MEMOS, E-MAILS, ETC.)

→Dear Mr. Lin:

As you requested, I am writing to request that you stop service to account number 3284. Full payment for our current bill is enclosed. Thank you for your help in this matter.

→Sincerely,

Ritu Gupta

APPLY CAPITALIZATION RULES

Edit the following letter for proper use of capitalization.

dear Ms. Gupta:

Please accept this letter as notice of termination of services to account number 3284. Our records show that you are due a refund, so I have enclosed a check for $49.50.

best regards,

Jim Lin

Practice 4

RULE 4: **In titles of publications, such as books, magazines, newspapers, songs, poems, plays, and articles, capitalize the first letter of the first and last words, the principal words, and the first word that comes after a semicolon or a colon.**

Do not capitalize the first letters of the following in titles, unless they are the first or last word or come after a semicolon or colon: articles (*a, an, the*), prepositions (such as *in, of,* and *with*), and conjunctions (such as *and, but,* and *for*). Keep in mind that capitalization styles for titles differ in certain academic disciplines, so always check with your teacher for style guidelines.

Article:

CAPITALIZE THE FIRST WORD AND PRINCIPAL WORDS IN A TITLE

"Dangerous Behaviors behind the Wheel"

UNLESS THEY ARE THE FIRST OR LAST WORD, DO NOT CAPITALIZE THE FIRST LETTER OF MINOR WORDS, ARTICLES, PREPOSITIONS, OR CONJUNCTIONS

Book:

ALWAYS CAPITALIZE THE FIRST LETTER OF THE PRINCIPAL WORDS IN A PUBLICATION TITLE

Privacy Lost: How Technology Is Endangering Your Privacy

Magazine:

Reader's Digest

Newspaper:

Washington Post

Play or Movie:

UNLESS THEY ARE THE FIRST OR LAST WORD, DO NOT CAPITALIZE THE FIRST LETTER OF MINOR WORDS IN TITLES: ARTICLES, PREPOSITIONS, OR CONJUNCTIONS

The True Story of the Internet

Poem or Short Story:

"Mending Wall"

Song:

"Digital Man"

Website:

Cellphonesafety.org

Note: Digital terms, such as Internet or the World Wide Web, use initial capitalization.

APPLY CAPITALIZATION RULES

Edit the following paragraph for proper use of capitalization in titles of publications.

(1) In 1818, the novel *frankenstein* warned about the moral dangers in the drive to advance technology. (2) That same year, the poem "ozymandias" was published; the poem is about the fall of a great king and his civilization, and it mocks human pride in human effort. (3) In 1844, the short story "rappaccini's daughter" raised the issue of corrupt medical research. (4) More recently, movies, such as *ender's game* have explored the dangers of technology. (5) For example, *jurassic park* imagined the effects of tinkering with genes and relying too much on computers. (6) Of course, we can't forget about *the terminator*, a nearly unstoppable killing machine. (7) Even comic books such as *iron man* question the moral use of technology. (8) Surely, the classic film *star wars* illustrates that technology can serve either good or evil. (9) This ongoing concern about moral values and technology is seen today in current websites, such as the ethics center at http://ethicscenter.net/.

Write a sentence that requires the appropriate use of capitalization. Suggested topic: Your favorite movie, song, or book.

RULE 5: **Capitalize the first letters in all essential words in proper nouns.**

Proper nouns name specific people, places, things, and events. Proper nouns include people's names; certain titles of people (see Rule 6 on page 238 for details), places, and regions; organizations and associations; and publications. Each of the examples in the chart below illustrates various rules for capitalizing proper nouns.

Note the capitalization of initials and abbreviations. Do not capitalize common nouns.

	Common Nouns	**Proper Nouns**
People	a man or woman a professor the name of a relative a believer of a religion member(s) of an organization	Mr. Bob Jones, Ms. R. A. Grove Professor Stevens Uncle Jeremy, Father Muslim, Christian, Buddhist Democrat, Girl Scout
Places	a country a street	England First Avenue
Things	a language an academic course a sacred text a god, a religion a group/organization a department, office, or institution a company	Spanish Biology 101 the Koran, the Torah, the Bible Christ, Christianity Red Hot Chili Peppers House of Representatives State Farm Insurance
Events	a day, a month	Monday, March
Times	an era	the Great Depression
Periods	a war a holiday	World War II Thanksgiving

▲ *Lincoln Memorial during the 1963 Civil Rights Protest*

Edit the following paragraph for proper use of capitalization.

In 1776 in our declaration of independence, thomas jefferson defined the promise of america as freedom and equality for all. The words rang hollow, however, for millions of people. african americans were held in slavery prior to the civil war, and later they were denied their rights by unjust laws and social customs. The national register of historic places tells their powerful story. The long struggle of african americans to achieve the bright promise of america led to the heroic era known as the civil rights movement. The national register of historic places lists many of the places where these crucial events occurred. This list can be found on the website *we shall overcome: historic places of the civil rights movement.*

Adapted from *We Shall Overcome: Historic Places of the Civil Rights Movement.* National Parks Service. Sept. 2008. http://www.nps.gov/history/nr/travel/civilrights/intro.htm

RULE 6: Capitalize the first letter of the title of a person when the title precedes the person's name.

Some writers capitalize the first letter of a title of very high rank even when it follows a proper name. Capitalization of the first letter of a title is also common if it appears at the end of a letter, e-mail, or other correspondence, following the person's name. Do not capitalize those titles when they appear on their own as common nouns (without modifying a particular person's name).

ALWAYS CAPITALIZE THE FIRST LETTER OF A PERSON'S TITLE WHEN IT APPEARS BEFORE THE PERSON'S NAME

↓

Dr. Mehmet Oz

WHEN A PERSON'S TITLE APPEARS AFTER HIS OR HER NAME, THE INITIAL LETTER OF THE TITLE REMAINS LOWERCASE

↓   ↓

Mehmet Oz, a medical doctor

CAPITALIZE THE FIRST LETTERS OF A PERSON'S TITLE

↓   ↓

Prime Minister Harper

IN SOME CASES, IF IT'S A HIGH-RANKING TITLE, WRITERS WILL CAPITALIZE A TITLE EVEN IF IT APPEARS AFTER THE NAME

↓   ↓

Stephen Harper, Prime Minister of Canada

Practice 7

APPLY CAPITALIZATION RULES

Edit the following paragraph for proper use of capitalization.

As a woman raised in the era of the equal rights amendment, I want to live up to my potential. So I have searched for positive women role models to teach me values. First, the stories in the bible about mary the Mother of jesus christ have taught me to have faith. Second, Nurse clara barton, founder of the red cross, has taught me to take action. Third, doctor marissa sanchez, the Pediatrician I went to as a child, has taught me to break barriers. She was the first woman Doctor in our small town. And professor b.j. ocha has taught me to love learning. Finally, my Mother always teaches me by her example to be Honest and Kind.

RULE 7: Capitalize proper adjectives. Proper adjectives are formed from proper nouns.

Proper Noun	Proper Adjective
Africa	African
America	American
Florida	Floridian
Japan	Japanese
Spain	Spanish
Shakespeare	Shakespearean

Use and capitalize brand-name trademarks as proper adjectives.

Kleenex tissue   Scotch tape

APPLY CAPITALIZATION RULES

Edit the following paragraph for proper use of capitalization.

Don Matthews has been all over the world. As a young soldier, he was held in a small vietnamese prison during the vietnam war. After the war, he joined the peace corps and worked as a Professor teaching english to children in china. There, he learned to love chinese food. Later, after a european tour of italy, france, and germany, he lived in the australian wilderness for several years.

Practice 8

CAPITALIZATION REVIEW

Write four sentences that require the use of capitalization. Suggested topics: Useful technology, good role models for youth, a place everyone should visit, and favorite songs. Exchange your work with a peer and edit each other's sentences.

1. ....

2. ....

3. ....

4. ....

Practice 9

Editing Assignments

MyWritingLab™
Complete this Exercise
on mywritinglab.com

Editing for Everyday Life

Assume your friend has written you an e-mail about what he did last night. Edit the paragraph for proper use of capitalization. Use your own paper or complete the exercise on MyWritingLab.com.

Hey Man, WHAT'S GOING ON? you won't believe what happened last night. After charles jimenez and i finished watching the movie ant man, we went to club royal and listened to the new band killer bs. I had too many miller lights, so chuck had to drive me home. he was the Designated Driver!

Editing for College Life

Assume you are writing about online relationships and technology for a college sociology class. Edit the paragraph for proper use of capitalization. Use your own paper or complete the exercise on MyWritingLab.com.

online relationships are here to stay. in his book *the interpersonal communication book,* joseph devito discusses relationships and technology. the number of internet users is rapidly growing. commercial websites for meeting people are exploding in number. books currently high on the amazon.com list include titles such as *online dating for dummies,* and afternoon talk shows like *ellen* and *dr. phil* often feature people who have met online. clearly many are turning to the internet to find a friend or romantic partner.

Editing for Working Life

Assume you are the owner of a cab company, and you are writing a memo to your employees about the use of cell phones while driving. Edit the paragraph for proper use of capitalization. Use your own paper or complete the exercise on MyWritingLab.com.

due to the accident involving one of our drivers, ahmed fahd, and the mayor of lake city, use of cell phones while driving is banned. although the accident was the fault of mayor harvey, the incident made clear the need for a formal policy on our part. the city cab employee handbook has been updated to include this policy. you can also access the entire handbook on our website citycab.com.

WHAT HAVE I LEARNED ABOUT CAPITALIZATION?

To test and track your understanding, answer the following questions.

1. Capitalize the .... of every sentence.

2. Capitalize the pronoun ....

3. Capitalize the first letter of the first words of .... and ....

4. Capitalize the first letter of .... words in ....

5. Capitalize the first letter of the .... of a person when the title

.... the person's name.

6. Capitalize the first letter of .... nouns. Do not capitalize .... nouns.

7. Capitalize the first letter of .... adjectives.

8. How will I use what I have learned about capitalization?
In your notebook, discuss how you will apply to your own writing what you have learned about capitalization.

9. What do I still need to study about capitalization?
In your notebook, describe your ongoing study needs by describing what, when, and how you will continue studying capitalization.

MyWritingLab™

Complete the Post-test for Chapter 15 in MyWritingLab.

16

Improving Your Spelling

LEARNING OUTCOMES

After studying this chapter, you should be able to:

L1 Answer the Question "What's the Point of Improving Your Spelling?"

L2 Take Five Steps to Improve Your Spelling

L3 Apply Eight Rules to Improve Your Spelling

To spell correctly is to understand the rules for properly arranging letters in a word.

Do you have trouble spelling words? If so, you are not alone. Many people have trouble spelling. Despite these difficulties, it is important to work toward accurate spelling because it is an important part of effective expression. Complete the following activity and answer the question "What's the point of improving your spelling?"

What's the Point of Improving Your Spelling?

Practice 1

Assume one of your friends has applied for a job. She has asked you to proofread her cover letter. Can you find the five misspelled words in this draft? What impact could misspelled words have on her job prospects?

> I beleive I can be a key player on your team, and I would like the chance to prove that to you in an interveiw. Within a short time of your recieving this letter, I'll contact you to arrange a meeting. Untill then, feel free to call me at the number listed above or e-mail me. Thank you for your time and concideration.

WRITING FROM LIFE

What's the point of improving your spelling?

_____

_____

_____

One Student Writer's Response

The following paragraph offers one writer's reaction to the spelling in the cover letter for the job opportunity.

> *The misspelled words in this letter make a poor impression. These mistakes will most likely hurt the writer's chances of being hired. If a person is careless about something as important as a cover letter, then how can that person be trusted to be a careful or knowledgeable worker? I am a horrible speller, too, so I always use a spell checker.*

You can improve your spelling by identifying and correcting patterns of misspellings in your writing. Each writer develops his or her own system for learning and using correct spelling. For example, some writers keep a vocabulary journal of new words or difficult-to-spell words, and most writers use a spell checker as a last step before publishing a piece of writing. The steps, rules, and practices in this chapter are designed to help you develop a system to improve your spelling.

LO2 Take Five Steps to Improve Your Spelling

Five of the best ways to improve your spelling are to use a spell checker, dictionary, mnemonics, spelling error tracking, and the writing process.

1. Use a Spell Checker

Computerized spell checkers are an asset to a writer. However, spell checkers seldom catch all errors in your writing. Consider the following tips when you use a spell checker:

- Be aware that spell checkers fail to spot words that sound alike but differ in meaning such as *to, too,* and *two* or *there* and *they're.*

- Note that spell checkers often flag proper nouns as misspellings even if they are spelled correctly.

- Carefully consider the reason a spell checker highlights a word.

- Be cautious about clicking the "change" or "change all" button too quickly.

2. Use a Dictionary

To look up misspelled words in a dictionary, consider the following tips:

- Print dictionaries have guide words at the top of each page to help you locate a word.

- Each entry gives the spelling of the main word first in bold type.

- The word is divided into syllables.

- The function or part of speech and the etymology (the history of the word's origin) are stated. Since many English words come from other languages, you will find the etymology helpful.

- Additional spellings or forms of the word appear at the end of the entry. This listing is most helpful when letters are dropped or added to create a new word or word form.

- Online dictionaries locate words through a search box instead of using guide words. If you misspell a word in the search box, online dictionaries offer sample spellings to aid in your search.

Study the following example from Merriam-Webster Online Dictionary, and think about how you will use a dictionary to improve your spelling.

---

harass

Main Entry: **ha·rass**

Pronunciation: \hə-ˈras; ˈher-əs, ˈha-res\

Function: *transitive verb*

Etymology: French *harasser*, from Middle French, from *harer* to set a dog on, from Old French *hare,* interjection used to incite dogs, of Germanic origin; akin to Old High German *hier* — more at HERE

Date: 1617

1 a: EXHAUST, FATIGUE **b (1):** to annoy persistently **(2):** to create an unpleasant or hostile situation for especially by uninvited and unwelcome verbal or physical conduct: to worry and impede by repeated raids <*harassed* the enemy>

synonyms see WORRY

— **ha·rass·er** *noun*

— **ha·rass·ment** \-mənt*noun*

Source: By permission. From *Merriam-Webster's Collegiate® Dictionary*, 11th Edition © 2015 by Merriam-Webster, Inc. (www.Merriam-Webster.com).

3. Use Mnemonics

Mnemonics are different types of memory tricks that can help you remember the correct spelling of words. For example:

- Create a mental or visual image: To spell *piece,* picture a **piece** of **pie.**

- Chunk a word into visual parts or look for smaller words in larger words: satisfactory = **sat is fact or y**

- Color-code trouble spots in a word: their (**not** *thier*).

- Create a silly saying using each letter of the word: The first letter of each word in the following sentence combines to spell **rhythm: R**hythm **H**as **Y**our **T**wo **H**ips **M**oving.

4. Track Spelling Errors

Identify your misspellings through teacher feedback, peer edits, or a spell checker. In a journal, create a list of words that you have misspelled. Contrast the way you misspell the word with the rule and the correct spelling. Identify information that helps you remember the correct spelling such as the word's function or etymology. Create a memory trick as needed. Choose from the headings in the following example to create your own journal system for improving your spelling.

Correct Spelling	Function	Etymology	My Misspelling	Spelling Rule	Memory Trick
friend	noun	Old English *frēon* to love	freind	*i* before *e* except after *c*	Friend to the end

5. Use the Writing Process to Improve Your Spelling

As you write, use these tips to ensure accurate spelling:

☐ **Decide when during the writing process you will identify and correct misspellings.**
Some writers who compose as they type or write pause frequently to revise and edit what they just wrote. Others prefer to complete a draft and then check for misspellings during the revision and proofreading phases of the writing process.

☐ **Identify and study specialized or difficult words that are connected to your writing assignment.**
Verify the spelling and etymology (how the word originated) of these words before you begin writing. Find correctly spelled synonyms (words that have similar meanings) for these words. Use this group of correctly spelled words to brainstorm additional details for your writing.

☐ **Use one proofreading session to focus only on spelling accuracy.**
By devoting time to proofreading your spelling, you are more likely to catch errors.

☐ **During the proofreading phase, edit on a printed copy of your writing if you are using a word processor.**
It's easy to overlook errors in text on a computer screen.

☐ **Decide how you will track your misspelling patterns as you write.**
Will you make a list as you go, or will you list troubling words after you have completed your final edit?

Commit to improving your spelling by creating an individual study process.

Practice 2

TAKE STEPS TO IMPROVE YOUR SPELLING

Write out the steps you will take to improve your spelling. When possible, tie your steps to the writing process: Prewriting, Drafting, Revising, and Editing. Include additional steps if necessary. Share and discuss your responses with your class or a peer.

Step 1 _____

_____

Step 2 _____

_____

Step 3 _____

_____

Step 4 _____

_____

Step 5 _____

_____

Apply Eight Rules to Improve Your Spelling L❸

Improving your spelling involves understanding rules about vowel and consonant patterns, as well as rules about the use of suffixes and prefixes.

Recognize Vowel and Consonant Patterns

Many spelling rules are based on the use of vowels and consonants to form words, so to improve your spelling, take note of the patterns of vowels and consonants in words. Take a moment to look at the following examples to refresh your memory about consonant (c) and vowel (v) patterns in words.

```
C V C         C CVC C        C V C V C V        V C V C C V
↓ ↓ ↓         ↓ ↓↓↓↓         ↓ ↓ ↓ ↓ ↓ ↓        ↓ ↓ ↓ ↓ ↓ ↓
h a t         b r i c k      p o t a t o        a g e n d a
```

Apply the Rules for Use of Suffixes

A **suffix** is added to the end of a **base word** (a word's original meaning) to change the use or meaning of the word. For example, the suffixes -ing or -ed can either change the tense of a verb or change the verb into a noun or an adjective. For example, *walk* is a verb, but adding -ing creates the present participle *walking;* adding -ed creates the past participle *walked*. The present and past participles can function as verbs, adjectives, or nouns depending on the context in which they are used.

Suffixes begin with either a vowel or a consonant, which affects the spelling rules for adding them to base words. You will learn about the specific ways in which vowels and consonants impact spelling throughout this chapter. The following chart lists a few common vowel and consonant suffixes, along with their meanings and examples.

Vowel Suffix	Meaning	Example
-able, -ible	able to	possible
-ed, -d	past tense of a verb	created
-en	present or past participle	forgotten
-er	one who is or does	painter
-er	comparison	larger
-es	plural of a noun	dishes
-es	singular present tense of a verb	fixes
-ous	full of	ambitious

Consonant Suffix	Meaning	Example
-ful	full of	hopeful
-ly or -y	like	harshly
-ment	state of	agreement
-ness	state of being	gentleness
-s	plural of a noun	girls
-s	singular present tense of a verb	talks

The rules of spelling words with suffixes vary. The next several sections explain and illustrate the various spelling rules for adding suffixes.

1. Add -s or -es to Form the Plural of Nouns and to Form the Singular Present Tense of Most Verbs

- Add -s to form the plural of most regular nouns, including those that end with *o*.

  studio + s ⟶ studios

- Add -es to nouns that end with a consonant immediately before a final *o*.

  ech o + es ⟶ echoes

Add -s to most regular verbs to form the singular present tense in the third person.

  give + s ⟶ gives

Add -es to form the plural of nouns and to third-person present tense verbs that end in *ch, sh, s, x,* or *z.*

Nouns

church + es	church es
dish + es	dish es
glass + es	glass es
fox + es	fox es
topaz + es	topaz es

Verbs

match + es	match es
fish + es	fish es
toss + es	toss es
fax + es	fax es
buzz + es	buzz es

ADD *-S* OR *-ES* TO NOUNS AND VERBS TO FORM THE PLURAL

Complete the chart by choosing the appropriate suffix to each of the following base words. Consult a dictionary to check your answers.

Base Words	Suffixes		Base Words	Suffixes	
	-s	-es		-s	-es
1. wrench			**11.** tell		
2. boy			**12.** hope		
3. hero			**13.** think		
4. mix			**14.** wish		
5. ask			**15.** fizz		
6. book			**16.** care		
7. pass			**17.** love		
8. video			**18.** circus		
9. wash			**19.** reflex		
10. brush			**20.** address		

2. Double the Final Consonant in Words with One Syllable

Many **one-syllable** words end in a **consonant** with a **vowel** immediately **before** it. (*Hint:* remember CVC.) For a word with one syllable, one consonant, and one vowel, double the final consonant when adding a vowel suffix. The final consonant is *not* doubled when adding a consonant suffix.

Exception: Do not double the final consonant of words that end in *w, x,* or *y* as in the following examples: snowing, boxer, obeys.

Complete the chart by adding each of the suffixes to the base words. Consult a dictionary to check your answers.

Base Words	Suffixes			
	-s	*-er*	*-ed*	*-ing*
1. bat				
2. knit				
3. run			— — —	
4. sit			— — —	
5. scan				
6. slug				
7. skin				
8. spot				
9. rub				
10. pat				

3. Double the Final Consonant in Words with More Than One Syllable

Words with more than one syllable often end with a vowel immediately before a **consonant**. (*Hint*: Remember VC.) If the final syllable is stressed or emphasized in its pronunciation, **double the final consonant**.

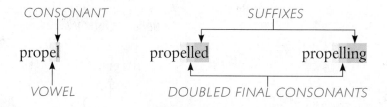

CONSONANT   SUFFIXES

propel   propelled   propelling

VOWEL   DOUBLED FINAL CONSONANTS

DOUBLE THE FINAL CONSONANT IN WORDS WITH MORE THAN ONE SYLLABLE

Complete the chart by adding the appropriate suffixes to the base words. Consult a dictionary to check your answers.

Base Words	Suffixes			
	-s	*-er*	*-ed*	*-ing*
1. admit				
2. begin			— — —	
3. control				
4. omit				
5. remit				
6. compel				
7. commit				
8. permit				
9. submit				
10. confer				

4. Drop or Keep the Final *E*

- Drop the *e* when the base *word ends* with a *silent e* and the *suffix begins* with a *vowel.*

  have + -ing ⟶ having

- Drop the *e* when a *vowel comes immediately before* the silent *e.*

  true + -ly ⟶ truly

- Keep the *e* when the base *word ends* with a **silent** *e* and the *suffix begins* with a *consonant.*

  state + -ment ⟶ statement

DROP OR KEEP THE FINAL *E*

Complete the chart by adding the appropriate suffixes to the base words. Consult a dictionary to check your answers.

Base Words	Suffixes				
	-s	*-ful*	*-ing*	*-ly*	*-ment*
1. argue		— — —		— — —	
2. brave		— — —			— — —
3. care				— — —	— — —
4. love		— — —			— — —
5. move		— — —		— — —	
6. taste				— — —	— — —
7. type		— — —		— — —	— — —
8. judge		— — —		— — —	
9. abase		— — —		— — —	
10. enable		— — —		— — —	

5. Change or Keep the Final Y

- When a *consonant* appears before the final *y*, change the *y* to *i*.

  carry + -ies ⟶ carries

- When a *vowel* appears before the final *y*, keep the *y*.

  play + -ed ⟶ played

- Keep the *y* when adding the suffix *-ing*.

  dry + -ing ⟶ drying

CHANGE OR KEEP THE FINAL Y

Complete the chart by adding each of the suffixes to the base words. Consult a dictionary to check your answers.

Base Words	Suffixes				
	-es	*-ed*	*-ier, -er*	*-est*	*-ing*
1. apply				— — —	
2. busy					
3. cry				— — —	
4. obey				— — —	
5. supply				— — —	
6. worry				— — —	
7. shy					
8. pry				— — —	
9. study				— — —	
10. marry			— — —	— — —	

6. Use Prefixes to Alter Meaning Not Spelling

A prefix added to the beginning of a base word changes the word's meaning, but it does not change the word's spelling. The following chart lists a few common prefixes, their meanings, and example words.

Prefix	Meaning	Example
bi-	two	bifocal
de-	not	depress
dis-	not	disconnect
im-	not	imperfect
mis-	not	misapplied
pre-	before	prewrite
re-	again	review
un-	not	unlisted

Adding a prefix to a word does not alter its spelling.

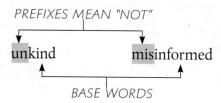

PREFIXES MEAN "NOT"

unkind   misinformed

BASE WORDS

Practice 8

USE PREFIXES TO BUILD AND CORRECTLY SPELL NEW WORDS

Use your dictionary to match words to the correct prefix. Complete the chart by writing the new words created by adding the appropriate prefixes. Consult a dictionary to check your answers.

Base Words	Prefixes				
	dis-	*pre-*	*pro-*	*re-*	*un-*
1. approved			— — —		
2. claimed		— — —			
3. engaged		— — —	— — —		
4. solved		— — —	— — —		
5. posed		— — —			
6. cover		— — —	— — —		
7. set	— — —		— — —		
8. fit	— — —	— — —			
9. created	— — —	— — —			
10. scribe				— — —	— — —

7. Choose *ie* or *ei*

A helpful way to remember how to use *ie* and *ei* in spelling is to think of the following rhyme:

"*i* before *e* except after *c* or when sounding like *ay* as in *neighbor* or *weigh*"

I BEFORE E...

↓

believe

... EXCEPT AFTER C ...

↓

conceit

... OR WHEN SOUNDING LIKE "AY"

↓

neighbor

There are, however, some exceptions to the *ie, ei* rule that should be memorized:

ie: species, science, conscience

ei: height, either, neither, leisure, seize, counterfeit, foreign, forfeit, sleight, weird

---

CHOOSE *IE* OR *EI*

Underline the correctly spelled word in each pair of words. Correctly spell the words that are misspelled. Consult a dictionary to check your answers.

1. *achieve* _____ *acheive* _____

2. *chief* _____ *cheif* _____

3. *ieght* _____ *eight* _____

4. *fiegn* _____ *feign* _____

5. *brief* _____ *breif* _____

6. *vien* _____ *vein* _____

7. *wiegh* _____ *weigh* _____

8. *receipt* _____ *reciept* _____

9. *cieling* _____ *ceiling* _____

10. *weird* _____ *wierd* _____

8. Memorize Commonly Misspelled Words

To aid in your efforts to improve your vocabulary, the following chart lists 60 of the most commonly misspelled words.

60 Commonly Misspelled Words				
absence	easily	interruption	original	recognize
acquire	embarrass	irritable	parallel	restaurant
advertise	environment	judgment	peculiar	sacrifice
apparent	excellent	knowledge	permanent	secretary
becoming	exercise	license	persevere	separate
business	explanation	loneliness	picture	sincerely
calendar	finally	mathematics	political	stopping
cemetery	generally	medicine	possible	succeed
criticize	guarantee	naturally	privilege	through
describe	humorous	noticeable	quiet	unusual
difference	imitation	occasion	quit	village
disappoint	incidentally	omission	quite	whether

Practice 10

CORRECT MISSPELLED WORDS

Edit the following sentences to correct misspelled words. Cross out each misspelled word and write the correct spelling above it.

1. To sucesfuly enter the busines world, you must exersise excelent judgement.

2. Preparation will garantee that you have the knowldge to suced.

3. You must match your pecular skills with the best posible job.

4. Don't be dissapointed if you don't aquire the first job you apply for.

5. Don't queit or lose hope but preserve until you find that perfect permnent job.

6. Once you are hired, be sure that no one can critisize you for excessive abcsences.

7. You will be sincerly appreciated if you contribute to a positive work envirenment.

8. Employees whose work ethic is noticeble are often the ones recogized with promotions.

9. Genrally, it is unsual to climb to the top of an organization without some sacrafice.

10. For example, beccoming the manager of a restarant, Raul easyly worked 60 hours a week.

SPELLING REVIEW

Edit the following sentences to correct misspelled words. Cross out each misspelled word and write the correct spelling above it.

1. An interveiw gives you the ocasion to showcase your qualifications to an employer, so it pays to be well prapard.

2. The following infermation provides some helpful hints.

3. First, learn about the organisation and have a specefic job or jobs in mind.

4. Reveiw your qualifications for the job; be ready to breifly discribe your expireince, showing how it relates to the job.

5. Be ready to answer broad questions, such as "Why should I hire you?" "Truely, why do you want this job?" and "What are your stregths and weekneses?"

6. Practice answering typecal questions that may be asked.

7. A prospective employer may make a judgement based on an apparant clue such as how you are dressed or if you are late for the meeting.

8. Takeing time to say thank you after the meeting shows that you are sincerly interested in the job.

9. Think about solveing problems for the company and proveing why you are the best candidate.

10. If you want to be thought of as an excelent candidate, then naturelly, you should be well prepared.

▼ *Woman researching company history in preparation for job interview*

Editing Assignments

MyWritingLab™
Complete this Exercise
on mywritinglab.com

Editing for Everyday Life

Assume you have been asked to write a letter of recommendation for a job for a young person you have known through volunteering for Habitat for Humanity. Edit the misspellings in the following draft. Use your own paper or complete the exercise on MyWritingLab.com.

> To Whom It May Concern:
>
> I write with great pleasure to recomend Hector Gonzales as an asistant manager for the Like Home Hotels in the Villages. I have had the pleasure of workking with Mr. Gonzales as we both volunterred with Habitat for Humanity. As our team leader, he dimonstated strong people skills and problem solving skills. He will be an aset to your organization.

Editing for College Life

Assume you are giving a speech using PowerPoint in a college business class. You have chosen to inform the class about the Department of Labor's Occupational Outlook Handbook. Edit the misspellings in the following PowerPoint slide. Use your own paper or complete the exercise on MyWritingLab.com.

> Information in *The Occupational Outlook Handbook*
>
> **Training, other Qualifications, and Advancment**
>
> - Education and trainning
> - Liscensure (or "Liscensure and certification" if a certfication is required)
> - Advancment (or "Certification and advancment" if voluntary certfications exist)

Editing for Working Life

Assume you have applied for a position advertised in the local newspaper. Edit the misspellings in the following draft. Use your own paper or complete the exercise on MyWritingLab.com.

> Dear Ms. Reynolds:
>
> The managment trainee position you advertized in today's Village Gazete greatly interestes me. The Like Home Hotels have always served as landmarks for me when I travel, and I would like to contribute to their continued growth. I have inclosed my résumé for your reveiw.

Academic Learning Log:
Chapter Review

WHAT HAVE I LEARNED ABOUT IMPROVING SPELLING?

To test and track your understanding, answer the following questions.

1. Add .... to form the plural of regular nouns and to form the singular third-person present tense of most regular verbs.

2. Add .... to nouns that end with a consonant immediately before a final *o*.

3. Add .... to form the plural of nouns and to the third-person present tense of verbs that end in *ch, sh, s, x,* or *z*.

4. When a word has one syllable and ends with a consonant with a vowel before it, ... the final consonant before adding the suffix.

5. When words with more than one syllable end with a .... immediately before a consonant and the final syllable is stressed, double the final consonant.

6. Drop the *e* when the base word ends with a .... *e* and the suffix begins with a vowel.

7. Drop the *e* when a .... comes immediately before the silent *e*.

8. Keep the *e* when the word ends with a silent *e* and the suffix begins with a ....

9. When a .... appears before the final *y*, change the *y* to *i*.

10. When a .... appears before the final *y*, keep the *y*.

11. Keep the *y* when adding the suffix ....

12. Adding a .... to a word does not alter its spelling.

13. "*I* before *e* except after *c* or when sounding like .... as in n*ei*ghbor or w*ei*gh."

14. **How will I use what I have learned about improving spelling?**
   In your notebook, discuss how you will apply to your own writing what you have learned about improving spelling.

15. **What do I still need to study about improving spelling?**
   In your notebook, write down your ongoing study needs by describing how you will continue to improve your spelling.

PORTFOLIO

MyWritingLab™

Complete the Post-test for Chapter 16 in MyWritingLab.

17

Mastering Often-Confused Words

Mastering often-confused words allows you to use words in a clear, understandable manner so that your writing is effective.

Do you ever confuse words that look alike or sound alike? It's not surprising if you do. The English language has many words that seem similar in sight, sound, or meaning, which makes it easy to use the wrong word when writing. Thinking about a real-life situation helps us to understand the importance of mastering often-confused words in our communication. Complete the following activity and answer the question "What's the point of mastering often-confused words?"

What's the Point of Mastering Often-Confused Words?

WRITING FROM LIFE

THE POINT OF MASTERING OFTEN-CONFUSED WORDS

Assume you are the office manager of a computer software company and you have recently interviewed several people for the position of assistant manager. The position offers a good salary with benefits. Two candidates have sent you thank you notes following the interview. Although the notes are similar, the note from Candidate 1 has errors due to the misuse of words. Compare the notes from both job candidates to find the errors, and then discuss the impact of the errors.

Note from Candidate 1:

Thank you for giving me so much of you're time. Beside my enthusiasm for performing good, I am already to use the company's computer software and no that I will be a good team player. I hope too here from you in the near future.

Note from Candidate 2:

Thank you for taking time out of your busy schedule to talk with me about the assistant manager position. Besides my computer software training, I have a strong desire to perform well, and I am all ready to start work. I look forward to hearing from you soon.

What's the point of mastering often-confused words?

One Student Writer's Response

The following paragraph offers one writer's reaction to the follow-up thank you notes.

I think the first note misused the words "you're," "beside," "good," "already," "no," "too," and "here." Even though the two notes said almost the same thing, the second note sounded better. It seems more professional. If I were doing the hiring, I would hire the person who wrote the second note.

Confusing words that are similar in sound, appearance, and meaning is a common problem for many writers that can be overcome by understanding the cause of such confusion. The following chart illustrates three major reasons words are confused.

L2 Identify Three Reasons for Word Confusion

REASON #1: Words sound alike but have different meanings.

Words that sound alike are called *homophones*. Although these words sound similar, they differ in meaning, function, and sometimes spelling.

Word		Meaning
Aloud	(adverb)	with the use of the voice, speaking, orally, loudly
Allowed	(verb)	permitted, planned for

ADVERB MEANING "SPEAKING"   *VERB MEANING "PLANNED FOR"*

He wondered aloud, "You should have allowed more time for the project."

REASON #2: Words sometimes have a similar meaning.

Some words differ in sound and spelling, but are close in meaning and sometimes serve the same function in a sentence.

Word		Meaning
Among	(preposition)	used to discuss a group of three or more people or things
Between	(preposition)	used to discuss a pair of (two) people or things

PREPOSITION INDICATING TWO OR MORE PEOPLE   *PREPOSITION INDICATING A GROUP OF THREE OR MORE*

Agreement is easier to achieve between two people than among a group.

REASON #3: Words are sometimes used improperly.

Words may sound alike, but they serve different functions in a sentence.

Improper Use of Pronouns	
Contractions	blend two words into one: **You're** is a contraction of the second-person pronoun you and the verb are.
Pronouns	act as replacements or substitutes for nouns or noun phrases: **Your** is the second-person possessive pronoun.

CONTRACTION MEANING "YOU ARE"   *SECOND-PERSON POSSESSIVE PRONOUN INDICATES THAT THE HOUSE BELONGS TO "YOU"*

You're going to your house.

Improper Use of Adjectives with Adverbs

ADJECTIVES describe nouns and pronouns: **Bad** means poor, unfavorable.

ADVERBS describe verbs, adjectives, and other adverbs, often with the *-ly* suffix: **Badly** means poorly, unfavorably, very much.

ADVERB MEANING "VERY MUCH" DESCRIBES PARTICIPLE "INJURED" *ADJECTIVE MEANING "UNFAVORABLE" DESCRIBES NOUN "RECORD"*

Badly injured, Jerome also faces a bad record for driving badly.

ADVERB MEANING "POORLY" DESCRIBES VERB "DRIVING"

Practice 2

OFTEN-CONFUSED WORDS

Create five sentences that correctly use words from the preceding charts. Answers may vary. Discuss your responses with a peer or your classmates. Suggested topic: The importance of hand washing.

1. ....
....

2. ....
....

3. ....
....

4. ....
....

5. ....
....

Correctly Use 30 Commonly Confused Words

L3

The rest of this chapter offers a glossary of 30 sets of commonly confused words, their definitions and functions, and examples of their proper use. The words are listed alphabetically and followed by practice activities. As you study these words, think about why they are often confused and how you will use them to achieve clear and effective expression.

Often-Confused Words	Part of Speech	Meaning
Accept, Except		
Accept	verb	to receive willingly
Except	preposition	but, not including

PREPOSITION MEANING "NOT INCLUDING"   *VERB MEANING "WILLINGLY RECEIVES"*

Everyone except Bob accepts responsibility.

Often-Confused Words	Part of Speech	Meaning
Advice, Advise		
Advice	noun	guidance
Advise	verb	to offer guidance, to recommend

VERB MEANING "RECOMMEND"   *NOUN MEANING "GUIDANCE"*

We advise you to follow the advice of your doctor.

Often-Confused Words	Part of Speech	Meaning
Affect, Effect		
Affect	verb	to influence
Effect	noun	result, outcome
Effect	verb	result in, cause to come into being

NOUN MEANING "RESULTS"   *VERB MEANING "INFLUENCE"*

The effects of the painkiller affect her emotions.

VERB MEANING "RESULTED IN"

Constant studying effected a high GPA.

Often-Confused Words	Part of Speech	Meaning
Allot, A lot		
Allot	verb	to assign portions of, to distribute
A lot	modifier	much, large amounts

NOUN MEANING "LARGE AMOUNTS"   *VERB MEANING "ASSIGN PORTIONS OF"*

The city wants a lot of power so officials can allot water for residential use.

Often-Confused Words	Part of Speech	Meaning
All ready, Already		
All ready	adverb	completely prepared
Already	adverb	previously, before now

ADVERB MEANING "PREVIOUSLY"   *ADVERB MEANING "COMPLETELY*
DESCRIBES VERB "HAS ASKED"   *PREPARED" DESCRIBES VERB "AM"*

He has already asked me if I am all ready for the cookout.

Beside, Besides		
Beside	preposition	by the side of
Besides	preposition	except, other than, together with

PREPOSITION MEANING "OTHER THAN"   *PREPOSITION MEANING "BY THE SIDE OF"*

Besides just visiting, Jordan takes a moment to sit beside his mother.

INTERJECTION MEANING   *PREPOSITION MEANING*   *VERB MEANING*
"FAREWELL"   *"BESIDE"*   *"TO PURCHASE"*

Tamar said "bye" to her friends and then drove by the house she wanted to buy.

Brake, Break		
Brake	verb	to stop
Brake	noun	a device that slows or stops
Break	verb	to smash, fracture, shatter
Break	noun	a time of rest

VERB MEANING   *NOUN MEANING*   *NOUN MEANING*
"FRACTURES"   *"DEVICE THAT STOPS A CAR"*   *"REST"*

Jon breaks his leg when his brakes fail, so he takes a break from work.

By, Bye, Buy		
By	preposition	near, beside, or through
Bye	interjection	farewell: an expression of leave-taking
Buy	verb	to purchase

Often-Confused Words	Part of Speech	Meaning
Clothes, Cloths		
Clothes	noun	garments, personal articles made of cloth
Cloths	noun	pliable material

NOUN MEANING "GARMENTS"   NOUN MEANING "PLIABLE MATERIAL"

These clothes are made of soft and silky cloths.

Coarse, Course		
Coarse	adjective	rough
Course	noun	path, direction, part of a meal, an academic class

ADJECTIVE MEANING "ROUGH" DESCRIBES NOUN "GRASS "NOUN MEANING "PATH"

He hit the ball into the coarse grass on the edge of the golf course.

NOUN MEANING "ACADEMIC CLASSES"   NOUN MEANING "PARTS OF A MEAL"

She took courses in gourmet cooking, so she learned to cook meals with five courses.

Farther, Further		
Farther	adverb	to a greater distance or more advanced point
Further	adjective	additional
Further	adverb	to advance

ADJECTIVE MEANING "ADDITIONAL"   ADVERB MEANING "TO A GREATER
DESCRIBES NOUN "STUDIES"   DISTANCE" DESCRIBES VERB "CAN TRAVEL"

Further studies will reveal how much farther we can travel in space.

Often-Confused Words	Part of Speech	Meaning
Fewer, Less		
Fewer	adjective	smaller number (count)
Less	adjective	smaller amount (noncount)

ADJECTIVE MEANING "SMALLER NUMBER" DESCRIBES NOUN "COMPLAINTS" ADJECTIVE MEANING "SMALLER AMOUNT" DESCRIBES NOUN "RESENTMENT"

Fewer complaints mean less resentment.

Often-Confused Words	Part of Speech	Meaning
Good, Well		
Good	adjective	having favorable qualities, excellent
Well	adverb	done in a good or proper manner

ADJECTIVE MEANING "EXCELLENT" DESCRIBES NOUN "STUDENT" ADVERB MEANING "IN A PROPER MANNER" DESCRIBES VERB "STUDIES"

The good student studies well.

Often-Confused Words	Part of Speech	Meaning
Hear, Here		
Hear	verb	to perceive sound
Here	adverb	in or at this place

ADVERB MEANING "AT THIS PLACE" DESCRIBES VERB "STAND" VERB MEANING "PERCEIVE SOUND"

Stand here to hear well.

Often-Confused Words	Part of Speech	Meaning
Its, It's		
Its	pronoun	singular third-person possessive case
It's	subject/verb	contraction of *it is*

CONTRACTION OF SUBJECT AND VERB "IT IS" POSSESSIVE PRONOUN "ITS" REFERS TO NOUN ANTECEDENT "DOG"

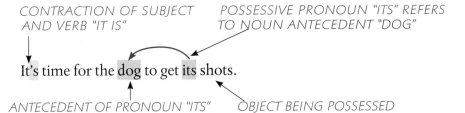

It's time for the dog to get its shots.

ANTECEDENT OF PRONOUN "ITS" OBJECT BEING POSSESSED

Often-Confused Words	Part of Speech	Meaning
Knew, New, Know, No		
Knew	verb, past tense	recognized, understood
New	adjective	recent, fresh
Know	verb, present tense	to recognize, understand
No	adverb	negative
No	adjective	not any

ADVERB MEANING "NEGATIVE" DESCRIBES VERB "DOUBTING"

ADJECTIVE MEANING "NOT ANY" DESCRIBES "NEW"

ADJECTIVE MEANING "RECENT" DESCRIBES NOUN "FACTS."

There's no doubting that I know now what you knew then; there are no new facts.

PRESENT TENSE VERB MEANING "UNDERSTAND"

PAST TENSE VERB MEANING "UNDERSTOOD"

Lay, Lie		
Lay	verb, present tense	to place
Lay	verb, past tense	reclined
Lie	verb, present tense	to recline
Lie	verb, present tense	to tell a falsehood
Lie	noun	a falsehood

PRESENT TENSE VERB MEANING "TELL A FALSEHOOD"

PAST TENSE VERB MEANING "RECLINE"

PRESENT TENSE VERB MEANING "PLACE"

I cannot lie; before, I lay in bed; now I lie on the sofa and lay the remote control nearby; that's no lie.

NOUN MEANING "FALSEHOOD"

PRESENT TENSE VERB MEANING "RECLINE"

Often-Confused Words	Part of Speech	Meaning
Passed, Past		
Passed	verb, past tense	moved, proceeded, went
Past	noun	a time gone by
Past	adjective	ago, just gone or elapsed
Past	preposition	beyond

NOUN MEANING "TIME GONE BY"   *PREPOSITION MEANING "BEYOND"*   *ADJECTIVE MEANING "ELAPSED" DESCRIBES NOUN "MONTH"*

In the past, Aleta couldn't get past her fear, but in the past month, she passed the test.

VERB MEANING "MOVED THROUGH"

Principal, Principle		
Principal	noun	a person, matter, or thing of chief importance or authority
Principal	adjective	most important
Principle	noun	a rule, code, or standard

NOUN MEANING "PERSON OF AUTHORITY"   *NOUN MEANING "RULES"*   *ADJECTIVE MEANING "MOST IMPORTANT" DESCRIBES NOUN "TASK"*

The principal is a person who sets helpful principles as his principal task.

Quiet, Quit, Quite		
Quiet	noun	silence
Quiet	verb	to silence
Quiet	adjective	silent
Quit	verb	to stop
Quite	adverb	wholly, completely to an extreme

VERB MEANING "SILENCE"   *ADVERB MEANING "COMPLETELY" DESCRIBES ADJECTIVE MEANING "SILENT"*

Quiet yourself: quit talking and be quite quiet to achieve quiet.

VERB MEANING "STOP"   *NOUN MEANING "SILENCE"*

Often-Confused Words	Part of Speech	Meaning
Raise, Rise		
Raise	verb	to cause to rise, to lift
Rise	verb	to assume an upright position from lying, kneeling, or sitting; to stand

VERB MEANING "STAND"   *VERB MEANING "LIFT"*

Rise to your feet and raise your right hand to take an oath.

Often-Confused Words	Part of Speech	Meaning
Sit, Set		
Sit	verb	to rest on the buttocks
Set	verb	to place

VERB MEANING "PLACE"   *VERB MEANING "REST ON YOUR BUTTOCKS"*

Set the program on the chair where you will sit.

Often-Confused Words	Part of Speech	Meaning
Than, Then		
Than	preposition	in comparison with
Then	adverb	at that time, following next, in that case

PREPOSITION MEANING "IN COMPARISON WITH"   *ADVERB MEANING "IN THAT CASE"*

If you like Chinese food better than Italian, then make reservations at the China Garden.

Often-Confused Words	Part of Speech	Meaning
Their, There, They're		
Their	pronoun	plural third-person possessive
There	adverb	in or at that place
They're	pronoun/verb	contraction of *they are*

CONTRACTION OF SUBJECT AND VERB "THEY ARE"   *ADVERB MEANING "THAT PLACE" REFERS TO VERB "GO"*   *POSSESSIVE PRONOUN "THEIR" REFERS TO PRONOUN ANTECEDENT "THEY"*

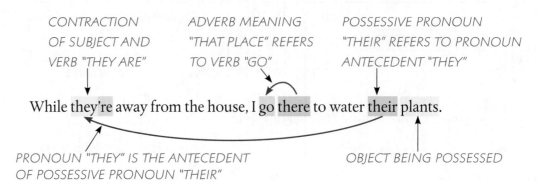

While they're away from the house, I go there to water their plants.

PRONOUN "THEY" IS THE ANTECEDENT OF POSSESSIVE PRONOUN "THEIR"   *OBJECT BEING POSSESSED*

Often-Confused Words	Part of Speech	Meaning
Threw, Through		
Threw	verb, past tense	to propel through the air
Through	preposition, adverb, adjective	in one side and out another

PAST TENSE VERB MEANING
"PROPELLED THROUGH THE AIR"   PREPOSITION MEANING "IN AND OUT"

Manny threw the ball through the hoop.

To, Too, Two		
To	preposition	movement toward, indicates direction
To	forms the infinitive	to be
Too	adverb	besides, also, excessively
Two	adjective, noun	one more in number than one

ADJECTIVE MEANING "ONE MORE IN NUMBER   ADVERB MEANING "EXCESSIVELY"
THAN ONE" DESCRIBES NOUN "TACOS"   DESCRIBES ADVERB "QUICKLY"

I went to the store to get two tacos; I ate them too quickly.

PREPOSITION MEANING   INFINITIVE VERB MEANING
"MOVEMENT TOWARD"   "THE ACT OF OBTAINING"

Waist, Waste		
Waist	noun	middle section of body between ribs and hips
Waste	noun	garbage, refuse
Waste	verb	to misuse, to ruin, to wear away

NOUN MEANING "GARBAGE"   NOUN MEANING "MID-SECTION OF THE BODY"

Leftover food that's thrown out creates waste. I am watching my waist.

The community wasted their resources.

VERB MEANING "RUINED"

Often-Confused Words	Part of Speech	Meaning
Wear, Where, Were, We're		
Wear	verb, present tense	to clothe, to put on
Where	adverb	at what place
Were	verb, past tense	plural past tense of *to be*
We're	pronoun/verb	contraction of *we are*

CONTRACTION OF PRONOUN AND VERB "WE ARE"　　　　*ADVERB MEANING "TO A PLACE" DESCRIBES VERB "ARE GOING"*

We were going to dress up, but now we're going where we can wear jeans.

PAST-TENSE VERB FORM OF "TO BE"　　　　*VERB MEANING "PUT ON"*

Weather, Whether		
Weather	noun	atmospheric conditions
Weather	verb	to endure
Whether	conjunction	if, alternative choices

CONJUNCTION MEANING "IF"　　*NOUN MEANING "ATMOSPHERIC CONDITIONS"*

Whether the weather is fair or not, we will play the match.

Whose, Who's		
Whose	pronoun	third-person possessive
Who's	pronoun/verb	contraction of *who is*

CONTRACTION OF PRONOUN AND VERB "WHO IS"

Who's going to find out whose jacket this is?

POSSESSIVE PRONOUN　OBJECT BEING POSSESSED

Circle the words that best complete the meaning of each sentence.

1. Hopefully, you are (already / all ready) in a healthy relationship, and you are (already / all ready) to be an (accepting / excepting) partner.

2. One piece of (advice / advise) suggests that couples could avoid (a lot / allot) of fights if they (a lot / allot) time for romance.

3. Some experts (advice / advise) you to consider the (affect / effect) of your words and actions, so you can (affect / effect) your relationship in a positive way.

4. Jazmen said "(bye / buy)" to her controlling partner; the (braking / breaking) point occurred when he made her (by / buy) (clothes / cloths) that were made from the cheapest (clothes / cloths).

5. She has decided to take a writing (course / coarse) at the college (besides / beside) her house.

6. A (good / well) fitting pair of shoes (fathers / furthers) foot health and allows you to walk (farther / further) distances without injury or pain.

7. Buy a shoe based on (it's / its) comfort and fit; if (it's / its) not comfortable and doesn't fit, don't buy it.

8. Experts understand a basic (principal / principle) about friendship: (know / no) fight ends until everyone says "I'm sorry."

9. For example, for months after I (knew / new) about the (lay / lie) my friend told me, I (lay / lie) awake at night stewing; I still can't (lay / lie) aside my hurt and disappointment.

10. Jeremy asked, "Are you (quite / quiet) pleased with yourself as you (lie / lay) in bed late into the morning?"

11. I replied, "Yes, I have had a (quite / quiet) morning; it has (past / passed) too quickly.

12. To soak feet, (set / sit) in a comfortable chair and (sit / set) your feet in a bowl of warm, soapy water; (their / there / they're) is no need to use Epsom salt.

13. People (raise / rise) early in the morning to shampoo, shower, shave, and style themselves, (than / then) rarely pay attention to (their / there / they're) feet.

14. Yesterday Jordon and her sister went (threw / through) the closets and (threw / through) away all smelly or tight shoes; today (their / there / they're) going to get a pedicure.

15. Discretion often affects (weather / whether) or not a relationship can (weather / whether) hardships; discuss private matters in private places (wear / where) they belong.

Practice 3

16. You (waist / waste) intimacy when you open your heart (to / too) the entire world, leaving nothing that is just for the (too / two) of you alone.

17. Spend some quality time with other couples (whose / who's) relationships are stable; look for another couple (whose / who's) a good match for both of you, (to / too).

18. Lenny and I (were / we're) always arguing about silly stuff like what we should (wear / where) or (wear / where) we should eat; now (were / we're) being patient and having fun with each other.

19.–20. Write two sentences correctly using one of the often-confused words from pages 264–272 in each sentence. Suggested topics: Advice everyone should follow, an ideal life partner, reasons friends fight, common foot problems, or a trait of a stable couple.

Practice 4

REVIEW OF OFTEN-CONFUSED WORDS

Circle the words that best complete the meaning of each sentence.

It is important that you try to (1) (accept / except) and validate your coworkers' feelings. Let them know that you (2) (hear / here) what they say. Communicate (3) (to / too) them that (4) (their / there) feelings make sense. (5) (Know / No), you don't have (6) (to / two) agree with them, but (7) (its / it's) important to understand (8) (their / they're) point of view. (9) (There / They're) is no more important task (10) (than / then) validating feelings. During (11) (brake/ break) time, you should (12) (allot / a lot) time to sit, be (13) (quiet / quite), and listen to them. Model the (14) (principal / principle) of caring. Let them (15) (know / no) that (16) (there / they're) important. Learn what (17) (affects / effects) them; think about what they go (18) (threw / through) on a daily basis. Darius (19) (raised / rose) the morale of his unit by giving and taking sound (20) (advice / advise).

Editing Assignments

MyWritingLab™
Complete this Exercise
on mywritinglab.com

Editing for Everyday Life

An intervention is a united effort of friends and family to confront the addiction of a loved one. Assume you and your friends are staging an intervention for another friend who is addicted to cocaine. On behalf of the group, you are writing a letter that explains your purpose to your troubled friend. Edit this draft for correct use of often-confused words.

You're use of cocaine has effected your relationships with allot of people. Your well health is our principle concern. We want you to brake the cycle of addiction. We also want to discuss ways that we can help you get and stay sober. Were hear to help. We no you feel badly. You can feel better. Please fight this addiction. We love you very much!

Editing for College Life

Assume you are writing a paper about the link between someone's personality and the shoes they wear for your college psychology class. Edit this draft of your introduction for correct use of often-confused words.

From Soul to Sole

The basic principal of shoes is to offer protection for the feet. However, allot of people wear shoes more to match they're personality then to protect their feet. For example, Converse are basketball shoes. They were developed, marketed, and endorsed by professional basketball players as high-performance athletic shoes. However, they have developed almost a cult following among youth and others who have no interest in basketball. Their now available in bright, stylish colors and worn with everything including tuxedoes, dresses, and jeans.

Academic Learning Log: Chapter Review

Editing for Working Life

Assume you work at a small local company that sent you to a workshop sponsored by the area's Workforce Coalition. You are expected to share what you have learned in a presentation to your coworkers. Edit this draft of a PowerPoint slide for correct use of often-confused words.

> **Improving You're Work Relationships**
> •
> Have a Positive Attitude: Except others.
> •
> Sit Boundaries: Focus on work rather then personal issues.
> •
> Resolve Conflicts: Be direct and polite; lie aside petty differences.

WHAT HAVE I LEARNED ABOUT MASTERING OFTEN-CONFUSED WORDS?

To test and track your understanding, answer the following questions. Fill in the blanks with information you have learned from this chapter.

1. (a) **Accept** _____ (b) **Except** but, not including

2. (a) **Advice** guidance (b) **Advise** _____

3. (a) **Affect** _____ (b) **Effect** result, outcome

4. (a) **Allot** _____ (b) **A lot** much, large amounts

5. (a) **All ready** prepared (b) **Already** _____

6. (a) **Beside** by the side of (b) _____ except, other than, together with

7. (a) **By** _____ (b) **Bye** farewell
   (c) **Buy** to purchase

8. (a) **Brake** to stop (b) **Break** _____

9. (a) _____ garments (b) **Cloths** pliable material

10. (a) **Coarse** _____ (b) **Course** path, direction, part of a meal, an academic class

11. (a) **Farther** to a greater distance (b) _____ additional, to advance

12. (a) **Fewer** count (b) **Less** _____

13. (a) **Good** favorable, best .... (b) **Well** ....

14. (a) .... to perceive sound .... (b) **Here** in or at this place

15. (a) **Its** possessive pronoun .... (b) **It's** ....

16. (a) **Knew** recognized, understood .... (b) **New** ....
    (c) **Know** to recognize .... (d) **No** negative, not any

17. (a) **Lay** .... (b) **Lie** recline, tell a falsehood, a falsehood

18. (a) .... moved, proceeded, ... (b) **Past** a time gone by, ago, elapsed, beyond
    went

19. (a) **Principal** of chief importance .... (b) .... rule, code, or standard

20. (a) **Quiet** silence, to silence, silent .... (b) **Quit** ....
    (c) **Quite** wholly, completely

21. (a) **Raise** .... (b) **Rise** to assume an upright position

22. (a) **Sit** to rest on the buttocks .... (b) .... to place

23. (a) .... in comparison with .... (b) **Then** at that time, following next, in that case

24. (a) **Their** plural third-person possessive .... (b) **There** ....
    (c) **They're** contraction of *they are*

25. (a) .... to propel through the air .... (b) **Through** in one side and out another

26. (a) **To** movement toward, indicates .... (b) **Too** besides, also, excessively
    direction, forms the infinitive

    (c) **Two** ....

27. (a) **Waist** middle of the body .... (b) **Waste** to ruin, wear away, ...

28. (a) **Wear** .... (b) **Where** at what place
    (c) **Were** plural past tense of *to be* .... (d) **We're** contraction of *we are*

29. (a) **Weather** atmospheric conditions .... (b) .... if, alternative choices

30. (a) **Whose** .... (b) **Who's** contraction of *who is*

How will I use what I have learned about mastering often-confused words?
In your notebook, discuss how you will apply to your own writing what you have learned about mastering often-confused words.

What do I still need to study about mastering often-confused words?
In your notebook, describe your ongoing study needs by describing what, when, and how you will continue mastering often-confused words.

Academic Learning Log: Chapter Review

PORTFOLIO

MyWritingLab™
Complete the Post-test for Chapter 17 in MyWritingLab.

18

Thinking Through the Writing Process

The writing process has four stages: prewriting, drafting, revising, and proofreading.

Writing develops, records, and communicates your thoughts to other people. Careful writers rely on the writing process to discover, organize, and record information in response to a specific writing situation.

What's the Point of the Writing Process?

LO 1

The following photographs document some of the situations in which we use writing in our everyday, college, and working lives. Write a caption for each picture that includes a reason for writing well in that situation. Then, state the point of writing well.

Practice 1

WRITING
FROM LIFE

PHOTOGRAPHIC ORGANIZER: REASONS TO WRITE

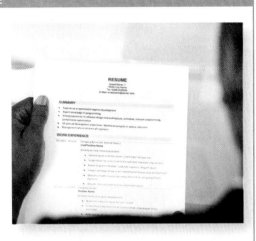

_____

_____

_____

_____

What's the point of writing well?

_____

_____

_____

My First Thoughts: A Prewriting Activity

PREWRITING

Set a time limit, such as five minutes, and jot down in your notebook your thoughts about the importance of writing. Do not let your pen or pencil stop, even if you must repeat ideas. Keep writing until the time limit is up.

One Student Writer's Response

The following paragraph is one writer's response to the question "What's the point of writing well?"

> *Writing is a necessary skill for success in college, everyday, and working life. Everyone knows that writing essays and reports is expected in the college classroom; however, writing is also important in other situations. For example, last week I got an e-mail from my cousin thanking me for the money I loaned him. His note meant so much to me that I printed it out and put it on the refrigerator as a daily reminder that I can make a difference in someone else's life. His note hangs right next to the newspaper clipping of a letter I wrote to the editor. A friend of mine was hurt in an accident due to a drunk driver, so I wrote a letter warning people against driving while under the influence. Finally, good writing is key to a successful career, too. An effective cover letter or resume can make a big difference in getting a job or promotion. Overall, writing helps me to learn and share ideas.*

L2 Assess the Writing Situation: Topic, Audience, and Purpose

When you write, you develop a point about a topic to fulfill a purpose for a specific audience. To develop your point, you need to think about two aspects of writing: the writing situation and the writing process.

A piece of writing develops in response to a specific **writing situation** that is composed of the **topic** (your subject), the **audience** (your reader), and the **purpose** for writing (your goal).

TOPIC
What you write

AUDIENCE
Who reads
your writing

PURPOSE
Why you write

The Topic: What You Write

When writing about situations in our personal lives, we may choose to compose a letter of complaint to a business or an e-mail to a friend. Often in these circumstances, the topic of our writing naturally emerges from our need to communicate.

However, when writing for college, many of us face writer's block in our search for a topic. You can break through writer's block by building a topic bank for college writing.

The following thinking guide can help you generate a bank of topics.

The Writing Situation Step by Step:

Topic

Build a bank of topics by listing ideas in a special section in your notebook. Use the following prompts to create several lists:

☐ Write down the major topics of importance in a specific course (such as biology, psychology, history).

☐ Find interesting or important current events.

   ☐ Topics most often covered in magazines and newspapers

   ☐ Controversial topics from television (such as news and talk shows)

   ☐ Topics about which you want to learn more

   ☐ Topics about which you feel deeply

   ☐ Hobbies and personal interests

☐ Share your lists with your classmates; use class discussion to generate more ideas.

☐ Review and expand your list on a regular basis.

As you continue to build your bank of general topics, read, read, and read some more. Read newspapers, magazines, and textbooks for additional topics. Many textbooks provide writing topics at the end of sections or chapters; in addition, headings and subheadings of chapters or sections are excellent sources of topics for your writing.

Practice 2

ASSESS THE WRITING SITUATION: TOPIC

Rank the following topics **1** through **5** to reflect your interest in each one, with **1** representing the least interesting topic and **5** representing the most interesting topic. Then, write a few sentences that explain the reasons for your ranking.

.... Reasons to raise minimum wage

.... Causes and effects of global warming

.... Ways to overcome stress

.... Icons of popular entertainment

.... A hard-to-learn lesson in life

Practice 3

Skim a newspaper, a magazine, and a textbook and write a list of five topics from each one. Then, share your list with your class or in a small group.

TOPICS FROM A NEWSPAPER: ....

....

TOPICS FROM A MAGAZINE: ....

....

TOPICS FROM A TEXTBOOK: ....

....

The Purpose: Why You Write

Good writing focuses on a goal or purpose. Your writing will flow much more easily when you write with purpose. The following chart presents four basic purposes for writing.

Informative When writing informatively, your purpose is to share, explain, or demonstrate information.  **EXAMPLE:** An **informative essay** that explains the cycles of grief to your reader; a paragraph that answers an exam question about the major causes of global warming.	**Persuasive** When writing persuasively, your purpose is to change your reader's opinion or call your reader to take action.  **EXAMPLE:** An **argumentative essay** that defends graffiti as an art form; a letter to the editor that argues for a midnight curfew for teenagers.	
Expressive When writing expressively, your purpose is to share with the reader your personal opinions, feelings, or reactions to a topic.  **EXAMPLE:** An **expressive piece** that conveys an emotion or insight about a particular topic in the form of a poem, short story, or personal essay.	**Reflective** When writing reflectively, your purpose is to record your understanding about what you have experienced or learned.  **EXAMPLE:** An **informal essay** that explores what you think is significant about a current event; a journal entry that discusses the strengths of a paper written by you or a peer.	

The following thinking guide can help you identify your purpose in writing.

The Writing Situation Step by Step:

Purpose

☐ Annotate the lists in your topic bank to indicate possible purposes for each topic: Beside each one write **I** for informative, **P** for persuasive, **E** for expressive, or **R** for reflective.

☐ Generate four sets of topics based on different purposes for writing, using "The Writing Situation: Step by Step: Topic" box on page 281 to guide your thinking.

☐ Select one topic for each of the four purposes and complete the following statements:

   ☐ This topic will inform the reader about…

   ☐ This topic will persuade the reader to…

   ☐ This topic will express…

   ☐ This topic will reflect upon…

Practice 4

ASSESS THE WRITING SITUATION: PURPOSE

State the purpose of each of the following topic sentences. Discuss with your class or in a small group how a writer's purposes may be combined in certain situations.

1. After examining the results of this week's quiz, I need to review the following topics.

2. Love forgives even when it can't forget.

3. Drug companies should not use animals to research or test products.

4. A few reasons for obesity include poor diet choices, inactivity, and increased stress levels that are linked to overeating.

5. The government must fund improvements for the nation's aging roads and bridges.

ASSESS THE WRITING SITUATION: PURPOSE

For each of the following topics, write a sentence that states a purpose you may have for writing about this subject. Discuss your answers with your class or in a small group.

1. Identity theft

----

2. Responsible use of cell phones

----

3. Steroids and athletes

----

4. How to earn an "A"

The Audience: Who Reads Your Writing

When we take part in a conversation, we know exactly to whom we are speaking, and we adjust our tone, word choice, and examples to match the situation. For example, contrast how you talk to a friend with the way you talk to the dean of your college. Audience has the same impact in the writing situation.

Assume that you have chosen to write about the topic of alcohol abuse. What main points do you want each of the following audiences to consider about alcohol abuse? Use the blanks below each picture to record your ideas.

--   --

--   --

--   --

The following thinking guide can help you identify your audience.

The Writing Situation Step by Step:

Audience

☐ Choose a specific topic and purpose for writing.

☐ List the traits of your audience that are relevant to your topic and purpose:

 ☐ Age

 ☐ Gender

 ☐ Education level

☐ If you are writing for a general audience of mixed traits, identify the main traits most relevant to your topic and purpose.

☐ Identify three or four points about the topic of most interest to a specific audience.

☐ Choose several key words to describe your topic and hook the interest of a specific audience. Use a thesaurus to find the words best suited for your audience.

Practice 6

Based on your first thoughts about the audiences represented by the four pictures on pages 284–285, write a brief response to the following questions. Then, discuss your answers with your class or in a small group.

• What are the most important traits of each audience represented by the pictures?

• Did your main points differ based on the audience? Why or why not?

• Will your word choice or examples differ based on the audience? Why or why not?

Practice 7

Each of the following four pieces of writing appeals to one of the audiences depicted by the photos on pages 284–285. Write the letter of the piece of writing in the picture that shows its audience.

A. Research indicates that alcohol abuse among youth can be reduced by initiating strong intervention policies. Therefore, the legal drinking age should not be lowered to 18, but must remain at 21.

B. By the time you become a teenager, you will most likely also become a binge drinker. You probably already know a teenager who abuses alcohol because 92% of American teenagers binge drink on a regular basis.

C. Did you know that binge drinking contributes to the three leading causes of death among young people: unintentional injury, homicide, and suicide? If you are a girl and drink more than three drinks in two hours, you are a binge drinker. If you are a guy and drink more than four drinks in two hours, you are a binge drinker. Now you know. So if you are a binge drinker, stop now! Save your life!

D. The well-being of our youth is the responsibility of the entire community. You, as a member of the business community, can help reduce binge drinking by being aware of the problem and being a part of the solution.

When student writers are asked "Who is your audience?" most reply, "The teacher." Of course, the teacher is your immediate audience, and you must carefully consider his or her expectations. However, many teachers understand the value of writing to a real-life audience. College is preparing you for success in life. You are learning to write for life.

ASSESS THE WRITING SITUATION: TOPIC AND AUDIENCE

The following writing prompts apply an academic topic to a real audience.

Write the name of the college course(s) for each prompt and describe the traits of each audience. Discuss your answers with your class or in a small group. Talk about how each audience affects the writer's choice of words and details.

1. Write a report for a bank to convince investors to finance your business plan.

COURSE(S): ....

AUDIENCE: ....

....

2. Write a letter to the editor of a newspaper to convince readers to "Go Green" by buying hybrid cars.

COURSE(S): ....

AUDIENCE: ....

....

3. Write a memo that explains the company's sexual harassment policies to a new, young sales clerk who works part time at a retail clothing store.

COURSE(S): ....

AUDIENCE: ....

....

4. Write an e-mail to a friend who is a victim of identity theft that explains the steps he needs to take to protect himself.

COURSE(S): ....

AUDIENCE: ....

....

L3 Use the Writing Process: Prewrite, Draft, Revise, and Proofread

Writing is a process that comprises a series of phases or steps. The process approach focuses on the writer, the way writing is produced, and how the writer can improve his or her personal writing process. The process approach is recursive; the writer may loop or combine any of the stages at any point during the writing process. The key outcome at the end of the process is a published piece of writing. Throughout each stage, think about the relationships among your topic, purpose, and audience.

👁 Watch the **Video** on **mywritinglab.com**

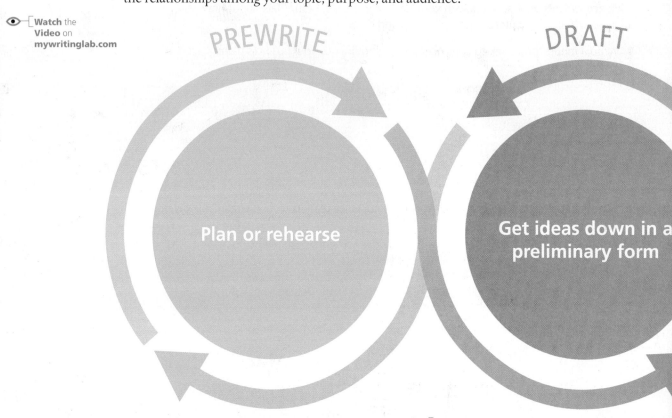

👁 Watch the **Video** on **mywritinglab.com**

👁 Watch the **Video** on **mywritinglab.com**

PREWRITE

During the prewriting stage, you create a plan for your piece of writing.

This phase of writing is made up of the following steps:

- Decide on a topic.
- Determine your purpose for writing.
- Gather information.
- Generate details by using clusters, lists, and freewrites.
- Organize the details into an outline.

The rest of this chapter covers specific prewriting techniques.

DRAFT

During the drafting stage, you create a draft of your writing.

This phase may include the following steps:

- Determine who is your audience.
- Choose a format (such as an essay or a letter).
- Create an introduction, body, and conclusion for longer pieces.

Chapters 19–20 guide you through the entire writing process as you learn how to write paragraphs.

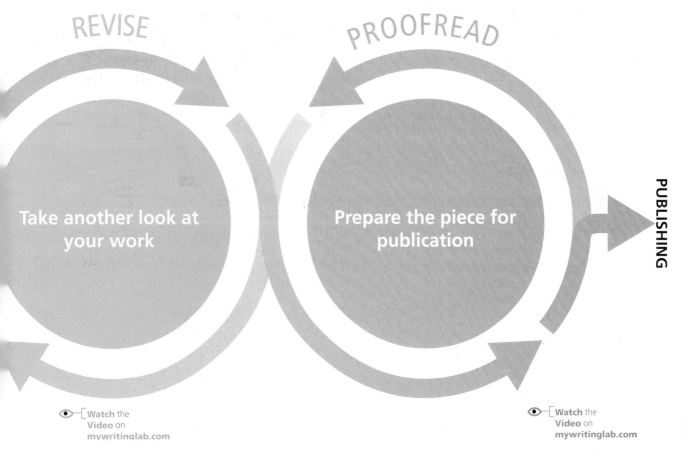

REVISE

PROOFREAD

Take another look at your work

Prepare the piece for publication

PUBLISHING

👁━│Watch the
Video on
mywritinglab.com

👁━│Watch the
Video on
mywritinglab.com

REVISE

During the revision phase, you fine tune the ideas in your essay. After you have written a draft, allow some time to pass so that you can examine your writing with fresh eyes.

This phase includes the following steps:

- Delete details that are not relevant.
- Add details to ideas that need more support.
- Reorder ideas for clarity.
- Insert transitions between details for a smooth flow of ideas.
- Replace vague or weak words with vivid, strong words.
- Write a new draft if necessary.

Part 6 covers specific skills to consider while revising.

PROOFREAD

During the editing phase of the writing process, you polish your draft so your reader will not be distracted or confused by careless errors.

This phase includes correcting errors such as:

- Fragments
- Fused sentences
- Shift in tenses
- Spelling
- Punctuation

Parts 2–4 cover the skills to consider during editing.

Prewrite

Carefully examine the cartoon. Then, in the space provided, write a few sentences explaining your understanding of what prewriting is.

Unfortunately, napkins hadn't been invented yet, so good ideas were quickly forgotten.

What is prewriting?

_____

_____

_____

_____

_____

_____

In general, writing occurs long before you pick up your pen or your fingers touch the keyboard. **Prewriting** includes reading, listening, discussing, and thinking about your topic before you write a rough draft that captures your prewriting thoughts on paper. It allows you to explore ideas and plan your strategies without worrying about polishing them.

Have you ever stared at a clean sheet of paper with a blank mind, unable to think of how to start a writing task? Or, have you ever had so many ideas that they jumble up in chaos so that you can't even begin to write? Finding those first few words to put on paper can grind a writer's thinking process to a complete halt.

If you face these problems, take heart; you are not alone! Even the best writers face writer's block now and then. Although no cure-all for writer's block exists, prewriting fuels thinking, triggers the writing process, and fires past the block. Experienced writers have learned to spend time thinking about what they are going to write before they begin drafting.

> **Prewriting** is the act of generating, exploring, developing, and roughly organizing ideas. Prewriting can help you choose a topic, narrow a topic, and put details related to a topic in logical order.

The rest of this section guides you through five prewriting techniques:

- Asking Questions:
    The Reporter's Questions
    Reflective Questions

- Freewriting
- Listing
- Concept Mapping
- Outlining

As you write for life, try out each one. Combine a few to stretch your thinking. Experiment with all of them. Discover which one(s) best suit you as a writer or in a particular writing situation.

Asking Questions

Asking questions helps you identify a topic and develop details about it based on thoughtful insights. Asking and answering questions helps you discover both what you already know and what you need to learn about the topic. Your goal as a writer is to share a point or main idea about a topic. Usually, a main idea or point is made up of the topic and the writer's opinion about the topic. Two types of questions enable you to explore topics and your opinions about those topics: the reporter's questions and reflective questions.

THE REPORTER'S QUESTIONS

To describe a newsworthy event, effective reporters gather the facts by asking six basic questions:

- Who?
- What?
- When?
- Where?
- Why?
- How?

At first, the answers to these questions may help you identify and narrow a topic that grabs your interest; once you have narrowed your topic, these questions also yield many details of support for your topic.

Practice 9

Assume you are preparing an informative speech for your college speech class on the issue of binge drinking among college students. You have decided to use a photograph as a visual aid to help make your point. Use this photo and the reporter's questions to brainstorm your first thoughts for your speech.

What is binge drinking?

Why is binge drinking a problem?

How should colleges deal with binge drinking?

REFLECTIVE QUESTIONS

Reflective questions also help you discover your purpose for writing by revealing your attitude toward a topic. By using these questions to reflect, identify, and add your opinion about a topic to your writing, you can also narrow a writing topic that is too general. For example, binge drinking is a controversial topic about which many disagree. For the purposes of narrowing this particular general topic, the following questions might help you identify your opinions about it:

- When, if ever, should parents be notified about a student's binge drinking?
- Who supports binge drinking? Why? Who opposes binge drinking? Why?
- In what ways do I agree or disagree with these opinions?
- How can I best express my point about binge drinking to someone with whom I disagree?

Answering these questions before writing will also guide you to make logical decisions about which details to select and highlight when you do begin to write.

When you are ready to explore ideas about a topic on paper, the following thinking guide can help you use questions as a prewriting technique.

The Writing Process Step by Step:

Prewriting by Asking Questions

Use the reporter's questions to identify a topic, purpose, and audience.

☐ What?

☐ Why?

☐ Who?

Use the reporter's questions to generate details about the topic.

☐ When?

☐ Where?

☐ How?

Use reflective questions to identify attitudes and generate additional details about the topic.

☐ What are my attitudes or feelings about this topic?

☐ What are my audience's attitudes or feelings about this topic?

☐ Why is this topic important?

☐ How will my audience respond to my point?

☐ How can I make this topic interesting and relevant to my audience?

USE THE WRITING PROCESS: PREWRITE BY QUESTIONING

Assume you are reporting on the influence of Hollywood on society. Using the box "The Writing Process Step by Step: Prewriting by Asking Questions," write a list of questions to identify your point and generate details. Share your ideas with the class or in a small group.

....

....

....

USE THE WRITING PROCESS: PREWRITE BY QUESTIONING

Ask questions to brainstorm your first thoughts about one of the following topics:

• Underage Drinking ....

• Tattoos ....

• Obesity ....

• Managing Stress ....

• Minimum Wage ....

Freewriting

During **freewriting**, you record your thoughts as they stream through your mind. The key to this brainstorming strategy, like all prewriting activities, is to turn off the critic inside your head. At this point, no thought is wrong, off base, or silly. The idea is to warm up your thinking muscles, flex your creativity, and set your ideas free. The following thinking guide can help you use freewriting as a prewriting technique.

The Writing Process Step by Step:

Prewriting by Freewriting

☐ Set a time limit, such as ten minutes, and write whatever comes to mind as fast as you can, without stopping at all.

☐ If you get stuck, write the same word or phrase until a new idea comes along. Do not stop writing. Do not worry about wording, organization, or grammar. Later in the writing process, you will organize and polish your ideas—tell that critic inside your head to pipe down for now.

☐ When the time limit is up, read what you wrote and underline interesting ideas.

☐ Use one of the ideas you underlined as a starting point for a focused freewrite. In a **focused freewrite** you write without stopping about a specific topic you have chosen or been assigned.

USE THE WRITING PROCESS: PREWRITE BY FREEWRITING

Read the following two freewrites. Discuss with your class or in a small group how ideas develop using freewriting and focused freewriting. What are the advantages of freewriting? What are the disadvantages?

Practice 12

| Freewrite 1 | I have tried to start writing several times, and each time I just draw a blank. So what do I do? I go to the net. Sure, my excuse is that I'm gonna look for topics to write about. My homepage is set to MSN, whatever that means, so sometimes I just click around on all the topics that snag my attention, and then those that didn't. Before I know it 30 minutes is gone and I have written nothing. So I try again, and again, nothing comes to me that seems worth writing down. After a few minutes of staring at a blank page and getting nowhere, I think I'll just check my Facebook page. In fact, I'm fighting the urge to stop writing and go look at it. (But I'm on a roll, so anyway, I go to Facebook and read new posts or click on friends and scroll through people's timelines. Before you know it, another 30 minutes or more is gone. And still I have written nothing, nothing. Just now, my phone beep with a message—I know the sound, it's Words with Friends. So I'll be right back...can't resist.) Okay, I'm back. It's too funny, this obsession with the social net!!! I'm not the only one I know who's like this. Most everyone I know is tech distracted. Look around right now. How many people do you see on a cell-phone... Even. When. Driving! Hey, that's a pretty good topic, Technology Distraction. |

| Freewrite 2 | Technology can be very distracting. A cellphone ringing in a theater during a movie takes attention away from the movie and ruins the moment. And it always seems to ring right at the most important, scary, or romantic moment in the movie. It's awful, too, when you think the ringing cell phone is yours. I'll never forget the time my brother and I went to see Jurassic Park. And during one frightful scene when a T-Rex appeared out of nowhere, a cellphone started ringing. It was my ring tone and so nearby that I began scrambling through my purse to find it and shut it off. My brother nudged me and smirked "the cell phone is ringing in the dinosaur's stomach. Remember when he ate the guy who was holding it in an earlier scene?" People around us told us to shush and watch the movie. Use of cellphones also distracts drivers from their driving. A driver takes his eyes off the road to look at his cellphone for any number of reasons. He dials a number, he sends a text, he reads a text, he drops his phone, he looks for it, he bends to pick it up, his car veers, he jerks it back. He does all this instead of watching the road or paying attention to the cars around him. A car also comes with technology that can be distracting. Drivers may fiddle with the radio or program the GPS to map out directions. Technology can also distract workers on a job. Companies lose hours and hours of work time because employees surf the Internet, maybe shop online, go to social networks, or read and write personal emails. Students are also distracted by technology. Many interrupt their studies to use social media or surf the net. |

USE THE WRITING PROCESS: PREWRITE BY FOCUSED FREEWRITING

Step 1: Choose one of the following topics and freewrite for five minutes. Ask and answer the reporter's and reflective questions before you begin freewriting.

- Peer Pressure

- Useful Technology

- Eating Disorders

- A Role Model

Step 2: Read your freewrite and highlight ideas. Write a focused freewrite for an additional five minutes using the idea(s) you highlighted.

Listing

A common way to brainstorm ideas is to **create a list**. If you have a free choice of topics, then create a topic bank: List ideas you want to learn more about or topics you already know something about and that you enjoy discussing. To create a list of topics for an academic course, look at the table of contents, the index, and the glossary of your textbook. Use these resources to create a list of topics based on what you will be studying throughout the semester. If you already have a topic, then create a list of everything that comes to mind as you think about your topic. Write your list as quickly as you can. Just as in freewriting, quiet your inner critic. Once you make a thorough list, then you can organize your ideas.

The Writing Process Step by Step:

Prewriting by Listing

☐ Write a topic at the top of your page.

☐ List ideas as quickly as possible in the order that they occur to you, using words or short phrases.

☐ List all ideas that occur to you; reject nothing.

☐ If you run out of ideas, choose one idea you have already recorded and begin a new list about that idea.

☐ Review your list and group ideas into logical relationships.

☐ Label each group of ideas as possible points of development for a piece of writing.

Practice 14

USE THE WRITING PROCESS: PREWRITE BY LISTING

Prewriting for an Academic Course: The following lists are based on the table of contents of two textbooks. Identify the academic courses to which each list is related. Then, brainstorm a list of additional writing topics based on an idea from each list.

COURSES: ....   COURSES: ....

List 1

The Great Depression
   Causes of the Crisis
   Surviving Hard Times
   The Dust Bowl
Presidential Responses to the Depression
   Herbert Hoover
   Franklin Delano Roosevelt

New Lists of Additional Ideas

....

....

....

List 2

Finding the Right Balance
   Promoting Healthy Behavior Change
   Mental, Emotional, Spiritual Wellness
   Violence and Abuse
Building Healthy Lifestyles
   Eating for Health
   Exercising for Personal Fitness

New Lists of Additional Ideas

....

....

....

Prewriting for Business Writing: Assume you are applying for a position as a loan officer at a local bank. You need to write a cover letter for your application. Read the description of the job and complete the prewriting activity. (Hint: If you prefer to find a different position to write about, go to the Department of Labor's Occupational Outlook Handbook and browse the A-Z index for additional job descriptions: http://www.bls.gov/oco/)

Education and Training: The position of loan officer requires a bachelor's degree in finance, economics, or a related field, or several years of work in another related occupation, such as teller or customer service representative.

Other Qualifications: An applicant should be good at working with others, confident, and highly motivated. Loan officers must be willing to attend community events as representatives of their employer. Sales ability, good interpersonal and communication skills, and a strong desire to succeed also are important qualities. Familiarity with computers and their applications in banking is preferred.

Step 1: Based on the job description, write a list of the skills you already possess that qualify you for the job.

Step 2: Choose three skills that are your strengths and list one example of how you learned or used each skill.

Step 3: List the skills you need to acquire or improve to qualify for the job.

Step 4: List the steps you will take to acquire or improve each skill you listed in Step 3.

Concept Mapping

Concept mapping, also known as **clustering** or **webbing**, creates a visual picture of the relationships among the ideas you generate. Think of what you already know about a map. Someone can tell you how to get somewhere, but it is much easier to understand the directions when you can study a map and see how each road connects to other roads. Likewise, a concept map shows how a topic connects to supporting details—how each idea connects to another idea and how the main idea connects to supporting details. Sometimes, as you use a concept map, the idea that first occurred to you might be a great example for a supporting detail. Rarely do ideas occur to us in a logical order. Concept mapping helps a writer figure out the logical order of ideas. Chapters 19–20 will show you how to adapt concept maps to specific writing situations and thought patterns.

The following thinking guide can help you use concept mapping as a prewriting technique.

The Writing Process Step by Step:

Prewriting by Concept Mapping

- [ ] Draw a circle in the middle of your page and write your topic in the circle.

- [ ] Write a word that relates to the topic, circle the word, and connect it to the topic circle with a line.

- [ ] Repeat this process so that a set of major supports radiates out from the topic circle.

- [ ] Write a word that relates to one of the major supports, circle it, and connect it to that major support circle.

- [ ] Repeat this process for each of the major supports to create clusters of minor supports.

Practice 16

USE THE WRITING PROCESS: PREWRITE BY MAPPING

The writer of the following paragraph used a concept map to brainstorm ideas. Read the paragraph. Then, recreate her concept map by filling in the appropriate blanks with ideas from her paragraph. Discuss how the concept map differs from her final draft.

Dear Ms. Gomez,

I would like to be considered for the position of manager that you advertised on the Glendale Mall website. I believe my experience, work ethic, and people skills make me a strong candidate for the position. For three years, I managed a kiosk for Kings Jewelry in Town Square Mall. For the past five years, I have worked in my current position as the assistant manager of Technology Town. I have solid experience in hiring, firing, creating work schedules, serving customers, completing sales transactions, bookkeeping, recruiting and training employees. My work ethic has been regularly noted in my job performance reviews. I have been awarded a series of merit pay raises as well. As an assistant manager, I have developed people skills to lead and motivate my team to work together, even under pressure or challenging situations. I communicate effectively with people in a friendly, professional way. I would like to discuss this opportunity further with you. Should you have any additional questions or comments, do not hesitate to contact me.

Sincerely,
Roberta Anderson

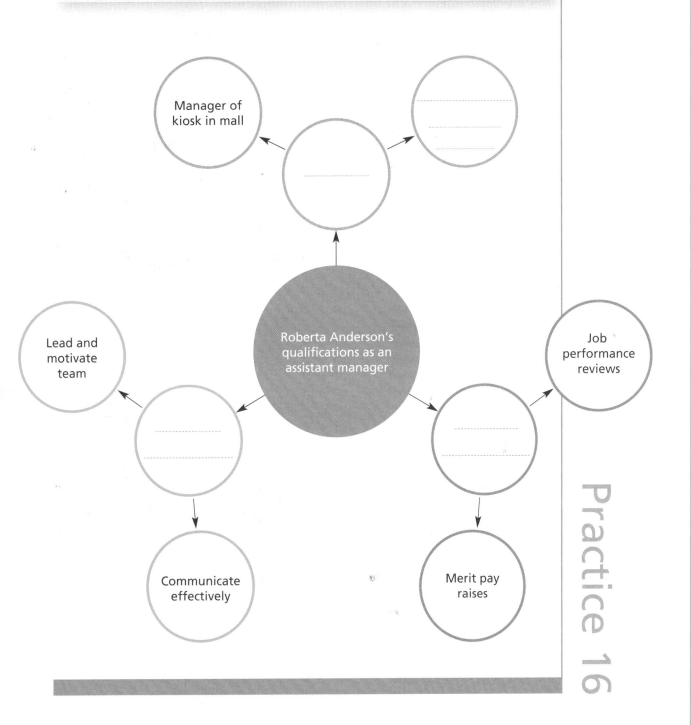

Practice 16

Practice 17

Using your own sheet of paper, create a concept map to brainstorm ideas for one of the following topics. Use circles and arrows to show your flow of ideas. Or feel free to use ideas generated in a freewrite that you created for Practices 11 and 13.

- Shocking Celebrity Behavior
- Minimum Wage
- Prescription Drug Abuse
- A Natural Disaster
- Balancing Work and School
- Gun Control
- Dieting
- College Stress

Outlining: A Writing Plan

In addition to brainstorming first thoughts, a prewrite also organizes ideas into a writing plan. A concept map is one way to create a writing plan because it shows the flow of ideas among the topic, major details, and minor details. An outline is another way to create a writing plan. An **outline** lists ideas in blocks of thought, as shown in the following outline for a paragraph.

Main Idea Statement: Topic Sentence

    A. Major supporting detail
      1. Minor detail
      2. Minor detail
    B. Major supporting detail
      1. Minor detail
      2. Minor detail
    C. Major supporting detail
      1. Minor detail
      2. Minor detail

The following thinking guide can help you use outlining as a prewriting technique.

The Writing Process Step by Step:

Prewriting by Outlining

☐ Create an outline from other prewriting activities such as freewrites, lists, and concept maps.

☐ List and identify each item with Roman numerals, capital letters, Arabic numerals, and lowercase letters, in that order, to show the flow of ideas, as illustrated below:

I. Main Idea

   A. Major supporting detail

      1. Minor supporting detail

        a. Subpoint

☐ Place a period after each numeral or letter.

☐ Capitalize each item.

☐ For topic outlines, state each item with a word or phrase.

☐ For sentence outlines, state each item as a complete thought.

USE THE WRITING PROCESS: PREWRITE BY OUTLINING

Practice 18

The following reflection and concept map were created by a student during the prewriting phase of an assignment. Complete the outline with ideas from the concept map.

Juan's First Thoughts:
I am going to write about the topic "Personal Boundaries." My psychology professor and classmates are my audience. I am going to focus my topic on the difference between healthy and unhealthy personal boundaries.

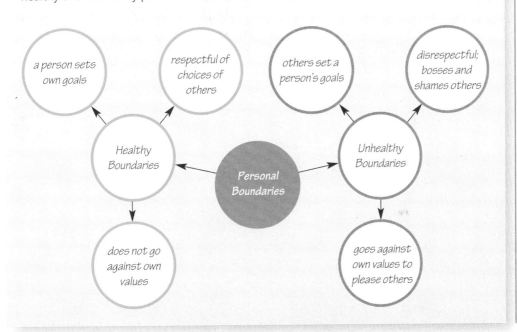

Main Idea Statement: Healthy and unhealthy boundaries differ in obvious ways.

A. _____

   1. _____

   2. A person is respectful of the choices of others.

   3. _____

B. _____

   1. Others set a person's goals.

   2. _____

   3. _____

USE THE WRITING PROCESS: PREWRITE BY CREATING A WRITING PLAN

Choose your own topic or select one of the following topics. Identify your audience and purpose. Then, generate major and supporting details using the outline. Use the reporter's questions *Who? What? When? Where? Why?* and *How?* to produce details.

- An important life lesson everyone needs to know

- Stem cell research

TOPIC: _____

AUDIENCE: _____

PURPOSE: _____

_____

_____

_____

TOPIC SENTENCE: _____

_____

_____

A. _____

   1. _____

   2. _____

Practice 19

B. ....

   1. ....

   2. ....

C. ....

   1. ....

   2. ....

Draft

The **drafting** stage of the writing process may include several tasks depending on the writing situation. An essay or letter may require the drafting of an introduction, a main idea, supporting details, and conclusion. A stand-alone paragraph may require only a main idea and supporting details.

> **Drafting** is putting your ideas into sentences and paragraphs.

Compose a Main Idea

The **main idea statement** for an essay is called a **thesis statement**. The main idea statement for a paragraph is called a **topic sentence**. Drafting an effective main idea statement requires several steps. Since our focus is the writing process, the steps for writing a topic sentence are explained, illustrated, and reinforced with in-depth practice activities on page 320. Likewise, the steps for writing a thesis statement are covered on page 487. The following discussion and activities introduce the concept of topic sentences and thesis statements to show when they are created during the writing process.

See the following for more information about Introductions: page 497, Conclusions: page 498, Topic Sentences: pages 483-484, Thesis Statements: pages 483-484

In general, the main idea sentence presents a topic and the point you are making about the topic, as in the following example:

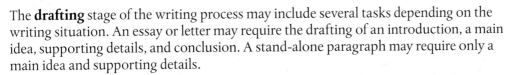

TOPIC

Guitars are versatile instruments that range in type of sounds such as acoustic, classical, and electric. ◄——— WRITER'S POINT ———

The writer's point focuses the general topic "Guitars" into a narrow topic for a discussion about three types of guitars. This main idea statement gives an overview of the paragraph or essay. The writer narrowed the topic "guitars" by stating the opinion "versatile" and by identifying three "types of sounds such as acoustic, classical, and electric."

The following thinking guide can help you draft a piece of writing.

The Writing Process Step by Step:
Drafting

☐ Write your main idea in a complete sentence. Make a specific statement rather than a vague, general statement.

☐ As you write a thesis statement or topic sentence, assert an idea instead of announcing your topic. Avoid the following announcements:

- "I am going to write about…"
- "My paragraph (or essay) is about…"
- "My topic is…."

☐ As you write your first draft, do not worry about issues such as spelling and grammar.

☐ Generate major and minor details to support your main idea.

☐ As you write, include new ideas as they occur to you without self-criticism or editing before you have a complete draft; this first draft does not need to be perfect. You will use the revision process to evaluate details for logic and relevance once your draft is complete.

☐ Use the first draft to discover how your ideas flow and fit together.

☐ Resolve to write multiple drafts to produce your best work.

USE THE WRITING PROCESS: DRAFT BY STATING THE MAIN IDEA

Complete the following set of exercises about main idea statements. Discuss your work with your class or in a small group.

A. Read the following main idea statements. Underline the subject once and underline the writer's point twice.

1. Road rage is a mental disorder that can be treated.

2. The twentieth century was a time of great scientific progress.

3. Dr. Martin Luther King had hope, strength, and courage.

4. *American Idol* remains popular for three reasons.

B. Revise the following main idea statements so they are more effectively expressed. Identify the hint you used to revise each one.

5. I am going to write about how regular exercise relieves stress and improves health.

....

....

Hint: ....

....

6. The benefits and responsibilities of owning a home.

Hint:

7. Many people participate in binge drinking.

Hint:

Write a Draft of Your Paragraph

A draft of a paragraph or essay is the result of careful thought based on prewriting activities. Creating a first or rough draft allows you to get a working copy of your ideas that can be improved upon during the revision process.

USE THE WRITING PROCESS: COMPOSE A TOPIC SENTENCE AND A DRAFT

Step 1. Choose a topic from a previous practice exercise and compose a main idea statement. (Remember that your **main idea statement** is also called a **topic sentence** if you are writing a paragraph. If you are writing an essay, your main idea statement is also called a **thesis statement**.)

Step 2. Write a draft using your own paper.

AUDIENCE AND PURPOSE:

TOPIC:

WRITER'S POINT:

MAIN IDEA STATEMENT (topic sentence or thesis statement):

Revise

Now that you have gotten your ideas on paper, you can review your work to make sure your paragraph offers a focused, unified, well-supported, and coherent chunk of information. As you revise your draft, review and apply what you have learned.

> **Revising** is re-seeing your work through the eyes of your reader. Revising is reworking your draft for clarity, logic, interest, and credibility.

The following thinking guide can help you revise a piece of writing.

The Writing Process Step by Step:

Revising

- [ ] Read your draft out loud (either on your own or to a peer). This is an easy way to identify parts of your draft that may be unclear or awkward.
- [ ] Make sure your main idea is stated clearly in a topic sentence or thesis statement.
- [ ] Make sure the details in the body of your paragraph or essay fully support your topic sentence or thesis statement.
- [ ] Make sure every sentence in a paragraph relates to your main idea so that a reader can easily follow the logic of your ideas.
- [ ] Move information as needed into the most logical order.
- [ ] Add transitions as needed to clarify the relationship between ideas.
- [ ] Add details and examples as needed to strengthen or clarify the main idea and supporting points.
- [ ] Replace vague words and details with vivid and precise expressions.
- [ ] Delete irrelevant details.
- [ ] If your paragraph or essay draft seems to end abruptly, add a concluding sentence (or paragraph, if you are writing an essay), restating and summing up your main points.

Read Juan's first draft of his paragraph "The Difference between Healthy and Unhealthy Boundaries." Then, complete the activity that follows. Share your work and thoughts with a small group of your peers.

The Differences between Healthy and Unhealthy Boundaries

(1) When we create clear boundaries, we define ourselves and how we relate to others. (2) When we don't create clear boundaries, we are more likely to suffer addiction or become codependent. (3) The difference between healthy and unhealthy boundaries is seen in three areas. (4) I learned about the difference between healthy and unhealthy boundaries from my counselor. (5) One issue about boundaries deals with goal setting. (6) When a person sets his or her own goals, that person has created a healthy boundary. (7) In contrast, a person who allows others to set his or her goals has got an unhealthy boundary. (8) A second boundary issue is about respect. (9) On the one hand, a person with healthy boundaries respects the choices, opinions, and feelings of others. (10) On the other hand, a person with unhealthy boundaries treats others with disrespect by bossing or embarrassing them. (11) For example, a person with a healthy boundary agrees to disagree while one with an unhealthy boundary uses name calling and eye rolling. (12) A vital boundary concerns a person's value system. (13) Someone who has healthy boundaries does not go against his or her own value system. (14) Someone who has unhealthy boundaries will go against his or her values to please others. (15) For example, a healthy person doesn't drink or take drugs just to be part of the crowd. (16) An unhealthy person will do so in the hopes of being accepted or liked by others. (17) If we want healthy relationships, we gotta establish healthy boundaries.

1. Locate the topic sentence by underlining the topic once and the writer's point about that topic twice.

2. Cross out any details that are not related to the topic sentence.

3. Circle any ideas that need more examples to fully support the main idea.

4. Choose three words to revise; cross out the words you chose and above them, write stronger or more vivid words. Use a thesaurus.

5. Insert the following transitions where they best show the logical flow of ideas: First, Finally, In contrast.

Practice 23

Review a draft you have written. Annotate or mark your paragraph with the changes you need to make, and write a journal entry about your revision. Do you need to brainstorm more details for certain ideas? Identify those ideas and describe or explain the kinds of details you need. Do you need to use a thesaurus to improve word choice? List and discuss the words that need to be replaced. Based on your review, revise to create a new draft of your work.

Proofread

Once you have revised your paragraph, take time to carefully proofread your work. Publishing a clean, error-free draft proves you are committed to excellence and that you take pride in your work. Many student writers struggle with common errors, and every writer has her or his own pattern or habit of careless errors. To create a polished draft, a careful writer masters the rules of writing and edits to eliminate careless errors.

> **Proofreading** is preparing your work for publication.
> Proofreading is correcting errors in punctuation, capitalization, mechanics, grammar, and spelling.

The following thinking guide can help you proofread a piece of writing.

The Writing Process Step by Step:
Proofreading

- [ ] Allow some time to pass between revising and proofreading.
- [ ] Read your work one sentence at a time from the *end* to the *beginning*. Reading your work from the end to the beginning allows you to focus on each sentence.
- [ ] Read again from the beginning with a blank paper that you slide down the page as you read so you can focus on one sentence at a time, covering the rest of the text.
- [ ] Use a highlighter to mark mistakes.
- [ ] Proofread more than once; focus on one type of error at a time.
- [ ] Proofread for the types of errors you commonly make.
- [ ] Use word processing spell checkers carefully (they don't know the difference between words such as *there, their,* or *they're*).
- [ ] Use a dictionary to double check your spelling.
- [ ] Have someone else read over your work.

The following draft by a student writer reveals her struggle with a common error: subject-verb agreement. The box below sums up the rules for subject-verb agreement and includes sentence examples that are correct. Read the rule and examples in the box, and then use them as a guide to correct three errors in subject-verb agreement in the student's draft.

Subject-Verb Agreement

If the subject of a sentence is singular, then the verb and object of the verb must be singular. If the subject of a sentence is plural, then the verb and object of the verb must be plural.

SINGULAR SUBJECT

CORRECT:

The lead driver rams his race car into the wall.

THIRD PERSON SINGULAR VERB (ADD "-S")

PLURAL SUBJECT

CORRECT:

Four other drivers lose control of their cars.

THIRD PERSON PLURAL VERB

Student draft

Learning the Value of Money

(1) When I lived with my mother, I didn't appreciate the value of money. (2) I never thought about how much food I was eating or how much it cost. (3) While shopping with her, I never looked at the prices. (4) I just threw items into the basket and never gave a thought about paying bills. (5) Now, being on my own, I watch what I spend. (6) My roommate and I shops for sale items. (7) We mostly buys Wal-Mart products. (8) Bills is another issue. (9) It's hard to keep up with all the due dates for bills, and there is no one to tell me when to pay them. (10) We've learned to pay our bills early to avoid late fees. (11) Now that I pay my own way, I appreciate the value of money.

Academic Learning Log:
Chapter Review

PORTFOLIO

To test and track your understanding of what you have studied, answer the following questions.

1. A piece of writing develops in response to a specific situation that is composed of the

   ...., the .... for writing, and the ....

2. The four basic purposes for writing are ...., ...,

   ...., and ....

3. The four phases of the writing process are ....,.........................,

   ...., and ....

4. The writing process is ....: any step can be repeated as necessary.

5. Several prewriting techniques include ....,.........................,

   ...., ..., and ....

6. Drafting is putting your ideas into .... and ....

7. Revising is .... your work through the eyes of your reader.

8. Revising is reworking your draft for ...., ...,

   ...., and ....

9. Proofreading is preparing your work for ....

10. Proofreading is correcting errors in ...., ...,

    ...., ..., and ....

Academic Learning Log: Chapter Review

11. How does this chapter relate to the information in Chapter 1? What have I learned based on my study of Chapter 18?

12. What about "thinking through the writing process" do I need to continue studying or practicing?

PORTFOLIO

MyWritingLab™

Complete the Post-test for Chapter 18 in MyWritingLab.

19

Understanding the Paragraph

A paragraph is a well-planned sequence of sentences joined together to support a narrowed topic.

All of us have had some experience reading, writing, or studying paragraphs. What do you already know about paragraphs? What are the traits of a paragraph?

A paragraph allows a writer to express clearly and powerfully one main idea about a narrowed subject. A well-written paragraph can express a valid consumer complaint, a compelling reason to be hired, a sincere apology to a loved one, or a concept tested by a written exam in a college course.

What's the Point of a Paragraph?

A paragraph is a well-thought-out chunk of information. A writer narrows a topic into a focused main idea, selects enough relevant details to support the main idea, and organizes these supporting details in a logical flow of information.

Three Levels of Information in a Paragraph

The following flow chart shows the three levels of information within a paragraph.

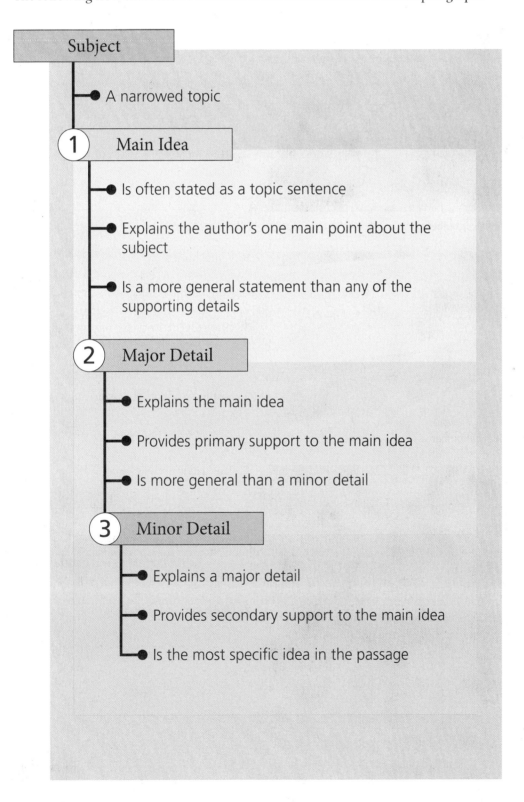

Subject
- A narrowed topic

① Main Idea
- Is often stated as a topic sentence
- Explains the author's one main point about the subject
- Is a more general statement than any of the supporting details

② Major Detail
- Explains the main idea
- Provides primary support to the main idea
- Is more general than a minor detail

③ Minor Detail
- Explains a major detail
- Provides secondary support to the main idea
- Is the most specific idea in the passage

Practice 1

WRITING
FROM LIFE

PHOTOGRAPHIC ORGANIZER: IDENTIFY LEVELS OF INFORMATION

Study the following outline of a student writer's paragraph for a sociology class. In the blanks, identify each piece of information as the narrowed topic, main idea, major supporting detail, or minor supporting detail.

Traits of Bullying Behavior ....

Bullying behavior can be physical, verbal, and psychological. ....

▲ **Physical bullies**

A. Physical bullies

1. use physical threats

2. attack victims regardless of the sex of their victims

▲ **Verbal bullies**

B. Verbal bullies

1. send cruel instant or e-mail messages

2. post insults about a person on a website

▲ **Psychological bullies**

C. Psychological bullies

1. exclude or gossip about victims

2. cause mental health problems

Practice 2

Read the paragraph developed from the previous outline. Circle the main idea. Underline the three sentences that state the major supports.

Types of Bullying Behavior

(1) Bullying is an ongoing act of abuse based on force and an imbalance of power. (2) Basically, bullying occurs as three basic types of abuse. (3) Bullying may be physical, verbal, and psychological. (4) The first type, physical bullying, includes hitting, kicking, shoving, and spitting. (5) Every afternoon, Lucas and his posse of peers hang out at a certain street corner. (6) Every afternoon, this group picks on Carl. (7) They take turns tripping, pushing, and slapping until he cries and begs them to stop. (8) The second type, verbal bullying, includes relentless teasing and insults, name calling, or spreading lies and false rumors. (9) Alicia constantly made fun of Raul by posting cruel remarks about him on Facebook. (10) In one post, she calls Raul "a wimpy nerd who will never get a date." (11) In another post, she falsely accuses Raul of being a "dummy who cheated to earn an A" on an assignment. (12) Unfortunately, many of her friends "like" her comments about Raul. (13) The third type, psychological bullying, includes gossip, isolation, and social rejection. (14) A popular cheerleader, Sandra, constantly gossips about Lydia. (15) Since Sandra is so well liked, many believe her gossip and reject Lydia as a friend. (16) As a result, Lydia is rarely invited to social events. (17) Bullying is abuse.

Read the following paragraph that gives advice to a young person about how to respond to bullies. Then, fill in the sentence outline with the main idea and missing supporting details.

Dealing with the Bullies

(1) Here are some things you can do to combat psychological and verbal bullying. (2) Ignore the bully and walk away. (3) It's definitely not a coward's response—sometimes it can be harder than losing your temper. (4) Bullies thrive on the reaction they get, and if you walk away, or ignore hurtful e-mails or instant messages, you're telling the bully that you just don't care. (5) Sooner or later the bully will probably get bored with trying to bother you. (6) Take charge of your life. (7) Think about ways to feel your best—and your strongest—so that other kids may give up the teasing. (8) Exercise is one way to feel strong and powerful; learn a martial art, or take a class like yoga. (9) Another way to gain confidence is to hone your skills in something like chess, art, music, computers, or writing. (10) Joining a class, club, or gym is a great way to make new friends and feel great about yourself. (11) Talk about it. (12) It may help to talk to a guidance counselor, teacher, or friend—anyone who can give you the support you need. (13) Talking can be a good outlet for the fears and frustrations that can build when you're being bullied.

–Adapted from Kidshealth. "Dealing with Bullies."© 1995–2012. The Nemours Foundation / Kidshealth® Reprinted with permission.

▲ **Ignore it**

▲ **Take charge of your life**

▲ **Talk about it**

Main idea (Topic Sentence): ....

....

A. Major support: ....

....

1. Minor support: It's definitely not a coward's response—sometimes it can be harder than losing your temper.

2. Minor support: Bullies thrive on the reaction they get, and if you walk away, or ignore hurtful e-mails or instant messages, you're telling the bully that you just don't care.

3. Minor support: ....

....

B. Major support: Take charge of your life.

1. Minor support: Think about ways to feel your best—and your strongest—so that other kids may give up the teasing.

2. Minor support: ....

....

3. Minor support: Another way to gain confidence is to hone your skills in something like chess, art, music, computers, or writing.

4. Minor support: Joining a class, club, or gym is a great way to make new friends and feel great about yourself.

C. Major support: ....

1. Minor support: It may help to talk to a guidance counselor, teacher, or friend—anyone who can give you the support you need.

2. Minor support: Talking can be a good outlet for the fears and frustrations that can build when you're being bullied.

Practice 3

L2 Identify the Three Parts of a Paragraph

A paragraph is a series of closely related sentences that develop and support the writer's point about a narrowed subject. Often, the paragraph serves as a building block for a longer piece of writing such as an essay, since an essay is composed of two, three, or more paragraphs. In many situations a writer can make a point through one well-developed paragraph. Sometimes, a writer provides a stand-alone paragraph with a title. In addition to a title, a paragraph has three basic parts:

A Beginning:
An introduction of one or more sentences: A topic sentence that states the author's purpose and main point

A Middle:
A body of major and minor details that support the topic sentence

An Ending:
A conclusion of one or more sentences that reinforces the author's purpose and main point

The following graphic describes the function of each part of a paragraph and shows the general format of a paragraph.

Title:
Use Key Words or a Phrase to Vividly Describe the Point of Your Paragraph

Introduction:
An introduction is usually one or more sentences that explain the importance of the topic or give necessary background information about the topic.
Your topic sentence states your narrowed subject and your point about the subject.

Body:
The body of a paragraph is made up of a series of sentences that offer major details in support of your topic sentence. If needed, provide minor details that support the major details. Link sentences within the paragraph with clear transitions so your reader can easily follow your thoughts.

Conclusion:
The conclusion restates or sums up your paragraph's main idea in one or more sentences.

Practice 4

IDENTIFY PARTS OF A PARAGRAPH

The following student essay by Michaelle Gilson illustrates the use of a title and the three parts of a paragraph. Underline the topic sentence. Circle each of the three parts of the paragraph: Introduction, Body, and Conclusion. Provide a title for the paragraph.

(1) Most people, regardless of race, age, or gender compare themselves to others, and some become obsessive about their looks. (2) This obsession can lead to three types of eating disorders. (3) One of the most common eating disorders, Anorexia Nervosa, occurs when people severely restrict their food intake; sometimes they stop eating altogether. (4) Also, anorexics often exercise excessively to control their weight. (5) Another common eating disorder is Bulimia Nervosa. (6) Bulimia can be described as self-induced vomiting after eating large amounts of food to avoid weight gain. (7) In addition, bulimics often use laxatives and enemas as part of their efforts to control their weight. (8) Anorexia and bulimia lead to unhealthy weight loss and even death without proper treatment and counseling. (9) A third common eating disorder, Compulsive Overeating is marked by uncontrollable eating and weight gain. (10) Compulsive eaters take in large amounts of food in a very short period of time. (11) This disorder leads to obesity; and obesity increases the risk of heart disease and cancer. (12) Ultimately, all three of these eating disorders can be cured with the proper treatment.

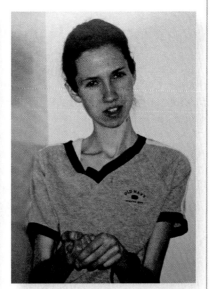
▲ Anorexia Nervosa

▲ Bulimia Nervosa

▲ Compulsive Overeating

Find more information and practice on each part of the paragraph in the following sections: Introductions— page 498. Conclusions— page 499.

An effective paragraph is *focused, detailed, logical,* and *well expressed.* A writer (1) composes a topic sentence; (2) creates logical order; (3) develops relevant and adequate details; and (4) uses effective expression through the purposeful choice of words, sentence structure, and grammar.

L3 Compose a Topic Sentence

A focused main idea presents a narrowed subject and the writer's controlling point about the narrowed subject. The controlling point often indicates both the writer's opinion and a pattern of organization. A topic sentence states the focused main idea in a complete sentence.

Narrow the Topic

Use the following suggestions to guide your thinking as you focus a general topic into a narrowed subject or topic.

- Narrow the topic based on your **opinion**. An opinion is expressed by using words such as *amazing, alarming, beautiful, best, likely, should,* or any other word that states personal values, judgments, or interpretations. Use questions, freewriting, mapping, listing, or another brainstorming technique to discover your opinion about a topic.

Example:	General Topic	Narrowed Subject
	Dieting	A healthful diet
		Dangerous diets

- Narrow the topic based on a **pattern of organization**. A writer may use a pattern of organization to narrow a subject and generate details. Patterns of organization are also used to develop, organize, and express a main idea, major details, and minor details in a logical order. The following list provides a few examples of patterns of organization and signal words for each one.

Pattern of Organization	Signal Words
Space Order	*above, below, next to, underneath, behind*
Time Order	*first, now, then, before, after, process, use*
Example	*for example, exemplify, includes, such as*
Classification	*types, kinds, levels*
Compare/Contrast	*similar, likewise, just as/however, in contrast*
Cause/Effect	*source, origin/results, impact*

Example:	General Topic	Narrowed Subject
	Exercise	The effect of exercise
		The types of exercise

- Combine topic, opinion, and pattern of organization to generate a narrowed subject.

Example:	General Topic	Narrowed Subject
	Dieting	Three steps to a healthful diet
		Dangerous types of diets
	Exercise	The benefits of weightlifting
		The difference between aerobic and anaerobic exercise

COMPOSE A TOPIC SENTENCE: FOCUS A TOPIC INTO A NARROWED SUBJECT

Combine the topic with an opinion and pattern of organization signal words to narrow the topic.

1. GENERAL TOPIC: *Health Issue: Walking*

   OPINION: *positive*　　　　　　SIGNAL WORD: *effects*

   NARROWED SUBJECT:

2. GENERAL TOPIC: *A Public Figure: Barack Obama*

   OPINION: *admirable*　　　　　　SIGNAL WORD: *traits*

   NARROWED SUBJECT:

3. GENERAL TOPIC: *Vacation destination: Blue Springs State Park*

   OPINION: *beautiful and peaceful*　　SIGNAL WORD: *scene*

   NARROWED SUBJECT:

4. GENERAL TOPIC: *Business: Opening a bank account*

   OPINION: *easy*　　　　　　SIGNAL WORD: *steps to*

   NARROWED SUBJECT:

5. GENERAL TOPIC: *Digital cable*

   OPINION: *efficient and clear signal*　SIGNAL WORD: *characteristics*

   NARROWED SUBJECT:

6. GENERAL TOPIC: *organic food*

   OPINION: *better*　　　　　　SIGNAL WORD: *leads to*

   NARROWED SUBJECT:

Write the Topic Sentence

Once you have focused a topic into a narrowed subject with your opinion and a pattern of organization, you are ready to write a complete sentence to state the main idea. Each of the following topic sentences offers a subject and a controlling point: a **topic** narrowed by the writer's **opinion** and a suggested **pattern of organization**.

WRITER'S OPINION   TOPIC   PATTERN OF ORGANIZATION

Create a healthful diet in three steps.

PATTERN OF ORGANIZATION   TOPIC   WRITER'S OPINION

Three types of diets are dangerous.

TOPIC   PATTERN OF ORGANIZATION   WRITER'S OPINION

Weightlifting offers several benefits.

WRITER'S OPINION   PATTERN OF ORGANIZATION   TOPIC

Important differences exist between aerobic and anaerobic exercise.

Practice 6

WRITE A TOPIC SENTENCE

Write topic sentences for each of the following narrowed subjects.

1. Narrowed Subject: Benefits of laughter

TOPIC SENTENCE: ....

....

2. Narrowed Subject: The admirable traits of a good parent

TOPIC SENTENCE: ....

....

3. Narrowed Subject: Disney World, expensive but fun

TOPIC SENTENCE: ....

....

4. Narrowed Subject: Easy steps to save money

TOPIC SENTENCE: ....

....

Create Logical Order

Use a writing plan to establish a logical order for details and a clear flow of ideas. A writing plan includes one or more of the following elements:

A *Pattern of Organization* As discussed on page 320, a writer uses a pattern of organization to arrange major details and minor details in a logical order. The following chart provides a few examples of patterns of organization and signal words for each one (see pages 332–369 for in-depth instruction about patterns of organization and signal words):

Patterns of Organization	Signal Words
Description (Space order)	*above, behind, below, next to, underneath*
Narrative/Process (Time order)	*after, before, first, next, now, stage, then*
Example	*exemplify, for example, includes, such as*
Classification	*kinds, levels, types*
Compare/Contrast	*in contrast, likewise/however, similar*
Cause/Effect	*impact, origin/results, reasons, source*

Order of Importance Often, a writer decides upon and arranges details according to his or her opinion about the importance of the details, known as **climactic order**. Usually, climactic order moves from the least important point and builds to the paragraph's climax, the most important point.

Order of Topic Sentence Often the controlling point of the topic sentence divides the subject into chunks of information. The order of the ideas in the topic sentence often reflects a pattern of organization or an order of importance for details.

LOGICAL ORDER

The following paragraph from a college textbook demonstrates a writing plan based on the logical order of a topic sentence and pattern of organization. Underline the topic sentence. Circle the pattern of organization's signal words.

Practice 7

(1) Jean Piaget, a Swiss psychologist, concluded that children go through four stages as they develop their ability to reason. (2) During the sensorimotor stage (from birth to about age 2), our understanding is limited to direct contact, such as sucking, touching, listening, and looking. (3) We aren't able to "think." (4) We do not know that our actions cause something to happen. (5) During the preoperational stage (from about age 2 to age 7), we develop the ability to use symbols. (6) However, we don't understand concepts such as size, speed, or cause and effect. (7) Nor can we take on the role of the other. (8) During the concrete operational stage (from the age of about 7 to 12), our reasoning abilities are more developed, but they remain concrete. (9) We now understand numbers, size, speed, and cause and effect, and we can take on the role of the other. (10) We still need concrete examples and have difficulty talking about concepts such as truth or honesty. (11) During the formal operational stage (after the age of 12), we are now capable of abstract thinking. (12) We can talk about concepts, come to conclusions based on general principles, and use rules to solve problems.

—Henslin, James M., *Essentials of Sociology; A Down-To-Earth Approach*, 10th. © N/A. Printed and Electronically reproduced by permission of Pearson Education, Inc., Upper Saddle River, New Jersey.

Practice 8

Study the following list of ideas. Label the major supports in each group A, B, and C to achieve the most logical order. Discuss the reasons for your choices with a small group of peers.

1. Writing for Everyday Life

Dear Kenesha, thank you for the surprise birthday party you organized for me.

.... the weeks of secret planning

.... the beautiful decorations and lovely gifts

.... the surprise of walking through the door

2. Writing for Working Life

To: Heather Brady. From: Nicolas Wienders, Supervisor. You are to be highly praised for your outstanding contributions to the team's project.

.... Ultimately, you suggested the best solution possible.

.... Throughout the project, you researched ways to solve the problem.

.... You identified a problem early on in the project.

3. Writing for College Life

Although not identical, weather and climate have much in common.

.... Thus, climate is the total of all statistical weather information that helps describe a place or region.

.... On the other hand, climate is often described as "average weather."

.... On the one hand, weather is the state of the atmosphere at a given time and place.

L5 Develop Relevant and Adequate Details

Relevant and adequate details support and develop the main idea. As you narrow a topic, usually you generate many ideas before you decide on one main point. You must evaluate each detail based on its relationship to the point you want to make.

Relevant details explain and support only the writer's point. Once you narrow a subject into a focused main idea, you then include only those details that relate to your opinion and pattern of organization.

Check for Relevant Details

Apply the following questions to each detail to see if it is relevant to a main idea. If the answers to these questions are "no," then the detail is most likely irrelevant and should not be included as a support.

- Does the detail reinforce the writer's opinion?
- Does the detail carry out the pattern of organization?
- Does the detail support the main idea?
- Does the detail support a major detail?

The following prewrite list includes a focused main idea and a set of details. Use the "Check for Relevant Details" questions given above to identify the irrelevant detail, and cross it out.

Main Idea: Follow these easy steps to save money.

Step 1: Look for a Bargain
- *Compare prices*
- *Use coupons*
- *Brand names are higher quality*

Step 2: Do It Yourself
- *Cook/eat at home*
- *Make your own coffee*

Step 3: Save Energy
- *Carpool*
- *Turn off unused appliances, devices, and lights*

Practice 9

Adequate details offer in-depth explanations and supports for the writer's opinion and pattern of organization. In-depth support of a main idea often requires both major and minor details. Major details directly support the main idea. Minor details support and explain the major details (review the chart on page 313 of this chapter).

Check for Adequate Details

Apply the following questions to see if you have adequate details to support your main idea. If the answer is "yes" to these questions, then additional details are most likely needed to fully support the main idea.

- Is more information needed to explain the writer's opinion?
- Is more information needed to carry out the pattern of organization?
- Does a major detail need a minor detail of support or explanation?

Practice 10

Practice 11

DEVELOP ADEQUATE DETAILS

The following list includes a main idea statement, three major supporting details, and minor details that support each major detail. Circle the major detail that needs more support. Add additional minor details of support for the idea you circled.

Main Idea: Disney World is expensive but fun.

Major Details: *Expensive*   *Fun*

Minor Details: • *admission tickets*   • *Magic Kingdom*
                                       • *Epcot*
                                       • *Animal Kingdom*
                                       • *Blizzard Beach, Typhoon Lagoon*

Many writers use concept maps and other brainstorming techniques to generate enough relevant details to convincingly support a point. Chapter 20 offers detailed instruction and practice with concept maps and other prewriting activities.

DEVELOP RELEVANT AND ADEQUATE DETAILS

Read the following rough draft of a paragraph. Cross out the irrelevant detail. Underline the point that needs more information to adequately support the main idea.

▲ **Gang graffiti**

▲ **Hip-hop Mural**

The Various Shades of Graffiti

(1) Graffiti is made up of the words, colors, and shapes drawn or scratched on buildings, overpasses, train cars, desks, and other public surfaces. (2) It is done without permission; it is against the law, and it is vandalism. (3) However, not all graffiti is the same. (4) Graffiti varies based on its purpose and style. (5) For example, the goal of Hip-hop graffiti is to gain fame for the individual style of the graffiti artist. (6) Hip-hop graffiti offers colorful and often artistic designs that range from simple tags, or signatures, to more complex pieces, such as murals. (7) In contrast, the purpose of gang graffiti is to build recognition, create fear, and mark the gang's turf or area. (8) Gang graffiti may list members, offer drugs for sale, or send warnings to rivals. (9) Gang graffiti differs from Hip-hop graffiti not only in its purpose, but also in its style. (10). Both Hip-hop graffiti and gang graffiti are statements of rebellion against authority.

Use Effective Expression

Effective expression enhances the writer's purpose through the precise choice and use of words, sentence structure, and grammar.

Word Choice

Precise word choice communicates exact meaning. Writers choose words that effectively communicate tone, purpose, and order. For example, strong transitions and signal words clue the audience into the logical order of the writer's thoughts. Another example of effective expression is the use of action verbs. In addition, words chosen for their emotional or visual impact create strong images in the reader's mind and carry out the writer's purpose.

Ineffective Expression

NON-ACTION VERBS

Leigh was glad when the race was over.

Effective Expression

ACTION VERBS

Leigh shouted in triumph when the race ended.

Sentence Structure

Four types of sentences serve as the basis for all sentences in the English language: simple, compound, complex, and compound-complex sentences. Effective expression uses a variety of sentence types to express ideas in clear and interesting statements. (To learn more about sentence structure, see Chapters 2–6.)

Simple Sentence

Jerome struggles with test anxiety.

Compound Sentence

Jerome knows the material, but he freezes up during an exam.

Complex Sentence

Because Jerome does not test well, he has created a test-taking plan to improve his scores.

Compound-Complex Sentence

For example, Jerome reads through the entire exam; then he answers all the easy questions so that he can accumulate points and gain confidence.

Grammar

Grammar is a tool of effective expression. Writers use grammar to clarify and polish ideas. Grammar includes a wide variety of language rules such as the following: tense, agreement, and punctuation. During the revision process, many writers focus on one element of expression at a time.

USE EFFECTIVE EXPRESSION

Revise the following paragraph for effective expression through word choice. With a small group of your peers, revise the underlined verbs of the following paragraph. Discuss how your revision improves the effectiveness of the paragraph.

A Survivor's Account

(1) The tornado tore through the neighborhood. (2) The funnel cloud <u>was huge</u> and roared like a train. (3) The wind <u>was blowing</u> so hard that the trees <u>were touching</u> the ground. (4) All around us, houses were splintering, and debris <u>was flying</u> through the air. (5) We barely made it out of our car and into the roadside ditch where we <u>were</u> flat on our stomachs. (6) We <u>were praying</u> for our lives.

Analyze the Effectiveness of a Paragraph

LO **7**

Workshop

Many student writers benefit from using a scoring guide. A scoring guide identifies and describes levels of writing effectiveness. The following scoring guide describes the traits of an effective paragraph as discussed earlier: A score of "5" indicates a highly effective paragraph. In a small group of your peers, discuss the differences between a "5" paragraph and a "3" paragraph.

Scoring Guide for a Paragraph

5 A focused main idea presents the narrowed subject and the writer's point, and suggests a pattern of organization. Relevant and in-depth details convincingly support and develop the main idea. Strong transitions indicate careful ordering of details based on a logical pattern of organization. Effective expression enhances the writer's purpose through the precise choice and use of words, sentence structure, and grammar.

4 A focused main idea presents the narrowed subject and the writer's opinion, and suggests a pattern of organization. Relevant and adequate details support and develop the main idea. Clear transitions indicate an order of details based on a logical pattern of organization. Effective expression carries out the writer's purpose through the competent use and choice of words, sentence structure, and grammar.

3 A focused main idea presents the narrowed subject and the writer's opinion or a pattern of organization. Relevant details offer enough support to develop the main idea. Occasional transitions indicate the use of a pattern of organization, but details are not always logically ordered. Expression does not interfere with the writer's purpose, even though occasional errors in use and choice of words, sentence structure, and grammar occur.

2 The main idea presents a general subject or a broad opinion. Details are generalized statements or lists that do not offer enough information to support the main idea. Weak or misused transitions and confused order of details indicate little use of a pattern of organization. Weak expression interferes with the writer's purpose through frequent errors in use and choice of words, sentence structure, and grammar.

1 The main idea presents a vague, weakly worded opinion about a general subject. Details are missing, superficial, or rambling. Lack of transitions and illogical order of details indicate no use of a pattern of organization. Confused expression interferes with the writer's purpose through pervasive errors in choice and use of words, sentence structure, and grammar.

Workshop

Use the scoring guide to assign a score to each of the following paragraphs written by students about the following topic: *A Behavior or Decision That Can Have Positive or Negative Effects*. Be prepared to discuss your reasons for each score.

_____ Living away from your country can be really interesting and unforgettable experience. At the same time, very important effects on one's life. Missing your friends and family, days goes fast when spending time with them and now everything is different here. Living far away from your family is really hard going to school, cleaning up your closet cook food for yourself, too much changelings. Living far from home, even for a short period of time, can be really hard.

_____ Procrastination of academic assignments is a negative behavior that I, like many others, struggle with. I keep telling myself that I will do the work later, or tomorrow, and the next thing I know, the assignment is due. Once, I had an exam for a business class, and I kept putting off studying. The weekend before the exam, I decided to go to Universal Studios and Disney World. I had planned to study Sunday night after I returned from the parks. However, I was exhausted after two long days of fun, so instead of studying, I slept. Suddenly, it was Monday morning and time for my exam. Of course, because I had not studied, I performed poorly on the exam. Unfortunately, procrastination is a clear path to failure.

_____ Exercise is good for you. Exercise makes your heart, muscles, and lungs strong. To get the benefit of exercise. You have to do it most every day. Good exercises are walking, swimming or a jog. We should exercise 5 days a week. There are many benefits to exercising but many people don't exercise.

_____ Success begins when you decide to be successful. Bill Gates is a perfect example of a person who made the decision to succeed. He knew what he wanted and failure wasn't going to stop him! Gates believed that on every office desk and in every home there should be a computer. If you look around almost everyone owns at least one computer, and Gates had something to do with it. He set out to make computers widely available and he ended up becoming one of richest persons in the world. Gates is only one man who had a dream and decided to achieve it. So make the decision to succeed and don't stop until you get the results you want.

_____ As a teenager one takes the first drink. Especially in high school, parties are taking place, "trying to fit in," or it's just something to do. As the partying continues and the fun reaches its peak, no one contemplates the effects alcohol has on the body. After a night of heavy drinking you might wake up with a hang over and throwing up all day with a headache. Little does one know that poison, alcohol, drank last night is damaging your vital organs, including liver, heart and pancreas. If one continues to drink, it could lead to alcoholism which can cause death. Keep in mind, every time an alcoholic drink enters your body it's being affected in some way.

Academic Learning Log: Chapter Review

UNDERSTANDING THE PARAGRAPH

To test and track your understanding of what you have studied, answer the following questions.

1. The three _____ in a paragraph are the main idea, the major details, and the minor details.

2. The three _____ are the beginning, middle, and end.

3. The _____ of a paragraph includes a title, the introduction, and the topic sentence.

4. The middle or the _____ of the paragraph offers major and minor details in support of the topic sentence.

5. The ending or _____ of the paragraph reinforces the author's main idea.

6. An _____ is focused, detailed, logical, and well expressed.

7. A _____, states the focused main idea in a complete sentence.

8. To establish _____, a writing plan includes one or more of the following: a pattern of organization, order of importance, and the order of the topic sentence.

9. _____ explain and support only the writer's point; _____ offer in-depth explanations and supports for the writer's point.

10. _____ enhances the writer's purpose through the precise choice of words, sentence structure, and grammar.

11. **How will I use what I have learned about the paragraph?**
In your notebook, discuss how you will apply to your own writing what you have learned about the paragraph.

12. **What do I still need to study about the paragraph?**
In your notebook, describe your ongoing study needs by describing what, when, and how you will continue studying the paragraph.

MyWritingLab™

Complete the Post-test for Chapter 19 in MyWritingLab.

20

LEARNING OUTCOMES

After studying this chapter you should be able to:

L❶ Answer the Question, "What's the Point of Using Patterns of Organization to Develop Paragraphs?"

L❷ Write a Descriptive Paragraph

L❸ Write a Narrative Paragraph

L❹ Write a Process Paragraph

L❺ Write an Example Paragraph

L❻ Write a Classification Paragraph

L❼ Write a Comparison and Contrast Paragraph

L❽ Write a Definition Paragraph

L❾ Write a Cause and Effect Paragraph

L❿ Write a Persuasive Paragraph

Using Patterns of Organization to Develop Your Paragraphs

Patterns of organization help a writer focus a topic.

Clear communication between a writer and a reader comes from clear organization. Clear organization is based on following familiar patterns of organization.

What's the Point of Using Patterns of Organization to Develop Paragraphs?   **L❶**

A **pattern of organization** arranges details into a specific logical order. For example, to tell a story or explain a process, a writer follows the time order pattern of organization. For the writer, a pattern of organization acts as a thinking guide, and helps a writer focus a topic and develop supporting details to make a specific point. Likewise, effective use of a pattern of organization helps the reader to understand and remember the writer's point. Once you understand a few basic patterns of organization, you can choose the best pattern to clearly present your ideas in a paragraph. This chapter explores nine basic patterns of organization to help you write with clarity and power.

Most of us look for patterns to help make sense of information. For example, study the photographs about working puzzles. In the spaces provided, answer the questions about the photographs. Then, answer the question "What's the point of using patterns of organization to develop paragraphs?"

WRITING
FROM LIFE

How would you use patterns to start a puzzle?

_____

_____

_____

How would you rely on patterns to join puzzle pieces?

_____

_____

_____

How are patterns in a puzzle used to create the bigger picture?

_____

_____

_____

How is working a puzzle similar to writing a paragraph?

_____

_____

What's the point of using a pattern of organization to develop your paragraph?

_____

_____

_____

L2 Write a Descriptive Paragraph

A description is an account that creates a powerful mental image. The writer uses sensory details such as sights, sounds, smells, tastes, feelings, and textures to create vivid images in the reader's mind. The writer often uses spatial order and time order to describe a person, place, object, or scene.

What's the Point of Description?

Getting a mental picture of the person, place, object, or scene helps a writer discover the point of the description. Study the following set of photographs of Eagle Rock at Topanga State Park in Los Angeles, California. Fill in each blank with a caption that best describes each part of Eagle Rock. Then, state in one sentence an overall main idea by answering the question "What's the point or impression you would make by describing the park?"

Practice 2

PHOTOGRAPHIC ORGANIZER: DESCRIPTION

The following pictures represent one student's effort to prepare to learn about writing. Write a caption for each photograph that identifies her efforts to prepare to learn.

Which signal word(s) describe this view?

_____

What are the sensory details?

_____

Which signal word(s) describe this view?

_____

What are the sensory details?

_____

Which signal word(s) describe this view?

_____

What are the sensory details?

_____

What's the point?

_____

One Student Writer's Response

The following descriptive paragraph offers one writer's point about Eagle Rock. Read this description and the explanations. Then, complete the activities in **bold** type given in the annotations.

Well Worth the Effort

(1) Located at the top of a hiking trail in Los Angeles' Topanga State Park, Eagle Rock offers a quiet place of rest and a spectacular view. (2) Eagle Rock is a boulder outcropping. (3) Centuries of weather have worn away some of its sandstone to create a shady cave of rest. (4) On the outside, the cave looks like part of a craggy skull with two empty eye sockets. (5) These sockets act as doors that allow the hiker to see and go through to the other side. (6) Inside, the cave is cool, the ground is smooth, and the walls are decorated with the colorful graffiti of previous hikers. (7) Beyond the cave, the wide-open view inspires awe. (8) Miles and miles of green tree tops rise and fall to reveal the peaks and valleys of the mountains below. (9) In the distance, the blue mountains line the horizon. (10) Eagle Rock is well worth the effort it takes to rest in its cave and enjoy its view.

Main Idea: The main idea is the point the writer is making. The topic is "Eagle Rock." **Underline the writer's point.**

Relevant Details: Relevant details describe the scene to support the writer's point. **Underline another major detail that supports the writer's point.**

Spatial Order: The phrase "on the outside" states spatial order. **Circle three more words or phrases that indicate spatial order.**

Effective Expression: Sensory details, like "cool," create a visual mental picture. **Place a check mark above 4 more sensory details.**

Writing Assignments

MyWritingLab™ Complete this Exercise on mywritinglab.com

Considering Audience and Purpose

Study the photographs in the photographic organizer. Assume you have joined a group to keep Topanga State Park open. Write a letter to the editor of a newspaper that describes the park's beauty.

Writing for Everyday Life

Assume you have cleaned out your home and are having a "virtual garage sale." Write a paragraph to post online that describes the most treasured or valuable possession you are selling.

Writing for College Life

Assume you are taking a science class and the current unit of study is about pollution. Describe in one paragraph an instance of pollution in your area.

Writing for Working Life

Assume you are a member of the Safety Committee for a small business such as a restaurant or clothing store. Identify and describe in one paragraph a hazard that needs to be addressed for the safety of employees and customers.

Workshop: Description Graphic Organizer and Writer's Journal

Descriptive transition words signal that the details follow a logical order based on the following: (1) the way a person, place, object, or scene is arranged in space; and (2) the starting point from which the writer begins the description.

Transition Words Used to Signal Visual Description

above	at the top	beyond	farther	left	right
across	back	by	front	middle	there
adjacent	behind	center	here	nearby	under
around	below	close to	in	next to	underneath
at the bottom	beneath	down	inside	outside	within

GRAPHIC ORGANIZER: DESCRIPTION

Use the following graphic organizer to either organize the ideas you have already created or generate details to support your point. (*Hint*: Fill in the "Where" column with spatial signal words such as *left*, *right*, *near*, *far*, *above*.)

Concept Chart: Description					
Topic:					
What's the point?					
Where	**Sight**	**Smell**	**Sound**	**Taste**	**Touch**

Review

WRITER'S JOURNAL FOR A DESCRIPTIVE PARAGRAPH

Use the following form to record your thinking about writing a descriptive paragraph.

 What is your point?

TOPIC, PERSON, PLACE, OBJECT, OR SCENE: ....

AUDIENCE: ....

PURPOSE: ....

State your main idea in a topic sentence.

Generate relevant details.

DETAILS BASED ON REPORTER'S QUESTIONS: WHO, WHAT, WHEN, WHERE, WHY, AND HOW? ....

....

Generate spatial and sensory details.

LOCATION (TOP, MIDDLE, BOTTOM, LEFT, RIGHT): ....

SIGHT, SMELL, SOUND, TASTE, TOUCH: ....

Use logical order. Use transition words to signal organization of details and relationships between ideas.

SPACE ORDER: ....

TIME ORDER: ....

Use effective expression. Proofread to eliminate errors.

ERRORS NOTED: ....

....

WRITER'S JOURNAL FOR A DESCRIPTIVE PARAGRAPH

L3 Write a Narrative Paragraph

Narration is an account of events told in chronological order to make a specific point. A narrative tells a story. To make a point by telling a story, a writer relies on relevant sensory details and time order. Time order is the logical sequence of events as they occur in time. Each event in a narrative is developed by describing the individual actions and details that make up the event.

What's the Point of Narration?

Getting a mental picture of an event helps a writer to discover the point he or she wishes to make. The following sequence of photographs documents a challenging kayak trip. Study each photograph in the timeline. Write a caption that states the action in each picture. Answer the question, "What's the point?" with a one-sentence statement of the overall main idea.

Practice 3

PHOTOGRAPHIC ORGANIZER: NARRATION

FIRST EVENT

▲ *Sea Kayaker at Sunset*

What happened?

_____

_____

SECOND EVENT

▲ *Sea Kayaker Paddling Through Waves*

What happened?

_____

_____

THIRD EVENT

▲ *Sea Kayaker Paddling Toward Islands*

What happened?

_____

_____

FOURTH EVENT

▲ *Sunrise*

What happened?

_____

_____

What's the point?

_____

One Student Writer's Response

The following paragraph offers one writer's narrative of her kayak trip. Read this narrative; then, read the explanations. Then, complete the activities in **bold** type given in the annotations.

My First Time Kayaking: A Long, Hard Night

(1) My first time in a kayak was unlike most kayaking trips. (2) An 8 mile, 3 hour kayak trip turned into ten hours of my most difficult challenge yet. (3) The sun had been sinking most of the time we were in the water. (4) There was a 30 mph wind, tall chop, and a strong current caused by a cold front moving in. (5) When the sun sank below the horizon, I got scared, turned at the wrong marker, and got us lost in a bay. (6) To get out, we circled the edges of the bay—hoping and searching for an opening that would lead back to the channel. (7) Hours later, we made it out. (8) Maybe we could have tied up to some of the mangroves and rested in our wet kayaks, but the cold air threatened hypothermia if we didn't keep moving. (9) Suddenly, the moon shown for a moment, revealing a silver strip straight ahead; it was beach! (10) Even though I had hit exhaustion hours ago, I paddled like there was a motor on my boat. (11) I have never felt so strong or helpless or happy to stand as I did that night. (12) The next day, we awoke with the sunrise to a remote paradise, untouched by most.

Main Idea:
The main idea is the point of the narration. The topic is a "kayak trip." **Underline the author's point.**

Relevant Details:
Relevant details describe the point about how challenging the trip was. **Underline another detail about the challenges she faced.**

Effective Expression:
In a narrative, effective expression often uses sensory details to describe the experience. **Place a check mark above three more sensory details.**

Chronological Order:
Time order is established with the word "when." **Circle three more words or phrases that indicate time order.**

Writing Assignments

MyWritingLab™
Complete this Exercise on mywritinglab.com

Considering Audience and Purpose

Study the photographs in the photographic organizer. Assume you are the historian of a local kayaking club. Write a narrative paragraph that documents a recent kayaking trip for the club's blog.

Writing for Everyday Life

Assume someone you know is receiving an award for accomplishing a good deed. You have been asked to present the award at a community banquet. To prepare for your speech, write a narrative paragraph that identifies the person and describes the good deed.

Writing for College Life

Assume you are taking a history class. Write a narrative paragraph about an event in the life of a person who has shaped history.

Writing for Working Life

Assume you are applying for a promotion. Write a paragraph that illustrates your strengths as a worker.

Workshop: Narrative Graphic Organizer and Writer's Journal

Time order transitions show the flow of events as they unfold in the narrative.

Transition Words Used to Show Time Order

after	during	later	previously	ultimately
afterward	eventually	meanwhile	second	until
as	finally	next	since	when
before	first	now	soon	while
currently	last	often	then	

GRAPHIC ORGANIZER: NARRATIVE

Use the following graphic organizer to either organize ideas you have already created or generate details to support your point.

What's the point?

TOPIC SENTENCE: _____

_____

_____

_____

What happened?

1

2

3

4

5

Review

WRITER'S JOURNAL FOR A NARRATIVE PARAGRAPH

Use the following form to record your thinking about writing a narrative paragraph.

PREWRITING DRAFTING   What is your point?

TOPIC, SITUATION, OR EVENT: ....

AUDIENCE: ....

PURPOSE: ....

PREWRITING DRAFTING   State your main idea in a topic sentence.

....

....

PREWRITING DRAFTING   Generate relevant details.

SENSORY DETAILS BASED ON REPORTER'S QUESTIONS: WHO, WHAT, WHEN, WHERE, WHY, AND HOW?

....

....

PREWRITING DRAFTING REVISING   Use logical order. Use transition words to signal organization of details and relationships between ideas.

SPACE ORDER: ....

TIME ORDER: ....

REVISING PROOFREADING   Use effective expression. Proofread to eliminate errors.

ERRORS NOTED: ....

....

....

L4 Write a Process Paragraph

A process is a series of steps, occurring in chronological order. A process shows how to do something or how something works. A process may also describe the phases, stages, or cycle of a recurring event such as the phases of the moon or the stages of grief. To describe a process, a writer uses chronological order (also called time order) and relevant concrete details.

What's the Point of Process?

Visualizing a process helps a writer discover his or her point about the procedure. The following sequence of photographs documents a series of steps to make a veggie breakfast wrap. Study each photograph in the timeline. Write a caption that briefly describes each step.

Practice 4

PHOTOGRAPHIC ORGANIZER: PROCESS

FIRST STEP

SECOND STEP

THIRD STEP

FOURTH STEP

FIFTH STEP

SIXTH STEP

One Student Writer's Response

Read the following paragraph written by student writer Hannah Davis that describes her way of making a healthy breakfast wrap. Read the process and the explanations. Then, complete the activities in **bold** type in the annotations.

A Heart Healthy Veggie Breakfast Wrap

(1) Consider taking just a few minutes to have a hearty meal without the hassle of standing over the stove for hours. (2) This easy to make veggie breakfast wrap gives breakfast a whole new twist without the added fat and calories. (3) To make a heart healthy veggie wrap just follow these easy steps. (4) First, gather the following items and place them on the kitchen counter: one large skillet, a carton of egg white substitute, 1 small can of tomatoes (or one Roma tomato), 2 medium chopped Bella mushrooms, one cup of shredded mozzarella cheese, 1/4 cup of diced onion, 1 teaspoon of olive oil, and one 10-inch whole wheat tortilla. (5) After collecting the ingredients, pour 1 teaspoon olive oil in the large skillet. (6) Then, place the skillet on the stovetop and set the temperature at medium-high heat. (7) Once the skillet is hot, add the 1/4 cup diced onion and cook for about 2 minutes until the onions begin to caramelize; make sure to stir frequently. (8) Next, add the chopped mushrooms and let simmer for an additional minute. (9) While the mushrooms and onions are cooking down, open the small can of tomatoes and drain (dice the Roma tomato if using this instead)—add the tomatoes to the onion and mushroom mixture. (10) After adding the tomato, pour 4 tablespoons of the egg white substitute into the skillet. (11) Stir the mixture until the entire egg white substitute is fluffy. (12) Now, it is time to assemble your heart healthy breakfast burrito. (13) Turn off the stove and set the skillet aside—sprinkle shredded mozzarella cheese on top and let the cheese melt on its own. (14) Meanwhile, warm the whole wheat tortilla in the microwave on a paper towel for 10 seconds. (15) For the final step, after tortilla is warm, place all of egg mixture into tortilla, and simply roll it up. (16) This quick and easy healthy breakfast burrito is both filling and good for your heart.

Effective Expression: The writer describes this process as "easy to make." **Place a check mark above three more words or phrases that describe this recipe as "easy to make."**

Main Idea: The main idea is the point the writer is making. The topic is "make a veggie wrap." **Underline the writer's point.**

Chronological Order: The transition "First" indicates time order. **Circle four more time order transitions.**

Adequate Details: The writer is describing the steps to make a veggie wrap. **Number each step by writing a number above the first word of each step.**

Writing Assignments

MyWritingLab™
Complete this Exercise on mywritinglab.com

Considering Audience and Purpose

Study the photographs in the photographic organizer. Assume you downloaded the writer's instructions from the website "Easy Recipes" and tried to make the dish, but it was not as easy as it sounded. Write a letter to the author, describing the problems you faced in each step.

Writing for Everyday Life

Assume you are in regular conflict with someone about whom you care deeply. To put a stop to the cycle of arguing, write a one-paragraph letter to that person; explain three steps you both can take to resolve conflict before, during, and after it happens.

Writing for College Life

Assume you have not done as well as you would like on an exam for a college class, such as Algebra, Biology, or English. Your professor has asked you to write a one-paragraph journal entry about the steps you took to study for the exam, and what additional steps you could take to master information.

Writing for Working Life

Assume you are the manager at a local grocery store. You have received several complaints from customers about the way most of your employees bag their groceries. Write a one-paragraph memo that describes the proper procedure to bag groceries.

Workshop: Process Graphic Organizer and Writer's Journal

A process describes the individual actions that make up each step or phase within the process. Time order words show the flow of events as the process unfolds. Strong transitions establish coherence—a clear and understandable flow of ideas.

Transition Words Used to Show Time Order

after	during	later	previously	ultimately
afterward	eventually	meanwhile	second	until
as	finally	next	since	when
before	first	now	soon	while
currently	last	often	then	

Workshop 3

GRAPHIC ORGANIZER: PROCESS

Use the following graphic organizer to either organize the ideas you have already created or generate details to support your point.

What's the point?

TOPIC SENTENCE: ....

....

....

What is happening?

First Step

Second Step

Third Step

Fourth Step

Review

Use the following form to record your thinking about writing a process paragraph.

PREWRITING DRAFTING   **What is your point?**

TOPIC, PROCESS OF STEPS OR PHASES: ....

AUDIFNCE: ....

PURPOSE: ....

PREWRITING DRAFTING   **State your main idea in a topic sentence.**

....

....

PREWRITING DRAFTING   **Generate relevant details.**

DETAILS BASED ON REPORTER'S QUESTIONS: WHO, WHAT, WHEN, WHERE, WHY, AND HOW? ....

....

....

....

PREWRITING DRAFTING REVISING   **Use logical order. Use transition words to signal organization of details and relationships between ideas.**

SPACE ORDER: ....

TIME ORDER: ....

REVISING PROOFREADING   **Use effective expression. Proofread to eliminate errors.**

ERRORS NOTED: ....

....

....

L5 Write an Example Paragraph

An example, also called an exemplification, is a specific illustration of a more general idea. An exemplification illustrates a main point with one or more examples. To exemplify a point, a writer lists examples, often according to the order of importance, and explains each example with relevant details.

What's the Point of Example?

Generating and organizing examples helps a writer to discover his or her point about a particular topic. Study the following photographs that illustrate one soldier's view of Iraq at night. Then, answer the question, "What's the point?" with a one-sentence statement of the overall main idea.

Practice 5

PHOTOGRAPHIC ORGANIZER: EXAMPLE

TOPIC

A Soldier's Night in Iraq

FIRST EXAMPLE

What does this illustrate?

_____

_____

SECOND EXAMPLE

What does this illustrate?

_____

_____

THIRD EXAMPLE

What does this illustrate?

_____

_____

_____

FOURTH EXAMPLE

What does this illustrate?

_____

_____

What's the point?

_____

One Student Writer's Response

The following paragraph by student writer Joshua Hartzell offers his view as a soldier of Iraq at night. Read his example paragraph and the explanations. Then, complete the activities in **bold** type given in the annotations.

A Soldier's Night

(1) Night time was the best time to work in the Iraq desert. (2) Unlike the day, at night Iraq was very cool, or at least it seemed that way after the one hundred plus degree days, beautiful, and even seemed peaceful. (3) For example, at night it was comfortable to wear all of the equipment that the army said we needed in order to look professional, as well as protect ourselves from the unknown dangers that came along with combat. (4) I loved the night patrol shifts. (5) For instance, every night after getting up and putting on my flak jacket and Kevlar helmet wrapped in desert colors, I picked up my M249 machine gun, lovingly referred to as "the saw," and walked to the hummer to meet with my assigned team. (6) As I stood behind my weapon in the military hummer, I could look up and see the stars that outnumbered the world population without the disruption of street lights. (7) At night, everything seemed beautiful. (8) For example, the Euphrates River that was drying up in the desert, and was anything but beautiful during the day was a wonder to look at during the night in the glow of the moon and stars. (9) Another example was the sight of tracer rounds from gunfire as rival clans fought with each other in the distance over their beliefs and differences. (10) In a way it almost reminded me of fireworks on the fourth of July. (11) Everything seemed so distant and peaceful at night.

Main Idea: The main idea is the writer's point about a topic. The topic "is Iraq at night." **Underline the writer's point.**

Effective Expression: To make his point about Iraq at night, the writer uses vivid descriptions and sensory details. **Place a check mark above two more vivid descriptions or sensory details.**

Example Transitions: The phrase "for example" is a transition that links a general statement to an example. **Circle three more transitional phrases that signal example.**

Relevant Details: Many of the details are examples of events or scenes that occur at night. **Underline two more details that are nighttime events or scenes.**

Writing Assignments

MyWritingLab™ Complete this Exercise on mywritinglab.com

Considering Audience and Purpose

Study the photographs about Iraq at night. Assume you are a friend or close relative of Joshua Hartzell or another soldier serving in a foreign country. Write a letter in response to his paragraph. Share your feelings or thoughts prompted by the images about his service, or the service of a soldier you know, to the country. Give examples.

Writing for Everyday Life

Assume that a person you know is facing a difficult time and needs to be encouraged. Write a one-paragraph letter of encouragement. Offer examples of other people who have overcome difficulties.

Writing for College Life

Assume you are taking a health course and the focus of the current unit of study is nutrition, obesity, and fast food in America. Write a one-paragraph report that offers examples of healthy fast food for those who are concerned about nutrition and weight control.

Writing for Working Life

Assume you are applying for a job as a firefighter. The job posting listed the following requirements: the ability to work as a team member and good communication skills. Write a one-paragraph letter of application. Include examples of how you fulfill these requirements.

Workshop: Example Graphic Organizer and Writer's Journal

A writer uses transitions to signal or list examples. Strong transitions establish coherence—a clear and understandable flow of ideas.

Transitions Used to Signal Examples

an illustration	for instance	once	to illustrate
for example	including	such as	typically

Transitions Used to List Examples

also	final	for one thing	last of all	second
and	finally	furthermore	moreover	third
another	first	in addition	next	
beside	first of all	last	one	

Workshop 4

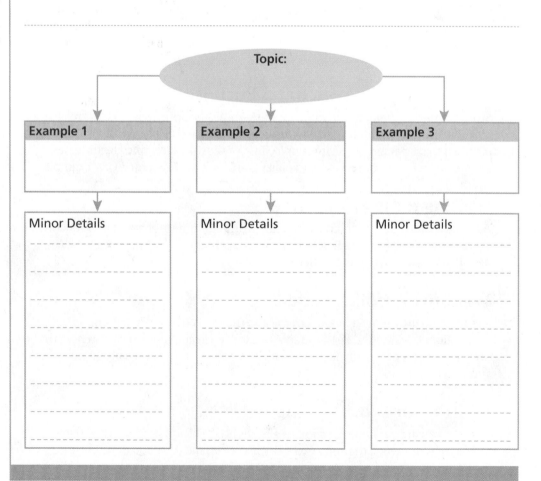

GRAPHIC ORGANIZER: EXAMPLE

Use the following graphic organizer to either organize ideas you have already created or generate details to support your point.

What's the point?

....

Topic:

Example 1	Example 2	Example 3

Minor Details	Minor Details	Minor Details

WRITER'S JOURNAL FOR AN EXAMPLE PARAGRAPH

Use the following form to record your thinking about writing an example paragraph.

What is your point?

TOPIC, EXAMPLES: ....

AUDIENCE: ....

PURPOSE: ....

State your main idea in a topic sentence.

Generate relevant details.

DETAILS BASED ON REPORTER'S QUESTIONS: WHO, WHAT, WHEN, WHERE, AND HOW? ....

CONCRETE EXAMPLES: ....

Use logical order. Use transition words to signal organization of details and relationships between ideas.

TRANSITIONS TO SIGNAL EXAMPLES: ....

TRANSITIONS TO LIST EXAMPLES: ....

Use effective expression. Proofread to eliminate errors.

ERRORS NOTED: ....

L6 6 Write a Classification Paragraph

A classification is a division of a topic into one or more subgroups. To support a point through classification, a writer divides a topic into subgroups based on common traits or principles, and then offers relevant concrete details of description and examples.

What's the Point of Classification?

Identifying and labeling groups or types helps a writer to discover his or her point about a particular topic. Study the following set of photographs. In the spaces provided (1) identify the type of music represented by each photograph. (2) Identify the traits of each type of music. Then, answer the question, "What's the point?" with a one-sentence statement of the overall main idea.

PHOTOGRAPHIC ORGANIZER: CLASSIFICATION

TYPES OF MUSIC

1st type

2nd type

3rd type

Type of music:

....

Traits:

....

....

Examples:

....

Type of music:

....

Traits:

....

....

Examples:

....

Type of music:

....

Traits:

....

....

Examples:

....

What's the point?

....

....

One Student Writer's Response

The following classification paragraph offers student writer Evan Praetorius's point about the types of music. Read this classification paragraph and the explanations. Then complete the activities in **bold** type given in the annotations.

Three Types of Music

(1) People enjoy listening to the types of music that most appeal to them. (2) Classical, Jazz, and Rock are three major types of music, each with distinct sounds, styles, and traits. (3) The first major type, classical music, is easily recognized by its use of classical instruments such as violins or clarinets and generally follows a classic structure. (4) People enjoy listening to classical music for the complex harmonies, rich history, and stirring movement. (5) Some subgroups include the ornamental baroque forms of Vivaldi and Bach or the more emotional romantic style of Beethoven and Schubert. (6) The second major type of music, jazz uses a mixture of classic and more contemporary instruments, such as the saxophone. (7) The style of jazz is more fluid and uses improvisation. (8) Drawn to its groovy sound, people listen to Jazz for anything from dancing to relaxation. (9) Two types of jazz are the upbeat danceable music of swing jazz by Duke Ellington and Count Basie and the more jarring and chromatic style of Charlie Parker and Thelonious Monk's bebop. (10) The third major type, rock music, is marked by using mostly electronic instruments and simple, catchy beats and harmonies. (11) Traits people enjoy in rock music are its catchy rhythms, harmonies, and lyrics. (12) Two styles of rock music are the blues inspired songs of Led Zeppelin and more pop influenced bands like Coldplay. (13) Many may argue about which type of music is best. (14) Ultimately, the best type of music is the kind that gives the listener the most enjoyment.

Main Idea:
The main idea is the writer's point about a topic. The topic is "types of music." **Underline the writer's point.**

Strong Transitions:
The transitional phrase "first major type" signals that ideas are organized by classification. **Circle two more transitional phrases that signal classification.**

Effective Expression:
The phrase "stirring movement" states an emotional appeal of classical music. **Place a check mark over two other phrases that state the emotional appeal of a type of music.**

Relevant Details:
The writer includes subgroups for each of the three major types of music. **Underline a subgroup of jazz and rock music.**

Writing Assignments

MyWritingLab™
Complete this Exercise on mywritinglab.com

Considering Audience and Purpose

Study the photographs about music. Assume you are a music critic. Write a review for a piece of music that you like or dislike. Identify it by type and discuss its traits.

Writing for Everyday Life

Assume you are shopping for a new car. To prepare for your purchase, write a one-paragraph entry in your personal journal that describes the kind of car you want, based on the kind of lifestyle you lead.

Writing for College Life

Assume you are a member of the Student Government Association at your college, and you are in charge of increasing student participation in campus activities. Write a one-paragraph article for the college's newspaper that describes several types of activities available to students.

Writing for Working Life

Assume you are an office manager, and it is time to submit a budget for equipment and supplies. Write a one-paragraph memo to request the type of equipment and supplies you need for each type of office task.

Workshop: Classification Graphic Organizer and Writer's Journal

To make a point using classification, a writer uses transitions to signal or list the groups, types, or traits. Strong transitions establish coherence—a clear and understandable flow of ideas.

Words That Are Used to Signal Groups, Types, or Traits

aspect	category	classify	ideal	rank	trait
attribute	characteristic	collection	kind	section	type
branch	class	division	level	set	typical
brand	classification	group	quality	style	

Transitions That Combine with Signal Words to List Groups, Types, or Traits

also	another	finally	for one thing	in addition	moreover	third
and	final	first	furthermore	last of all	second	

Workshop 5

GRAPHIC ORGANIZER: CLASSIFICATION

Use the following graphic organizer to either organize ideas you have already created or generate details to support your point.

Types (groups) of

1st Type/group	2nd Type/group	3rd Type/group
Traits:	Traits:	Traits:
Examples:	Examples:	Examples:

What's the point?

WRITER'S JOURNAL FOR A CLASSIFICATION PARAGRAPH

Use the following form to record your thoughts about writing a classification paragraph.

  What is your point?

TOPIC, GROUPS, TYPES, TRAITS: ....

AUDIENCE: ....

PURPOSE: ....

State your main idea in a topic sentence.

....

....

Generate relevant details.

DETAILS BASED ON REPORTER'S QUESTIONS: WHO, WHAT, WHEN, WHERE, AND HOW? ....

....

SUBGROUPS (USE VIVID LABELS FOR EACH GROUP): ....

TYPES: ....

TRAITS: ....

Use logical order. Use transition words to signal organization of details and relationships between ideas.

TRANSITIONS TO LIST SUBGROUPS, TYPES, OR TRAITS: ....

TRANSITIONS TO SIGNAL EXAMPLES: ....

Use effective expression. Proofread to eliminate errors.

ERRORS NOTED: ....

....

L7 Write a Comparison and Contrast Paragraph

A comparison makes a point by discussing the similarities between two or more topics. A contrast makes a point by discussing the differences between two or more topics. To support a point through comparison or contrast, a writer identifies the comparable points of the topic and gives concrete descriptions and examples for each comparable point.

What's the Point of Comparison and Contrast?

Often ideas become clearer when they are studied based on how they relate to one another. The following set of photographs shows the differences between two southern landmarks: the Lighthouse Pier and visitor's center in Biloxi, Mississippi, and the Superdome, in New Orleans, Louisiana before and after they were hit by Hurricane Katrina. Study the set of images. Write a caption that describes each comparable point. Then, state in one sentence an overall main idea by answering the question "What's the point about the before-and-after images of the landmarks?"

Practice 7

PHOTOGRAPHIC ORGANIZER: COMPARISON AND CONTRAST

SIMILAR TO OR DIFFERENT FROM

BEFORE HURRICANE

AFTER HURRICANE

SIMILAR TO OR DIFFERENT FROM

BEFORE HURRICANE

AFTER HURRICANE

What's the point?

One Student Writer's Response

The following paragraph offers one writer's point about the differences in the two landmarks before and after they were hit by Hurricane Katrina. Read the paragraph and the annotations. Then, complete the activities in **bold** type given in the annotations.

The Devastating Differences

(1) The difference between two landmarks before and after they were hit by Hurricane Katrina reveal the devastating power of the storm. (2) Before the hurricane, locals and visitors enjoyed fun and beautiful landmarks such as the pristine visitor center and boardwalk at Lighthouse Pier, and the grand Superdome arena. (3) In shocking contrast, these same two structures after the hurricane stood in ruins. (4) The Lighthouse Pier and Visitor Center were completely washed away. (5) Likewise, the force of the rushing winds broke and peeled the Superdome's roof, which was built to withstand 200 mph winds. (6) The destruction was so severe that light from outside can be seen pouring to the arena from above. (7) Before the hurricane, these two landmarks attracted large and profitable crowds. (8) In contrast, after the hurricane, these two beloved landmarks were no longer able to host their many visitors. (9) Instead, only empty spaces, destruction, and debris remain.

Main Idea:
The main idea is the point the writer is making about the "two landmarks." **Circle the two ideas being compared and contrasted, and underline the writer's point.**

Logical Order:
Words of comparison or contrast signal similarities or differences. **Draw a box around three more transitions of comparison and contrast.**

Effective Expression:
Sensory details help the reader see the writer's point. **Place a check mark above two more sensory details.**

Relevant Details:
Relevant details include descriptive details about similarities or differences between comparable points. **Underline two more details of similarities or differences.**

Writing Assignments

MyWritingLab™
Complete this Exercise on mywritinglab.com

Considering Audience and Purpose

Study the photographs about the differences between the Biloxi, Mississippi, Lighthouse Pier and the Louisiana Superdome before and after Hurricane Katrina. Identify a landmark in your community that needs to be restored. You plan to help raise money for the effort, and you need to attract donors. Write a paragraph describing how you would want to rebuild the landmark. Discuss how it will be better or safer then the original building.

Writing for Everyday Life

Assume your family is shopping for a product such as a cell phone. You have done some research comparing products and prices. Write a one-paragraph e-mail to your family members summing up the similarities and differences in price and features between two cell phones (or product of your choice).

Writing for College Life

Assume you are taking a college psychology class, and you are studying human emotions. Write a paragraph about the differences between infatuation and love.

Writing for Working Life

Assume you own a small business, such as a computer repair shop. You need to hire highly skilled workers, but you are competing against large corporations like Best Buy for employees. Write a one-paragraph advertisement that contrasts the benefits of working with a small firm over a large corporation.

Workshop: Comparison and Contrast Graphic Organizer and Writer's Journal

Words That Signal Comparison

alike	equally	just like	likewise	similar(ly)
as	just as	like	same	similarity

Words That Signal Contrast

although	despite	even though	nevertheless	still
at the same time	difference	in contrast	on the one hand	unlike
but	different(ly)	instead	on the other hand	yet

GRAPHIC ORGANIZER: COMPARISON AND CONTRAST

Use the following graphic organizer to either organize the ideas you have already created or generate details to support your point.

CONCEPT CHART: COMPARISON/CONTRAST				
Comparable topics:	**Topic A**	**Like or unlike**		**Topic B**
1st attribute, point, basis of comparison		Like or unlike		
2nd attribute, point, basis of comparison		Like or unlike		
3rd attribute, point, basis of comparison		Like or unlike		

What's the point?

_____

_____

Review

WRITER'S JOURNAL FOR A COMPARISON AND CONTRAST PARAGRAPH

Use the following form to record your thinking about writing a comparison or contrast paragraph.

 What is your point?

TWO (OR MORE) COMPARABLE TOPICS: ....

AUDIENCE: ....

PURPOSE: ....

State your main idea in a topic sentence.

....

....

Generate relevant details.

DETAILS BASED ON REPORTER'S QUESTIONS: WHO, WHAT, WHEN, WHERE, AND HOW? ....

....

POINTS OF SIMILARITIES: ....

POINTS OF DIFFERENCE: ....

Use logical order. Use transition words to signal organization of details and relationships between ideas.

TRANSITIONS OF COMPARISON: ....

TRANSITIONS OF CONTRAST: ....

Use effective expression. Proofread to eliminate errors.

ERRORS NOTED: ....

....

....

L8 Write a Definition Paragraph

A definition explains what a word or concept means. A definition makes a point by classifying a concept, describing its traits, describing what it is not like, and illustrating it with examples.

What's the Point of Definition?

The following definition-concept map shows three visual examples of a concept and one visual example of what the concept is not. Study the chart and the visual examples. Write answers to the questions in the chart. Then, answer the question, "What's the point?" with a one-sentence statement of the overall main idea.

PHOTOGRAPHIC ORGANIZER: DEFINITION

WHAT IS BEING DEFINED?

WHAT IT IS NOT?

WHAT ARE THE TRAITS OF THESE EXAMPLES?

Traits? _____

Traits? _____

Traits? _____

What's the point?

_____

_____

_____

_____

One Student Writer's Response

The following paragraph offers one writer's point about the concept depicted in the photographic organizer. Read the definition and the paragraph's annotations. Complete the activities in **bold** type in the annotations.

The Master Student

(1) To get the most from the cost of a college education, every student should strive to be a master student. (2) A master student is an active learner who plans for success. (3) First, a master student is actively involved in the classroom. (4) This student attends class regularly, listens, takes notes, and asks questions. (5) Additionally, being a master student means working on assignments outside of class. (6) Sometimes homework requires independent work; other times, study groups are more effective and enjoyable. (7) Another trait of a master student is the ability to manage time wisely by creating a study plan; the master student makes a calendar that includes study times and due dates for each class. (8) Most importantly, a master student is not a cheater. (9) This student does not copy homework or cheat on exams. (10) A master student refuses to cheat herself or her classmates by looking for easy shortcuts that undercut a good education.

Main Idea: The main idea states the writer's point about a concept. The concept being defined is a "master student." **Underline the writer's point about the concept.**

Listing Order: The transition "First" indicates a list of traits and examples. **Circle two other transitions that introduce supporting details.**

Relevant Details: Relevant details include descriptive details about traits and examples. **Underline two additional traits of a master student.**

Effective Expression: The use of active verbs makes a definition more interesting to read. **Place a check mark above two more active verbs.**

Writing Assignments

MyWritingLab™ Complete this Exercise on mywritinglab.com

Considering Audience and Purpose

Study the set of photographs about the master student. Assume you have been invited to speak to a group of teenagers about the value of higher education. Write a paragraph that defines the value of education.

Writing for Everyday Life

Assume a friend of yours has given you assistance or encouragement. Write a one-paragraph thank you note to your friend. In your note, define the concept of "an excellent friend" and explain how your friend exemplifies the concept.

Writing for College Life

Assume you are taking a college government course, and you are currently studying the role of the President in the United States government. Write a paragraph that defines the role of the President of the United States.

Writing for Working Life

Assume you are ready to start your career, and you are creating a resume and general cover letter that you can easily revise to fit a specific job opportunity. Write a paragraph that defines you as a worker, or define the ideal job that you are seeking.

Workshop: Definition Graphic Organizer and Writer's Journal

Strong signal words establish coherence—a clear and understandable flow of ideas.

Key Words That Signal Definition

are	defined as	is	means
consists of	indicates	is not	suggests

Transitions That Signal Definition

also	for example	in particular	one trait
another trait	in addition	like	such as

Workshop 7

GRAPHIC ORGANIZER: DEFINITION

Use the following graphic organizer to either organize ideas you have already created or generate ideas to support your main point.

What is being defined?

What it is NOT

Trait:

Example:

Trait:

Example:

What's the point?

Trait:

Example:

Review

WRITER'S JOURNAL FOR A DEFINITION PARAGRAPH

Use the following form to record your thinking about writing a definition paragraph.

What is your point?

CONCEPT TO BE DEFINED: ....

AUDIENCE: ....

PURPOSE: ....

State your main idea in a topic sentence.

....

....

Generate relevant details.

DETAILS BASED ON REPORTER'S QUESTIONS: WHO, WHAT, WHEN, WHERE, AND HOW? ....

....

TRAITS OF THE CONCEPT: ....

WHAT THE CONCEPT IS NOT: ....

EXAMPLES OF THE CONCEPT: ....

Use logical order. Use transition words to signal organization of details and relationships between ideas.

TRANSITIONS OF COMPARISON: ....

TRANSITIONS OF CONTRAST: ....

Use effective expression. Proofread to eliminate errors.

ERRORS NOTED: ....

....

Practice 9

L9 Write a Cause and Effect Paragraph

A cause and effect paragraph makes a point by discussing the reasons and results among a set of events, objects, or factors. To support a point through cause and effect, a writer tests each reason and result to separate true causes and effects from coincidence.

What's the Point of Cause and Effect?

Often ideas become clearer when they are thought about based on how they relate to one another. Study the images and write captions that identify the cause and effect relationships shown by the photographs. Answer the question, "What's the point?" with a one-sentence statement of the overall main idea.

PHOTOGRAPHIC ORGANIZER: CAUSE AND EFFECT

CAUSE

EFFECT

EFFECT

EFFECT

What's the point?

One Student Writer's Response

The following paragraph offers one writer's point about the positive benefits of owning a dog. Read the paragraph and the annotations. Then, complete the activities in **bold** type in the annotations.

Good Reasons to Adopt a Dog

(1) Some experts say that around 6 million dogs will die this year in animal shelters in the United States, yet these dogs have much to offer would-be owners. (2) The benefits of owning a dog increase the quality of our lives. (3) One benefit of owning a dog is the companionship of a loyal friend. (4) Dogs offer unconditional love. (5) And they show their love every time we walk through our front doors. (6) Another benefit is physical exercise. (7) It is a well-known fact that even 20 minutes of walking a day improves our overall health. (8) And walking a dog makes regular exercise much more likely and enjoyable. (9) A third benefit is the protection a dog provides. (10) From large guard dogs to small lap dogs, dogs are territorial; their barks alert us to possible threats and scare away intruders. (11) Every time one of us adopts a dog from a shelter, we improve our own lives as we save theirs.

Main Idea:
The main idea is the point the writer makes about a topic. The topic is "owning a dog." **Underline the writer's point.**

Strong Transitions:
The word "one" signals an effect or benefit. **Circle two more strong transitions.**

Relevant Details:
"Companionship" is one effect. **Underline two more effects of owning a dog.**

Effective Expression:
The writer uses the first person plural pronoun to connect with the reader. **Place a check mark above all the first person pronouns.** Discuss with your classmates how the wording would change with the use of the second person "you."

Writing Assignments

MyWritingLab™
Complete this Exercise on mywritinglab.com

Considering Audience and Purpose

Study the photographs about the benefits of owning a dog. Assume you are the parent of a young person who wants to adopt a dog. Write a paragraph that describes the effects of the responsibility and limitations of pet ownership.

Writing for Everyday Life

Assume you are a person who relies on public transportation to get to school and work. The city has decided to cut back on these services. Write a one-paragraph letter to the editor of the newspaper in protest of the cutbacks. Discuss the reasons you use public transportation and the negative effect of the loss of the services.

Writing for College Life

Assume you are taking a college course on finance, and you are studying about the use of credit cards. Write a one-paragraph report that describes the benefits or dangers of using credit cards.

Writing for Working Life

Assume you are a manager for a local department store such as Wal-Mart or Target. This month's training session for your employees is about "Service with a Smile." Write a memo that explains the benefits of a positive attitude of the associates on sales.

Workshop: Cause and Effect Graphic Organizer and Writer's Journal

A writer uses transitions to signal causes, effects, and examples. Strong transitions establish coherence—a clear and understandable flow of ideas.

Transitions That Signal Cause and Effect

as a result	consequently	for that reason	leads to	since ,	thus
because of	due to	if…then	results in	so	therefore

GRAPHIC ORGANIZER: CAUSE AND EFFECT

Use the following graphic organizer to either organize the ideas you have already created or generate details to support your point.

Effect

Cause

Effect

Effect

What's the point?

Use the following form to record your thinking about writing a cause and effect paragraph.

What is your point?

CAUSES (REASONS FOR AN EVENT, OBJECTS, OR FACTOR): ....

EFFECTS (REASONS FOR AN EVENT, OBJECTS, OR FACTOR): ....

CAUSES LEADING TO EFFECTS: ....

AUDIENCE: ....

PURPOSE: ....

State your main idea in a topic sentence.

Generate relevant details.

DETAILS BASED ON REPORTER'S QUESTIONS: WHO, WHAT, WHEN, WHERE, AND HOW? ....

Use logical order. Use transition words to signal organization of details and relationships between ideas.

TRANSITIONS THAT SIGNAL CAUSES: ....

TRANSITIONS THAT SIGNAL EFFECTS: ....

Use effective expression. Proofread to eliminate errors.

ERRORS NOTED: ....

L⑩ Write a Persuasive Paragraph

To be persuasive, a writer takes a strong stand on one side of a debatable issue and then supports that stand by offering convincing reasons or supporting points. A strong stand often states and disproves an opposing point.

What's the Point of Persuasion?

The purpose of persuasion is to convince the reader to agree with a particular point or claim about a debatable topic. Persuasion is a call to action or a call to a change of mind. The following images are about "Be Green." Study the pictures and write captions for each image. Answer the question, "What's the point?" with a sentence that states a strong stand about "Be Green."

PHOTOGRAPHIC ORGANIZER: PERSUASION

SUPPORTING POINT

OPPOSING POINT

SUPPORTING POINT

DEBATABLE TOPIC

Save Planet Earth

REBUTTAL OF OPPOSING POINT

SUPPORTING POINT

What's the point or claim?

One Student Writer's Response

The following paragraph states a strong stand about saving the environment. Read the persuasive paragraph and the annotations. Then, complete the activities in **bold** type in the annotations.

Just Be Green!

(1) Several urgent conditions in our world demand that we must "be green." (2) First, did you know that currently there are over 7 billion people living on Earth? (3) And that number is expected to explode to over 9 billion by 2050. (4) As the number of people grows, so do the demands on our Earth, which brings up the second urgent reason to be green. (5) Right now, our landfills are overflowing. (6) In fact, one of the greatest threats to our future resources comes from our toxic trash. (7) For example, household batteries, chemicals, and electronic waste can leak through barriers and pollute ground and water. (8) Finally, while our population and the trash we create are growing, our natural resources are not. (9) There are only so many forests, rivers, and lakes on Earth, and once they are polluted or gone, then what will we do? (10) The critics of "green" living say that it costs too much to change. (11) It's probably true, green technology and recycling plants may be costly. (12) But saving our Earth—that's priceless!

Main Idea:
The main idea is the point or claim the writer is making about the topic. The topic is "be green." **Underline the writer's point about the topic.**

Strong Transitions:
"First" signals a reason of support. **Circle two more transitional words or phrases that signal reasons of support.**

Effective Expression:
To be persuasive, a writer uses biased words for emotional appeal. **Place a check mark above three more biased words or phrases.**

Relevant Details:
In persuasion, a writer often states and responds to an opposing point. **Underline a sentence that responds to the opposing point.**

Writing Assignments

MyWritingLab™
Complete this Exercise on mywritinglab.com

Considering Audience and Purpose

Study the set of photographs about "Be Green." Do you agree or disagree with the student author? Write a one-paragraph letter to the editor of your local newspaper that explains how one person can "be green" and make a difference.

Writing for Everyday Life

Assume the town or neighborhood you live in has decided to install security cameras in an effort to reduce crime. Take a stand either for or against the installation of the security cameras. Write a one-paragraph letter to your local officials in support or protest of this decision.

Writing for College Life

Assume your college proposes a 10% raise in tuition, and you are going to take a strong stand in a one-paragraph article for the college's newspaper: Assume you are an administrator who supports this action. Or assume you are a self-supporting student who opposes the higher tuition.

Writing for Working Life

Assume you own a business in the service industry such as a salon or a gym. You have recently relocated to an area that offered you a better deal on rent; however, most of your clients will have to travel an additional 30 minutes to your new location. Write a one-paragraph flier that convinces clients to support you in your new location.

Workshop: Persuasion Graphic Organizer and Writer's Journal

The writer's persuasive opinion is frequently signaled by biased words or phrases. These biased words qualify an idea as debatable.

Words That Signal Persuasion

all	may	must not	ought to	think
always	might	never	possibly, possible	too
believe	must	only	probably, probable	

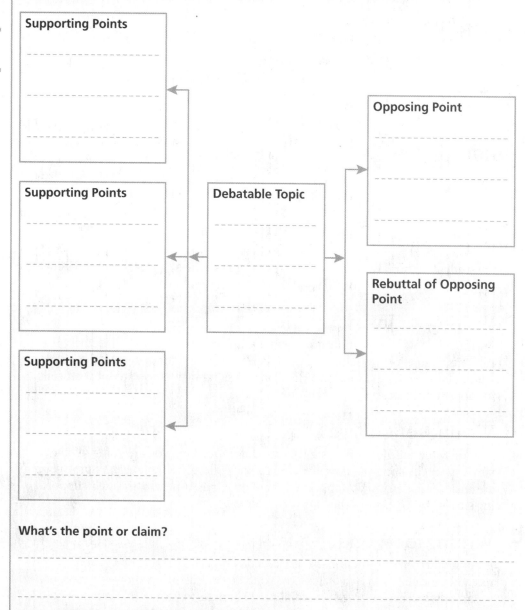

GRAPHIC ORGANIZER: PERSUASION

Use the following graphic organizer to either organize the ideas you have already created or generate details to support your point.

Supporting Points

Supporting Points

Supporting Points

Debatable Topic

Opposing Point

Rebuttal of Opposing Point

What's the point or claim?

WRITER'S JOURNAL FOR A PERSUASIVE PARAGRAPH

Use the following form to record your thinking about writing a persuasive paragraph.

 What is your point?

DEBATABLE CLAIM: ....

AUDIENCE: ....

PURPOSE: ....

 State your main idea in a topic sentence.

....

....

 Generate relevant details.

DETAILS BASED ON REPORTER'S QUESTIONS: WHO, WHAT, WHEN, WHERE, AND HOW? ....

....

OPPOSING POINTS: ....

SUPPORTS THAT REFUTE OPPOSING POINTS: ....

 Use logical order. Use transition words to signal organization of details and relationships between ideas.

TRANSITIONS THAT SIGNAL PERSUASION: ....

 Use effective expression. Proofread to eliminate errors.

ERRORS NOTED: ....

....

MyWritingLab™

Complete the Post-test for Chapter 20 in MyWritingLab.

21

LEARNING OUTCOMES

After studying this chapter, you should be able to:

L1 Answer the Question "What's the Point of Sentence Variety?"

L2 Vary Sentence Purpose

L3 Vary Sentence Types

L4 Vary Sentence Openings

Sentence Variety

Sentence variety is the use of sentences of different lengths, types, and purposes.

Communicating about a real-life situation helps us to understand the purpose of sentence variety. The photograph on the facing page illustrates a family day trip to a local landmark. Read the accompanying short paragraph about the landmark in Practice 1, complete the activities, and answer the question "What's the point of sentence variety?"

What's the Point of Sentence Variety?

LO 1

Practice 1

Read the following short paragraph. What do all the sentences have in common? Describe the overall effect of the paragraph.

The Ponce de Leon Inlet Lighthouse was built in 1884. The lighthouse is 175 feet tall. The lighthouse is the second highest lighthouse on the East Coast. The lighthouse is a very highly visited site. It has many resources. It has lots of old photographs. It has a visitor's video about its history.

What is the point of sentence variety?

WRITING
FROM LIFE

One Student Writer's Response

The following paragraph records one writer's thoughts about the point of sentence variety in the paragraph in Practice 1.

In the paragraph about the lighthouse, every sentence after the first one starts with the words "the lighthouse" or the pronoun "it," and most of the sentences use the same verbs "is" and "has." In addition, the sentences are all simple and about the same length, using four to ten words. The paragraph seems flat and dull.

Sentence variety adds interest and power to your writing. You can achieve sentence variety by varying the purposes, types, and openings of your sentences.

L2 Vary Sentence Purpose

Every sentence expresses a purpose.

For more about sentence purposes, see Chapter 17.

1. Declarative sentences make a statement to share information and are punctuated with a period. Declarative sentences are often used to state a main idea and supporting details.

A mayday call signals a life-threatening emergency.

2. Interrogative sentences ask a question and are punctuated with a question mark. Usually, the writer also provides an answer to the question. An interrogative sentence may be used to introduce a topic and lead into a topic sentence.

What is your emergency?

3. Imperative sentences give a command that demands an action and are punctuated with a period. Imperative sentences are often used to give directions to complete a process or persuade a reader to take action.

You must tell us your position.

4. Exclamatory sentences express a strong emotion and are punctuated with an exclamation point. Exclamatory sentences emphasize a significant point.

Mayday, mayday, our boat is flooding!

Most often, you will rely upon the declarative sentence to share information with your reader. However, thoughtful use of a question, command, or exclamation gives your writing variety and adds interest to your ideas.

VARY SENTENCE PURPOSE

Read the following paragraph, adapted from "Disaster by the Late Storm: Awful Shipwreck at Minot's Ledge," an 1849 newspaper article. Identify the purpose of each sentence.

Awful Shipwreck at Minot's Ledge

(1) Who can imagine such a tragedy? (2) When the Saint John struck, her small boat was got ready, but was swamped by a large number jumping into her. (3) Shortly after, the long boat broke her fastening and floated off. (4) After the ship struck the rocks, she thumped awhile. (5) But shortly she went to pieces, holding together not more than sixty minutes. (6) Seven women and three men came ashore on pieces of the wreck, alive, but very much exhausted. (7) Towards nightfall, the bodies began to come ashore, and quite a number were taken from the surf, all, however, dead. (8) Dead bodies would be thrown upon the rocks, but before they could be reached, the sea would carry them back again. (9) Ninety-nine people perished! (10) We must honor the loss of these poor souls; we must never forget this tragedy.

Practice 2

Sentence 1. _____	Sentence 6. _____
Sentence 2. _____	Sentence 7. _____
Sentence 3. _____	Sentence 8. _____
Sentence 4. _____	Sentence 9. _____
Sentence 5. _____	Sentence 10. _____

Vary Sentence Types

LO3

You learned in Chapters 5 and 6 about the four types of sentences: simple, compound, complex, and compound-complex. When writers rely on one type of sentence more than the others, their work becomes dull and flat, like a speaker delivering a speech in a monotone. As writers combine sentences, they must decide if the combined ideas are equal in importance, or if one idea is more important than another.

Coordinating ideas makes each idea equal in importance. To combine coordinate ideas, use a comma and a coordinating conjunction (FANBOYS: *for, and, nor, but, or, yet,* or *so*).

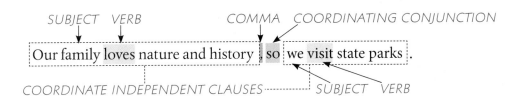

Subordinating ideas makes one idea dependent on (and less important than) another idea. To make an idea subordinate, use a subordinating conjunction (*after, although, as, because, before, since, unless,* etc.). If the new subordinate clause begins the sentence as an introductory element, include a comma at the end of that clause to set it off from the main independent clause.

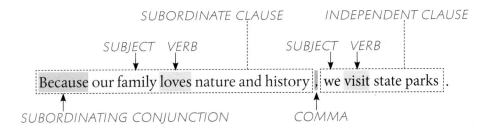

As you study methods of combining sentences, you will learn how to coordinate or subordinate ideas. To add interest and emphasis to your writing, vary the type of your sentences. Many writers use the revision process to combine sentences to achieve variety and interest.

Combine Two or More Simple Sentences into One Simple Sentence

A series of short simple sentences often creates a choppy flow of ideas. Combining closely related short simple sentences into one simple sentence creates a smooth flow of ideas. Short simple sentences can be combined in several ways.

Combine Sentences with a Compound Subject

For more about subject-verb agreement, see pages 166–185.

When two separate simple sentences possess the same verb, they can become one sentence with a compound subject. A **compound subject** is two or more nouns or pronouns joined by the coordinating conjunction **and**. Note that the verb form of a compound subject must be plural. This method of coordinating ideas places equal emphasis on each subject.

Original Sentences:

SUBJECT VERB   *SUBJECT REPEATED VERB*

Hiking is one fun activity at a state park. Kayaking is another fun activity.

Visiting museums at a state park is also fun.

SUBJECT   REPEATED VERB

Sentences Combined with a Compound Subject:

COMPOUND SUBJECTS   PLURAL VERB

Hiking, kayaking, and visiting museums are fun activities at a state park.

COMMAS   COORDINATING CONJUNCTION

Practice 3

VARY SENTENCE TYPES

Combine the following simple sentences into a new simple sentence using compound subjects. *Hint*: Delete words or reword ideas as needed to create a smooth flow of ideas.

1. The Fairchild Oak is located in Bulow State Park. The ruins of a sugar cane plantation are also in the park.

2. The 400-year-old Fairchild Oak is impressive. The Bulow ruins are also remarkable.

3. Originally, American Indians inhabited Bulow Woods. Later, Europeans inhabited the woods.

4. In the 1800s, Charles Bulow established a plantation in Bulow Woods. John Bulow had a plantation there. John Bunch also owned a plantation in Bulow. Colonel Thomas Dummett had a plantation there, too.

----

5. Indigo was one crop grown on the plantations. Sugar cane was another. Cotton was also grown in Bulow Woods.

----

6. Dr. David Fairchild, a botanist, frequently visited Bulow Woods to study its plant life. Oak Ames, from Harvard University, also studied the plant life at Bulow Woods. In addition, naturalist John Audubon made several trips to Bulow Woods to study its wildlife.

----

7. The Dummett Mill ruins remain a local landmark. The original north wall is still standing. Two chimneys are also still there.

----

8. The plantation was destroyed in 1826 by raiding Seminole Indians. The sugar mill was left in ruins. A spring house was destroyed. Slave cabins were also severely damaged.

----

9. Canoeing is a popular activity at Bulow Woods State Park. So is hiking. Visitors also enjoy picnicking and bicycling.

----

10. White-tailed deer live in Bulow Woods. Barred owls thrive in the woods. Raccoons also live there.

Practice 3

Combine Sentences with a Compound Verb

When two separate simple sentences possess the same subject, they can become one sentence with a **compound verb**, two or more verbs joined by a coordinating conjunction of addition or contrast: *and, or, but,* or *yet.* When only two verbs are joined, no comma is needed before the conjunction. This method of coordinating ideas places equal emphasis on each verb.

Original Sentences:

Stephen Crane wrote powerful stories. Stephen Crane lived a dramatic life.

Sentences Combined with a Compound Verb:

Stephen Crane wrote powerful stories and lived a dramatic life.

Practice 4

VARY SENTENCE TYPES

Combine the following simple sentences into a new simple sentence using compound verbs.

1. Crane was a journalist. Crane really wanted to report on the freedom fighters in Cuba.

----

2. Smugglers used the steam tug *Commodore* to run guns to the Cuban freedom fighters. They hired Crane as an able seaman.

----

3. On the way to Cuba, Crane's boat sank off the coast of Florida. The sinking left him adrift for several days.

----

4. The famous short story by Stephen Crane, "The Open Boat," was based on his experience of surviving the shipwreck off the coast of Florida. "The Open Boat" was published in *Scribner's Magazine.*

----

5. While in Jacksonville, Crane met Cora Taylor, the madam of a brothel. He began a lifelong relationship with her.

6. During the final years of his life, Crane covered conflicts in Greece. He also lived in England with Cora.

7. Crane suffered financial difficulties. He died of tuberculosis at the age of 29.

8. Crane never married Cora. He left her everything in his will.

9. Crane published numerous novels, poems, and short stories. He is mainly remembered for *The Red Badge of Courage*.

10. Renowned writer James Conrad hailed Crane as an innovative and gifted writer. Another famous writer, H. G. Wells, also greatly admired Crane for his innovations and talent.

Practice 4

Combine Sentences with a Phrase

A phrase is a group of related words that lacks both a subject and a verb. Because it lacks a subject and a verb, it cannot act as a sentence. A phrase acts as a single part of speech in a sentence; for example, a phrase can function as an adjective. The use of commas depends upon where the phrase appears. This sentence combination subordinates an idea by placing less emphasis on the idea in the phrase.

Original Sentences:

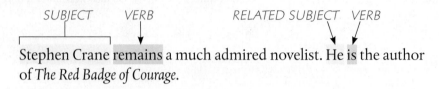

SUBJECT   VERB   RELATED SUBJECT   VERB

Stephen Crane remains a much admired novelist. He is the author of *The Red Badge of Courage.*

Revised with phrase at the beginning of sentence:

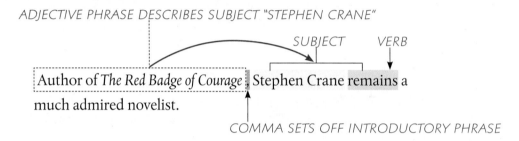

ADJECTIVE PHRASE DESCRIBES SUBJECT "STEPHEN CRANE"

SUBJECT   VERB

Author of *The Red Badge of Courage,* Stephen Crane remains a much admired novelist.

COMMA SETS OFF INTRODUCTORY PHRASE

Revised with phrase in the middle of sentence:

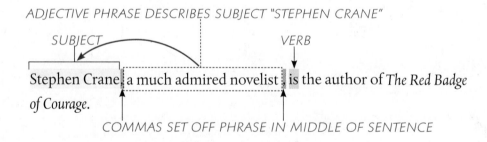

ADJECTIVE PHRASE DESCRIBES SUBJECT "STEPHEN CRANE"

SUBJECT   VERB

Stephen Crane, a much admired novelist, is the author of *The Red Badge of Courage.*

COMMAS SET OFF PHRASE IN MIDDLE OF SENTENCE

Revised with phrase at the end of sentence:

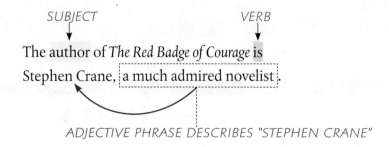

SUBJECT   VERB

The author of *The Red Badge of Courage* is Stephen Crane, a much admired novelist.

ADJECTIVE PHRASE DESCRIBES "STEPHEN CRANE"

Practice 5

VARY SIMPLE SENTENCES

In each of the items below, combine the given simple sentences into one new sentence using a phrase. In your answers, follow the placement of the phrase suggested in parentheses at the end of each item. Use appropriate punctuation.

◄ Lighthouse staircase ►

1. The earliest lighthouses were simply bonfires. These bonfires were built on hillsides to guide ships. (end of sentence)

---

2. The first lighthouse was built in 285 BCE. It was serving the old world city of Alexandria. (beginning of sentence)

---

3. The first American lighthouse came into service in 1716. It was at Boston Harbor. (end of sentence)

---

4. The lantern was typically a round, square, octagonal, or decagonal-shaped cast-iron house for a lens. It was surrounded by an exterior stone or cast-iron gallery with railing. (beginning of sentence)

---

5. Stairs gave access to the lantern at the top of the tower. The stairs were winding around a central column or spiral inside the tower wall. (middle of sentence)

---

6. The Boston Light was kept by George Worthylake. He was the nation's first lightkeeper. (end of sentence)

----

7. A cannon served as the first fog horn. It was installed in 1719. (middle of sentence)

----

8. Onshore lights were lighthouses built on land. They made up the majority of lighthouses in America.

----

9. Most lighthouses were made of wood, stone masonry, brick, or cast-iron plates. Most lighthouses were straight piles built in the form of a cone. (beginning of sentence)

----

10. The screw-pile lighthouse stands on metal piles that are screwed into sandy or muddy sea or river bottoms. The screw-pile lighthouse was designed and built by the blind engineer Alexander Mitchell. (beginning of sentence)

Practice 5

Combine Ideas Using Compound and Complex Sentence Types

For information on how to create compound and complex sentences, see pages 100–117.

Combine ideas of equal importance using **coordination**, joining independent clauses into a **compound sentence**. Combine ideas of unequal importance—a main idea and a subordinate, or minor, idea—using **subordination**, joining an independent clause with a dependent clause into a **complex sentence**.

VARY SIMPLE SENTENCES

Use subordination and coordination to logically combine the ideas in the twelve sentences below into five sentences. Punctuate properly. (*Note:* For more help on how to create compound and complex sentences and punctuate them correctly, see Chapter 6.)

(1) We were fighting a war in Iraq. (2) I was deployed several times. (3) I was in the Army. (4) I have gone through a lot of emotions and experiences because of the war. (5) I read Stephen Crane's novel *The Red Badge of Courage*. (6) *The Red Badge of Courage* is about the Civil War. (7) It is supposed to be a realistic view of war. (8) I read with great interest. (9) I compared my experiences to the experiences of Henry Fleming. (10) He is the main character. (11) The novel makes a good point. (12) Youths must quickly mature in order to survive.

Vary Sentence Openings

LO4

Most often, we begin our sentences with the subject followed by the verb. To add interest and to shift the emphasis of an idea, you can vary the ways in which you begin a sentence. You have already worked with two types of sentence openings: phrases and dependent clauses. Two additional ways to begin a sentence include using adverbs and prepositional phrases. As introductory elements in a sentence, both an adverb and a prepositional phrase are set off with a comma.

Adverb

- Describes or modifies another adverb, a verb, or an adjective
- Answers the questions: *How? How often? How much? When? Where?* and *Why?*
- Usually ends in *-ly: angrily, beautifully, frequently*

ADVERB   COMMA SETS OFF INTRODUCTORY ELEMENT

Patiently, Liza listened to the speaker.

Prepositional Phrase

- Begins with a preposition and ends with a noun or pronoun, the object of the preposition
- Object of the preposition describes or modifies another word in the sentence
- Common prepositions and objects: *about the time, at the store, by the door, in the house, on the way, to the corner, with you*

PREPOSITIONAL PHRASE   COMMA SETS OFF INTRODUCTORY ELEMENT

After the lecture, Liza recopied her notes.

VARY SENTENCE OPENINGS

Revise the openings of the sentences to vary emphasis and expression. Move the position of the adverb or prepositional phrase to the beginning of a sentence as appropriate.

Angel Oak Tree ▶

1. Angel Oak, outside Charleston, South Carolina, is the oldest thing east of the Rockies.

2. Angel Oak is apparently around 1,500 years old.

3. Angel Oak, over 65 feet high, sprouted 1,000 years before Columbus came to the New World.

4. Angel Oak, in modern times, has become a popular tourist attraction.

5. It has impressively survived hurricanes, floods, and earthquakes.

6. The General Sherman is a giant sequoia tree with a height of 275 feet and a diameter between 25 to 36 feet located in Sequoia National Park in California.

7. The Grizzly Giant stands as one of the oldest and largest giant sequoias in Yosemite National Park.

8. Methuselah is amazingly a 5,000-year-old Great Basin Bristlecone.

9. Methuselah's exact location remains a secret for protection against vandalism.

10. The Mississippi Petrified Forest is currently a private park open to the public.

Editing Assignments

MyWritingLab™
Complete this Exercise
on mywritinglab.com

Editing for Everyday Life

Revise the following letter to create a variety of purposes, types, patterns, openings, and lengths of sentences. Use your own paper or complete the exercise on MyWritingLab.com.

Dear Maxine,

It was so good to be with you during our family vacation. We enjoyed all the activities that you planned for us. We were surprised by the Fairchild Oak. We were impressed with its size and beauty. Your Uncle Adolph is still talking about the Ponce de Leon Lighthouse. He is a history buff. He was fascinated. He especially liked learning about the shipwreck experiences of the author Stephen Crane. We enjoyed the sightseeing. We enjoyed reconnecting with family most of all. Thank you so much for all you did for us. You now need to come see us.

All our love, Aunt Frances

Editing for College Life

Your humanities teacher has assigned a short response paper about the significance of a local landmark. Assume you have composed the following piece of writing. Revise the draft to create a variety of purposes, types, patterns, openings, and lengths of sentences. Use your own paper or complete the exercise on MyWritingLab.com.

> The Alamo is located in San Antonio, Texas. The Alamo was originally called Mission San Antonio de Valero. It was the home of Native Americans. They had been converted to Christianity. The Spanish military set up a station there. They were stationed there in the early 1800s. The Alamo, in time, became a place for Mexican Revolutionaries. Mexican Revolutionaries fought for Mexico's independence from Spain. Texan and Tejano volunteers fought Mexican troops during the Texas Revolution. A group of volunteers took over the Alamo. They took it over in 1835. They defended the Alamo against Santa Ana's army. They would not surrender. They were defeated. The year was 1836. The Alamo honors the struggle against overwhelming odds. The Alamo honors the love for liberty.

Editing for Working Life

Revise the following draft of a letter of application to create a variety of purposes, types, patterns, openings, and lengths of sentences. Use your own paper or complete the exercise on MyWritingLab.com.

To Whom It May Concern:

I am applying for the position of front office manager in your organization. I received my Master of Business Administration from the University of Sindh Jamshoro, Pakistan. I worked as a travel guide with Waljis Travel. Waljis Travel is a well-known tour company in Pakistan. I also worked in media management with Spanish television in Pakistan. I also worked as an administrative officer with Snow Land Trek and Tour at Skardu. I am ready to take a challenging job. I am eager to take a job where my skills and knowledge will benefit the company.

Best Regards,

Shamshad Hussain

Academic Learning Log: Chapter Review

WHAT HAVE I LEARNED?

To test and track your understanding of sentence variety, answer the following questions.

1. What are the four purposes for sentences? ...., ..., ..., ...

2. What are the four ways to combine simple sentences? ...., ..., ..., ...

3. What are four ways to vary sentence openings? ...., ..., ..., ...

4. Why is it important to vary sentence length? ....

5. **How will I use what I have learned?**
   In your notebook, discuss how you will apply to your own writing what you have learned about sentence variety. When will you apply this knowledge during the writing process?

6. **What do I still need to study about sentence variety?**
   In your notebook, discuss your ongoing study needs by describing what, when, and how you will continue studying and using sentence variety.

MyWritingLab™

Complete the Post-test for Chapter 21 in MyWritingLab.

22

Sentence Clarity: Point of View, Number, and Tense

LEARNING OUTCOMES

After studying this chapter, you should be able to:

1 Answer the Question "What's the Point of Sentence Clarity?"

2 Use Consistent Person and Point of View

3 Use Consistent Number

4 Use Consistent Tense

Sentence clarity creates a logical flow of ideas through consistency in person, point of view, number, and tense.

Communicating about a real-life situation helps us to understand the purpose of sentence clarity. The photograph on the facing page captures two young men break dancing. Read the accompanying original and revised sentences about the young men in Practice 1, complete the activities, and answer the question "What's the point of sentence clarity?"

What's the Point of Sentence Clarity?

PHOTOGRAPHIC ORGANIZER: SENTENCE CLARITY

Practice 1

WRITING
FROM LIFE

▲ Hip-hop Dancers

What do you think the following sentence means? How could the sentence seem confusing to some readers?

Original Sentence: Juan and Tomas often listened to Hip-hop music and practice his dance moves.

Is the above sentence describing a current or a past event? Whose dance moves are being discussed—Juan's, Tomas's, or both?

Below, the sentence has been revised for clarity. Circle the words that have been revised. How do these revised words clarify the meaning of the sentence?

Revised Sentence: Juan and Tomas often listen to Hip-hop music and practice their dance moves.

What is the point of sentence clarity?

....

....

....

One Student Writer's Response

The following paragraph offers one writer's reaction to the clarity of the sentence about the dancers.

I was confused by the first sentence. I didn't know when the action took place. Did the men get together in the past or is this something they do now? Also, the wording made me wonder who was practicing dance moves. The revised sentence answered my questions by changing two words. Changing "listened" to "listen" made it clear that this takes place in the present. And changing "his" to "their" made it clear that both of them practice dance moves.

Sentence clarity is the precise choice of the form and arrangement of words and groups of words within a sentence. A clearly stated sentence is consistent in person, point of view, number, and tense. As a result, sentence clarity creates a coherent flow of ideas within and among sentences. Often, sentence and paragraph clarity emerge during the revision process. As you study the sentence clarity techniques in this chapter, revise pieces of your own writing and peer edit for a classmate. Apply and track what you are learning as you go.

L2 Use Consistent Person and Point of View

The term **person** refers to the use of pronouns to identify the difference between the writer or speaker, the one being written or spoken to, and the one being written about or spoken of. **Point of view** is the position from which something is considered, evaluated, or discussed; point of view is identified as first person, second person, or third person. Person and point of view also communicate tone.

Three Points of View

Person	Traits	Pronouns
First Person	The writer or speaker; informal, conversational tone	singular: *I, me* plural: *we, our*
Second Person	The one being written or spoken to; can remain unstated; informal, conversational tone	singular: *you* plural: *you*
Third Person	The one being written about or spoken of; formal, academic tone	singular: *he, she, it, one* plural: *they*

Illogical Shift in Person

An abrupt or **unnecessary shift in person or point of view** causes a break in the logical flow of ideas. The key is to use the same phrasing throughout a paragraph.

For more information about subject-verb agreement, see pages 166–185.

Illogical Shift in Person:

Anyone can learn to dance despite your age.

↑ THIRD PERSON   ↑ SECOND PERSON

Revisions:

Anyone can learn to dance despite his or her age.

↑ THIRD PERSON   ↑ THIRD PERSON

You can learn to dance despite your age.

↑ SECOND PERSON   ↑ SECOND PERSON

Practice 2

USE CONSISTENT PERSON AND POINT OF VIEW

Edit the following statements to ensure consistent use of person in each sentence.

1. Dancers develop self-confidence; therefore, you are more outgoing.

2. A dancer can truly reflect your feelings through your body movements.

3. Dancing helps your circulatory system as it makes one's heart pump blood faster.

4. One can control their weight and improve your overall fitness by burning off calories while dancing.

5. For many people, dance becomes more than your hobby; it provides you with a new lifestyle based on confidence and fitness.

6. Dance improves our memory by making you recall steps and routines.

7. Balancing yourself in one position may seem easy, but balancing oneself in a variety of positions while dancing builds core strength.

8. A dancer may try several types of dance before they find the type they prefer.

9. If you like to improvise, a person may prefer jazz dance.

10. If people like to create timely beats and rhythmic patterns, he may enjoy tap dancing.

L3 Use Consistent Number

The term *number* refers to the difference between a singular noun or pronoun and plural nouns and pronouns. Once you choose a point of view, carefully edit your writing to ensure **consistent use of number:** singular pronouns refer to singular nouns, and plural pronouns refer to plural nouns.

	Singular	Plural
First Person	I, me, my, mine	we, our, ours
	myself	ourselves
Second Person	you, yours, yourself	you, yours, yourselves
Third Person	he, she, it	they
	him, her	them
	his, hers, its	theirs
	himself, herself, itself	themselves
	one, everyone, none	

Illogical Shift in Number

When pronouns act as the subject of a verb, they, too, must agree in number. An abrupt or **unnecessary shift in number** causes a break in the logical flow of ideas.

Illogical Shift in Number:

SINGULAR NOUN   PLURAL, THIRD-PERSON PRONOUN

Hip-hop is a form of urban youth culture; they include rap music, graffiti, and break dancing.

PLURAL VERB

Revision:

SINGULAR NOUN   SINGULAR, THIRD-PERSON PRONOUN

Hip-hop is a form of urban youth culture; it includes rap music, graffiti, and break dancing.

SINGULAR VERB

Practice 3

USE CONSISTENT NUMBER

Edit the following statements to ensure consistency in number within each sentence.

1. Break dancing has four basic elements; it is toprock, downrock, power moves, and freezes.

2. A male break dancer is called a b-boy because they can express themselves through the four elements of break dancing.

3. A b-boy uses toprock moves to show their ability to rock the beat while they are standing up.

4. B-boys use downrock to show off its speed and agility by using his hands and feet on the floor.

5. Power moves are borrowed from gymnastics; it requires upper body strength and momentum.

6. A freeze halts all movement in a freestanding pose; they are often handstands or pikes.

7. A break dancer begins with toprock moves; they start with any string of steps to express their feelings; they also use toprock to link together other types of moves.

8. Downrock is based on dancers' mastery of the six-step and his flexibility.

9. Power moves and freezes are show-off moves; it requires a great deal of strength, flexibility, and balance.

10. As a break dancer combines these four elements in their routines, it is fun to watch them move up and down in the levels of heights.

USE CONSISTENT NUMBER

Revise the following paragraph to change the point of view from third person to second person. Change nouns, pronouns, and verbs as needed for consistency in point of view and number.

How to Break Dance Using the Six-Step

(1) Roxanne practices these six steps to master the basic footwork of break dancing. (2) Starting in a push-up position with her legs spread apart shoulder width, she lifts her right hand and puts her left leg where her right hand was. (3) Next, she brings her right leg behind her left knee and points her right hand to the sky. (4) Then, she steps her left foot out and brings her right hand back down to the floor. (5) At this point, her back is facing the floor, and both of her knees are bent. (6) Her fourth move is to put her right foot in front of her left foot. (7) Then, she steps her left foot away while she shifts her weight onto her right arm and left foot. (8) Finally, she brings her right foot under her left foot as she brings her left hand back to the ground in front of her so she is back into the push-up position.

L4 Use Consistent Tense

Consistent tense expresses the logical sequence of events or existence. Verb *tense* expresses the time or duration of an action or state of being. Primary tenses include three timeframes: The **past** *was*; the **present** *is*; the **future** *will be*. The following chart offers definitions, examples, and possible signal words for the three primary tenses of verbs in English.

Primary Verb Tenses		
Past	**Present**	**Future**
Action or state of being ended at a certain point in the past	Action or state of being exists or is repeated	Action or state of being occurs in the future
danced	**dance/dances**	**will dance**
Past Tense Signal Words	Present Tense Signal Words	Future Tense Signal Words
• before • for several days, weeks, etc. • last week, month, year • one hour, day, week, year ago • yesterday	• always • every day, week, month, year • frequently • now • sometimes • usually	• in the future • later • next week, month, year, etc. • soon • tomorrow • tonight

Illogical Shift in Tense

An abrupt change from one verb tense to another without a logical reason, also called an **illogical shift in tense**, breaks the logical flow of ideas and causes confusion.

Illogical Shift in Tense:

PRESENT TENSE
↓

Music exerts a powerful influence on her physically; soothing music lowered her blood pressure.

PAST TENSE

Revisions:

PRESENT TENSE
↓

Music exerts a powerful influence on her physically; soothing music lowers her blood pressure.

PRESENT TENSE

PAST TENSE
↓

Music exerted a powerful influence on her physically; soothing music lowered her blood pressure.

PAST TENSE

USE CONSISTENT TENSE

Edit the following sentences to ensure consistency in tense.

1. Before Shannon passes the final exam, her heart rate raced with stress.

2. Every time she takes a test, she feared it.

3. Shannon learned that music helps her older sister to relax before taking an exam.

4. After Shannon learns about her sister's experience, she listened to music before the exam.

5. From now on, Shannon not only will study but also listens to classical music before an exam.

6. Research indicates that music with a strong beat stimulated brainwaves.

7. Faster beats sharpen concentration and caused alert thinking; in contrast, slower beats promoted a calm state.

8. Bodily functions controlled by the autonomic nervous system, such as breathing and heart rate, are improved by music; thus music prevented the damaging effects of chronic stress.

9. Listening to music boosts the immune system and eased muscle tension.

10. Music therapy is a popular treatment; many hospitals used music therapy for pain management.

Logical Shift in Tenses

Frequently, a writer states the logical movement from one tense to another tense. Often signal words indicate this logical shift in tense.

Past to Present Tense: Jay-Z and Beyoncé dated for years; they are now a married couple.

Present to Future Tense: They are a power couple who will only become richer in the future.

Jay-Z and Beyoncé ▶

USE CONSISTENT TENSE

Edit the following paragraph to ensure consistency in tense.

(1) Jay-Z is the stage name of Shawn Corey Carter, who was born December 4, 1969. (2) Jay-Z was a rapper, songwriter, record producer, and savvy businessman. (3) As of 2010 his net worth is over $450 million. (4) Jay-Z says his earliest musical experience is listening to his parents' record collection, which contains soul music. (5) In 2008, Jay-Z married R&B singer Beyoncé Knowles. (6) In 2012, they have a baby girl that they name Blue Ivy. (7) Two days later, Jay-Z releases "Glory," a song dedicated to his newborn daughter. (8) Since Blue's cries are recorded on the song, she was given official credit. (9) Blue Ivy Carter becomes the youngest person to appear on a Billboard chart. (10) Becoming a parent changed Jay-Z, who said in 2012 that in the future he stopped using the "B" word.

SENTENCE CLARITY REVIEW

Revise the following student paragraph for consistent use of point of view, number, and tense.

RAPPING: THE TRUTH HURTS

(1) Many people cry out against Hip-hop music. (2) Critics say that Hip-hop music passed on the wrong message to young people. (3) One of the reasons people opposed Hip-hop was because of the curse words used by many rap artists. (4) But rappers used these words to capture the anger and frustration of people in their neighborhoods. (5) Critics also complain about the graphic sexual content of lyrics, and many lyrics put women down through the use of crude names. (6) Rapper David Banner says that the words are honest. (7) The lyrics only describe a certain type of women, and other women should not be offended. (8) He also point out that sex sells. (9) Hip-hop musicians see himselves as artists. (10) He sees his job as to capture the reality of the society as they see it. (11) They expect to offend you if you don't want to know the truth.

Revise the following student paragraph for consistent use of point of view, number, and tense.

IT'S A WOMAN'S WORLD, TOO

(1) Hip-hop is often seen as a man's world. (2) But three women prove that Hip-hop is a woman's world, too. (3) Nicki Minaj dreams of being a famous singer. (4) Then in 2010, she burst on the music scene with her hit single "Super Bass." (5) The album *Pink Friday* sold millions worldwide and earns her several awards. (6) Her rap skills and colorful, eccentric costumes have made her an icon. (7) You may not think that Rihanna is as good as she can be, but her single "Diamonds" delivers a powerful beat and made good use of her deep voice. (8) In the future, she only improves. (9) In fact, since the release of her debut album *Music of the Sun* in 2005, Rihanna has turned out many hit singles worldwide. (10) Finally, Beyoncé is the queen of Hip-hop. (11) First, she rose to fame as the lead singer of Destiny's Child; then she starts a successful solo career. (12) You have to admire her sex appeal and amazing voice. (13) In 2013 and 2014, she is named one of the most influential people in the world by *Time Magazine*. (14) These women rock!

Editing Assignments

MyWritingLab™
Complete this Exercise
on mywritinglab.com

Editing for Everyday Life

Revise the following paragraph, written as a posting to a Facebook blog, for sentence clarity. Use your own paper or complete the exercise on MyWritingLab.com.

Over the past three months, I have gotten in shape and reduced my stress, and I now wanted to help someone else do the same in their lives. I used *Hip-hop Cardio and Strength Building* videos and got fantastic results. Each video was a 45-minute workout routine. There are five DVDs. First you learned the basic six-step. They develop your balance and strengthens your core. Then over the course of several weeks, you learned the hottest dance moves. Soon, you are dancing like a pro. The hard-driving beat of the music is a great outlet for all my pent up frustration and worries. Since the DVDs help me, I know they help someone else.

Editing for College Life

Edit the following paragraph, written in response to a short-answer question on a college humanities exam, for sentence clarity.

Test Question: What is the difference between Rap and Hip-hop?

Student Answer: *Rap is something you do; Hip-hop is something you live. Hip-hop is a label for a lifestyle. They include DJing, music, break dancing, graffiti, and clothing. This lifestyle is based on the belief that a person has the right to live their lives in any way they choose. Hip-hop will celebrate emotional release and fully living every moment. Rap is the musical element of the Hip-hop culture. Rap began in the urban setting of the Bronx. During the 1970s, DJs and emcees give toasts; they half-sang, half spoke rhymes in a rapid-fire beat. Rap reflected the values of the Hip-hop lifestyle. Sometimes, rap is a social protest; other times it was an honest picture of urban life; often it is bitter and angry.*

Editing for Working Life

The following letter requests permission to use a song in a fundraising presentation. Edit the letter for sentence clarity.

Dear Mr. Smith:

I work for the non-profit organization "Youth Rock." We sponsored urban centers that provide computers, tutoring, and counseling to urban youth. We are putting together a multimedia presentation to raise funds. We understand that you are the owner of the copyright in the musical composition "Rock On," and we want to use the entire song in the presentation. Since we was on a limited budget, we hoped that you will allow us this use without any charge. If a fee was required, please let us know the amount. Your signature below, under "confirmed by," will indicate that you agreed to permit this use without payment of a fee. Thank you for your help with this matter, and we look forward to hearing from you.

Sincerely,
Wayne Scroggins

WHAT HAVE I LEARNED ABOUT SENTENCE CLARITY?

To test and track your understanding of sentence clarity, answer the following questions. Use several sentences as needed for each response.

1. What is sentence clarity?

_____

_____

2. What are three techniques used to achieve sentence clarity?

(a) _____   (b) _____

(c) _____

3. How will I use what I have learned?
In your notebook, discuss how you will apply to your own writing what you have learned about sentence clarity. When will you apply this knowledge during the writing process?

4. What do I still need to study about sentence clarity?
In your notebook, describe your ongoing study needs by describing what, when, and how you will continue studying and using sentence clarity.

PORTFOLIO

MyWritingLab™
Complete the Post-test for Chapter 22 in MyWritingLab.

23

Dialects and Standard English

Dialects are regional speech patterns that differ in grammar, vocabulary, and pronunciation based on social and geographical influences.

Standard English is the form of English commonly accepted and used as a model for speech and writing.

Are you able to tell where someone comes from based on his or her speech pattern? If so, you recognize that person's dialect. Everyone speaks a dialect or a variation of a language. Thinking about a real-life situation helps us to understand the relationship between a dialect and Standard English in our communication. Complete the following activity and answer the question "What's the point of dialects and Standard English?"

What's the Point of Dialects and Standard English?

PHOTOGRAPHIC ORGANIZER: THE POINT OF DIALECTS AND STANDARD ENGLISH

Assume someone you know is injured in a car accident. He asks you to read the accident report that he has completed for the insurance company. As you read his draft, you notice he has written in a dialect. Would you advise him to revise? Why or why not?

> I had gone down to a meetin but ain't nobody there. So I decided to go see my Dad and was drivin down I-287. I weren't going fast. I saw a deer runnin cross the road. Right direckly the other truck try to miss the deer and got into my lane and ran into me. He knocked me clean off the road.

WRITING
FROM LIFE

What's the point of dialects and Standard English?

....

....

....

One Student Writer's Response

The following paragraph offers one writer's reaction to the car accident report.

> I actually found the paragraph interesting. The way he used language kept me interested in what he was saying. However, I would advise him to revise because of his audience. He is dealing with a legal matter, and some people might not listen to him, or they may try to take advantage of him if they think they can. People might not take him seriously. I would be respectful, but I would still tell him that people might think he isn't very smart or well educated because of the way he writes.

A **dialect** is the spoken language of a particular group of people in a particular region. Dialects are speech patterns that differ in grammar, vocabulary, and pronunciation based on social and geographical influences. For example, the Midwestern English dialect uses the phrase *don't cha* for *don't you* or the word *ya* for *you*. The Appalachian English dialect uses *you was* and *y'all were* to indicate the singular and plural of *you*. The Southern dialect often omits the ends of words as in *fishin* (fishing). Dialects arise from and reflect specific cultures, so no dialect is superior to another. In fact, understanding a dialect and its relationship to Standard English will deepen your knowledge about how language works.

Standard English is the form of English commonly accepted and used as a model for speech and writing.

No one has to give up a dialect to master Standard English. Instead, Standard English can be added to expand a person's use of language so that the person can communicate effectively and powerfully in all situations. Understanding four basic grammatical elements of Standard English will aid in the mastery of Standard English: articles and nouns, the sequence of verb tenses, prepositions, and idioms.

L❷ Apply General Guidelines for Use of Articles and Nouns

An article, such as *a*, *an*, or *the*, is a type of adjective that indicates whether a noun is **general** or **specific**, **count** or **noncount**, and **singular** or **plural**. The guidelines below describe these types of nouns and explain their relationship with articles.

General Guidelines for Articles and Nouns

• A **count noun** names something that can be counted.

COUNT NOUN

The two pencils are on the desk.

• A **noncount noun** names something that cannot be counted or is referred to as a whole.

NONCOUNT NOUN

water

• A **general noun** names any member of a larger group.

GENERAL NOUNS

a pen, an eraser

• A **specific noun** names a particular member of a group.

SPECIFIC NOUN

the eraser

- **Indefinite Articles:** *A* and *an* are indefinite articles that are used before a singular count noun that refers to any member of a **general** group; *a* or *an* indicates **one out of many**. An indefinite article often introduces a **general** noun for the first time in the discussion.

    a. Use *a* before a count noun that begins with a consonant.

    a student

    b. Use *an* before a count noun that begins with a vowel.

    an exam

- **Definite Article:** *The* is a definite article. It is used before a *specific* noun; *the* indicates *this particular one*, as in the following instances:

    a. A plural count noun that refers to *those specific things*

    "THE" REFERS TO PLURAL COUNT NOUN "CHILDREN" (A SPECIFIC GROUP OF CHILDREN)

    The children are in the yard.

    b. A plural proper noun

    "THE" REFERS TO PLURAL PROPER NOUN "SMITHS"

    The Smiths live next door.

    c. A singular count noun that refers to a *specific member* of the larger group

    "THE" REFERS TO SINGULAR COUNT NOUN "CAT" (A SPECIFIC CAT)

    The cat looks hungry.

    d. A noncount noun limited by a modifier

    "THE" REFERS TO NONCOUNT NOUN "COFFEE"

    The coffee from Starbucks is delicious.

    e. A noun that refers to something unique

    "THE" REFERS TO UNIQUE NOUN "INTERNET"

    The Internet connects us to information.

    f. A noun that has already been introduced into the discussion

    INDEFINITE ARTICLE "A" INTRODUCES GENERAL NOUN "PACKAGE"; DEFINITE ARTICLE "THE" REFERS TO THE PREVIOUSLY INTRODUCED NOUN

    A package is at the front door; the package looks damaged.

- **Zero Article:** When no article is used before the noun, it is a zero article. Zero article implies *all of them everywhere* and may indicate a proper noun.

    a. Use zero article to refer to the entire general group or idea

    ZERO ARTICLE USED WITH NOUN THAT REFERS TO THE ENTIRE GENERAL CATEGORY OF CATS

    ↓

    Cats are easy to own.

    b. Use zero article to refer to noncount general nouns

    ZERO ARTICLE USED WITH NONCOUNT GENERAL NOUN "COFFEE"

    ↓

    Coffee is delicious.

    c. Use zero article to refer to proper nouns

    ZERO ARTICLE USED WITH PROPER NOUNS

    ↓   ↓

    Janice Smith, Drexel Avenue

Practice 2

APPLY THE GENERAL GUIDELINES: COUNT AND NONCOUNT NOUNS

Identify the nouns in bold print as count or noncount. Fill in each blank with **C** for count noun or **N** for noncount noun. Then, underline the proper article.

.... **1.** We can train (a, an, the, zero article) **animal** to help us.

.... **2.** (A, An, the, zero article) **Pork Chop** has been trained.

.... **3.** He is (a, an, the, zero article) **beagle**.

.... **4.** He is trained to collect (a, an, the, zero article) **money**.

.... **5.** He collects for (a, an, the, zero article) **charity**.

.... **6.** Boots was (a, an, the, zero article) **veteran dog actor** of the 1940s.

.... **7.** Boots helped raise more than $9 million in bonds to support (a, an, the, zero article) **American war effort** during World War II.

.... **8.** Boots appeared before troops at more than (a, an, the, zero article) **150 locations.**

.... **9.** He also performed before (a, an, the, zero article) **President Roosevelt.**

.... **10.** Boots was (a, an, the, zero article) **amazing trick dog** and fundraiser.

An article indicates the position of a noun within its larger group. The following graphic visualizes the movement from using an indefinite article with a general noun to using the definite article with a specific noun.

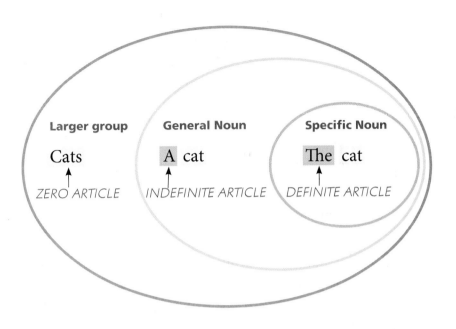

APPLY THE GENERAL GUIDELINES: GENERAL AND SPECIFIC NOUNS

Identify the nouns in bold print as larger group, general, or specific. Fill in each blank with **L** for larger group, **G** for general noun, or **S** for specific noun. Then, underline the proper article.

.... **1.** All (a, an, the, zero article) **cats** are playful and curious.

.... **2.** (A, An, The, zero article) **cat** likes to investigate.

.... **3.** (A, An, The, zero article) **cat** seems content.

.... **4.** It is acting like (a, an, the, zero article) typical **cat.**

.... **5.** (A, An, The, zero article) **Brutus** is playful and curious.

.... **6.** (A, An, The, zero article) Maine Coon **cats** are one of the largest breeds of domestic cats.

.... **7.** Males can weigh up to 25 pounds and grow up to 16 inches in height and 40 inches in length, including (a, an, the, zero article) **tail.**

.... **8.** Tommy, our cat, is (a, an, the, zero article) young Maine Coon **cat.**

.... **9.** He is (a, an, the, zero article) gentle **giant** with above average intelligence.

.... **10.** Tommy is (a, an, the, zero article) best feline **friend** I have ever had.

Deciding which article to use with a noun is a challenge for many writers. The choice becomes even more complicated when an adjective describing the noun is involved. The following chart illustrates the most common and correct combinations of articles, adjectives, and nouns.

Articles: *A, An, The,* Zero			
A	An	The	Zero
Singular count noun beginning with a consonant (any such item)	Singular count noun beginning with a vowel (any such item)	Singular count noun (that specific thing)	Plural count noun (the entire group)
A cell phone	An iPhone	The cell phone	Cell phones
Adjective beginning with a consonant placed between article and noun (any such item)	Adjective beginning with a vowel placed between article and noun (any such item)	Plural count noun (those specific things)	Noncount noun
A recycled iPhone	An easy-to-use cell phone	The cell phones	Communication

APPLY THE GENERAL GUIDELINES: SELECT THE CORRECT ARTICLE

Read the following paragraph. Fill in the blanks with the proper article: *a, an,* or *the.* Mark *X* in the blank for zero article.

One can usually find (1) _____ Starbucks coffee shop in (2) _____ shopping mall. (3) _____ People go to Starbucks for (4) _____ delicious cup of coffee. Because (5) _____ coffee is so popular, (6) _____ shop is always busy. (7) _____ Gibsons go to (8) _____ Starbucks in (9) _____ shopping mall on (10) _____ Mason Avenue. Mr. Gibson always orders (11) _____ iced coffee with milk. Mrs. Gibson prefers (12) _____ Caramel Macchiato. Their daughter Kim doesn't like (13) _____ coffee, so she gets (14) _____ order of cold apple juice. (15) _____ family also enjoys (16) _____ food at Starbucks. Their favorite is (17) _____ Chicken Sausage Breakfast Wrap. In some cities, Starbucks also sells (18) _____ beer and wine. (19) _____ company also purchased (20) _____ fresh juice company.

Use the Logical Sequence of Verb Tenses   **L3**

The tense of a verb states the basic time of an event or state of being. In English, there are three basic tenses: **past**, **present**, and **future**. In addition, each of these basic tenses has a perfect form: **past perfect**, **present perfect**, and **future perfect**. The perfect tenses indicate the timing of one action in relationship to another action.

Tenses are formed through the use of helping verbs like *will, had,* or *have* and verb endings like *-s, -es, -ed, -en,* and *-ing*. Various dialects often drop certain verb endings, such as *-s* or *-ing*; however, Standard English requires their use. As you study the following chart that lists and defines these six basic tenses, notice the use of helping verbs and verb endings to mark each tense.

Six Basic Verb Tenses and Definitions		
Present: Third-person singular often ends in *-s* or *-es*	An action performed habitually	He walks to work every day.
	An unchanging truth	Effort accomplishes results.
	A general statement of fact	Walking builds bones.
Past: Often ends in *-ed*	A action completed before now	He walked to the store.
Future: *will*	An action that has not yet occurred	He will walk tomorrow.
Present Perfect: *have/has*	An action repeated several times before now	He has walked every day for weeks.
	An action completed at an unspecified time before now	He has lost weight.
	An action not completed in the past	He has dropped 30 pounds so far.
Past Perfect: *had*	An action completed in the past before another past action	He had walked before he ate.
Future Perfect: *will have*	An action that will occur before some future time	He will have lost another 10 pounds before summer begins.

In addition to these six basic tenses, the English language also includes the progressive tenses formed with *to be* helping verbs and the *-ing* suffix to indicate ongoing or continuous action. The progressive tenses include all six of the basic tenses:

Present progressive	I am writing a letter.
Past progressive	I was writing a report.
Future progressive	I will be writing thank you notes.
Present perfect progressive	I have been writing for hours.
Past perfect progressive	I had been writing for years.
Future perfect progressive	I will have been writing this book for three years.

Practice 5

IDENTIFY THE VERB TENSE

Identify the tense of the verbs in bold print.

1. Serena Williams **is** a world-famous tennis player. ....

2. She **has won** over two dozen career Grand Slams. ....

3. Currently, her wins **include** 64 single, 2 mixed double, and 22 women's double titles.

   ....

4. She **has decided** to use her wealth and fame to help others. ....

5. The Serena Williams Foundation **was established** to accomplish two main goals.

   ....

6. The first goal **is** to give aid to youth affected by violent crimes. ....

7. The second **is** to provide an education to underprivileged youth around the

   world. ....

8. The Foundation **will supply** counseling, housing, food, and education to youth affected
   by violence in the United States. ....

9. The Foundation **will** also **provide** grants and scholarships to deserving high school
   students around the world. ....

10. Write a sentence that uses the future tense. Suggested topic: A personal goal.

    ....

    ....

Verb tenses are often marked by words and phrases that indicate a time sequence such as *before, now,* and *after.* These time markers can help you visualize the sequence of the verbs and use the correct tense. The following timeline illustrates the sequence of the six basic tenses with example time markers.

Sequence of Six Basic Verb Tenses					
Before; Yesterday	Yesterday	*Since;* Yesterday	*Now;* Today	Tomorrow	*Before;* Tomorrow
had worked	worked	have worked	work	will work	will have worked
Past Perfect	Past	Present Perfect	Present	Future	Future Perfect

The difficulty in using the correct verb sequence usually occurs when using perfect tenses in complex sentences. To use correct verb sequence, identify independent and dependent clauses within a complex sentence. A **complex sentence** contains one independent clause and at least one dependent clause. An **independent clause** includes a subject and a verb that expresses a complete thought.

In contrast, a **dependent clause** includes a subject and a verb that does not express a complete thought. An independent clause expresses the main idea of the sentence; a dependent clause expresses a subordinate idea.

To use the correct verb sequence, identify independent and dependent clauses. The sequence of tenses in complex sentences is usually determined by the tense of the verb in the independent clause.

"ALREADY," "BEFORE," AND PAST PERFECT TENSE INDICATE ACTION IN THE INDEPENDENT CLAUSE WAS COMPLETED BEFORE THE PAST TENSE ACTION IN THE DEPENDENT CLAUSE

Serena already had earned $34.7 million in prize money before she reached the age of 30.

DEPENDENT CLAUSE   INDEPENDENT CLAUSE

USE LOGICAL VERB FORM

In each blank, write the verb form that logically completes the sentence.

1. Before the hurricane hit land, we _____ all our preparations.

   a. make   b. had made   c. will make

2. We _____ since the beginning of this year's hurricane season.

   a. have been prepared   b. are prepared   c. were prepared

3. By the time we finish shopping for supplies, we _____ all our shelves.

   a. stocked   b. have stocked   c. will have stocked

4. We have boarded up our windows several times since the hurricane season _____ .

   a. begins   b. began   c. will begin

5. After this hurricane season ends, I _____ to another state.

   a. moved   b. will be moving   c. will have been moving

6. When you _____ a hurricane, you know to listen to warnings.

   a. survive   b. will survive   c. have survived

7. Since we _____ Hurricane Andrew, we knew about the need to be prepared.

   a. experienced   b. had experienced   c. will experience

8. Before you go through a hurricane, you think it _____ fun and exciting.

   a. is   b. has been   c. will be

9. As hurricane winds push toward the shore, the ocean's surge _____ heights of 20 feet or more.

   a. reaches   b. have reached   c. will have reached

10. Within 12 hours after a hurricane _____ landfall, wind speeds usually decrease greatly.

   a. makes   b. had made   c. will have made

L④ Use Prepositions to Express Relationships among Ideas

The word **preposition** comes from two Latin words that mean *placed before*. A preposition is a word that is *placed before* a noun or pronoun. The noun or pronoun following the preposition is called the **object of the preposition**. The function of a **preposition** is to state the relationship between the object of the preposition and some other word in the sentence. This relationship is expressed in a **prepositional phrase** that begins with the preposition and ends with its object. For example, when we use the prepositional phrase "a letter in an envelope," the word "in" is a preposition. "In" states a relationship based on location between *letter* and the object of the preposition *envelope*. The key to the correct use of prepositions is to understand the types of relationships they state.

Common Prepositions and the Relationships They Express					
Direction, Movement	**Location, Place**		**Time**	**Possession**	**Responsibility**
from in regard to into onto through to toward	aboard about above across against around at at the back of at the bottom of at the top of behind below beneath beside between beyond by down in in front of inside	in the middle of near next to off on on the corner of on the side of on the other side of on top of opposite out out of outside over to the left of to the right of through under underneath up upon	after around at before between by during for from in on out past since through till until within	of with without	according to by for
Addition, Exclusion				**Comparison, Contrast**	**Cause, Effect**
besides except in addition to				instead of in place of in spite of like over	because of by the way of on account of

USE PREPOSITIONS

The following sentences describe the photograph about the dog, Pork Chop. Fill in each blank with a preposition that best completes the sentence. Discuss your answers with a classmate.

1. _____ working hard all day, Pork Chop lays _____ a hat full _____ money.

2. Some of the money is still _____ the hat.

3. Sometimes money spills _____ the floor _____ the hat.

4. _____ this evening, Pork Chop and his owner will have collected enough money to pay _____ Little League uniforms.

5. Well-groomed _____ his owner, Pork Chop has a healthy and shiny coat of fur.

6. Pork Chop is owned _____ Priscilla Aimes.

7. Ms. Aimes followed the rules _____ effective dog training.

8. She never punished Pork Chop _____ yelling _____ him.

9. She started _____ the simplest commands.

10. _____ treats, she rewarded him _____ affection every time he obeyed.

A few prepositions are particularly confusing. For example, the prepositions *at*, *on*, and *in* are commonly used to indicate either place or time depending on the context. And the time prepositions *during* and *for* are often confused because they seem similar in meaning in certain contexts. The next several sections examine these prepositions based on their use.

Place: *At, On, In*

The most commonly used place prepositions are *at, on,* and *in.* Your choice of any of these prepositions depends on your intended meaning. The following chart illustrates the meanings and uses of these three prepositions.

Place Prepositions: *At, On, In*		
At	**On**	**In**
a specific place	a place that is physically on top of a place	a place that is enclosed or within boundaries
at Starbucks	on the table	in the box

PLACE PREPOSITION INDICATING AN ENCLOSED PLACE

PLACE PREPOSITION INDICATING A SPECIFIC PLACE

PLACE PREPOSITION INDICATING A PHYSICAL SPACE ON TOP OF A PLACE

The customers in the shop sit at the table. Their coffee cups are on the table.

Practice 8

USE PLACE PREPOSITIONS

▲ A view of the Thames

The following sentences describe the photograph of a view of the Thames. Fill in each blank with a preposition that best completes the sentence. Discuss your answers with a classmate.

The people are sitting (1) _____ a lounge (2) _____ benches. They are looking (3) _____ St. Paul's Cathedral (4) _____ Ludgate Hill (5) _____ London, England. One man stands (6) _____ the front, not looking (7) _____ the scenery. He looks (8) _____ the people nearby. He has chosen to stand (9) _____ the window. The steeple that sits (10) _____ top of the cathedral seems to touch the sky.

Time: *At, On, In*

The most commonly used time prepositions are *at, on,* and *in*. The following chart illustrates the meanings and uses of these three prepositions.

Time Prepositions: *At, On, In*		
At	**On**	**In**
a specific time	days and dates	period of time: days, years, months, seasons
at 5:00 PM	on Valentine's Day	in a few minutes

TIME PREPOSITION
INDICATING A SEASON

TIME PREPOSITION
INDICATING A DATE

TIME PREPOSITION
INDICATING A SPECIFIC TIME

In the winter, on February 14, 2008, at midnight, I broke my leg.

USE TIME PREPOSITIONS

The following sentences describe the Parthenon in Athens, Greece. Fill in each blank with a preposition that best completes the sentence. Discuss your answers with a classmate.

(1) _____ this day, the sky is unblemished. The Parthenon is beautiful (2) _____ the evening. It will be dark (3) _____ a few minutes (4) _____ 9:21 PM. (5) _____ the meantime, the light (6) _____ dusk is mesmerizing. The building of the Parthenon began (7) _____ 447 BCE as a temple to the Greek goddess Athena. The temple was completed (8) _____ 438 BCE. (9) _____ that time, Greek culture was at the height of power. (10) _____ September 26, 1687 CE, an explosion of ammunition severely damaged the temple.

More Time Prepositions: *During, For*

Two additional commonly used time prepositions are *during* and *for*. The chart below illustrates their meanings and use.

Time Prepositions: *During, For*	
During	**For**
throughout the length of	a length of time
during the storm	for the past hour

TIME PREPOSITION INDICATING A LENGTH OF TIME

TIME PREPOSITION MEANING "THROUGHOUT THE LENGTH OF" A SPECIFIC TIME SPACE

He kept falling asleep for a few minutes during the movie.

Practice 10

USE THE CORRECT PREPOSITION

Fill in each blank with a preposition that best completes the sentence. Discuss your answers with a classmate.

1. The wind and rain of the hurricane lasted .... hours.

2. Some people tried to escape .... the storm surge.

3. .... the drive out of town, we watched the water rise to cover the road.

4. We drove very slowly .... a long time.

5. My heart was racing .... the entire treacherous drive.

L5 Revise Idioms into Standard English

An **idiom** is a group of words that, when used together, have a meaning that is different than the meanings of the individual words used. For example, to most English speakers, the idiom "kick the bucket" means to die, yet the individual words in this phrase do not have the same meaning. Idioms enrich informal conversations, and some have become ingrained in Standard English. Consider the following commonly used idioms and their meanings:

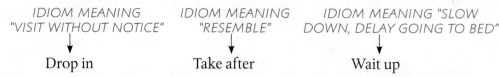

IDIOM MEANING "VISIT WITHOUT NOTICE"

IDIOM MEANING "RESEMBLE"

IDIOM MEANING "SLOW DOWN, DELAY GOING TO BED"

Drop in   Take after   Wait up

The meaning of these phrases is hard to grasp based on the meanings of the individual words. To effectively use idioms, you need to know about literal and figurative language. **Literal language** uses the exact meaning of a word or phrase. **Figurative language** uses a word or phrase to imply or mean something different from its literal definition. A particular type of figurative language, such as an idiom, is also known as a "figure of speech." So the idiom "kick the bucket" is figurative speech, and its meaning "die" is literal language.

The proper use of idioms is made difficult by the wide range of idioms and their various forms. For example, there are animal idioms such as "quiet as a mouse," body idioms like "a pain in the neck" or sports idioms like "behind the eight ball." These are just a few of the countless idioms used in the English language.

Some of the most common idioms are formed by combining a verb and a preposition. The following chart defines and illustrates just a few of the most common idioms formed with only five specific verbs: *back, carry, come, get,* and *take.*

Common Idioms		
Idiom	**Literal Meaning**	**Example**
Back down	retreat from	I won't back down.
Back out, Back out of	desert, to break a promise, move backwards	He backed out of going. She slowly backed out of the driveway.
Back up	alternative plan or copy	You better back up your work.
Carry on	continue	Carry on with your studies.
Carry out	fulfill, accomplish, perform, food ordered to go	She carried out her duties. We ordered carry out.
Carry over	carry, continue at another time or place	The meeting carried over into the weekend.
Come about	happen, occur	She feared what came about.
Come across	find by accident	He came across a long-lost friend.
Come along	accompany, make progress	Come along with us.
Come back	return	I will come back later.
Come by	visit	They came by yesterday.
Come down with	become ill	He came down with the flu.
Come out with	say, produce	Apple came out with the iPad.
Come over	go to where someone is	She will come over later.
Come through	succeed	I knew you would come through.
Come to	regain awareness, become aware	He came to after surgery.
Come up with	think, produce	Where do they come up with their ideas?
Get across	cause understanding	Am I getting across to you?
Get ahead	make progress	He wants to get ahead at work.
Get along	be friendly	They get along well.
Get around	move, navigate	She gets around well.
Get away	escape	The prisoner got away.

Idiom	Literal Meaning	Example
Get by	survive, manage, cope	They get by on very little.
Get in	enter	I always get in trouble.
Get off	descend, dismount	She gets off the horse.
Get on	enter a vehicle, mount	Get on the bus.
Get through	finish, endure	We will get through this ordeal.
Get up	rise	He gets up early.
Take back	retract a statement, return	Take back what you said! I am going to take back this dress.
Take down	remove from a high place, record in writing	Let's take down the banner. Take down this memo.
Take in	understand, accept, deceive, make smaller	She takes in foster children. She was taken in by a scam artist. I had my dress taken in.
Take off	leave, leave the ground	The plane took off safely.
Take over	assume control of, take	The inmates took over the prison.

Use the revision phase of the writing process to edit idioms into Standard English.

Original Sentence:

IDIOM MEANING "AN UNINVITED VISIT"   IDIOM MEANING "LINGER"

I plan to drop in at the ranch and just hang around with my friends, so I am not going to dress up.

IDIOM MEANING "WEAR FORMAL CLOTHES"

Revised to Standard English:

I plan a surprise visit to the ranch to spend time with my friends, so I am going to dress casually.

CORRECTING IDIOMS

Revise each sentence into Standard English by eliminating the idioms. Discuss your answers with a classmate.

1. Many people find it difficult to carry on after going through a traumatic loss.

2. Loss can take you down, and anger can take over your life.

Practice 11

3. People in grief often wish they could take back past actions or words.

4. They can't seem to get around the guilt of getting on with their lives.

5. Some grief-stricken people try to get by through alcohol or drug abuse.

6. They find it hard to take in the reality of the loss.

7. If you are suffering a loss, support groups can help you get through the grief.

8. Talking with others will help you come to your senses.

9. You just need to get up and get in the flow of everyday life.

10. You will get through this difficult time.

DIALECTS AND STANDARD ENGLISH REVIEW

Edit the paragraph for use of Standard English.

Depression differs with grief. Clinical depression affects a whole body. It can take over how you think and feel. Depression had the following traits. One trait is an sad, anxious, or empty feeling. Besides a change in sleep patterns, loss of appetite, weight loss, and gloomy thoughts have occurred. There are several steps one can take to get through depression. While there are no quick fixes, there will be a workable solution. The solution will work if a person understood and applied it. One part of solution involves building supportive relationships. Another part is a challenging negative thinking. Regular exercise, the healthful diet, and plenty of rest help prevent the depression. For the lowest cycle of depression, one should get in touch with friends and family. Person who is depressed will feel like he or she has been beyond help.

Editing Assignments

Editing for Everyday Life

Assume you are writing a letter to the editor of your local newspaper about the litter problem in your neighborhood. Edit this draft using Standard English.

> Litter is collected with the sides of the road for the past several weeks. The litter includes the broken beer bottles, fast food cartons, and cigarettes. Most alarmingly, I have seen discarded needles. Every day, children rode their bikes and walk to school on these streets. The litter gets across a bad example for our youth.

Editing for College Life

Assume you are writing an e-mail to your instructor asking for a recommendation. Edit this draft using Standard English.

> Dear Professor Ries,
>
> I have to come up with an recommendation letter so I can get in a University of Florida and carry on my studies next year. Would you please write an recommendation letter to me?

Editing for Working Life

Assume you are working on an advertising campaign for the restaurant you manage. Edit the following draft using Standard English.

> Drop in for an elegant meal or carry out some great tasting sandwiches. Our servers want to get along with you because we want you to come back many times as the happy customer.

Academic Learning Log: Chapter Review

WHAT HAVE I LEARNED ABOUT DIALECTS AND STANDARD ENGLISH?

To test and track your understanding, answer the following questions.

1. *A* or *an* is used before a singular .... noun that refers to any member of a general group.

2. *The* is used before a .... noun and indicates *this particular one*.

3. Six basic verb tenses in English include the ...., ..., ..., ..., ..., and ....

4. The sequence of tenses in complex sentences is usually determined by the tense of the verb in the .... clause.

5. A preposition states the relationship between the .... of the preposition and another word in the sentence.

6. Some of the relationships prepositions express include ...., ..., ..., ..., ..., ..., and ....

7. Five often confused prepositions are ...., ..., ..., ..., and ....

8. Literal language uses the .... meaning of a word or phrase.

9. .... language uses a word or phrase to imply or mean something different from its literal meaning.

10. An .... is a phrase that cannot be understood based on the meanings of the individual words in the phrase.

11. **How will I use what I have learned about dialects and Standard English?**
In your notebook, discuss how you will apply to your own writing what you have learned about dialects and Standard English.

12. **What do I still need to study about dialects and Standard English?**
In your notebook, describe your ongoing study needs by describing what, when, and how you will continue studying dialects and Standard English.

PORTFOLIO

MyWritingLab™

Complete the Post-test for Chapter 23 in MyWritingLab.

24

Revising for Effective Expression

LEARNING OUTCOMES

After studying this chapter, you should be able to:

1 Answer the Question "What's the Point of Revising for Effective Expression?"

2 Use Concise Language

3 Use Active and Positive Language

4 Use Concrete Language

5 Use Fresh Language

Effective expression makes language clear and interesting.

Have you ever noticed how some speakers and writers use wordy or tired and worn out expressions? Have you been confused or discouraged by a person's negative, fuzzy, or vague wording? Take a moment to think about the need for effective expression in the messages we send to others. Complete the following activity and answer the question "What's the point of effective expression?"

What's the Point of Revising for Effective Expression?

PHOTOGRAPHIC ORGANIZER: EFFECTIVE EXPRESSION

Assume you received the following e-mail from a coworker. What is your impression of the person based on the language used in the e-mail?

Practice 1

WRITING
FROM LIFE

FROM: Kendis Moore Kendis@ITsolutions.com

Date: January 15, 2016

TO: Dwayne <Dwayne@ITsolutions.com>

SUBJECT: FW: A Good Cause

To: All Employees

The reason why I am writing is to give advance notice of the fundraiser drive we will be doing in the upcoming months for the Red Cross. At this point in time, there is no doubt that we are facing a very unique situation. Terrible storms have destroyed countless in number of homes, business, and lives in the recent past years. Due to this fact, we need to raise a large in size donation for the Red Cross. Let me repeat again that in my personal opinion I believe that we have the ability to make a difference.

Please, give!

Kendis Moore
Assistant Manager
IT Solutions

What's the point of revising for effective expression?

One Student Writer's Response

The following paragraph offers one writer's reaction to the e-mail from the coworker.

> *This memo sounds like the writer wants to sound important. But the message comes across as empty and insincere. I most likely would not respond to this message. It's just not professional or thoughtful.*

Effective expression is a result of thoughtful word choice. Mark Twain once said, "The difference between the almost right word and the right word is really a large matter—it's the difference between the lightning bug and the lightning." During early drafts, writers often relate thoughts and ideas without concern for word choice. Words or phrases are needlessly repeated. Clichés (overused expressions or ideas) are sometimes included in the draft. This rush to record ideas as they occur makes good use of the writing process. However, we must take time to revise for effective expression after we have completed a draft. Effective expression involves concise, active, positive, concrete, and fresh writing. Use the revision process to achieve effective expression.

L2 Use Concise Language

The most effective writing is concise and to the point. Concise language avoids wordiness—the repetition of words and phrases that add nothing to the writer's meaning. The following example shows the difference between wordiness and concise writing.

Wordy

The reason why Jamie was calling was to give advance warning about the storm.

Concise

Jamie called to warn about the storm.

Examples of Wordy Expressions with Revisions for Conciseness			
Wordy	**Concise**	**Wordy**	**Concise**
absolutely certain	certain	in today's world	today; currently
advance notice	notice	personal opinion	opinion
has the ability	can	personally, I think	I think
he is a man who; she is a woman who	he; she	refer back	refer
		repeat again	repeat
during the same time that	when	summarize briefly	summarize
given the fact that	because	very unique	unique
in this day and age	today	whole entire	whole; entire

USE CONCISE LANGUAGE

Revise each sentence using concise language. Share your work with a peer or small group of classmates.

1. In this day and age, we need a hero who is good and inspiring.

2. In my personal opinion, we need a hero with the very unique goodness of someone like Clara Barton who was the woman who founded the Red Cross.

3. In Clara Barton's personal opinion, there are two "rules of action."

4. For one, we must have the ability to practice "control under pressure."

5. In addition, we must be able to focus on what we can do with an "unconcern for what cannot be helped."

6. Barton had always had a very unique ability for nursing.

7. Her brother referred back to the time that she was 11 years old and she already had the nursing ability to save his life.

8. Given the fact that Barton established the American Red Cross in 1881, her work has had the ability to continue to impact people even in this day and age.

9. I personally believe with absolute certainty that Clara Barton is an American hero.

10. To summarize briefly, Clara Barton dedicated her whole entire life to helping others.

L❸ Use Active and Positive Language

The most effective writing uses active, positive language to state ideas. The **active voice** states what somebody or something did. The **passive voice** states what was done to someone or something. Sentences written in the active voice are more concise because the active voice uses fewer words to state an action, and it clearly states the relationship between the subject and the action. In contrast, the passive voice uses more words to state an action, and the relationship between the subject and the action is less clear. The active voice is more direct and more powerful than the passive voice.

Active Voice

THE SUBJECT "RED CROSS" PERFORMS THE ACTION.

The Red Cross helps millions of people.

Passive Voice

THE SUBJECT "MILLIONS" RECEIVES THE ACTION PERFORMED BY SOMEONE ELSE.

Millions of people are helped by the Red Cross.

Practice 3

USE ACTIVE VOICE

Revise these sentences from passive to active voice. Share and discuss your answers with a peer or your class.

1. Each year in America, 70,000 disasters are responded to by the American Red Cross.

2. Victims of house and apartment fires are helped by Red Cross volunteers.

3. Millions of patients are given blood collected by the Red Cross's blood drives.

4. The American Red Cross was established on May 21, 1881, by Clara Barton.

5. Relief to victims who have been afflicted by disaster across the world is provided by more than a million Red Cross volunteers.

6. Hurricanes, floods, house fires, and other natural or manmade disasters are responded to by the Red Cross.

7. When Haiti was devastated by an earthquake in 2010, $314.7 million was allocated by the Red Cross for relief.

8. Reducing deaths by measles worldwide has been targeted by Red Cross International Services.

9. Vaccination drives have been supported in over 60 countries by the Measles Initiative sponsored by Red Cross.

10. Millions of lives have been touched by the Red Cross.

Effective writing also involves stating ideas in the positive, which is more powerful than stating them in the negative. Too often, the use of a negative expression makes language seem unclear. The following charts offer some tips and examples for creating positive language.

Tips for Creating a Positive Voice
• Say what something **is** instead of what it **is not**. *Negative:* Your actions are not funny. *Positive:* Your actions are serious.
• Say what **can** be done instead of what **cannot** or **should not** be done. *Negative:* The witness cannot lie. *Positive:* The witness must tell the truth.
• Propose an **action** in addition to offering an **apology** or **explanation**. *Negative:* Sorry, we cannot respond until our computer is online. *Positive:* Sorry, we will respond as soon as our computer is online.

The following chart lists negative expressions in one column and positive revisions to those expressions in the other column.

Examples of Negative Expressions with Revisions to the Positive	
Negative Expression	**Positive Expression**
cannot lie	must tell the truth
cannot reconnect without	reconnect by
cannot waste resources	value resources
do not forget	remember
do not be late	be on time
do not be negative	be positive
never delay a response	respond quickly
never be rude	be polite
sorry, we cannot respond until	we will respond by
you misunderstood	let me clarify

Practice 4

USE POSITIVE LANGUAGE

Revise these sentences from negative statements to positive statements. Share and discuss your answers with a peer or your class.

1. We must not ignore those who need help.

....

2. The Red Cross is not able to do its job without volunteers and donations.

....

3. Joseph cannot give a donation until his next paycheck.

....

4. We must not forget about the victims of the 2010 Haiti earthquake.

....

5. The world did not delay in responding to Haiti in the aftermath of the earthquake.

....

6. The people of Haiti have not wasted the resources provided by other countries.

....

7. Two years after the earthquake, half of the debris had not been cleared by workers and a half million people had not yet moved out of tents into homes.

....

....

8. A cholera epidemic did not take long to occur in Haiti, and the disease took a long time to control.

....

....

9. A cholera epidemic could not be stopped without clean drinking water and a safe sewage system.

....

....

10. We must not misunderstand the need for long-term commitment to recovery efforts.

....

....

Practice 4

Use Concrete Language

Another key to effective writing is using **concrete language**. When writers use concrete language, they give readers vivid descriptions that can be visualized. Concrete language is the result of the thoughtful choice of nouns, verbs, adjectives, and adverbs. Your choice of words can mean the difference between writing that is **abstract** (vague, nonspecific writing) and writing that is concrete. Let's look at the difference between abstract and concrete nouns, verbs, adjectives, and adverbs.

An **abstract noun** names an emotion, feeling, idea, or trait detached from the five senses. A **concrete noun** names an animal, person, place, or object that the reader can see, touch, taste, hear, or smell (sensory details). The following chart illustrates the difference between concrete and abstract nouns.

Abstract Noun	Concrete Noun
Justice	Judge
Truth	Lie detector test

An **abstract verb** or verb phrase tells about a state of being or describes a general or nonspecific action. A **concrete verb** or verb phrase shows a specific action or creates a clear picture for the reader. The following chart illustrates the difference between abstract and concrete verbs and verb phrases.

Abstract Verb	Concrete Verb
She is afraid.	She screams in fear.
He got a raise.	He earned a raise.
Tashika went down the road.	Tashika drove down the road.

An **abstract adjective** is a broad and general description that is open to interpretation based on opinion. A **concrete adjective** shows a specific trait or sensory detail and is not open to interpretation. The best writing relies on the strength of concrete nouns and verbs, so use adjectives only when necessary.

Abstract Adjective	Concrete Adjective
awesome waves	20-foot waves
bad meat	rotted meat

An **abstract adverb** is a broad and general description that is open to interpretation based on opinion. A **concrete adverb** shows a specific trait or sensory detail and is not open to interpretation. The best writing relies on the strength of concrete nouns and verbs, so use adverbs only when necessary.

Abstract Adverb	Concrete Adverb
He has to eat a lot.	He has to eat hourly.
He kind of exercises.	He walks once a week.

Practice 5

USE CONCRETE LANGUAGE

▲ *Destruction caused by Hurricane Ike in Galveston*

Revise these sentences from abstract language to concrete language. Share and discuss your answers with a peer or your class.

1. Hurricane Ike caused a lot of damage to Galveston, Texas.

2. Pretty much all the buildings were really affected.

3. The coast of Texas got a lot of wind from Hurricane Ike.

4. The wind sounded awesome.

5. A Category 4 hurricane is a pretty strong storm.

6. Damage from a Category 4 hurricane can cost a lot of money.

7. Because we didn't evacuate, we went in the bathtub and were afraid for our lives.

8. A Category 4 hurricane usually causes a huge storm surge to crash into the coast.

9. A lot of people can be without power for a long time.

10. Even four years after Hurricane Ike, Galveston was still kind of recovering.

Practice 5

Use Fresh Language

L5

Effective writing also relies on using fresh language as opposed to clichés. Clichés are weak statements because they have lost their originality and forcefulness. See the example below.

Cliché:

You can't judge a book by its cover.

Fresh Language:

Outward appearance does not always provide a correct view of a person or object.

The following chart lists some popular clichés and their meanings.

Examples of Clichés and Their Meanings	
Cliché	**Meaning**
all bent out of shape	angry, upset
back against the wall	no escape, no options
call it a day	stop working
doesn't have a prayer	no hope or chance for success
easy as A, B, C	get organized or prepared
get your ducks in a row	simple, very easy
keep your chin up	be confident
missed the boat	lost opportunity
pain in the neck	a nuisance, a cause of trouble or concern
sharp as a tack	smart, witty, intelligent
wasted	drunk, intoxicated

Instead of relying on clichés such as the ones presented here, use fresh language as you revise your writing. When logical, create your own similes and metaphors to express your meaning.

Practice 6

USE FRESH LANGUAGE

Revise the following sentences by replacing clichés with fresh language. Share and discuss your answers with a peer or your class.

1. Maya is keeping her chin up as she prepares to evacuate before the storm.

2. She doesn't want to be caught with her back against the wall when the storm comes onshore.

3. During the last storm, she felt like she missed the boat because she waited too long to evacuate.

4. Evacuating is a pain in the neck, but it doesn't help to get bent out of shape about it.

5. Hundreds of people stock up with supplies and call it a day.

6. Once the storm hits, you need to remain calm; do not get all bent out of shape.

7. Families in one- or two-story homes built in low-lying areas didn't have a prayer unless they evacuated.

8. Some people endure a storm by getting wasted.

9. Preparing for a storm may not be as easy as A, B, C, but it could save your life.

10. After the storm destroyed his home, Lamar kept his chin up and began the recovery process.

EFFECTIVE EXPRESSION REVIEW

Revise the following sentences for effective expression. Remember to use the key ingredients of effective expression—concise, active, positive, concrete, and fresh language.

1. In this day and age, we need leaders who are busy as bees and sharp as tacks.

2. Our whole entire country is challenged by a lot of awesome natural disasters.

3. We must not be weak; we must not be afraid; we must not delay our action.

4. Given the fact that so many are in need, we cannot waste our resources.

5. We are absolutely certain that we will be confronted by another disaster.

6. Given the fact that severe weather occurs more frequently in this day and age, we must not delay in creating a disaster plan.

7. We don't want to repeat again the bad response to Hurricane Katrina.

8. In today's world, we have advanced notice of dangerous storms from sophisticated storm tracking systems.

9. Do not delay your response to a storm warning.

10. Don't forget, getting your ducks in a row before the storm hits may save your life.

Editing Assignments

MyWritingLab™
Complete this Exercise
on mywritinglab.com

Editing for Everyday Life

Assume you are writing a thank you note for a housewarming gift. Revise the note for effective expression. Use your own paper or complete the exercise on MyWritingLab.com.

> Dear Aunt Jo,
>
> I just wanted to drop you a line to thank you for the very unique lamp we got from you for our porch. I have never ever before seen a lamp made from a water pump. You can bet your bottom dollar that we love the lamp. We are always delighted with your really unusual and fun gifts.

Editing for College Life

Assume you are taking a sociology class, and you are studying the impact of a trauma, such as a natural disaster. Revise for effective expression.

> To summarize briefly, there are two types of trauma: physical and mental. Physical trauma is caused by serious injury and threat. Mental trauma has the ability to cause frightening thoughts and painful feelings. They are the mind's response to very serious injury. Strong feelings can be produced by mental trauma. Extreme behavior can be caused by it, too. Trauma makes people feel like they are off their rocker as they feel intense fear or helplessness, withdrawal, lack of the ability to concentration, being irritable, sleep problems, anger, or flashbacks.

Editing for Working Life

Assume you are applying for a job, and you have written a cover letter. Revise for effective expression.

> Dear Ms. Matthews:
>
> I am writing to apply for the position of office manager. In this day and age, there is a need for very creative and hardworking employees. You better believe that I am a worker who thinks outside the box and who is willing to roll up her sleeves and get to work. I am absolutely certain that my experience and education have made me the exact right choice for this position. Don't hesitate to contact me if you need more information.

WHAT HAVE I LEARNED ABOUT USING EFFECTIVE EXPRESSION?

To test and track your understanding, answer the following questions.

1. The most effective writing is .... and to the point.

2. .... avoids wordiness.

3. .... is the use of unnecessary or redundant words and phrases that add nothing to the writer's meaning.

4. The .... voice states what somebody or something did.

5. The .... voice states what was done to somebody or something.

6. Stating ideas in the .... is much more powerful than stating them in

   the ....

7. .... language is the result of the thoughtful choice of nouns,

   ...., adjectives, and adverbs.

8. A .... is a trite or overused expression.

9. **How will I use what I have learned about effective expression?**
   In your notebook, discuss how you will apply to your own writing what you have learned about effective expression. When during the writing process will you apply this knowledge?

10. **What do I still need to study about effective expression?**
    In your notebook, describe your ongoing study needs by describing what, when, and how you will continue studying effective expression.

Academic Learning Log: Chapter Review

PORTFOLIO

MyWritingLab™

Complete the Post-test for Chapter 24 in MyWritingLab.

Reading Selections

Reading and writing are mirror reflections of the thinking process.

The connection between reading and writing is a natural one. Effective writers are often avid readers. They know that reading and studying well-written pieces by other writers is one way to become a better writer. To begin your thinking about the connection between reading and writing, complete the following activity.

What's the Connection Between Reading and Writing?

Practice 1

YOUR COLLEGE EXPERIENCE REQUIRES THAT YOU READ AND WRITE.

Many students agree that reading and writing are related, but often, they do not actively make use of the connection. To gauge your own understanding and use of the connection between reading and writing, answer the following questions in your notebook. Brainstorm or share your answers in a small group discussion.

• Do you enjoy reading? Why or why not?

• Do you think reading is an important activity? Why or why not?

• Do you enjoy writing? Why or why not?

• Do you think writing is an important activity? Why or why not?

• What do you read for school? For work? For personal enjoyment? For general information?

• If you don't read much, what could or should you read for school, work, personal enjoyment, or general information?

• How often do you write? Why? What kind of writing do you do: journal writing, creative writing, academic assignments, business reports and letters, e-mailing or blogging?

• What are some specific ways you think reading can help a writer?

Make the Connection Between Reading and Writing

Reading benefits a writer in many ways. For example, by reading, a writer gains the following:

- New vocabulary
- Different opinions on a topic
- Additional facts about a topic
- Details that support an opinion
- Varying ways to apply writing techniques
  - Ways to use punctuation
  - Ways to use fresh or creative expressions
  - Ways to write sentences
  - Ways to organize ideas
  - Ways to open and close an essay

The more you read, the more you know and the more you have to write about.

A major similarity between reading and writing is that each is a thinking process best accomplished in specific stages; careful thought before, during, and after reading a selection or writing a piece improves your ability to do both. The following chart correlates the stages of the reading and the writing processes by listing the similarities between each of their phases.

The Connection Between Reading and Writing

	Reading	Writing
Phase 1:	Preread: Ask questions and skim details to discover the writer's purpose and point	Prewrite: Ask questions to generate details to discover your purpose and point for writing; read for information to use in your writing
Phase 2:	Read: Comprehend the writer's purpose and point; take note of key words, main ideas, major supports	Draft: Communicate your purpose and point with the use of key words, main ideas, and supporting details
Phase 3:	Review and Reflect: Achieve and reinforce clear understanding of the writer's purpose and point; adjust your views based on new information gained through reading	Revise: Rephrase or re-organize ideas to clearly support your point; ensure the reader's understanding of your purpose and point
Phase 4:	Record: Discuss changes in your thinking based on new information learned through reading; respond to the writer's ideas with your new insights based on new understandings; use all the phases of the writing process	Edit: Create an error-free draft that reflects your new insights and skills as a writer

As you can see, reading and writing mirror each other. Becoming strong in one makes you strong in the other.

Practice 2

Choose a selection from the eighteen reading selections. Working together with a small group of your peers, use the reporter's questions (*Who? What? When? Where? How? Why?*) to generate prereading and prewriting questions. Create general questions about the writer's purpose, main idea, supporting details, logical order, or word choice. Use your own paper.

The basic connection between reading and writing is thinking: thinking about the meaning of what you read and what you say, and thinking about the connection between what you read and what you write. To fully realize the connection between reading and writing, you need to be an active and focused thinker. Two active thinking-reading-writing tasks are annotating a text and writing a summary. The following discussions take you through several steps that show you how to think, read, think again, reread, and then write—as a strategy to improve your writing.

How to Annotate a Text

Use your writing skills throughout the reading process to ensure that you are an active thinker. Annotate the text, take notes, and write journal entries, summaries, and critical responses to what you read. Annotating the text before and during reading is an active thinking-reading-writing strategy. You have been taught to ask questions as a prereading thinking task. When you read, annotate your text as you find the answers to your questions.

The word *annotate* suggests that you "take notes" on the page of the text. Writing notes in the margin of the page as you read focuses your attention and improves your concentration. Annotating also will improve your understanding of the writer's purpose and point. You can note questions or answers quickly where they occur, move on in your reading, and later return to those details for clarification. In addition to writing notes, you can underline, circle, or highlight important terms, definitions, examples, or other key ideas. After reading, a review of your annotations will make responding to the material easier and more efficient. The following techniques are often used to annotate a text. Use these as guidelines to develop your own system for annotating a text.

Annotation Techniques
• Underline the main idea once.
• Underline major supporting details twice.
• Circle or highlight key words or special terms.
• Place small question marks above unknown words.
• Signal steps in a process or list by using numbers.
• Point out important concepts with symbols such as a star or a check.
• Write recall questions in the margin where the answer is found.
• Write a statement for an implied idea.
• Write a summary.

Use your annotations to guide your written response to a piece of writing. The following selection has been annotated for you as an illustration.

What's the difference between stress and a challenge?

What Is Job Stress?

Job stress can be defined as the harmful physical and emotional responses that occur when the requirements of the job do not match the *abilities?* capabilities, resources, or needs of the worker. Job stress can lead to poor health and even injury. The concept of job stress is often confused with challenge, but these concepts are not the same. *mentally?* Challenge energizes us psychologically and physically, and it motivates us to learn new skills and master our jobs. When a challenge is met, we feel relaxed and satisfied. *useful? large amounts of work?* Thus, challenge is an important ingredient for healthy and productive work. The importance of challenge in our work lives is probably what people are referring to when they say "a little bit of stress is good for you."

—Centers for Disease Control and Prevention. "Stress . . . at Work." National Institute for Occupational Safety and Health. Publication No. 99-101. 11 Dec. 2008. <http://www.cdc.gov/niosh/stresswk.html#c>.

Practice 3

Reread the selection you chose for Practice 2. As you read, annotate the text. After you have annotated the text, recall and record in your notebook what you remember about the selection.

How to Write a Summary

A summary includes only the most important points of a text. A summary is a restatement of the main idea and the major supporting details. The length of the summary should reflect the length of the passage you are trying to understand. For example, a paragraph might be summarized in a sentence or two; an article might be summarized in a paragraph, and a much longer document might be summarized in several paragraphs.

Writing a summary by relying on the annotations you make during reading is an excellent way to check your understanding of what you read. Always use the writer's name and the title of the text in your summary. The following summary is based on the annotations of the piece on job stress.

According to the article "What Is Job Stress?" job stress occurs when the abilities, assets, or goals of the worker differ from the demands of the job. The physical and emotional reactions to job stress can injure the health of the worker. Job stress differs from a challenge, which may require hard work, but brings satisfaction.

Write a summary based on the annotations you made for the reading selection you used in Practice 3. Use your own paper.

Practice 4

A Reading Strategy for a Writer

As you read the eighteen selections included in this section, use the following reading strategy to make the connection between reading and writing. Read each selection three times. Read it once just to enjoy the writing. Then, reread the piece to annotate it for understanding. Then, read a third time to study the piece more closely to prepare for a written response. The following steps are a guide to how to get the most out of your reading.

Reading Like a Writer

Before Reading Write a journal entry about the topic, title, and vocabulary. What do you already know, believe, or feel about the topic? Skim the text to identify and look up new or difficult words.

During Reading Annotate the text. Underline or highlight key terms, definitions, and main ideas. Generate questions to guide your thinking as you read; these questions will help you recall information after you read. Look for the answers to these questions and annotate the text when you come across the answers. Many college textbooks provide comprehension questions after a section of information. Feel free to use these after reading questions to focus your attention as you read.

After Reading Think, discuss, and write about what you read. Each of the eighteen reading selections has four discussion questions about the writer's main idea, relevant details, logical order, and effective expression. These directed thinking activities are called "After Reading Discussion Questions: Meaning, Structure, and Expression." Your writing will improve as you learn how other writers handle these elements.

- **Discuss it** Use your annotations to compare your views about a text with those of your classmates. Be open to ideas you had not considered. Add information to your notes. Discuss possible written responses.

- **Write about it** Respond in writing to the text. Each of the eighteen reading selections has two activities called "Thinking Prompts to Move from Reading to Writing."

Eighteen Reading Selections

Description

Water

RACHEL SCHNELLER

The Peace Corps Experience Award is presented yearly to a Peace Corps Volunteer or staff member, past or present, who has written the best short description of life in the Peace Corps. The subject matter can be any aspect of the daily life of the Peace Corps experience. In the following essay, 1998 Peace Corps Experience Award winner Rachel Schneller describes her observations of women carrying water in Kenya.

Before Reading Have you or someone you know struggled to complete a difficult physical task? Or have you ever seen a person whose physical appearance reveals his or her struggle? Write a journal entry that describes a person facing a difficulty or challenge.

1   When a woman carries water on her head, you see her neck bend outward behind her like a crossbow. Ten liters of water weighs twenty-two pounds, a fifth of a woman's body weight, and I've seen women carry at least twenty liters in aluminum pots large enough to hold a television set.

2   To get the water from the cement floor surrounding the outdoor hand pump to the top of your head, you need help from the other women. You and another woman grab the pot's edges and lift it straight up between you. When you get it to head height, you duck underneath the pot and place it on the wad of rolled up cloth you always wear there when fetching water. This is the cushion between your skull and the metal pot full of water. Then your friend lets go. Spend a few seconds finding your balance. Then with one hand steadying the load, turn around and start your way home. It might be a twenty-minute walk through mud huts and donkey manure. All of this is done without words.

3   It is an action repeated so many times during the day that even though I have never carried water on my head, I know exactly how it is done.

4   Do not worry that no one will be at the pump to help you. The pump is the only source of clean drinking water for the village of three thousand people. Your family,

your husband and children rely on the water on your head. Maybe ten people will drink the water you carry. Pump water, everyone knows, is clean. Drinking well water will make you sick. People here die every month from diarrhea and dehydration.

The pump is also where you hear gossip of the women from the other side of the village. Your trip to the pump may be your only excuse for going outside of your family's Muslim home alone. When a woman finds her balance under forty pounds of water, I see her eyes roll to their corners in concentration. Her head makes the small movements of the hands of someone driving a car: constant correction. The biggest challenge is to turn all the way around from the pump in order to go home again. It is a small portion of the ocean, and it swirls and lurches on her head with long movements.

It looks painful and complicated and horrible for the posture and unhealthy for the vertebrae, but I wish I could do it. I have lived in this West African village for two years, but cannot even balance something solid, like a mango, on my head, let alone an object filled with liquid. When I lug my ten-liter plastic jug of water to my house by hand, it is only a hundred meters, but the container is heavy and unwieldy. Changing the jug from one hand to the other helps, but it is a change necessary every twenty meters. Handles do not balance. On your head, the water is symmetrical like the star on top of a Christmas tree. Because my life has never depended on it, I have never learned to balance.

—Rachel Schneller, "Water" in Peace Corps Experience Award Winner, July 1998 issue of RPCV Writers and Readers. Copyright © 1998. Reprinted by permission of the author.

Vocabulary
Before, during, and after reading the selection, annotate the text and write in your journal. Create a list of vocabulary words, along with their definitions. Give examples of their use from the selection you just read.

After Reading Discussion Questions: Meaning, Structure, and Expression

1. **Main Idea:** Work as a group to write a summary that answers the following questions: What purpose did Rachel Schneller have for writing this essay? Who is her intended audience? What is the main idea of the essay?

2. **Relevant Details:** Schneller uses vivid sensory details to describe the sights, sounds, and feelings of a woman carrying water on her head in a West African village. Identify these vivid sensory details, and discuss their impact on you as a reader. Which sensory details are the most effective? Why?

3. **Logical Order:** The third paragraph is a one-sentence statement about the author's personal experience. Why does she include this statement at this point in the essay? Why does she set it off in its own paragraph? How does this statement relate to the essay's conclusion? Is this statement a necessary detail? Why or why not?

4. **Effective Expression:** Throughout the essay, the author moves between the uses of first person "I," second person "you," and third person "a woman" or "her." For example, paragraph 5 combines all three points of view. Why did the author choose to shift between these points of view? Are the shifts in viewpoint confusing or effective? Why?

Thinking Prompts to Move from Reading to Writing

1. In her essay, Schneller vividly shows the difficulty of a process or task by describing the physical effects of performing that task. Write an essay that describes the physical effects of a difficult or stressful task or situation. Assume you are writing an essay for a college psychology or health class.

2. Schneller's description of a woman carrying water reveals much about the small African village in which she worked. Write a descriptive essay about an aspect of daily life that reveals something about your neighborhood, town, or city. Assume you are writing an article for your local newspaper.

Rain of Fire

EVAN THOMAS

Born in 1951 in Huntington, New York, Evan Thomas is a journalist and author. A graduate of Harvard University and the University of Virginia School of Law, he is the Editor at Large of *Newsweek*. Thomas has won many journalism awards. For example, his reports on the terror events of September 11 and the Iraq War helped *Newsweek* win the National Magazine Award for General Excellence for 2002 and 2004. The following selection is Part IV of a longer article called "The Day That Changed America" that appeared in *Newsweek* in 2001.

Before Reading Have you or someone you know ever been involved in a frightening or threatening situation? Describe what occurred and discuss how you or others felt and reacted.

1. A self-described workaholic, Virginia DiChiara was normally out of her house and on her way to work by 7 A.M. But the morning of September 11 was so brilliantly beautiful that DiChiara decided to dawdle. She let her two golden retrievers play in the yard, cooked herself some eggs, poured herself a cup of coffee. "I was just moseying along," she says. "I didn't feel like rushing." She left her Bloomfield, N.J., home at 7:40, a 40-minute delay that would end up saving her life.

2. It was a little after 8:40 when she entered the lobby of the North Tower of the World Trade Center. Together, with a Cantor Fitzgerald co-worker, she rode the elevator up to the 78th floor, where she crossed a lobby to take a second elevator the rest of the way to her office on the 101st floor. The elevator door opened and she pressed the button for 101. It was 8:46 A.M.

3. As the elevator doors closed, Flight 11 plowed into the northern face of Tower I some 20 floors above. The elevator went black and "bounced around like a ball," DiChiara recalls. "I remember seeing two lines shooting around the top of the elevator"—electrical cables that had come loose and were spitting current—and "everybody started screaming." In front of her was a man named Roy Bell, who later said that the sound of impact was "deafening," like someone banging a 2-by-2-foot sheet of aluminum with a hammer "six inches from your head." The right wall of the elevator car crashed into Bell, breaking several of his fingers and flinging him to the left side. Miraculously, the elevator doors remained open about a foot. Within seconds, Bell "just sprinted" out of the elevator, he recalls. "Inside was not where you wanted to be."

4. DiChiara had crouched down behind Bell. She saw Bell go through, and thought, "*I don't hear any screaming, so I know he's not on fire ... I'm outta her*e." She decided to go for it. But as she gathered herself, huge blue flames—translucent teardrops of fire, a foot in diameter—began falling in a steady curtain. DiChiara dropped her bag, covered her face with her palms and squeezed through the door, her elbows pushing the black rubber guards on the elevator doors. Left behind was her Cantor co-worker. DiChiara never saw her again; at times she feels guilty that she made it out and her co-worker did not.

5. DiChiara was aflame when she emerged from the elevator. "I remember hearing my hair on fire," she says. (She later joked, "I must have put on some extra hair spray.") With her hands she tapped out the fire. "I got it out, I got it," she said to herself. Then, feeling something else, she looked back and saw flames rising from her shoulder. In that instant, she remembered the old lesson from grade school: stop, drop, and roll. She threw herself to the carpeted floor and rolled over and over, frantically patting out the flames. "I remember getting up and just looking at myself," she says. "'OK, everything's out.' And then sort of laughing, almost like a hysteria, like a little giggle, like, 'Oh my God, let me do it again just in case I missed it.' I was so scared, like there was an ember on my body that was still going to go up."

6. DiChiara crawled some 20 feet down the hallway and sat with her back propped against a wall. She was wearing a sleeveless cotton shirt that day, and her arms and hands were seared with third-degree burns. In shock, she did not feel the pain—yet. Improbably prosaic thoughts crossed her mind. In the

briefcase she'd left on the elevator were some airplane tickets recently purchased for a vacation jaunt to the Florida Keys, as well as a wad of cash. Should she go back and retrieve it? "No," she thought to herself. "Just stay right where you are."

Then she spotted a co-worker, Ari Schonbrun, head of global accounts receivable at Cantor. "Ari!" she called out. He turned around and looked at her. "Virginia! Oh my God!" he said. "Ari, I'm badly burned," Virginia told him. She was gradually realizing how grave her condition truly was, and beginning to feel it as well. "I'm in so much pain," she said. Schonbrun was horrified. "The skin was peeled off her arms," he says. "You knew this woman was in trouble." DiChiara read his expression. "I knew by the look on his face that I was bad," she says. Schonbrun told her, "Virginia, take it easy. We're going to get help. Don't worry. You're going to be fine." She begged, "Whatever you do, don't leave me." Schonbrun reassured her, "I'm not going to leave you. I'll be with you."

The hallways were smoky, suffused with the nauseating smell of burned jet fuel, littered with debris, and completely dark save for some outdoor light filtering in from windows at the end of the hall. Schonbrun gently guided DiChiara toward a small security office behind the elevator banks where the lights still worked. About a dozen people were huddled there, including two security guards. DiChiara lay down on the floor, on the verge of passing out. A woman sitting nearby was crying. One of the security guards was furiously dialing for help on the office phone but couldn't get through. The other guard had a radio, but she was paralyzed, crying. Schonbrun told her, "You've got to calm down. You've got to get on that radio and get us help." The guard tried, but the only sound coming over the radio was a cacophony of screams.

Singed by his narrow escape through the elevator doors, Bell had also made it to the security office. His doctors would later tell him that the few seconds between his exit and DiChiara's made the difference between his second-degree and her third-degree burns. Suddenly, a man appeared saying that he was a fire warden. There was a stairwell in the middle of the tower that they could use, he announced. Schonbrun leaned over DiChiara and laid out the options: either they could wait for someone to rescue them, or they could start heading down by foot.

For DiChiara, there was no choice. No way was she going to sit there and wait. Gritting her teeth, she got up and headed for the stairwell.

—Evan Thomas, "The Day That Changed America, Part IV 'Rain of Fire'" From Newsweek 12/31/01 © 2001 IBT Media. all rights reserved. Used by permission and protected by the Copyright laws of the United States. The printing, copying, redistribution, or retransmission of this Content without express written permission is prohibited.

Vocabulary Before, during, and after reading the selection, annotate the text and write in your journal. Create a list of vocabulary words, along with their definitions. Give examples of their use from the selection you just read.

After Reading Discussion Questions: Meaning, Structure, and Expression

1. **Main Idea:** Work as a group to write a summary that answers the following questions: What purpose did Evan Thomas have for writing this essay? Who is his intended audience? What is the main idea of the essay?

2. **Relevant Details:** The opening paragraph gives a detailed description of Virginia DiChiara's morning activities before she went to work. Thomas could have easily omitted these details and simply told us that DiChiara came in later than usual on that fateful day. Why did he choose to include these details? How do these details help Thomas make his point?

3. **Logical Order:** The vivid description of the sights, sounds, and smells of the situation give this selection its power. However, Thomas organized his description through the use of another pattern of organization. What other pattern of organization did Thomas use? Why did Thomas use both patterns of organization? Would his essay have been as powerful if he had only used description? Why or why not?

4. **Effective Expression:** Thomas paints a graphic and unforgettable scene with dramatic language such as this expression from paragraph 4: "huge blue flames—translucent teardrops of fire, a foot in diameter—began falling in a steady curtain." Find three more uses of dramatic language and discuss their impact. How does each expression help Thomas make his point?

Thinking Prompts to Move from Reading to Writing

1. The essay "Rain of Fire" describes a man-made disaster and the ordeal of a woman who survived. Many of us have lived through natural disasters such as earthquakes, tornadoes, hurricanes, floods, or wildfires. Write an essay that describes a natural disaster and the suffering it caused either during or after the event. Assume you are writing an entry to post on your personal blog which has several hundred followers.

2. Through Evan Thomas's description, we see Virginia DiChiara go through a range of strong emotions including fear, panic, hysteria, courage, and determination. Think of a time when you or someone you know experienced similar strong emotions. Write an essay that describes a person experiencing a wide range of emotions. Assume you are writing an essay for a college psychology class.

Narration

For My Indian Daughter

LEWIS SAWAQUAT

Lewis Sawaquat, a Native American, was born on February 16, 1935, in Harbor Springs, Michigan. However, he was long known as Lewis Johnson. Like many other Native Americans, he had been assigned this more "acceptable" last name by the United States government. The government also forced him to attend a Catholic boarding school and to cut ties with his cultural roots. In 1986, Sawaquat won the National Essay of the Year award for the account of his life that he wrote for his young daughter. "For My Indian Daughter" was originally published in *Newsweek*.

Before Reading Have you or someone you know ever felt like an outsider? Did you try to change in order to fit in? Did you feel like an outsider because of your religion, race, or gender? Write a journal entry that describes how well you or someone you know fits into your peer group.

My little girl is singing herself to sleep upstairs, her voice mingling with the sounds of the birds outside in the old maple trees. She is two, and I am nearly 50, and I am very taken with her. She came along late in my life, unexpected and unbidden, a startling gift. 1

Today at the beach my chubby-legged, brown-skinned daughter ran laughing into the water as fast as she could. My wife and I laughed watching her, until we heard behind us a low guttural curse and then an unpleasant voice raised in an imitation war whoop. 2

I turned to see a fat man in a bathing suit, white and soft as a grub, as he covered his mouth and prepared to make the Indian war cry again. He was middle-aged, younger than I, and had three little children lined up next to him, grinning foolishly. My wife suggested we leave the beach, and I agreed. 3

I knew the man was not unusual in his feelings against Indians. His beach behavior might have been socially unacceptable to more civilized whites, but his basic view of Indians is expressed daily in our small town, frequently on the editorial pages of the county newspaper, as white people speak out against Indian fishing rights and land rights, saying in essence, "Those Indians are taking our fish, our land." It doesn't matter to them that we were here first, that the U.S. Supreme Court has ruled in our favor. It matters to them that we have something they want, and they hate us for it. Backlash is the common explanation of the attacks on Indians, the bumper stickers that say, "Spear an Indian, Save a Fish," but 4

I know better. The hatred of Indians goes back to the beginning when white people came to this country. For me it goes back to my childhood in Harbor Springs, Mich.

Theft. Harbor Springs is now a summer resort for the very affluent, but a hundred years ago it was the Indian village of my Ottawa ancestors. My grandmother, Anna Showanessy, and other Indians like her, had their land there taken by treaty, by fraud, by violence, by theft. They remembered how whites had burned down the village at Burt Lake in 1900 and pushed the Indians out. These were the stories in my family.

When I was a boy, my mother told me to walk down the alleys in Harbor Springs and not to wear my orange football sweater out of the house. This way I would not stand out, not be noticed, and not be a target.

I wore my orange sweater anyway and deliberately avoided the alleys. I was the biggest person I knew and wasn't really afraid. But I met my comeuppance when I enlisted in the U.S. Army. One night all the men in my barracks gathered together and, gang fashion, pulled me into the shower and scrubbed me down with rough brushes used for floors, saying, "We won't have any dirty Indians in our outfit." It is a point of irony that I was cleaner than any of them. Later in Korea I learned how to kill, how to bully, how to hate Koreans. I came out of the war tougher than ever and, strangely, white.

I went to college, got married, lived in La Porte, Ind., worked as a surveyor and raised three boys. I headed Boy Scout groups, never thinking it odd when the Scouts did imitation Indian dances, imitation Indian lore.

One day when I was 35 or thereabouts I heard about an Indian powwow. My father used to attend them, and so with great curiosity and a strange joy at discovering a part of my heritage, I decided the thing to do to get ready for this big event was to have my friend make me a spear in his forge. The steel was fine and blue and iridescent. The feathers on the shaft were bright and proud.

In a dusty state fairground in southern Indiana, I found white people dressed as Indians. I learned they were "hobbyists," that is, it was their hobby and leisure pastime to masquerade as Indians on weekends. I felt ridiculous with my spear, and I left.

It was years before I could tell anyone of the embarrassment of this weekend and see any humor in it. But in a way it was that weekend, for all its silliness, that was my awakening. I realized I didn't know who I was. I didn't have an Indian name. I didn't speak the Indian language. I didn't know the Indian customs. Dimly I remembered the Ottawa word for dog, but it was a baby word, *kahgee*, not the full word, *muhkahgee*, which I was later to learn. Even more hazily I remembered a naming ceremony (my own). I remembered legs dancing around me, dust. Where had that been? Who had I been? "Sawaquat," my mother told me when I asked, "where the tree begins to grow."

That was 1968, and I was not the only Indian in the country who was feeling the need to remember who he or she was. There were others. They had powwows, real ones, and eventually I found them. Together we researched our past, a search that for me culminated in the Longest Walk, a march on Washington in 1978. Maybe because I now know what it means to be Indian, it surprises me that others don't. Of course there aren't very many of us left. The chances of an average person knowing an average Indian in an average lifetime are pretty slim.

Circle. Still, I was amused one day when my small, four-year-old neighbor looked at me as I was hoeing in my garden and said, "You aren't a real Indian, are you?" Scotty is little, talkative, likable. Finally I said, "I'm a real Indian." He looked at me for a moment and then said, squinting into the sun, "Then where's your horse and feathers?" The child was simply a smaller, whiter version of my own ignorant self years before. We'd both seen too much TV, that's all. He was not to be blamed. And so, in a way, the moronic man on the beach today is blameless. We come full circle to realize other people are like ourselves, as discomfiting as that may be sometimes.

As I sit in my old chair on my porch, in a light that is fading so the leaves are barely distinguishable against the sky, I can picture my girl asleep upstairs. I would like to prepare her for what's to come, take her each step of the way saying, there's a place to avoid, here's what I know about this, but much of what's before her she must go through alone. She must pass through pain and joy and solitude and community to discover her own inner self that is unlike any other and come through that passage to the place where she sees all people are one, and in so seeing may live her life in a brighter future.

—Lewis Sawaquat, "For My Indian Daughter" is reprinted by permission of The Estate of Lewis Sawaquat.

Vocabulary Before, during, and after reading the selection, annotate the text and write in your journal. Create a list of vocabulary words, along with their definitions. Give examples of their use from the selection you just read.

After Reading Discussion Questions: Meaning, Structure, and Expression

1. **Main Idea:** Work as a group to write a summary that answers the following questions: What purpose did Lewis Sawaquat have for writing this essay? Who is his intended audience? What is the main idea of the essay?

2. **Relevant Details:** In paragraph 13, Sawaquat states, "The child was simply a smaller, whiter version of my own ignorant self years before. We'd both seen too much TV, that's all." How is television relevant to the point he is making?

3. **Logical Order:** Sawaquat organizes his ideas into three sections. Paragraphs 1–4 give background information. Then, he labels the next two sections "Theft" (paragraphs 5–12) and "Circle" (paragraphs 13–14). Why did he use these labels to divide his story into phases? Why is the second section longer than the other two?

4. **Effective Expression:** Sawaquat chooses his words to convey strong emotions and biases. For example, in paragraph 3 he uses the words "fat . . . grub . . . foolishly" to describe the white man and his family. Identify three other uses of emotional or biased language. Discuss his reasons for choosing those words and examine the impact those words have on the reader.

Thinking Prompts to Move from Reading to Writing

1. In his conclusion, Sawaquat states that his daughter "must pass through pain and joy and solitude and community to discover her own inner self." His essay tells of his own journey of self-discovery. Write your own essay about a journey of self-discovery. Share an incident that forced you or someone you know to grow up or become independent. Assume you are writing in a journal that you intend to pass on to your children and grandchildren.

2. In paragraphs 6–7, Sawaquat deals with instances of bullying because he was different—a Native American. Bullying is a common problem that many still face. Write a story about an incident in which a person is bullied because he or she is different. Assume you are writing a letter to your local school board to raise awareness about the problems of bullying.

Fish Cheeks

AMY TAN

Born in Oakland, California, in 1952 to immigrant parents from China, Amy Tan is the award-winning author of several novels, including her widely popular and critically acclaimed novel *The Joy Luck Club*. Tan's work explores the challenges of growing up as a first-generation Asian American. The following essay was published in her first nonfiction book, *The Opposite of Fate: A Book of Musings*, about her own life and family.

Before Reading Write a journal entry about the "shame of being different." Why is it hard to be different from the larger group? Why do we feel the need to belong? What are some differences that might cause a person to feel isolated or ashamed? How hard is it for someone from another country to be considered part of American society?

I fell in love with the minister's son the winter I turned 14. He was not Chinese, but as white as Mary in the manger. For Christmas I prayed for this blond-haired boy, Robert, and a slim new American nose.   1

When I found out that my parents had invited the minister's family over for Christmas Eve dinner, I cried. What would Robert think of our shabby Chinese Christmas? What would he think of our noisy Chinese relatives who lacked proper American manners? What terrible disappointment would he feel upon seeing not a roast turkey and sweet potatoes but Chinese food?   2

On Christmas Eve I saw that my mother had outdone herself in creating a strange menu. She was pulling black veins out of the backs of prawns. The kitchen was littered with appalling mounds of raw food: a slimy rock cod with bulging fish eyes that pleaded not to be thrown in a pan of hot oil. Tofu, which looked like stacked wedges of rubbery white sponges. A bowl soaking dried fungus back to life. A plate of squid, their backs crisscrossed with knife markings so they resembled bicycle tires.   3

And then they arrived—the minister's family and all my relatives in a clamor of doorbells and rumpled Christmas packages. Robert grunted hello, and I pretended he was not worthy of existence.   4

Dinner threw me deeper into despair. My relatives licked the ends of their chopsticks and reached across the table, dipping them into the dozen or so plates of food. Robert and his family waited patiently for platters to be passed to them. My relatives murmured with pleasure when my mother brought out the whole steamed fish. Robert grimaced. Then my father poked his chopsticks just below the fish eye and plucked out the soft meat. "Amy, your favorite," he said, offering me the tender fish cheek. I wanted to disappear.   5

At the end of the meal my father leaned back and belched loudly, thanking my mother for her fine cooking. "It's a polite Chinese custom to show you are satisfied," explained my father to our astonished guests. Robert was looking down at his plate with a reddened face. The minister managed to muster up a quiet burp. I was stunned into silence for the rest of the night.   6

After everyone had gone, my mother said to me, "You want be the same as American girls on the outside." She handed me an early gift. It was a miniskirt in beige tweed. "But inside you must always be Chinese. You must be proud to be different. Your only shame is to have a shame."   7

And even though I didn't agree with her then, I knew that she understood how much I had suffered during the evening's dinner. It wasn't until many years later—long after I had gotten over my crush on Robert—that I was able to appreciate fully her lesson and the true purpose behind our particular menu. For Christmas Eve that year, she had chosen all my favorite foods.   8

—"Fish Cheeks" by Amy Tan. Copyright © 1987 by Amy Tan. first appeared in *Seventeen Magazine*. Reprinted by permission of the author and the Sandra Dijkstra Literary Agency.

Vocabulary Before, during, and after reading the selection, annotate the text and write in your journal. Create a list of vocabulary words, along with their definitions. Give examples of their use from the selection you just read.

After Reading Discussion Questions: Meaning, Structure, and Expression

1. **Main Idea:** Work as a group to write a summary that answers the following questions: What purpose did Amy Tan have for writing this piece? Who is her intended audience? What is the main idea of the essay?

2. **Relevant Details:** In paragraph 8, Tan admits that she "had suffered during the evening's dinner." Identify the details that caused her suffering. Why did these details cause her to "cry" or feel "despair" or "want to disappear"?

3. **Logical Order:** What is the significance of the last sentence of the essay? Why does Amy Tan wait until the end of the essay to reveal this detail? Would the essay have been more effective if she had made this statement earlier? Why or why not?

4. **Effective Expression:** In paragraph 3, Tan vividly describes the foods her mother prepared. Are her descriptions positive or negative? Give examples and explain. Compare her descriptions of the food to the last sentence of the essay. Why do you think she describes her "favorite foods" as she does in paragraph 3? Why did her mother prepare all her favorite foods that Christmas Eve?

Thinking Prompts to Move from Reading to Writing

1. In this essay, Amy Tan describes her youthful struggle with being different and her shame of her family's culture. Have you or someone you know struggled with being "different"? Write a narrative essay about a specific event or struggle with being different or trying to fit in. Assume you are writing an essay to post on a blog that is read by teenagers from all over the world.

2. Amy Tan's narrative recreates a vivid scene of a dinner that reveals both the family's culture and the personalities of the family members. Write a narrative that captures your family's culture and personality, or describe a family you know. Like Tan, include details about the food and table manners to reveal cultural and personality traits. Assume you are writing in a journal that you intend to pass down to your children and grandchildren.

Process

Getting Coffee Is Hard to Do

STANLEY FISH

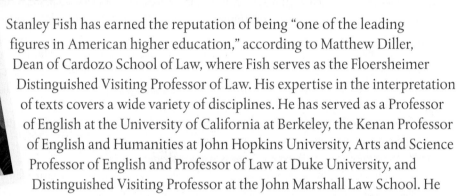

Stanley Fish has earned the reputation of being "one of the leading figures in American higher education," according to Matthew Diller, Dean of Cardozo School of Law, where Fish serves as the Floersheimer Distinguished Visiting Professor of Law. His expertise in the interpretation of texts covers a wide variety of disciplines. He has served as a Professor of English at the University of California at Berkeley, the Kenan Professor of English and Humanities at John Hopkins University, Arts and Science Professor of English and Professor of Law at Duke University, and Distinguished Visiting Professor at the John Marshall Law School. He also served as Dean of the College of Liberal Arts and Sciences at the University of Illinois. A prolific writer, he has published over 200 scholarly books and articles and contributes to "The Opinionator" blog for the *New York Times*. In the following column, he describes a process that was once easy but has become more complicated.

Before Reading Write a journal entry about the process of buying a particular product or service. How easy is it to make the purchase? What steps do you go through to make the purchase? How could the process be made easier for the customer?

A coordination problem (a term of art in economics and management) occurs when you have a task to perform, the task has multiple and shifting components, the time for completion is limited, and your performance is affected by the order and sequence of the actions you take. The trick is to manage it so that the components don't bump into each other in ways that produce confusion, frustration and inefficiency.   1

You will face a coordination problem if you are a general deploying troops, tanks, helicopters, food, tents and medical supplies, or if you are the C.E.O. of a large company juggling the demands of design, personnel, inventory and production.   2

And these days, you will face a coordination problem if you want to get a cup of coffee.   3

It used to be that when you wanted a cup of coffee you went into a nondescript place fitted out largely in linoleum, Formica and neon, sat down at a counter, and, in response to a brisk "What'll you have,   4 dear?" said, "Coffee and a cheese Danish." Twenty seconds later, tops, they arrived, just as you were settling into the sports page.

Now it's all wood or concrete floors, lots of earth tones, soft, high-style lighting, open barrels of coffee beans, folk-rock and indie music, photographs of urban landscapes, and copies of The Onion. As you walk in, everything is saying, "This is very sophisticated, and you'd better be up to it." 5

It turns out to be hard. First you have to get in line, and you may have one or two people in front of you who are ordering a drink with more parts than an internal combustion engine, something about "double shot," "skinny," "breve," "grande," "au lait" and a lot of other words that never pass my lips. If you are patient and stay in line (no bathroom breaks), you get to put in your order, but then you have to find a place to stand while you wait for it. There is no such place. So you shift your body, first here and then there, trying not to get in the way of those you can't help get in the way of. 6

Finally, the coffee arrives. 7

But then your real problems begin when you turn, holding your prize, and make your way to where the accessories — things you put in, on and around your coffee — are to be found. There is a staggering array of them, and the order of their placement seems random in relation to the order of your needs. There is no "right" place to start, so you lunge after one thing and then after another with awkward reaches. 8

Unfortunately, two or three other people are doing the same thing, and each is doing it in a different sequence. So there is an endless round of "excuse me," "no, excuse me," as if you were in an old Steve Martin routine. 9

But no amount of politeness and care is enough. After all, there are so many items to reach for — lids, cup jackets, straws, napkins, stirrers, milk, half and half, water, sugar, Splenda, the wastepaper basket, spoons. You and your companions may strive for a ballet of courtesy, but what you end up performing is more like bumper cars. It's just a question of what will happen first — getting what you want or spilling the coffee you are trying to balance in one hand on the guy reaching over you. 10

I won't even talk about the problem of finding a seat. 11

And two things add to your pain and trouble. First, it costs a lot, $3 and up. And worst of all, what you're paying for is the privilege of doing the work that should be done by those who take your money. The coffee shop experience is just one instance of the growing practice of shifting the burden of labor to the consumer—gas stations, grocery and drug stores, bagel shops (why should I put on my own cream cheese?), airline check-ins, parking lots. It's insert this, swipe that, choose credit or debit, enter your PIN, push the red button, error, start again. At least when you go on a "vacation" that involves working on a ranch, the work is something you've chosen. But none of us has chosen to take over the jobs of those we pay to serve us. 12

Well, it's Sunday morning, and you're probably reading this with a cup of coffee. I hope it was easy to get. 13

—Stanley Fish, Getting Coffee Is Hard to Do, *The New York Times*, August 5, 2007.

Vocabulary Before, during, and after reading the selection, annotate the text and write in your journal. Create a list of vocabulary words, along with their definitions. Give examples of their use from the selection you just read.

After Reading Discussion Questions: Meaning, Structure, and Expression

1. **Central Idea:** Work as a group to write a summary that answers the following questions: What purpose did Stanley Fish have for writing this piece? Who is the intended audience? What is the central idea of the essay? What is the significance of the title of the piece?

2. **Relevant Details:** Fish describes in detail the steps in the current process of getting a cup of coffee as an example of his central point. Identify and discuss three specific steps that support his central idea.

3. **Logical Order:** Fish asserts his central idea in paragraph 12, the next to last paragraph of his column. Why did he wait so late in the essay to state his central idea? Would the essay have been more effective if he had stated his central point in the first paragraph? Why or why not?

4. **Effective Expression:** How would you describe the tone of this column? Is it objective, angry, amused? What words or expressions establish the tone? For example, what tone is established by the contrast of ideas between paragraphs 2 and 3?

Thinking Prompts to Move from Reading to Writing

1. Assume you are writing an essay for a college course in sociology. Your topic is Changes in Society. In his column, Fish describes changes in the process of ordering a cup of coffee. In addition, in paragraph 12, he lists a number of other places where processes have changed, such as at gas stations, grocery and drug stores, and so on. Choose one of these shopping experiences or a similar one and describe how the process has changed. What was it like before and what is it like now? Is the new way easier or better than the old way? Why or why not?

2. Assume you are the manager of a coffee shop. As you read this column, you realized that your coffee shop and customers' experiences are similar to the one described by Fish. Based on the details in Fish's column, describe the steps you will take as manager to improve customer service. Write your ideas in the form of a memo that you will send out to your staff about the necessary changes in service and the reasons for the changes.

An American Slave: Written by Himself, Chapter VII

FREDERICK DOUGLASS

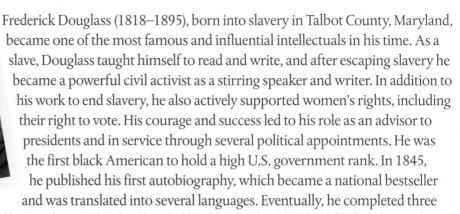

Frederick Douglass (1818–1895), born into slavery in Talbot County, Maryland, became one of the most famous and influential intellectuals in his time. As a slave, Douglass taught himself to read and write, and after escaping slavery he became a powerful civil activist as a stirring speaker and writer. In addition to his work to end slavery, he also actively supported women's rights, including their right to vote. His courage and success led to his role as an advisor to presidents and in service through several political appointments. He was the first black American to hold a high U.S. government rank. In 1845, he published his first autobiography, which became a national bestseller and was translated into several languages. Eventually, he completed three versions of his autobiography that detailed his life as a slave and his life after the Civil War. The following passage is an excerpt from his first autobiography.

Before Reading Write a journal entry about how an individual learns to read and write. When does this process of learning to read and write usually begin? What steps does a person usually go through? What type of help do most people need to learn how to read and write?

Very soon after I went to live with Mr. and Mrs. Auld, she very kindly commenced to teach me the A, B, C. After I had learned this, she assisted me in learning to spell words of three or four letters. Just at this point of my progress, Mr. Auld found out what was going on, and at once forbade Mrs. Auld to instruct me further, telling her, among other things, that it was unlawful, as well as unsafe, to teach a slave to read. 1

"It would forever unfit him to be a slave. He would at once become unmanageable, and of no value to his master. As to himself, it could do him no good, but a great deal of harm. It would make him discontented and unhappy." These words sank deep into my heart, stirred up sentiments within that lay slumbering, and called into existence an entirely new train of thought. It was a new and special revelation, explaining dark and mysterious things, with which my youthful understanding had struggled, but struggled in vain. I now understood what had been to me a most perplexing difficulty—to wit, the white man's power to enslave the black man. It was a grand achievement, and I prized it highly. From that 2 moment, I understood the pathway from slavery to freedom. It was just what I wanted, and I got it at a time when I the least expected it. Whilst I was saddened by the thought of losing the aid of my kind mistress, I was gladdened by the invaluable instruction which, by the merest accident, I had gained from my master.

* * *

Though conscious of the difficulty of learning without a teacher, I set out with high hope, and a fixed purpose, at whatever cost of trouble, to learn how to read.

3

* * *

The first step had been taken. Mistress, in teaching me the alphabet, had given me the *inch*, and no precaution could prevent me from taking the *ell*.

4

The plan which I adopted, and the one by which I was most successful, was that of making friends of all the little white boys whom I met in the street. As many of these as I could, I converted into teachers. With their kindly aid, obtained at different times and in different places, I finally succeeded in learning to read. When I was sent of errands, I always took my book with me, and by going one part of my errand quickly, I found time to get a lesson before my return. I used also to carry bread with me, enough of which was always in the house, and to which I was always welcome; for I was much better off in this regard than many of the poor white children in our neighborhood. This bread I used to bestow upon the hungry little urchins, who, in return, would give me that more valuable bread of knowledge. I am strongly tempted to give the names of two or three of those little boys, as a testimonial of the gratitude and affection I bear them; but prudence forbids;—not that it would injure me, but it might embarrass them; for it is almost an unpardonable offence to teach slaves to read in this Christian country.

5

* * *

The idea as to how I might learn to write was suggested to me by being in Durgin and Bailey's ship yard, and frequently seeing the ship carpenters, after hewing, and getting a piece of timber ready for use, write on the timber the name of that part of the ship for which it was intended. When a piece of timber was intended for the larboard side, it would be marked thus—"L." When a piece was for the starboard side, it would be marked thus-—"S." A piece for the larboard side forward, would be marked thus— "L. F." When a piece was for starboard side forward, it would be marked thus—"S. F." For larboard aft, it would be marked thus—"L. A." For starboard aft, it would be marked thus—"S. A." I soon learned the names of these letters, and for what they were intended when placed upon a piece of timber in the ship-yard. I immediately commenced copying them, and in a short time was able to make the four letters named. After that, when I met with any boy who I knew could write, I would tell him I could write as well as he. The next word would be, "I don't believe you. Let me see you try it." I would then make the letters which I had been so fortunate as to learn, and ask him to beat that. In this way I got a good many lessons in writing, which it is quite possible I should never have gotten in any other way.

6

During this time, my copy-book was the board fence, brick wall, and pavement; my pen and ink was a lump of chalk. With these, I learned mainly how to write. I then commenced and continued copying the Italics in Webster's Spelling Book, until I could make them all without looking on the book. By this time, my little Master Thomas had gone to school, and learned how to write, and had written over a number of copy-books. These had been brought home, and shown to some of our near neighbors, and then laid aside. My mistress used to go to class meeting at the Wilk Street meeting house every Monday afternoon, and leave me to take care of the house. When left thus, I used to spend the time in writing in the spaces left in Master Thomas's copy-book, copying what he had written. I continued to do this until I could write a hand very similar to that of Master Thomas. Thus, after a long, tedious effort for years, I finally succeeded in learning how to write.

7

—Chapter VII in *Narrative of the Life of Frederick Douglass, An American Slave, Written by Himself* by Frederick Douglass.

Vocabulary
Before, during, and after reading the selection, annotate the text and write in your journal. Create a list of vocabulary words, along with their definitions. Give examples of their use from the selection you just read.

After Reading Discussion Questions: Meaning, Structure, and Expression

1. **Main Idea:** Work as a group to write a summary that answers the following questions: What purpose did Frederick Douglass have for writing this piece? Who is the intended audience? What is the main idea of the essay? What is the significance of the title of the piece?

2. **Relevant Details:** What do you consider to be the most significant detail in this passage? Why is this detail so significant? How would the omission of this detail affect the effectiveness of the passage?

3. **Logical Order:** In this selection, Douglass combines narration and process as primary patterns of organization supported by cause and effect. Identify specific uses of each of these patterns of organization: narration, process, and cause/effect. Using the examples you identified, explain why each pattern was necessary to explain his experience.

4. **Effective Expression:** What is the tone of this selection? Is the tone matter-of-fact, bitter, proud, joyful, or some other tone or combination of tones? Which words establish his tone? Why did he choose the tone he did? How does his tone support his purpose for writing about his experiences to a general audience?

Thinking Prompts to Move from Reading to Writing

1. Assume you are writing about a key issue for a college course in social science. Your professor requires that you find and respond to a piece of text about a topic that has great social importance. You have chosen to write about the importance of literacy. In paragraph 2, Douglass describes his understanding about the importance of reading and writing as "the pathway from slavery to freedom." Explain how reading and writing may lead to independence and freedom. Consider how reading and writing was a path for Douglass to become a free man, or explain how reading and writing may be a path of freedom from poverty, prejudice, addiction, or other conditions that impede a person's progress and well being.

2. Assume you serve as volunteer at a local organization that works with at-risk students in an after school program. You have been asked to give a speech to the youth to encourage them to value literacy. Write a speech that explains steps the audience members can take to improve their reading and writing skills. Use details from Frederick Douglass to inspire and motivate your audience.

Illustration

What's Wrong with These Bleeping People?

KATHLEEN PARKER

An American journalist, Parker started her column in 1987 as a staff writer for *The Orlando Sentinel.* Her column was nationally syndicated in 1995. She joined The Washington Post Writers Group in 2006. In addition, she has contributed articles to *The Weekly Standard, Time, Town & Country, Cosmopolitan,* and *Fortune Small Business.* She also serves on the Board of Contributors for *USA Today* and writes for that newspaper's op-ed page. She is a regular guest on "The Chris Matthews Show" on NBC. In 2008, Random House published her book *Why Men Matter, Why Women Should Care.* In 2010, Parker won the Pulitzer Prize for Commentary with a selection of political opinion columns. In the following piece, she shares her opinion about public profanity.

Before Reading Write a journal entry about the public use of profane or obscene language. Do you think it is ever appropriate to use swear words or obscene language in public places? Why or why not?

1   Scene: An elevator in New York Presbyterian Hospital where several others and I were temporary hostages of a filthy-mouthed woman who was profanely berating her male companion. It wasn't possible to discern whether he was her mate or her son, but his attire (baggy drawers) and insolent disposition seemed to suggest the latter.

Every other word out of the woman's mouth was mother—, presumably a coincidental reference to any familial relationship. Finally, she shared with us bystanders her belief that said mother— would not be welcome in her house (Hark! Good news at last!) and that he could very well seek shelter at his mother—ing father's house. Aha, family ties established. 2

At this point, in a variation of deus ex machina, the elevator doors opened and we, the numb majority, were able to escape our too-close quarters, but not the diatribe, which continued unabated down the hallway, through the exit and onto the sidewalk. 3

A few of us made eye contact and returned the stare of recognition common among hostages. The understood sentiment is helpless indignation. What, really, can one do under such circumstances? 4

It was comical in a way. Seven or eight adults standing at attention, eyes forward, pretending that nothing is amiss or untoward, figuring we'd just get through this and thanking the stars and the moon that no children were on board and that this woman would not much longer be part of our lives. Our better sense instructed us that interference would not be rewarded with contrition. But what if she had decided to punch him? Then what? 5

Her exit and our release were accepted with silent gratitude, but I have been fuming ever since because, though she was gone, she didn't really exit our lives. She managed in those fleeting moments to make a mark, to alter our lives in some way. A vile invader, she made coarse and unlovely a period that was not her own. What gave her the right? And what about those other dozen or so people who dropped the F-word along those same hospital corridors as the hours passed? 6

I can't claim virginity in these matters, I should confess. But the elevator incident was so profoundly unpleasant that I've done a little soul-searching. How easy it is to casually let slip a word without thinking how it makes others feel. Perhaps relevant to my sensitivity, I was in the hospital that day for the birth of my great-niece. There's nothing like following the intimate miracle of childbirth to make one wish for a gentler world. 7

Public profanity is nothing new, of course, but it inarguably has gotten worse. It was hilarious (and shocking) in the 1970s when comedian George Carlin poked fun at our cultural aversion to the seven words you can't say on television. His act now can be viewed as a period piece. We can say most anything anywhere now, and we do. Penalties may arise from behavior that accompanies foul language, but the words themselves are constitutionally protected. As they should be, I hasten to add. Like most Americans, I'm willing to have my sensibilities offended rather than surrender the freedoms that permit such offense. 8

Context is everything, and (non-obstetric) delivery matters. I attended a tea not long ago when the subject of Tiger Woods came up. A British woman, in her refined accent, said: "Oh, he's such an ahs-hoal." I told her we could use that word in any circumstance if only we pronounced it the way she did. Pinkies extended, all together now. 9

Let's just say, the woman on the elevator had context and delivery issues. Her verbal fusillade may have been a random event, but her actions were neither singular nor disconnected from a broader range of cultural pathologies. Lack of civility in words bleeds into a lack of decency in behavior, and so it goes. 10

Good behavior is nothing but good manners, simply consideration of others. Recently out of vogue, manners get hauled out the way most people attend church—at Easter and Christmastime. But manners aren't just gray-haired pretensions practiced by smug elites on special occasions. They are the daily tithes we willingly surrender to civilization. 11

An "MF" here or an "FU" there might not constitute the unraveling of society, but each one uttered in another's involuntary presence is a tiny act of violence against kindness, of which we surely could use more. 12

Vocabulary

Before, during, and after reading the selection, annotate the text and write in your journal. Create a list of vocabulary words, along with their definitions. Give examples of their use from the selection you just read.

After Reading Questions: Meaning, Structure, and Expression

1. **Main Idea:** Work as a group to write a summary that answers the following questions: What purpose did Kathleen Parker have for writing this piece? Who is the intended audience? What is the main idea of the essay? What is the significance of the title of the piece?

2. **Relevant Details:** In paragraph 3, Parker compares the elevator doors opening to a "deus ex machina." What is the meaning of "deus ex machina"? If you don't know, do a word search on the Internet using a search engine such as Google. Why did Parker choose to use this detail to make her point?

3. **Logical Order:** Parker begins her essay by sharing an incident that illustrates her main point. She does not state her main idea until much later in the essay. Why did Parker begin with an illustration? Would her essay have been more effective had she stated her main idea before the illustration? Why or why not?

4. **Effective Expression:** Based on Parker's choice of words, how would you describe the main tone of this essay? For example, is her tone objective, sad, humorous, sarcastic, or alarmed? Give and explain examples to support your thoughts about the essay's tone.

Writing Prompts to Move from Reading to Writing

1. Reread the last paragraph in the essay. Write a response to Parker that agrees or disagrees with her concluding view. Assume you will post your response on the *Washington Post*'s comments section.

2. Assume you work as a volunteer with a youth group in your area, such as the Boys Club, the Girls Club, Boy Scouts, Girl Scouts, or the afterschool program at the YMCA. During your work with youth, you overhear their consistent use of profane language. In your role as a volunteer mentor, you have asked and received approval to conduct a workshop about the power and appropriate use of language. You have asked several members from the community, such as successful business leaders and the mayor. Write a speech to introduce the workshop to the youth who will participate. In your speech, state the purpose and need for the workshop and what you hope youth will gain from the experience.

The Whistle

BENJAMIN FRANKLIN

Born in Boston on January 6, 1706, Benjamin Franklin was one of the most remarkable people of Colonial times. He was a writer, inventor, scientist, philosopher, economist, diplomat, and revolutionary. Franklin swayed the destiny of the American colonies. He gave much to society. For example, he invented the first lightning rod, Franklin stove, bifocals, catheter, swim fins, and odometer. He started the first public library, the first volunteer fire company, the American fire insurance company, and the first hospital. He was also the first postmaster general. He founded the American Philosophical Society and The Academy and College of Philadelphia. This college later became the University of Pennsylvania. The following is an excerpt from a letter he wrote to his good friend Madame Brillon.

Before Reading Every day, we have the opportunity to learn important lessons from life. Write a journal entry that identifies and explains some of these important lessons.

In my opinion we might all draw more good from [this world] than we do, and suffer less evil, if we would take care not to give too much for whistles. For to me it seems that most of the unhappy people we meet with are become so by neglect of that caution.

1

You ask what I mean? You love stories, and will excuse my telling one of myself. 2

When I was a child of seven years old, my friends, on a holiday, filled my pocket with coppers. I went 3
directly to a shop where they sold toys for children; and being charmed with the sound of a *whistle*, that
I met by the way in the hands of another boy, I voluntarily offered and gave all my money for one. I then
came home, and went whistling all over the house, much pleased with my *whistle*, but disturbing all
the family. My brothers, and sisters, and cousins, understanding the bargain I had made, told me I had
given four times as much for it as it was worth; put me in mind what good things I might have bought
with the rest of the money; and laughed at me so much for my folly, that I cried with vexation; and the
reflection gave me more chagrin than the whistle gave me pleasure.

This, however, was afterwards of use to me, the impression continuing on my mind; so that often, 4
when I was tempted to buy some unnecessary thing, I said to myself, "Don't give too much for the
whistle"; and I saved my money.

As I grew up, came into the world, and observed the actions of men, I thought I met with many, very 5
many, who *gave too much for the whistle*.

When I saw one too ambitious of court favor, sacrificing his time in attendance on levees, his repose, 6
his liberty, his virtue, and perhaps his friends, to attain it, I have said to myself, "This man gives too
much for his whistle."

When I saw another fond of popularity, constantly employing himself in political bustles, neglecting 7
his own affairs, and ruining them by that neglect, "He pays, indeed," said I, "too much for his whistle."

If I knew a miser, who gave up every kind of comfortable living, all the pleasure of doing good 8
to others, all the esteem of his fellow-citizens, and the joys of benevolent friendship, for the sake of
accumulating wealth, "Poor man," said I, "you pay too much for your whistle."

When I met with a man of pleasure, sacrificing every laudable improvement of the mind, or of his 9
fortune, to mere corporeal sensations, and ruining his health in their pursuit, "Mistaken man," said I,
"you are providing pain for yourself, instead of pleasure; you give too much for your whistle."

If I see one fond of appearance, or fine clothes, fine houses, fine furniture, fine equipages, all above 10
his fortune, for which he contracts debts, and ends his career in prison, "Alas," say I, "he has paid dear,
very dear, for his whistle."

When I see a beautiful, sweet-tempered girl married to an ill-natured brute of a husband, "What a 11
pity," say I," "that she should pay so much for a whistle!"

In short, I conceive that great part of the miseries of mankind are brought upon them by the false 12
estimates they have made of the value of things, and by their *giving too much for their whistles*.

—Benjamin Franklin, "The Whistle," *The Oxford Book of American Essays*. (Matthews, Brander ed., 1914).

Vocabulary

Before, during, and after reading the selection, annotate the text and
write in your journal. Create a list of vocabulary words, along with their definitions. Give
examples of their use from the selection you just read.

After Reading Discussion Questions: Meaning, Structure, and Expression

1. **Main Idea:** Work as a group to write a summary that answers the following questions: What
   purpose did Benjamin Franklin have for writing this piece? Who is his intended audience? What
   is the main idea of the selection?

2. **Relevant Details:** Franklin offers a wide variety of examples to make his point. Identify all the
   examples he uses. Does he use too many or too few? How do all these examples work together
   to support his point?

3. **Logical Order:** Franklin uses a whistle as an example of a lesson he learned as a child. He opens his
   essay with this example, offers other examples, and then states his main idea near the end of his essay.
   Why did he choose this order to organize his thoughts? Would his point have been stronger had he
   stated his main idea in the first paragraph? Why or why not?

4. **Effective Expression:** Franklin repeats the idea "too much for a whistle" throughout the essay.
   How and why does he change the wording of this idea? Why did he repeat this idea? Describe
   the effect of a repeating idea in an essay.

Thinking Prompts to Move from Reading to Writing

1. Think of a lesson you have learned through experience. Write an essay that illustrates the importance of this lesson. Assume you are writing a letter to a good friend.

2. In the concluding paragraph, Franklin states that people are unhappy because of "the false estimates they have made of the value of things." Write an essay that illustrates this point. Consider using the following phrase to give credit to Mr. Franklin: "In his essay 'The Whistle,' Benjamin Franklin . . . ." Complete the sentence with your own words to introduce your main point. Assume you are writing an essay for a college humanities class.

Classification

Birth Order—Does It Really Make Any Sense?

KEVIN LEMAN

Originally from Williamsville, New York, Kevin Leman is an internationally known psychologist, humorist, and radio and TV personality, as well as a bestselling author of over 35 books. He is a former consulting psychologist for *Good Morning America*, and is a recurring guest for *The View, Today, The Early Show*, and *Focus on the Family*. A specialist in birth order and family relationships, Dr. Leman received his doctorate degree in clinical psychology from the University of Arizona. He is also a founding faculty member of iQuestions. com and the founder and president of Couples of Promise, an organization that helps couples remain happily married. The following selection is an excerpt from his bestselling book *The Birth Order Book: Why You Are the Way You Are*.

Before Reading Are you the oldest, middle, youngest, or only child in your family? Have you noticed that the oldest child or only child has different traits than a middle or youngest child? Write a journal entry about your birth order and the traits you developed as an oldest, middle, youngest, or only child.

Birth Order—Does It Really Make Any Sense?

I'm glad you asked. As North America's "pop" birth order psychologist, I get that question a lot. I'd really rather be called "one of North America's leading authorities on birth order, who makes a lot of sense." But, as a baby of the family with a strong drive to be entertaining and a little outrageous, I guess I can understand and put up with the "pop" label. After all, as I've crisscrossed the talk-show circuit countless times over the last twenty years, I often have to answer the question, Does birth order make any sense? My first response usually runs along the lines of "Does a bear go potty in the woods?" 1

Yes, birth order makes sense most of the time for a vast majority of people. The first thing that makes it intriguing is wrestling with the question: How can three or four or even eight little cubs be so different and yet come from the very same den? Yes, there are exceptions to the standard birth order rules but the exceptions are explainable when you understand how birth order works. Even the exceptions develop because of when you were born into your family. I call it your "branch on the family tree" and that branch has had a great deal to do with why you are the way you are today. 2

Nonetheless, as I give seminars or conduct counseling sessions, I still hear: "Birth order—isn't that like astrology? I'm a Sagittarius myself and my husband is a Libra—is that why he's driving me crazy?" 3

I smile and resist the strong temptation to say, "Astrology is really not my thing—I'm into pork bellies on the short term." Instead I reply kindly, "Birth order has no connection to astrology but it can 4 give you some important clues about your personality, your spouse, your children, the kind of job you have, and even how well you get along with your Maker if you happen to believe you have one."

"Okay, okay," my questioner might reply, "so what is birth order then, and why should I be interested?"   5

I then explain that birth order is the science of understanding your place in the family line. Were you   6
born first? second? third? or even farther down that line? Wherever you landed, it has affected your life in countless ways. Throughout my career as a psychologist, I've used the theory of birth order on a daily basis to help people understand themselves and solve their problems.

Which Traits Fit You Best?

To introduce my clients to birth order, I often give them a little quiz: Which of the following sets of   7
personality traits fits you the best? (Anyone taking this quiz must understand that he or she doesn't have to be everything in a certain list of traits. Just pick the list that has the most items that seem to describe you and your way of operating in life.)

A. perfectionist, reliable, conscientious, list maker, well organized, hard driving, natural leader, critical, serious, scholarly, logical, doesn't like surprises, loves computers

B. mediator, compromising, diplomatic, avoids conflict, independent, loyal to peers, many friends, a maverick, secretive, unspoiled

C. manipulative, charming, blames others, attention seeker, tenacious, people person, natural salesperson, precocious, engaging, affectionate, loves surprises

D. little adult by age seven; very thorough; deliberate; high achiever; self-motivated; fearful; cautious; voracious reader; black and white thinker; uses "very," "extremely," "exactly," a lot; can't bear to fail; has very high expectations for self; more comfortable with people who are older or younger

If you noted that this test seemed rather easy because A, B, and C listed traits of the oldest right   8
on down to the youngest in the family, you're right. If you picked list A, it's a very good bet you are a first born in your family. If you chose list B, chances are you are a middle child (second born of three children, or possibly third born of four). If list C seemed to relate best to who you are, it's likely you are the baby in the family and are not at all happy that this book has no pictures. (Just kidding—I like to have a little fun with last borns because I'm one myself, but more on that later.)

But what about list D? It describes the only child, and I threw it in because in recent years I have been   9
getting more and more questions from only children who know they are "first borns" but want to know how they are different from people who have siblings. Well, one way they are different is that the only child is a super or extreme version of a first born. They have many of the same characteristics of first borns, but in many ways they're in a class by themselves.

Notice, regarding each major birth order, I always qualify the characteristics by saying "good bet"   10
or "chances are." Not all characteristics fit each person in that birth order. In fact a first born may have baby characteristics, a last born can sometimes act like a first born in certain areas, and middle children may seem to be first borns. I've seen onlies who you would swear were youngest children. There are reasons for these inconsistencies, which I will explain as we go along. Birth order continues to be revealing when you look at who is in what occupation. For example, statistics show that first borns often fill positions of high authority or achievement. *Who's Who in America* or *American Men and Women in Science* both contain a high percentage of first borns. You will also find them more than well represented among Rhodes scholars and university professors.

What Do Presidents and Pastors Have in Common?

As for presidents and pastors, you guessed it, a great number of them are first borns. The way I   11
define a first born, twenty-three out of forty-one U.S. presidents (56 percent) have been first borns or functional first borns. A number of our presidents were born later than number one in their families. In some cases, they were born last, but in all cases they were the first-born *males* in the family. That tells me they had excellent chances of developing first-born traits and *functioning* as first borns, which undoubtedly helped them be effective in their role of president and leader.

Of course, many of our presidents have been middle children, and a few have been last borns, including   12
Ronald Reagan, the actor who made good in Washington. The big three of birth order—first born, middle

child, and baby—was vividly represented during the 1992 presidential campaign when incumbent George Bush, Bill Clinton, and Ross Perot squared off in a televised debate. Clinton, the first born, was suave, confident, loaded with answers, and projected strong leadership abilities. Bush, the middle child, used a mediating negotiating style, even while in debate. Perot, the last born, was an outrageous baby and then some—hard hitting, outspoken, asked lots of embarrassing questions of his opponents, and often had the audience in stitches. In regard to pastors, I was speaking to a group of fifty ministers and commented in passing, "Pastors, you know, are predominantly first borns." The skeptical looks on their faces told me that I might have wandered dangerously close to some kind of heresy, so I decided to poll the entire group and see if I was right. It turned out that forty-three out of the fifty were first-born sons or only children.

Research bears out that first borns are more highly motivated to achieve than later borns. A much greater proportion of first borns wind up in professions such as science, medicine, or law. You also find them in greater numbers among accountants, bookkeepers, executive secretaries, engineers, and computer specialists. And, oh yes, of the first twenty-three American astronauts sent into outer space, twenty-one were first borns and the other two were only children. All seven astronauts in the original Mercury program were first borns! 13

Even Christa McAuliffe, the teacher who died in the ill-fated *Challenger* space shuttle crash in 1986, was a first born who had four siblings. 14

—Kevin Leman, Excerpt (pp 13-16) from *The Birth Order Book*. Copyright © 2009 Reprinted by permission of Baker Publishing Group.

Vocabulary
Before, during, and after reading the selection, annotate the text and write in your journal. Create a list of vocabulary words, along with their definitions. Give examples of their use from the selection you just read.

After Reading Discussion Questions: Meaning, Structure, and Expression

1. **Main Idea:** Work as a group to write a summary that answers the following questions: What purpose did Dr. Leman have for writing this piece? Who is his intended audience? What is the main idea of the selection?

2. **Relevant Details:** Although the entire selection is an introduction to birth order, Dr. Leman devoted the last section of the piece to first borns. What is the purpose of giving so many details about first borns at this point in his discussion?

3. **Logical Order:** In paragraph 7, Dr. Leman introduces a quiz about birth order in which he asks, "Which of the following sets of personality traits fits you the best?" Then, he admits in paragraph 8 that the quiz was "rather easy" because it listed traits from the oldest to the youngest. Do you think that the quiz is most effective in this order? Or would it be a more effective test if he had randomly mixed the birth orders? Explain why.

4. **Effective Expression:** Dr. Leman is known for using humor to make his point. Find two examples of his use of humor. Why are these expressions humorous? Does his humor add to or detract from his point? Explain why.

Thinking Prompts to Move from Reading to Writing

1. In paragraph 6, Dr. Leman states that he uses the theory of birth order "to help people understand themselves." Analyze your family or a family you know by describing each family member by his or her personality traits based on birth order. Assume you are writing a journal that you will pass down to your children and grandchildren.

2. In paragraph 7, Dr. Leman gives a list of personality traits based on birth order, with each birth order category having its own strengths and weaknesses. Using this list of traits, describe your strengths as a possible employee. Assume you are writing a cover letter to apply for a job with a local business.

Why I Want a Wife

JUDY BRADY

In August 1970, Judy Brady was known as Judy Syfers, a married mother of two. She stood before a crowd that had gathered in San Francisco to celebrate the 50th anniversary of the 19th amendment, which gave women the right to vote, and read her now-famous essay "Why I Want a Wife." Although Judy was heckled by men in the audience, her work powerfully voiced the frustration of women in the emerging feminist movement. The essay was published in the first issue of *Ms.* magazine in 1971.

Before Reading All of us play many different roles in our lives, such as student, child, sibling, parent, employee, boss, or friend. Does each role have its own distinct traits? How do our behaviors change as our role changes? Write a journal entry about the types of roles performed by you or someone you know.

1 I belong to that classification of people known as wives. I am A Wife. And, not altogether incidentally, I am a mother.

2 Not too long ago a male friend of mine appeared on the scene fresh from a recent divorce. He had one child, who is, of course, with his ex-wife. He is looking for another wife. As I thought about him while I was ironing one evening, it suddenly occurred to me that I, too, would like to have a wife. Why do I want a wife?

3 I would like to go back to school so that I can become economically independent, support myself, and, if need be, support those dependent upon me. I want a wife who will work and send me to school. And while I am going to school, I want a wife to take care of my children. I want a wife to keep track of the children's doctor and dentist appointments. And to keep track of mine, too. I want a wife to make sure my children eat properly and are kept clean. I want a wife who will wash the children's clothes and keep them mended. I want a wife who is a good nurturant attendant to my children, who arranges for their schooling, makes sure that they have an adequate social life with their peers, takes them to the park, the zoo, etc. I want a wife who takes care of the children when they are sick, a wife who arranges to be around when the children need special care, because, of course, I cannot miss classes at school. My wife must arrange to lose time at work and not lose the job. It may mean a small cut in my wife's income from time to time, but I guess I can tolerate that. Needless to say, my wife will arrange and pay for the care of the children while my wife is working.

4 I want a wife who will take care of *my* physical needs. I want a wife who will keep my house clean. A wife who will pick up after my children, a wife who will pick up after me. I want a wife who will keep my clothes clean, ironed, mended, replaced when need be, and who will see to it that my personal things are kept in their proper place so that I can find what I need the minute I need it. I want a wife who cooks the meals, a wife who is a *good* cook. I want a wife who will plan the menus, do the necessary grocery shopping, prepare the meals, serve them pleasantly, and then do the cleaning up while I do my studying. I want a wife who will care for me when I am sick and sympathize with my pain and loss of time from school. I want a wife to go along when our family takes a vacation so that someone can continue to care for me and my children when I need a rest and change of scene.

5 I want a wife who will not bother me with rambling complaints about a wife's duties. But I want a wife who will listen to me when I feel the need to explain a rather difficult point I have come across in my course of studies. And I want a wife who will type my papers for me when I have written them.

6 I want a wife who will take care of the details of my social life. When my wife and I are invited out by my friends, I want a wife who will take care of the babysitting arrangements. When I meet people at school that I like and want to entertain, I want a wife who will have the house clean, will prepare a special meal, serve it to me and my friends, and not interrupt when I talk about things that interest me and my friends. I want a wife who will have arranged that the children are fed and ready for bed before my guests

arrive so that the children do not bother us. I want a wife who takes care of the needs of my guests so that they feel comfortable, who makes sure that they have an ashtray, that they are passed the hors d' oeuvres, that they are offered a second helping of the food, that their wine glasses are replenished when necessary, that their coffee is served to them as they like it. And I want a wife who knows that sometimes I need a night out by myself.

I want a wife who is sensitive to my sexual needs, a wife who makes love passionately and eagerly when I feel like it, a wife who makes sure that I am satisfied. And, of course, I want a wife who will not demand sexual attention when I am not in the mood for it. I want a wife who assumes the complete responsibility for birth control, because I do not want more children. I want a wife who will remain sexually faithful to me so that I do not have to clutter up my intellectual life with jealousies. And I want a wife who understands that *my* sexual needs may entail more than strict adherence to monogamy. I must, after all, be able to relate to people as fully as possible. 7

If, by chance, I find another person more suitable as a wife than the wife I already have, I want the liberty to replace my present wife with another one. Naturally, I will expect a fresh, new life; my wife will take the children and be solely responsible for them so that I am left free. 8

When I am through with school and have a job, I want my wife to quit working and remain at home so that my wife can more fully and completely take care of a wife's duties. 9

My God, who *wouldn't* want a wife? 10

—Judy Brady, "I Want a Wife." Originally appeared in *Ms. Magazine.* © Judy Brady. Reprinted by permission of the author.

Vocabulary Before, during, and after reading the selection, annotate the text and write in your journal. Create a list of vocabulary words, along with their definitions. Give examples of their use from the selection you just read.

After Reading Discussion Questions: Meaning, Structure, and Expression

1. **Main Idea:** Work as a group to write a summary that answers the following questions: What purpose did Judy Brady have for writing this piece? Who is her intended audience? What is the main idea of the selection?

2. **Relevant Details:** The details that Judy Brady uses to classify a wife come from her experiences in the 1960s. Her essay was published in 1971. Are the details still relevant? Are the roles of a wife today still the same? If not, how have they changed?

3. **Logical Order:** Underline the topic sentences for each of the body paragraphs 3 through 9. Based on the topic sentences, list the roles of a wife in the order she discusses them. Why did she choose this order for her ideas? Do you agree with this order of ideas? Why or why not?

4. **Effective Expression:** Judy Brady uses parallel expressions throughout her essay. Parallelism repeats the structure or wording of a phrase or clause. For example, she repeats the clause "I want a wife who . . . ." What is the impact of using parallel expressions? Would the essay be stronger if she had used fewer parallel expressions? Why or why not?

Thinking Prompts to Move from Reading to Writing

1. Write an essay that describes the qualities of a particular role a person fulfills in today's culture. For example, what are the current roles played by a wife, husband, significant other, friend, teacher, or student? Assume you are writing an article for your college's newspaper.

2. Write an essay that describes the various roles in life played by you or someone you know. Assume you are writing a posting for your blog on Facebook or MySpace.

Comparison-Contrast

Grant and Lee: A Study in Contrasts

BRUCE CATTON

Charles Bruce Catton (1899–1978) was an American historian and journalist. He is best known for his books on the American Civil War. He won a Pulitzer Prize in 1954 for *A Stillness in Appomattox,* his study of the final battle of the Civil War in Virginia. "Grant and Lee: A Study in Contrast" was written as a chapter of *The American Story,* a collection of essays by noted historians. In his essay, Catton skillfully contrasts and compares two great leaders on opposing sides of the Civil War.

Before Reading Write a journal entry about what you already know about the Civil War. What was the core issue that divided the country and caused the Civil War?

1   When Ulysses S. Grant and Robert E. Lee met in the parlor of a modest house at Appomattox Court House, Virginia, on April 9, 1865, to work out the terms for the surrender of Lee's Army of Northern Virginia, a great chapter on American life came to a close, and a great new chapter began.

2   These men were bringing the Civil War to its virtual finish. To be sure, other armies had yet to surrender, and for a few days the fugitive Confederate government would struggle desperately and vainly, trying to find some way to go on living now that its chief support was gone. But in effect it was all over when Grant and Lee signed the papers. And the little room where they wrote out the terms was the scene of one of the poignant, dramatic contrasts in American History.

3   They were two strong men these oddly different generals, and they represented the strengths of two conflicting currents that through them, had come into final collision.

4   Back of Robert E. Lee was the notion that the old aristocratic concept might somehow survive and be dominant in American life.

5   Lee was tidewater Virginia, and in his background were family, culture, and tradition . . . the age of chivalry transplanted to a New World which was making its own legends and its own myths. He embodied a way of life that had come down through the age of knighthood and the English country squire. America was a land that was beginning all over again, dedicated to nothing much more complicated than the rather hazy belief that all men had equal rights and should have an equal chance in the world. In such a land Lee stood for the feeling that it was somehow of advantage to human society to have a pronounced inequality in the social structure. There should be a leisure class, backed by ownership of land; in turn, society itself should be tied to the land as the chief source of wealth and influence. It would bring forth (according to this ideal) a class of men with a strong sense of obligation to the community; men who lived not to gain advantage for themselves, but to meet the solemn obligations which had been laid on them by the very fact that they were privileged. From them the country would get its leadership to them it could look for higher values—of thought, of conduct, or personal deportment—to give it strength and virtue.

6   Lee embodied the noblest elements of this aristocratic ideal. Through him, the landed nobility justified itself. For four years, the Southern states had fought a desperate war to uphold the ideals for which Lee stood. In the end, it almost seemed as if the Confederacy fought for Lee; as if he himself was the Confederacy . . . the best thing that the way of life for which the Confederacy stood could ever have to offer. He had passed into legend before Appomattox. Thousands of tired, underfed, poorly clothed Confederate soldiers, long since past the simple enthusiasm of the early days of the struggle, somehow considered Lee the symbol of everything for which they had been willing to die. But they could not quite put this feeling into words. If the Lost Cause, sanctified by so much heroism and so many deaths, had a living justification, its justification was General Lee.

Grant, the son of a tanner on the Western frontier, was everything Lee was not. He had come up the hard way and embodied nothing in particular except the eternal toughness and sinewy fiber of the men who grew up beyond the mountains. He was one of a body of men who owed reverence and obeisance to no one, who were self-reliant to a fault, who cared hardly anything for the past but who had a sharp eye for the future. 7

These frontier men were the precise opposites of the tidewater aristocrats. Back of them, in the great surge that had taken people over the Alleghenies and into the opening Western country, there was a deep, implicit dissatisfaction with a past that had settled into grooves. They stood for democracy, not from any reasoned conclusion about the proper ordering of human society, but simply because they had grown up in the middle of democracy and knew how it worked. Their society might have privileges, but they would be privileges each man had won for himself. Forms and patterns meant nothing. No man was born to anything, except perhaps to a chance to show how far he could rise. Life was competition. 8

Yet along with this feeling had come a deep sense of belonging to a national community. The Westerner who developed a farm, opened a shop, or set up in business as a trader could hope to prosper only as his own community prospered—and his community ran from the Atlantic to the Pacific and from Canada down to Mexico. If the land was settled, with towns and highways and accessible markets, he could better himself. He saw his fate in terms of the nation's own destiny. As its horizons expanded, so did his. He had, in other words, an acute dollars-and-cents stake in the continued growth and development of his country. 9

And that, perhaps, is where the contrast between Grant and Lee becomes most striking. The Virginia aristocrat, inevitably, saw himself in relation to his own region. He lived in a static society which could endure almost anything except change. Instinctively, his first loyalty would go to the locality in which that society existed. He would fight to the limit of endurance to defend it, because in defending it he was defending everything that gave his own life its deepest meaning. 10

The Westerner, on the other hand, would fight with an equal tenacity for the broader concept of society. He fought so because everything he lived by was tied to growth, expansion, and a constantly widening horizon. What he lived by would survive or fall with the nation itself. He could not possibly stand by unmoved in the face of an attempt to destroy the Union. He would combat it with everything he had, because he could only see it as an effort to cut the ground out from under his feet. 11

So Grant and Lee were in complete contrast, representing two diametrically opposed elements in American life. Grant was the modern man emerging; beyond him, ready to come on the stage was the great age of steel and machinery, of crowded cities and a restless burgeoning vitality. Lee might have ridden down from the old age of chivalry, lance in hand, silken banner fluttering over his head. Each man was the perfect champion for his cause, drawing both his strengths and his weaknesses from the people he led. 12

Yet it was not all contrast, after all. Different as they were—in background, in personality, in underlying aspiration—these two great soldiers had much in common. Under everything else, they were marvelous fighters. Furthermore, their fighting qualities were really very much alike. 13

Each man had, to begin with, the great virtue of utter tenacity and fidelity. Grant fought his way down the Mississippi Valley in spite of acute personal discouragement and profound military handicaps. Lee hung on in the trench at Petersburg after hope born of a fighter's refusal to give up as long as he can still remain on his feet and lift his two fists. 14

Daring and resourcefulness they had, too: the ability to think faster and move faster than the enemy. These were the qualities which gave Lee the dazzling campaigns of Second Manassas and Chancellorsville and won Vicksburg for Grant. 15

Lastly, and perhaps greatest of all, there was the ability, at the end, to turn quickly from the war to peace once the fighting was over. Out of the way these two men behaved at Appomattox came the possibility of peace of reconciliation. It was a possibility not wholly realized, in the year to come, but which did, in the end, help the two sections to become one nation again . . . after a war whose bitterness might have seemed to make such a reunion wholly impossible. No part of either man's life became him more than the part he played in their brief meeting in the McLean house at Appomattox. Their behavior there put all succeeding generations of Americans in their debt. Two great Americans, Grant and Lee—very different, yet under everything very much alike. Their encounter at Appomattox was one of the great moments of American history. 16

—Bruce Catton, "Grant and Lee: A Study in Contrast" in *The American Story*, edited by Earl Schneck Miers. Copyright USCHS; all rights reserved. Reprinted with permission.

Vocabulary   Before, during, and after reading the selection, annotate the text and write in your journal. Create a list of vocabulary words, along with their definitions. Give examples of their use from the selection you just read.

After Reading Discussion Questions: Meaning, Structure, and Expression

1. **Main Idea:** Work as a group to write a summary that answers the following questions: What purpose did Catton have for writing this piece? Who is the intended audience? What is the main idea of the essay? What is the significance of the title of the piece?

2. **Relevant Details:** Nowhere in the essay does Catton directly address the issue of slavery. Why do you think he omits any direct discussion of slavery? Where and how in the essay is the issue indirectly addressed? Do you think the issue of slavery should have been included to make his central point? Why or why not?

3. **Logical Order:** The overall pattern of organization is a carefully constructed contrast and comparison between these two military leaders. Identify the major points of contrast and comparison between the two men. Then, create an outline to show Catton's effective use of contrast and comparison.

4. **Effective Expression:** Throughout the essay, Catton uses vivid descriptions to express the differences in the men's attitudes, values, and lifestyles. For example, Catton refers to Lee as embodying "the age of knighthood." He then describes Grant as "a frontier man." Find at least two more vivid descriptions of each man. Then, discuss the impact of Catton's word choice in these descriptions. Did these vivid images help you better understand the differences between the two men? Why or why not?

Thinking Prompts to Move from Reading to Writing

1. Assume you are taking a college course in business, and you are studying the concept of leadership. Modeling Catton's use of comparison and contrast, write an essay that compares and contrasts an effective leader with an ineffective leader.

2. In paragraphs 10 and 11, Catton expresses the "most striking" contrast between Lee and Grant. Lee fought against change, for an old way of life; Grant fought for change for a new way of life. Assume you are writing a family history as a legacy for future generations. Interview an elder in your family. Contrast an "old way" of life experienced by your elder to the "new way" of life you now experience.

Gen X Is From Mars, Gen Y Is From Venus: A Primer on How to Motivate a Millennial

ROB ASGHAR

Based in Las Angeles, Rob Asghar is a writer and management and communications consultant. He has written for more than 30 publications around the world, including the *Chicago Tribune, Christian Science Monitor* and *Japan Times.* He also serves as a University Fellow at USC's Center for Public Diplomacy and is a member of the Pacific Council for International Policy. In 2014, Figueroa Press published his book *Leadership Is Hell,* and all proceeds benefit programs that make college accessible to promising Los Angeles urban school children. The following article, which appeared on Forbes .com, discusses the differences among generations of workers.

Before Reading   Write a journal entry about the differences between generations. How do younger people differ from older people in their views about work or authority figures?

Baby boomers made a deafening noise as they came of age, demanding that the world bend in their direction. Now here's a shock: They raised their kids to have pretty much the same expectations. Those kids are now known as the Millennial Generation or Generation Y, spanning the early 20s to early 30s, and they're driving many of their elders nuts—particularly those who belong to Generation X, which roughly spans the ages of mid-30s through late 40s.

Jamie Gutfreund of the Intelligence Group spends a great deal of time examining the differing motivations and preferences of the generations. Gutfreund (herself a member of Generation X) says it's important to bear in mind that Xers were culturally different from the Baby Boom Generation that preceded them.

While boomers insisted on being heard by the world, "we [Xers] were a smaller generation [less than half the size of the boomer generation] who felt no one was listening to us," she says. "We felt we had to fight" to have a voice, to make an impact, to earn a seat at the table of power.

"Generation Y was raised with a different perspective," she says. "Their Boomer parents taught them that their opinions are important. So they have an expectation to have a stake in outcomes."

In a wide-ranging interview last week, Gen Xer Gutfreund and her millennial colleague Shara Senderoff (CEO of Intern Sushi) offered me some shrewd insights into how and why Xers and millennials differ, summarized below.

1. A Different Concept of Authority

Gutfreund says that Xers view the boss as an expert—someone whose hard-earned experience and skill demand consideration and deference. Access to authority is limited and must be earned. By contrast, Senderoff says, "Millennials think they can go in on the first day and talk to the CEO about what's on their mind. The Generation X manager thinks, 'What are you doing??'"

But she and Gutfreund note that it's only natural for millennials to feel that way, given how their Boomer parents raised them to believe that their voice matters.

If a manager asks a Generation X employee to jump, the employee jumps and then asks, "Was that high enough?" But if a manager asks a millennial employee to jump, the employee is more likely to furrow an eyebrow and ask, "*Why...?*"

Senderoff says that even her best millennial employees will react in that manner. She adds that this may feel like a mutiny, but it's not. The millennial has been raised in an environment in which she's encouraged to engage and question authority; why would she accept a lesser bargain in the workplace?

Bear in mind again that millennials are the offspring of the Boomer parents who spent their formative adult years questioning authority. Gutfreund says that managers thus need to understand the benefit of shifting from "a command and control" style to a more inclusive management philosophy.

2. A Different Set of Motivations

Gutfreund describes Xers as a "very individualistic generation. They were very independent. They wanted to get the corner office and the trappings of success." Millennials, by contrast, want to find purpose in their toil and their career, she says, which does not necessarily come from getting the highest possible salary or nicest office.

"Generation X lives to work," she observes. "Generation Y works to live." Generation Y has multiple passions and is more global than any of its predecessors, as 70% of them say they would like to work abroad sometime over the course of their lives.

"Millennials are focused on making meaning, not just making money." This may well strike Xer managers and HR personnel as too precious and lofty an attitude for the real world, but that's the reality that organizations have to come to grips with.

3. A Desire for a Different Sort of Work Environment

Gen X tends to be structured and punctual and linear. Millennials can be unstructured and nonlinear, which can be maddening to the Xers.

Also, millennials are motivated by autonomy. They're not clock-watching pencil-pushers, and they're not lazy; they fully expect to be available to work 24/7, Gutfreund and Senderoff say, but they also expect the ability to leave the desk behind and take a walk.

Gutfreund says that, when you ask millennials where they'd like to work, the answer is generally: 16
First, Google; second, Apple; and third, for *themselves*.

Indeed, both companies project a mission to change the world or at least make it a more interesting 17
place. And Google's freewheeling but intense and highly productive culture speaks to most millennials, what with the many perks that seem to make the corporate campus more like a college campus.

But Senderoff clarifies, "It's not about free stuff [like lavish cafeterias and on-site massage 18
therapists]. It 100% comes down to culture."

She also says you can't motivate millennials to join your company just by posting a generic job 19
listing that may suit their skills. They want to sense what the larger company is about in terms of its mission and its values and they want to see it modeled by its leaders.

"They want to know," she says, "how close would they be to executives they can hear and learn from." 20
They need a vivid picture in their head of how working for you would make their lives and their world better.

4. A Different Concept of Progress on a Project

Gen Xers famously bemoan the "flakiness" of millennials. Senderoff suggests that this is actually a 21
result of speaking a language that millennials aren't wired to understand.

"Millennials move through things quickly," she says. "They think very quickly, and they're used to 22
doing so many things at one time." The upshot, she says, is that they may deliver a prototype when the Xer manager expects a more polished finished prototype.

In this case, she says the manager needs to communicate her needs more clearly, while also understanding 23
that the millennial appreciates regular feedback and coaching throughout the process.

Are we ready for a change in the workplace that allows millennials to bring their full talents to bear 24
on our organizations?

Gutfreund says we aren't as far along as we should be. "Many senior execs who run companies are 25
delaying changes that need to happen," she says, ". . . such as HR and performance reviews, because of short-term imperatives."

And she suggests that a focus on long-term growth demands that the necessary culture changes be 26
given greater priority.

—Rob Ashgar, "Gen X Is From Mars, Gen Y Is From Venus: A Primer On How to Motivate a Millenial," *Forbes*, January 14, 2014.

Vocabulary
Before, during, and after reading the selection, annotate the text and write in your journal. Create a list of vocabulary words, along with their definitions. Give examples of their use from the selection you just read.

After Reading Discussion Questions: Meaning, Structure, and Expression

1. **Central Idea:** Work as a group to write a summary that answers the following questions: What purpose did Rob Asghar have for writing this piece? Who is the intended audience? What is the central idea of the essay? What is the significance of the title of the piece?

2. **Relevant Details:** What were the four major details of contrast Asghar discussed? Why did he choose these particular major details? Are there other differences between generations that should have been discussed? If so, what other details should he have included and why?

3. **Logical Order:** Which method of contrast did Asghar choose to use? Did he discuss differences point by point or block of ideas by block of ideas? Was his choice of organization effective? Why or why not?

4. **Effective Expression:** Throughout the article, the author and the experts he quotes use vivid images or memorable phrases to show the supposed differences among generations. For example, Asghar refers to "a deafening noise" made by Baby Boomers. And Senderoff uses the phrase "feels like a mutiny" to describe millennials. Identify and discuss the effectiveness of three more vivid or memorable expressions.

Thinking Prompts to Move from Reading to Writing

1. Assume you are writing a response to this article for a college course in business management. Your professor requires that you read and respond in writing to articles about key issues in the workplace. Use the following prewriting questions: What is the issue? Why is this an important issue? How will the issue affect the relationship between a manager and his or her employees? How will this information help a manager be more effective?

2. Assume you are applying for a job as a manager trainee at the BestBean Coffee Company. Read the company's mission statement that follows. Then, write a letter of application for the job. Write your letter from the viewpoint of a Baby Boomer, a Generation Xer, or a Millennial. Use information from Asghar's article to describe your strengths as a candidate.

> Best Bean Coffee Company's mission is. . . To provide our guests with the ultimate customer experience in a friendly and inviting atmosphere. . . To offer the highest quality of food and service at the most reasonable price. . . To manage our staff with a true team approach in a creative and exciting workplace. . . To give back to our communities and to protect our environment."

Definition

All About Jazz, Uniquely American Music

MOIRA E. McLAUGHLIN

Moira E. McLaughlin is a reporter for the *Washington Post*. She serves as primary writer for the KidsPost section, web and print. In addition, she is a freelance writer who contributes to multiple sections of the *Washington Post* such as Style, Metro, Weekend, Book World, Real Estate, and Health. She has also written for the *Catholic Standard*, the *Alexandria Times*, and *Classical Singer* magazine. The following online article was posted in the KidsPost section of the *Washington Post*. Read to see how she defines the elements of jazz.

Before Reading Write a journal entry about your current understanding of jazz. What is jazz? How is jazz different from other types of music? If you are not familiar with jazz, write about the type of music you most enjoy. How would you define your favorite type of music? How is it different from other types of music?

Risky. Dangerous. Scary. A way to break the rules.   1

We're not talking about failing to study for your final math test or disobeying your parents. We're   2
talking about a type of music called jazz.

Some people say that jazz is America's only true art form. That's because it began here, hundreds of   3
years ago, in the fields where black people worked as slaves and made up songs to pass time, to express
themselves and to keep alive the culture and traditions of their African homelands. It wasn't called jazz
then, but the way the slaves were playing and singing music was different and special.

The music of America's black people came to be called jazz in the South in the early 1900s; New   4
Orleans, Louisiana, is often called the birthplace of jazz. Despite slavery's having ended in 1865, African
Americans still didn't have the same rights as white Americans. But jazz was music that both black and
white people could enjoy. By the 1920s, jazz was growing in popularity and included influences from
Europe as well as Africa.

Jazz has all the elements that other music has: It has *melody*; that's the tune of the song, the part you're most likely to remember. It has *harmony*, the notes that make the melody sound fuller. It has *rhythm*, which is the heartbeat of the song. But what sets jazz apart is this cool thing called *improvisation*. That means making it up on the spot. No music in front of you. No long discussion with your bandmates. You just play. 5

"It's more free. It's more soulful," says Geoffrey Gallante, 11, a sixth-grader at Stratford Landing Elementary School in Alexandria. Geoffrey is such a good musician that he has appeared at the Kennedy Center and has been on television lots of times; he has even played with the band on "The Tonight Show With Jay Leno." 6

In jazz, Geoffrey says, "it's easy to express your emotions. In classical, . . . you get the sheet music and you read it top to bottom. You're more focused on technically making it perfect. . . . In jazz, your main focus is . . . being creative and using your imagination." 7

What makes jazz unique

It's not that jazz songs don't have recognizable melodies. They do, but that's just a small part of it. In jazz, a melody begins a song, but then each musician will take turns improvising, playing all kinds of crazy notes: high, low, long, short, gravelly and clear. 8

The performers who are not soloing are playing quietly in the background, or *comping*, short for accompanying. Then at the end of the song, the melody returns. Improvising is what makes a jazz song different every time you hear it, unlike any pop song you hear on the radio. 9

Another thing that sets jazz apart is its approach to rhythm. Think of "The Star-Spangled Banner." When you hear that song, it probably doesn't make you want to tap your foot. There are no rhythmic surprises, or what is called syncopation, in most presentations of "The Star-Spangled Banner." Jazz musicians, on the other hand, "swing" notes, which means they change the length of notes, holding some longer and making others shorter. 10

Jazz and D.C.

Washington has an important place in jazz history. In 1920, the city had the largest population of black people in the country. That's around the time that a very famous jazz piano player, Duke Ellington, was playing around town. 11

Born in Washington in 1899, Ellington as a kid wanted to play baseball instead of the piano. That's why he sold peanuts, popcorn and candy at the games of the Washington Senators. (That was the baseball team here then.) But his parents played the piano, and so he started taking lessons when he was 7 or 8 years old. 12

By 1920, he was playing small shows at the Howard Theatre, where black musicians played to mostly black audiences. When he was 24, he moved to New York, but he didn't forget his home town. He called his band the Washingtonians and later he returned to perform at another famous Washington spot, the Lincoln Theatre. (Both the Lincoln Theatre and the Howard Theatre, where a statue of Ellington stands, still exist.) 13

Why is jazz cool?

Geoffrey Gallante was 4 years old when he picked up the trumpet. Now he practices three hours a day, mostly classical pieces. But what he really loves playing is jazz. It's the spontaneity of jazz—that means there's no planning ahead of time—that he really loves. He can walk into a club that he has never visited, with guys he has never seen, and just play. 14

"The [band leader] says, 'What do you want to play, and what key?' [I] can get up there and have a blast. With classical, you have to plan everything. You need to practice. . . . It's a whole big production. With jazz, you just walk up and you say, 'Hey, I want to do this. . . . Let's go.' " 15

—Moira E. McLaughlin, "All About Jazz, Uniquely American Music," *The Washington Post*, May 24, 2012.

Vocabulary   Before, during, and after reading the selection, annotate the text and write in your journal. Create a list of vocabulary words, along with their definitions. Give examples of their use from the selection you just read.

After Reading Discussion Questions: Meaning, Structure, and Expression

1. **Central Idea:** Work as a group to write a summary that answers the following questions: What purpose did Moira McLaughlin have for writing this piece? Who is the intended audience? What is the central idea of the essay? What is the significance of the title of the piece?

2. **Relevant Details:** McLaughlin only discusses two jazz musicians—Duke Ellington and Geoffrey Gallante. Why do you think she chose to focus on these two specific jazz artists?

3. **Logical Order:** Compare paragraph 1 to paragraph 16. How are the introduction and conclusion similar? Does the body of the article support the use of the words *risky, dangerous, scary*? Are McLaughlin's introduction and conclusion effective? Why or why not?

4. **Effective Expression:** How would you describe the tone of this passage? Is it objective, admiring, or critical? Identify three expressions that establish the tone of the article. Explain the tone and impact of each expression you chose.

Thinking Prompts to Move from Reading to Writing

1. Assume you are writing a report for a college course in humanities. You have chosen to write about the importance of music. You may pull examples from McLaughlin's article to use in your writing. Use the following prewriting questions: What is a definition of music? What inspires music? What is not music? What is the purpose or effect of music? What are the different forms of music?

2. Assume you are the parent of children in an elementary school that is considering cutting out the school's music program. Write a letter to the president of the Parent-Teacher's Association in support of keeping the music program. In your letter, explain the various important lessons students may learn or advantages they may gain from music. Use details from McLaughlin's article to support your central idea.

What Is a Friend?

BILLIE JEAN YOUNG

Actor, activist, poet, and educator Billie Jean Young works at home and abroad on behalf of social and economic justice for all people. A MacArthur Fellow, she has educated and inspired hundreds of audiences the world over through her poetry, lectures, drama workshops, and community organizing. For over two decades, she has shared with the world the life story of human rights activist and sharecropper from Sunflower County, Mississippi, Mrs. Fannie Lou Hamer. In her moving performances of her award-winning one-woman play *Fannie Lou Hamer: This Little Light* and in her efforts to give voice to the social and economic injustices currently affecting the people of the Black Belt region of the deep South, Billie Jean Young seeks to make change in the world in the spirit of Fannie Lou Hamer. Her works include nonfiction—*Now How you Do? A Memoir*, a volume of poetry—*Fear Not the Fall*, three plays including—*JimmyLee* and *Three Women Talking*, and one novel—*Family Secrets*. Young lives in the Black Belt of Alabama in Perry County, hometown of Coretta Scott King and Albert Turner, Sr. She was Artist-in-Residence at Judson College, Marion, Alabama. In the following essay, Young uses her poetic voice to express her definition of a friend.

Before Reading Write a journal entry about your experiences with friends. Have you thought someone was your friend only to find out later he or she betrayed you? How would you answer the question "What is a friend?"

> To my sweetheart,
> "Roses are red
> Violets are blue
> Sugar is sweet
> And so are you."

It was a note my best friend, Joanne, had written to her new boyfriend. She passed it to me to read. When I started to write a note on the bottom to ask her who it was for, I felt Mrs. Maye standing over me. I looked up. She was holding out her hand asking for the note. I froze. She reached down and picked up the note and read it anyway. I was eight years old. The teacher read the letter to the class and I got a whipping on my legs in front of everybody for writing a love letter. Joanne never said a mumbling word. 1

What is a friend? A friend is someone who steps in when others step out. A friend is usually the first one to get to you if you are in trouble. A friend will be there in person, in spirit, in word or deed—however. A friend is there. And you will know it; you will know that your friend is there with you. A friend does not use a megaphone to herald her arrival. A friend is simply there when trouble comes; a friend seeks you out. 2

A friend knows you. She may not have seen you for twenty years but when she does the conversation can pick up as if it were already begun. It can pick up where you left off. There is no need for great explanations about your actions or inaction to a friend—the whys and wherefores—even the seemingly insane. A friend knows you: she knows who you are, what you will do, what you are capable of doing. She does not have to ask others about you. 3

A friend listens to you. A friend does not try to speak for you. She listens to you, hears what you have to say, knows that you are telling her the truth. A friend will speak truth to you; she will not gloss over truth just because she knows it is what you want to hear. A friend will tell you the truth. A friend will speak truth to you about situations, events, others in your life. A friend is not jealous; a true friend loves you and welcomes, rejoices, even, in all your accomplishments. A friend only wants the best for you. 4

I could not tell the teacher that it was not my letter because then I would have to tattle on my best friend, Joanne, so I took the licking in silence. (Do you think Joanne and I remained best friends?) 5

—Billie Jean Young, "What is a Friend?" ://www.billiejeanyoung.com.

Vocabulary Before, during, and after reading the selection, annotate the text and write in your journal. Create a list of vocabulary words, along with their definitions. Give examples of their use from the selection you just read.

After Reading Questions: Meaning, Structure, and Expression

1. **Main Idea:** Work as a group to write a summary that answers the following questions: What purpose did Billie Jean Young have for writing this piece? Who is the intended audience? What is the main idea of the essay? What is the significance of the title of the piece?

2. **Relevant Details:** A strong definition offers an example or illustration. Identify Young's use of examples or illustrations. Is her use of examples or illustrations effective? Why or why not?

3. **Logical Order:** Young introduces and concludes her definition of a friend with a story from her childhood. What does this story illustrate? Why do you think Young used the story as the introduction and conclusion? Was this an effective way to organize the essay? Why or why not?

4. **Effective Expression:** How would you describe the tone of the article? Is it informal or formal, conversational or academic, biased or neutral? What words clue you into her tone? Is her use of language fresh and relevant to today's audience? Why or why not?

Writing Prompts to Move from Reading to Writing

1. Assume you are taking a college course in sociology. To prepare you to study about culture, your professor has asked you to identify and define key human characters (hypocrite, friend, mother, father, etc.) or values (power, self-control, freedom, success, etc.). Write a short essay that defines a key human character or value.

2. Assume you are a friend or relative of a teenager who is struggling with a problem, such as drug or alcohol abuse, bullying, body image/self-esteem, or depression. Write a letter to the teen in which you define the problem and offer encouragement.

Cause-Effect

Why War Is Never a Good Idea

ALICE WALKER

Alice Walker is a widely acclaimed and highly respected American author, poet, and activist. She has published seven novels, four collections of short stories, four children's books, and volumes of essays and poetry. She's best known for *The Color Purple*, the 1983 novel for which she won the Pulitzer Prize and the National Book Award. Her work has been translated into more than two dozen languages, and her books have sold more than fifteen million copies. The following essay is from her 2013 book *The Cushion in the Road: Meditation and Wandering as the Whole World Awakens to Being in Harm's Way*. In this essay, Walker explains why she wrote the children's book *Why War Is Never a Good Idea*.

Before Reading Write a journal entry about the causes and effects of war. Why do most wars occur? Are there worthwhile reasons to go to war? What are the effects of war on the land, on businesses, and on people?

When I wrote Why *War Is Never a Good Idea* I was thinking about children who play "war" long before they have any understanding of its meaning. Their parents buy toys for them that are miniature rifles, tanks, and bombs. Small babies are dressed in military print. They lie in their cribs grinning up at the adults of the world, without a clue that they are being set up to fight other young people, in not so many years, who would more sensibly be their playmates. I wanted to write a book for small children that would begin to counter the entrenched belief that it is all right for small children to think positively about war. It isn't all right, and the adults of the world must say so. 1

We've all heard of "the good war," presumably a war that is righteous and just. However, seen from the perspective of my children's book, there is no such thing as a "good" war because war of any kind is immoral in its behavior. It lands heavily on the good and the not good with equal impact. It kills humans and other animals and destroys crops. It ignites and decimates forests and it pollutes rivers. It obliterates beauty, whether in landscape, species, or field. It leaves poison in its wake. Grief. Suffering. When war enters the scene, no clean water anywhere is safe. No fresh air can survive. War attacks not just people, "the other," or "enemy"; it attacks Life itself: everything that humans and other species hold sacred and dear. A war on a people anywhere is a war on the Life of the planet everywhere. It doesn't matter what the politics are, because though politics might divide us, the air and the water do not. We are all equally connected to the life support system of planet Earth, and war is notorious for destroying this fragile system. 2

Our only hope of maintaining a livable planet lies in teaching our children to honor nonviolence, especially when it comes to caring for Nature, which keeps us going with such grace and faithfulness. *Why War Is Never a Good Idea* doesn't take sides because we are ultimately on the same side: the side of keeping our home, Earth, safe from attack. We cannot live healthy lives without a healthy Earth ever supporting and inspiring us, in all her unspoiled radiant generosity.

—Alice Walker, excerpt from *Why War Is Never a Good Idea.* Copyright 2007. Used by permission of HarperCollins Publishers.

Vocabulary   Before, during, and after reading the selection, annotate the text and write in your journal. Create a list of vocabulary words, along with their definitions. Give examples of their use from the selection you just read.

After Reading Discussion Questions: Meaning, Structure, and Expression

1. **Central Idea:** Work as a group to write a summary that answers the following questions: What purpose did Alice Walker have for writing this piece? Who is the intended audience? What is the central idea of the essay? What is the significance of the title of the piece?

2. **Relevant Details:** Walker gives many details about the negative effects of war, but she barely mentions the concrete causes or reasons for war. For example, in the second paragraph, she briefly mentions, "the good war. . . that is righteous and just." However, she doesn't give any examples or details about this type of war. Why does she omit these details?

3. **Logical Order:** Walker begins her essay by describing how parents teach children to believe war is positive. Why does she focus on this early learning process? Is this an effective introduction? Why or why not?

4. **Effective Expression:** How would you describe the overall tone of this essay? Is it objective, bitter, hopeful, or does it reveal some other tone or emotion? Does Walker's tone change based on what she is describing? For example, does the tone of paragraph 2 differ from or remain the same as the tone in paragraph 3? Identify and discuss three examples of words or phrases Walker uses to set a tone.

Thinking Prompts to Move from Reading to Writing

1. Assume you are writing an essay for a college course in sociology. Reading Walker's essay brings to mind a variety of activities that parents or youth engage in that affect the way youth grow to view the world. Use Walker's title to brainstorm a topic and develop details for your essay. Focus on the positive or negative causes/effects of an activity in which youth engage. Use one of the following topics, or create your own: Why Spanking is Never a Good Idea, Why Spanking Is a Good Idea, Why Video Games Are Never a Good Idea, Why Video Games Are a Good Idea, Why Social Media Is Not a Good Idea, Why Social Media Is a Good Idea.

2. Assume you write a blog about key issues concerning young people. Walker's essay has made you think about Hollywood movies that depict war such as *The Hunger Games* series, starring Jennifer Lawrence, Brad Pitt's movie *Fury* about World War II, or the classic *Gone with the Wind* about the Civil War. Write a posting for your blog in which you agree or disagree with Walker's belief that "War Is Never a Good Idea." Use examples from a Hollywood war movie of your choice to support your view.

Lifetime Effects of Stress and What Causes It

REBECCA J. DONATELLE

Rebecca Donatelle has served since 1990 as the Associate Professor and Coordinator of the Health Promotion and Health Behavior Programs in the Department of Health at Oregon State University. She has widely published in professional journals and is well known for her college textbooks on health. The following passage is an excerpt from her textbook *Health: The Basics*. In this passage, Donatelle describes ways to manage stress.

Before Reading Write a journal entry about the effects of stress and the various reasons we feel stress. How does stress affect most people? What are the main causes of stress in everyday life, college life, or working life?

Lifetime Effects of Stress

Stress is often described as a "disease of prolonged arousal" that leads to a cascade of negative health effects. The longer you are chronically stressed, the more likely there will be negative health effects. 1

Physical Effects of Stress

The higher the levels of stress you experience and the longer that stress continues, the greater the likelihood of damage to your physical health. In addition to the physical disease threats we've discussed, increases in rates of suicide, homicide, hate crimes, alcohol and drug abuse, and domestic violence are symptoms of a nation that is chronically stressed. 2

Stress and Cardiovascular Disease Perhaps the most studied and documented health consequence of unresolved stress is cardiovascular disease (CVD). Research on CVD demonstrates the impact of chronic stress on heart rate, blood pressure, heart attack, and stroke. 3

Historically, the increased risk of CVD from chronic stress has been linked to increased arterial plaque buildup due to elevated cholesterol, hardening of the arteries, increases in inflammatory responses in the body, alterations in heart rhythm, increased and fluctuating blood pressures, and difficulties in cardiovascular responsiveness due to all of the above. In the past two decades, research in the relationship between stress and CVD contributors has shown direct links between the incidence and progression of CVD and stressors such as job strain, caregiving, bereavement and natural disasters. 4

Stress and Weight Gain Are you a "*stress*" or "*emotional eater*"? Do you run for the refrigerator when you are under pressure or feeling anxious or down? If you think that when you are emotionally stressed you tend to eat more and gain weight, you didn't imagine it. We comfort ourselves with things we love. Hence that bag of chips or ice cream sundae may be just the thing to distract us. But there is more to stress eating than soothing our emotions. 5

"Higher stress levels may drive us toward food because they may increase cortisol levels in the bloodstream. Because cortisol contributes to increased hunger and seems to activate fat storing enzymes, people who are stressed may get a double whammy of risks from higher-circulating cortisol levels. High cortisol may also increase cravings for salty and sweet foods. Animal and human studies, including those in which subjects suffer from post-traumatic stress, seem to support the theory that cortisol plays a role in laying down extra belly fat and increasing eating behaviors. 6

Stress and Alcohol Dependence New research has found that a specific stress hormone, the corticotropin-releasing factor (CRF), is key to the development and maintenance of alcohol dependence in animals. CRF is a natural substance involved in the body's stress response, stimulating the secretion of various stress hormones. If proven to be true in humans, options for dealing with stress and alcohol may increase dramatically. 7

Stress and Hair Loss Too much stress can lead to thinning hair and even baldness in men and women. The most common type of stress-induced hair loss is *telogen effluvium*. Often seen in individuals who have lost a loved one or experienced severe weight loss or other trauma, this condition pushes colonies of hair into a resting phase. Over time, hair begins to fall out. A similar stress-related condition known as *alopecia areata* occurs when stress triggers white blood cells to attack and destroy hair follicles, usually in patches.

8

Stress and Diabetes Controlling stress levels is critical for preventing weight gain and other risk factors for type 2 diabetes, as well as for successful short- and long-term diabetes management. People under lots of stress often don't get enough sleep, don't eat well, and may drink or take other drugs to help them get through a stressful time. All of these behaviors can alter blood sugar levels and promote development of diabetes.

9

Stress and Digestive Problems Digestive disorders are physical conditions for which the causes are often unknown. It is widely assumed that an underlying illness, pathogen, injury, or inflammation is already present when stress triggers nausea, vomiting, stomach cramps and gut pain, or diarrhea. Although stress doesn't directly cause these symptoms, it is clearly related and may actually make your risk of having symptoms worse. For example, people with depression or anxiety, or who feel tense, angry, or overwhelmed, are more susceptible to dehydration, inflammation and other digestive problems. Irritable bowel syndrome may be more likely, in part, because stress stimulates colon spasms by means of the nervous system. Some relaxation techniques and mindfulness training may be helpful in coping with stressors that irritate your digestive system. These relaxation techniques reduce the activity of the sympathetic nervous system, leading to decreases in heart rate, blood pressure, and other stress responses. They also appear to reduce gastrointestinal reactivity and decrease your risks of gastrointestinal tract flare-ups.

10

Stress and Impaired Immunity A growing area of scientific investigation known as *psychoneuroimmunology* (PNI) analyzes the intricate relationship between the mind's response to stress and the immune system's ability to function effectively. Several recent reviews of research linking stress to adverse health consequences suggest that too much stress over a long period can negatively affect various aspects of the cellular immune response. This increases risks for upper respiratory infections and certain chronic conditions, increases adverse fetal development and birth outcomes, and exacerbates problems for children and adults suffering from post-traumatic stress. More prolonged stressors, such as the loss of a loved one, caregiving, living with a handicap, and unemployment, also have been shown to impair the natural immune response among various populations over time.

11

Intellectual Effects of Stress

In a recent national survey of college students, more than half of the respondents said that they had felt overwhelmed by all that they had to do within the past 2 weeks, 48.3 percent reported being exhausted, and 19.2 percent felt overwhelmed by anxiety in the same time period. About 37 percent of students felt they had been under more-than-average stress in the past 12 months, whereas over 10 percent reported being under tremendous stress during that same time period. Not surprisingly, these same students rated stress as their number one impediment to academic performance, followed by lack of sleep and anxiety. Stress can play a huge role in whether students stay in school, get good grades, and succeed on their career path. It can also wreak havoc on students' ability to concentrate, affect memory, and decrease ability to understand and retain information.

12

Stress, Memory, and Concentration Although the exact reasons stress can affect grades and job performance are complex, new research has provided possible clues. Animal studies have provided compelling indicators of how glucocorticoids—stress hormones released from the adrenal cortex—are believed to affect memory. In humans, acute stress has been shown to impair short-term memory, particularly verbal memory. Recent laboratory studies with rats have linked prolonged exposure to cortisol (a key stress hormone) to actual shrinking of the hippocampus, the brain's major memory center.

13

Psychological Effects of Stress Stress may be one of the single greatest contributors to mental disability and emotional dysfunction in industrialized nations. Studies have shown that the rates of mental disorders, particularly depression and anxiety, are associated with various environmental stressors." College students not only face pressure to get good grades, they also face additional new

14

stressors stemming from housing searches, becoming financially independent, career choices and employment (or the lack thereof), relationships, interactions with family and peers, and perceived environmental threats. Coping skills and social support from family, friends, and community services can buffer the negative effects of stress overload.

What Causes Stress?

On any given day, we all experience eustress and distress, usually from a wide range of sources. One of the most comprehensive studies examining sources of stress among various populations is conducted annually by the American Psychological Association. The 2012 survey found that concerns over money, work, the economy, and relationships were the biggest reported causes of stress for Americans. College students, in particular, face stressors that come from internal sources, as well as external pressures to succeed in a competitive environment. Awareness of the sources of stress can do much to help you develop a plan to avoid, prevent, or control the things that cause you stress.

15

Psychosocial Stressors

Psychosocial stressors refer to the factors in our daily routines and in our social and physical environments that cause us to experience stress. Key psychosocial stressors include adjustment to change, hassles, interpersonal relationships, academic and career pressures, frustrations and conflicts, overload, and stressful environments.

16

Adjustment to Change Anytime change, whether good or bad, occurs in your normal routine, you experience stress. The more changes you experience and the more adjustments you must make, the greater the chances are that stress will have an impact on your health. Unfortunately, although your first days on campus can be exciting, they can also be among the most stressful you will face in your life. Moving away from home, trying to fit in and make new friends from diverse backgrounds, adjusting to a new schedule, and learning to live with strangers in housing that is often lacking in the comforts of home can all cause sleeplessness and anxiety and keep your body in a continual fight-or-flight mode.

17

Hassles: Little Things That Bug You Some psychologists have proposed that the little stressors, frustrations, and petty annoyances, known collectively as hassles, can add up and be just as stressful as major life changes. Put another way, cumulative hassles add up. They tax the physiological systems of the body and cause stress-related wear and tear, known as an ***allostatic load,*** on the body. Listening to others monopolize class time, not finding parking on campus, continual drops on your cell phone connections, and a host of other irritants can push your buttons and trigger an acute fight-or-flight response. For many people, electronic devices that are supposed to be fun can cause anxiety and zap time.

18

The Toll of Relationships Let's face it, relationships can trigger some of the biggest fight-or-flight reactions of all time. Although romantic relationships are the ones we often think of first—the wild, exhilarating feeling of new love and the excruciating pain of breakups—relationships with friends, family, and coworkers can be sources of struggles, just as they can be sources of support. These relationships can make us strive to be the best that we can be and give us hope for the future, or they can diminish our self-esteem and leave us reeling from destructive interactions. A recent comparison of nearly 80 studies of stress and work provides strong evidence that work situations with high demands, little control, and coworkers who are difficult to get along with increase the likelihood of employee complaints about gastrointestinal ailments and sleep difficulties. Competition for rewards and systems that favor certain classes of employees or pit workers against one another are among the most stressful job situations.

19

Academic and Financial Pressure It isn't surprising that today's college and university students face mind-boggling amounts of pressure while competing for grades, internships, athletic positions, and jobs. Challenging classes can be tough enough, but many students must juggle studies with work to pay the bills, and an economic downturn can make student dreams seem unobtainable. Increasing reports of mental health problems on college campuses may be one result of too much stress and no clear way of finding relief.

20

Frustrations and Conflicts Whenever there is a disparity between our goals (what we hope to obtain in life) and our behaviors (actions that may or may not lead to these goals), frustration can occur. For example, you realize that you must get good grades in college to enter graduate school, which is your ultimate goal. If your social life is cutting into your studying time, you may find your goals slipping away, leading to increased stress.

21

Conflicts occur when we are forced to decide among competing motives, impulses, desires, and behaviors (for example, go out partying or study) or when we are forced to face pressures or demands that are incompatible with our own values and sense of importance (for example, get good grades or play on an all-star sports team). College students who are away from their families for the first time may face a variety of conflicts among parental values, their own beliefs, and the beliefs of others who are very different from themselves. 22

Overload We've all experienced times in our lives when the demands of work, responsibilities, deadlines, and relationships all seem to be pulling us underwater. *Overload* occurs when we are overextended and, try as we might, there are not enough hours in the day to do what we must get done. Students suffering from overload may experience depression, sleeplessness, mood swings, frustration, anxiety, or a host of other symptoms. Binge drinking, high consumption of junk food, lack of money, and arguments can all add fuel to the overload fire. Unrelenting stress and overload can lead to a state of physical and mental exhaustion known as *burnout*. 23

Stressful Environments For many students, where they live and the environment around them cause significant levels of stress. Perhaps you cannot afford quality housing, a bad roommate is producing major environmental stress, or loud neighbors are keeping you up at night. Maybe it isn't safe to walk to your car after dark on campus, or you have to leave your bicycle in a prime "rip-off" location during classes. Seemingly unending inconveniences and minor threats can wear you down. 24

Unexpected natural disasters that affect you or others can cause great emotional upset. Superstorm Sandy and Hurricane Katrina; the Sumatra, Japan, and Haiti earthquakes; killer tornadoes in Oklahoma, Iowa, and Kansas; as well as human disasters such as the Gulf Oil Spill have threatened millions with mayhem and death, disrupted lives, and damaged ecosystems for the foreseeable future. Even after the initial images of suffering pass and the crisis has subsided, shortages of vital resources such as gasoline, clean water, food, housing, health care, sewage disposal, and other necessities, as well as electricity outages and transportation problems, can wreak havoc in local communities and on campuses. Although not as newsworthy as major disasters, *background distressors* in the environment, such as noise, air, and water pollution; allergy-aggravating pollen and dust; unsafe food; or environmental tobacco smoke can also be incredibly stressful. Campus violence, shootings, and highly charged political clashes on campus can also be sources of anxiety as students worry about safety. 25

Bias and Discrimination Racial and ethnic diversity of students, faculty members, and staff enriches everyone's educational experiences. It also challenges us to examine our personal attitudes, beliefs, and biases. As campuses become more internationalized, a diverse cultural base of vastly different life experiences, languages, and customs is emerging. Often, those perceived as dissimilar may become victims of subtle and not-so-subtle forms of bigotry, insensitivity, harassment, or hostility, or they may simply be ignored. Race, ethnicity, religious affiliation, age, sexual orientation, gender, or other differences may hang like a dark cloud over these students. 26

Evidence of the health effects of excessive stress in minority groups abounds. For example, African Americans suffer higher rates of hypertension, CVD, and most cancers than do whites. Poverty and socioeconomic status have been blamed for much of the spike in hypertension rates for African Americans and other marginalized groups. Instead, chronic, physically debilitating stress among these groups may reflect the real and perceived effects of institutional racism. More research is necessary to show direct associations between racism, stress, and hypertension; however, it is important to realize that all types of "isms" may influence stress-related hypertension and make it more difficult for those affected to engage in healthy lifestyle behavior. 27

—Donatelle, Rebecca J. *Health: The Basics*, 11th ed., © 2015, pp 75–82. Reprinted and Electronically reproduced by permission of Pearson Education, Inc., New York, NY.

Vocabulary Before, during, and after reading the selection, annotate the text and write in your journal. Create a list of vocabulary words, along with their definitions. Give examples of their use from the selection you just read.

After Reading Discussion Questions: Meaning, Structure, and Expression

1. **Central Idea:** Work as a group to write a summary that answers the following questions: What purpose did Rebecca Donatelle have for writing this piece? Who is the intended audience? What is the central idea of the passage? What is the significance of the title of the piece?

2. **Relevant Details:** Donatelle offers many examples that illustrate the effects or causes of stress. Identify three examples and explain the effect or cause each one illustrates.

3. **Logical Order:** In this passage, Donatelle discusses the effects of stress before she explains the causes of stress. Should she have talked about the causes first, and then explained the effects? Why or why not?

4. **Effective Expression:** Often formal writing that is published for a general audience uses third person pronouns, such as *everyone, one, he, she, they,* and so on, to establish an objective, unbiased tone. However, in this passage, Donatelle uses the informal and subjective pronoun *you.* Why does she use the pronoun *you* in her discussion? What effect did she intend to have on her audience by using the pronoun *you?*

Thinking Prompts to Move from Reading to Writing

1. Assume you are taking a college health course. Your professor has given you the following study questions for an essay exam. Answer the question with information from the passage. Use your own words. Study Question: *What are some of the health risks that result from chronic stress and what factors cause stress?*

2. Assume you are a peer tutor in the learning center on your campus. The learning center is conducting a campaign to raise awareness about stress. You have been asked to create a brochure that describes the three most common causes of stress and the three most dangerous effects of stress. Use information from the passage to create your brochure.

Persuasion

It's Time to Ban High School Football

KEN REED

Ken Reed is Sports Policy Director for the League of Fans. Founded by public interest activist Ralph Nader, the goal of this organization is to reform sports and to encourage civic responsibility in sports. Reed is a long-time consultant, instructor, sports analyst, columnist, and author in the field of sports. The following column appeared in the *Chicago Tribune*. In his column, Reed makes a case against high school football.

Before Reading Write a journal entry about the dangers of playing high school football. Do you think football is too dangerous for high school athletes to play? Why or why not?

Across the United States approximately 1.3 million high school football players are busy practicing in preparation for a new season.

They shouldn't be. A growing mound of research makes it clear that football is too dangerous for the human brain. It's hazardous to one's health, just like smoking.

Once the evidence on smoking was clear we banned it from our high school campuses. The same fate should now happen to football. It hurts me to come to this conclusion. My dad was a football coach and I played the sport for six years. I enjoy watching football—at all levels. But I don't see any other way we can adequately protect the brains of young football players. It's important to note that young athletes' brains are more vulnerable to brain trauma than those of adults.

There aren't enough safety measures we can implement to overcome the fact that the brain isn't built to withstand the repetitive brain trauma inherent in a game built around violent collisions.

According to the Brain Injury Research Institute, in any given season, 20 percent of high school players sustain brain injuries. More than 40.5 percent of high school athletes who have suffered concussions return to action prematurely, which can lead to death from Second Impact Syndrome, a condition in which the brain swells, shutting down the brain stem and resulting in respiratory failure.

It's not just concussions we're concerned about. Purdue University researchers recently compared changes in the brains of high school football players who had suffered concussions with the brains of players who were concussion-free and found brain tissue damage in both. That's scary stuff. That means brain injuries are occurring without players, coaches or parents being aware of it.

Repetitive subconcussive hits to the head can cause as much damage as concussion-causing hits. A growing focus in the brain trauma field is chronic traumatic encephalopathy, a brain degeneration disease. It has many symptoms similar to Alzheimer's and other neurological diseases, however it isn't the result of some endogenous disease but due to brain injury—being hit too many times in the head.

Now consider that the average high school football lineman receives 1,000 to 1,500 shots to the head during a single football season, based on estimates by Boston University researchers.

Moreover, the effects of football-induced brain trauma often get worse over time. Consider that the number of former NFL players between the ages 30 and 49 who have received a diagnosis of "dementia, Alzheimer's disease or other memory-related disease" is 19 times the national average for that age group. Moreover, players who have suffered multiple concussions are three times more likely to suffer depression.

Clearly, football has a serious problem here. And there's no fix unless we eliminate blocking and tackling and go to flag football. Football is the lone high school sport where inflicting physical punishment on one's opponent is a primary objective.

Helmets are of little or no help. They're great at preventing skull fractures and lacerations but terrible at preventing brain damage. The reason is that the brain is like Jell-O bouncing up against the walls of the skull. It's a whiplash effect that leads to concussions. That's why players can receive concussions without even being hit in the head. A blow to the chest can send the brain splashing against the skull with as much force as a head-to-head shot. Undeniably, the demise of high school football will be a culture shock for schools and communities around the country. Culture change experts say it takes seven years to fully adapt to major change. But using taxpayer-dollars to fund a school activity that is clearly detrimental to the brain simply isn't justifiable.

Football proponents will argue that the game imparts lessons on the gridiron that can't be learned anywhere else. But life lessons like teamwork, leadership, perseverance, sacrifice, etc., can be just as easily and effectively acquired by participating in sports other than football.

Let's face it, football at the high school level is doomed. If parents don't rise up to stop it—in a Mothers Against Drunk Driving mode—insurance companies will. Inevitably, the new brain research will lead to lawsuits at all levels of the game. Football-related risk and liability will be hard to contain for school districts. And, when risk and liability can't be contained, insurance premium costs will shoot up, making the sponsoring of football cost prohibitive for high schools.

It may be 10 years, 20 years or 40 years before high school football's gone, but it will be gone. We can't put the medical research we're now aware of back in the bottle. But why do we have to wait? Let's act now and spare numerous young athletes—and their families—from dealing with the tragedies associated with football-induced brain trauma.

—Ken Reed, "It's Time to Ban High School Football," *Chicago Tribune*, August 29, 2012.

14

Vocabulary Before, during, and after reading the selection, annotate the text and write in your journal. Create a list of vocabulary words, along with their definitions. Give examples of their use from the selection you just read.

After Reading Discussion Questions: Meaning, Structure, and Expression

1. **Central Idea:** Work as a group to write a summary that answers the following questions: What purpose did Ken Reed have for writing this piece? Who is the intended audience? What is the main idea of the essay? What is the significance of the title of the piece?

2. **Relevant Details:** A sound argument offers and disproves an opposing point. Identify and evaluate Reed's opposing point. Did Reed choose a relevant opposing point? Did he effectively show why this point is not a solid reason to support high school football? Why or why not?

3. **Logical Order:** To make his argument, Reed describes the problems caused by high school football and the solution to the problems. Identify the logical flow of his ideas by outlining the harmful effects of football and the solution he suggests. Do you agree with the order of his details? For example, is the placement of his discussion of helmets and the opposing view effective? Why or why not?

4. **Effective Expression:** Reed uses comparisons and vivid images to express his view. For example, in paragraph 3, he compares the dangers of high school football to smoking. Identify two other comparisons he uses to make his point memorable. Why is each of these three comparisons effective?

Thinking Prompts to Move from Reading to Writing

1. Assume you are writing about a controversial issue for a college course in sociology. Your professor requires that you find and respond to an article about a current topic of debate in society. Respond to this article by agreeing or disagreeing with Reed's central idea. Choose specific points to support or oppose in your response. If appropriate, consider using details from the article "The Benefits of Playing Sports Aren't Just Physical" by the American Orthopaedic Society for Sports Medicine. (p. 477).

2. Assume the school board of your county's public school system is proposing a ban on high school football. Write a letter to the chair of the school board supporting this ban. To support your view, consider using details from this article or the article ""The Benefits of Playing Sports Aren't Just Physical" by the American Orthopaedic Society for Sports Medicine (p. 477).

The Benefits of Playing Sports Aren't Just Physical!

THE AMERICAN ORTHOPAEDIC SOCIETY FOR SPORTS MEDICINE

The following article appeared in the U.S. Department of Health and Human Services *Be Active Your Way Blog* for Physical Activity Guidelines for Americans (PAG). According to the homepage of PAG, the guidelines and blog are "based on the latest science" and "provide guidance on how children and adults can improve their health through physical activity." This article was contributed to the blog by the American Orthopaedic Society for Sports Medicine to encourage Americans to participate in youth sports.

Before Reading Write a journal entry about the controversy of playing sports such as high school football. What are the benefits of playing sports in high school? Do the benefits outweigh the dangers? Why or why not?

1   Sports participation in the United States has reached record levels. And high school-level sports participation continues to rise. In fact, the National Federation of State High School Associations estimates that more than 7.6 million high school students (over 55% of all students) played sports during the 2010–2011 academic year.

2   As orthopaedic surgeons, we are all too familiar with injuries that can occur in sports. But the benefits far outweigh the potential for injury. We are wrapping up National Physical Fitness and Sports Month. At this time, the American Orthopedic Society for Sports Medicine would like to focus on the many positive benefits of sports. We want to encourage Americans to participate.

3   The physical benefits of competitive sports are the most obvious. Much attention has been given to the role of sports and exercise in decreasing the rates of obesity in our nation's youth. Lower body mass among athletes is certainly a desirable marker, but it is not the only advantage of regular exercise that comes with sports participation. Athletes experience lower rates of diabetes and high blood pressure. They also improve their cardiovascular and pulmonary (lung) function.

4   However, the benefits of sports are not simply limited to physical health. Here are just a few reasons to consider playing sports or encouraging your children to play sports.

Social Benefits

5   A study published in *Pediatric and Adolescent Medicine* reported that out of 14,000 high school athletes, the ones who regularly played sports were less likely to use drugs. Likewise, a survey performed by the National Household Survey of Drug Abuse showed that students who played sports were less likely to have smoked cigarettes or used drugs. And they were more likely to disapprove of others using them. Also, the Women's Sports Foundation has stated that female high school athletes are 80% less likely to become pregnant than non-athletes.

Academic Benefits

6   Studies performed among students in multiple states—including Wyoming, Iowa, and Colorado—have shown that playing sports can actually increase success in the classroom. Various data reveal that athletes have higher grade point averages, higher standardized test scores, better attendance, lower dropout rates, and a better chance of going to college.

Career Benefits

A survey of individuals at the level of executive Vice President of 75 Fortune 500 companies showed that 95% of them played sports in high school. It might be hard to argue that sports participation could guarantee higher incomes, promotions, and better jobs. Yet, the leadership skills and development of teamwork, hard work, and determination might help prepare students to be leaders at work and in their communities later in life.   7

It is important for adults to be aware of the risks of injuries in various sports, both for themselves and for their kids. However, it is also important to remember that there are many great reasons to play them as well! How are you encouraging your family and friends to get involved in sports?   8

—AOSSM. "The Benefits of Playing Sports Aren't Just Physical!" U.S. Department of Health and Human Services. May 30, 2012. The Benefits of Playing Sports Aren't Just Physical!

Vocabulary
Before, during, and after reading the selection, annotate the text and write in your journal. Create a list of vocabulary words, along with their definitions. Give examples of their use from the selection you just read.

After Reading Discussion Questions: Meaning, Structure, and Expression

1. **Central Idea:** Work as a group to write a summary that answers the following questions: What purpose did the author have for writing this piece? Who is the intended audience? What is the central idea of the essay? What is the significance of the title of the piece?

2. **Relevant Details:** A sound argument offers and disproves an opposing point. Identify and evaluate the author's opposing point or points. How many relevant opposing points are offered? Is the opposing point(s) adequately explained to overcome a reader's objection to youth participation in sports? Why or why not?

3. **Logical Order:** To make an argument, the author discusses the benefits of youth sports. Identify the logical flow of the ideas by outlining the beneficial effects of participating in sports. For example, are the benefits listed in order of importance or in time order from immediate to long term? Do you agree with the order of the details? Why or why not?

4. **Effective Expression:** What are the viewpoint and tone of this essay? Does the author assume an objective viewpoint and tone or a subjective viewpoint and tone? Which words establish this viewpoint and tone? Do you think this viewpoint and tone are effective? Why or why not?

Thinking Prompts to Move from Reading to Writing

1. Assume you are writing about a controversial issue for a college course in sociology. Your professor requires that you find and respond to an article about a current topic of debate in society. Respond to this article by agreeing or disagreeing with the author's central idea. Choose specific points to support or oppose in your response. If appropriate, consider using details from the article "It's Time to Ban High School Football" by Ken Reed.

2. Assume the school board of your county's public school system is proposing to cut funding for high school sports to save money. Write a letter to the chair of the school board opposing this cut to funding high school sports.

Writing an Essay

An essay is a series of closely related ideas.

LEARNING OUTCOMES

After studying this chapter, you should be able to

① Answer the Question "What's the Point of an Essay?"

② Recognize the Parts of an Essay and Their Levels of Information

③ Write an Essay Step by Step

④ Use Effective Titles, Introductions, and Conclusions

All of us of have had some experience studying, writing, or reading essays. What do you already know about essays? Where have you seen essays? What are the traits of an essay?

Perhaps the most common and flexible form of writing, an essay allows powerful personal expression. The essay is used for academic papers, business reports, business letters, newspaper and magazine articles, Web articles, and personal letters, as well as letters to the editor of a newspaper or journal. By mastering the task of writing an essay, you empower your ability to think, to reason, and to communicate.

L① What's the Point of an Essay?

Like a paragraph, an **essay** is a series of closely related ideas that develop and support the writer's point about a topic. In fact, the paragraph serves as a building block for an essay since an essay is composed of two, three, or more paragraphs. Therefore, the skills you developed to write a paragraph will also help you write an effective essay.

Read the following essay, which was written as an article for a college newspaper to inform the local seaside community about the threat of sharks. Study the annotations and complete the activities that are highlighted in **bold** in the annotations. Then, answer the question "What's the point of an essay?"

Practice 1

PHOTOGRAPHIC ORGANIZER: THE ESSAY

Three Types of Sharks and Their Traits of Threat

by Heather Brady

(1) Most beach goers consider the ocean a refuge from the summer heat. (2) However, when a swimmer enters the ocean, she is entering a wild and natural world full of animals that are unfamiliar with humans. (3) Largely due to myth and movies, sharks are among the most feared species that inhabit the ocean. (4) However, a person is more likely to be killed by lightning than by a shark. (5) Experts have reported that out of more than 400 different species of shark only a dozen are dangerous to humans. (6) Of the most dangerous are the tiger shark, the white shark, and the bull shark.

The Title:
The writer sums up the point of her essay in just a few words. **Underline the words that narrow the topic "Sharks."**

The Introduction:
The writer begins with interesting background information to hook the reader's interest and introduce the main idea. **Underline the thesis statement.**

Tiger Shark ▶

▲ White Shark

Bull Shark ▶

(7) The threat these types of sharks pose is largely due to the animals' size, curiosity, and habitat. (8) First, the large size of these sharks prompts them to hunt larger prey. (9) Humans swimming on the ocean surface, splashing and sending out vibrations, may appear similar to other large animals the sharks may hunt. (10) The sharks' large size also means that an attack will cause more serious injury. (11) The teeth structure of the tiger shark, coupled with its size, enables it to kill almost everything it attacks. (12) Secondly, these types of sharks are curious by nature. (13) For example, a white shark will feel an unfamiliar prey with its jaws, tasting it to determine if it is fit for a meal. (14) This is a natural trait of the shark, not an aggressive attack; however these events can be deadly. (15) In addition, the tiger shark has the ability to change its diet to feed on what is available. (16) Thirdly, the environment plays a large part in how sharks encounter and attack swimmers. (17) The bull shark has the ability to live in both the ocean and brackish waters of river estuaries. (18) This animal also prefers the shallow waters closer to the shore, which means contact with a person is more likely. (19) Similarly, tiger sharks live in warm waters making them likely to confront more people. (20) Large white sharks can travel the world's oceans. (21) They live close to shore and swim near the surface looking for prey, which makes them more likely to encounter a surfer or two.

(22) Although there are hundreds of sharks in the oceans, only a small fraction of them pose a threat to people who enjoy the ocean. (23) The threat these top predators pose is not based on a greedy taste for human blood, but is largely due to encounters caused by the increasing number of people who invade the large sharks' natural habitat. (24) These animals are not beasts, but do share aggressive traits that have kept them at the top of the food chain for ages.

What's the point of an essay?

....

....

The Body:
The writer uses one extended paragraph to support the thesis statement. Underline the topic sentence and the three major supporting details. Circle the words that indicate each major support.

The Conclusion:
This essay ends by restating the writer's main idea. Underline the words that restate the essay's thesis.

Practice 1

My First Thought Box: A Prewriting Activity

Set a time limit, such as five minutes, and write without stopping about the essay you just read. Even if you must repeat ideas, keep writing until the time limit is up. Freewriting is a great way to start the writing and learning process.

One Student Writer's Response

It was really helpful to study Heather Brady's essay. I like the way she used the title to let me know what her topic and focus was. Her introduction was really interesting, but I think it could have been a little bit shorter. It was also helpful to see how she used transitions in the body of the essay to point out each major detail. She had a strong conclusion, too. She ended by restating the point about how it's the nature of sharks to be aggressive.

L2 Recognize the Parts of an Essay and Their Levels of Information

An essay has several basic parts: a **title**; a beginning, made up of an **introductory paragraph** that often includes a stated main idea or **thesis statement**; a middle, made up of **body paragraphs**; and an ending, often made up of a **concluding paragraph**. The following chart shows the general format of an essay.

The Title

**Hook the reader's interest.
Use key words or a phrase to
vividly describe your essay.**

The Introduction

An introduction usually consists of a brief paragraph in which you do the following: Introduce the topic. Explain the importance of the topic or give necessary background information about the topic. Hook the reader's interest.

Thesis Statement

State your main idea in a thesis statement—a sentence that contains your topic and your point about the topic.

The Body

The body of an essay is usually made up of a series of longer paragraphs. Most body paragraphs follow a similar pattern. Focus on one aspect of your main idea. State the focus of the paragraph in a topic sentence. Use the topic sentence to state the point you are making in the paragraph and relate the point of the paragraph to your thesis statement. Offer major details that support the topic sentence. If needed, offer minor details that support the major details. Link body paragraphs with clear transitions so your reader can easily follow your thoughts.

The Conclusion

The conclusion restates or sums up the essay's main idea. In longer essays, the conclusion may be a separate paragraph. In shorter essays, the conclusion may be a powerful sentence or two at the end of the last body paragraph.

For more on creating effective titles, introductions, and conclusions, see pages 497–500.

In addition to being made up of several parts, an essay offers several levels of information that range from general to specific. Understanding these levels of information helps a writer create and organize ideas throughout the writing process.

Titles, Introductions, and Conclusions

Titles, introductions, and conclusions introduce and summarize ideas.

Thesis Statements

The thesis statement is a one-sentence summary of the main idea of the essay. All the details in the body paragraphs support the thesis statement. A **thesis statement** shares the same traits of a topic sentence for a paragraph. Just as the topic sentence states the main idea of a paragraph, the thesis sentence states the main idea of the essay. Both statements answer the question "What's the point?" This point is the opinion about the topic that you are explaining and supporting in the essay. In fact, your point further narrows your topic. The writer's point or opinion is generally referred to as the *controlling idea*.

The controlling idea often includes a pattern of organization as well as the writer's opinion. You learned about patterns of organization as you studied how to develop paragraphs in Chapter 20. The following graphic illustrates an effective thesis statement.

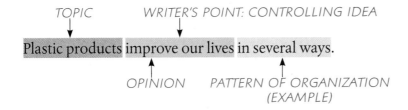

TOPIC   WRITER'S POINT: CONTROLLING IDEA

Plastic products improve our lives in several ways.

OPINION   PATTERN OF ORGANIZATION (EXAMPLE)

Types of Supporting Ideas

Two types of details are often needed to thoroughly explain a main idea: primary and secondary details. **Primary details** directly explain or support the thesis statement. **Secondary details** indirectly support the thesis statement. In an essay, topic sentences of the body paragraphs are the primary supports for the thesis statement. The examples, reasons, and facts within the body of a paragraph support the topic sentence. They serve as secondary details that support the thesis statement.

Levels of Supporting Ideas

Secondary supports can also be divided into two levels: major details and minor details. A **major detail** supports a topic sentence. A **minor detail** supports a major detail. Thus, a topic sentence supports the thesis statement, and secondary supports explain a topic sentence. The following flow chart illustrates these levels of information in an essay. This chart represents a basic three-paragraph essay. This format is often expanded to include two or more body paragraphs.

THE LEVELS OF INFORMATION IN AN ESSAY

Compare this chart to the chart about levels of information in a paragraph on page 313.

Introduction
Explains importance of topic and writer's point.

Offers background information about the topic.

Hooks reader's interest.

Thesis Statement
States the main idea in a complete sentence.

Uses specific, effective wording.

Relates to all the details in the essay.

The Body

Topic Sentence
States the main idea of the paragraph.

Offers one primary support for the thesis statement.

Relates to all the details in the paragraph.

Major Detail
Supports the topic sentence.

Is a secondary support for the thesis statement.

Is more general than a minor detail.

Minor Detail
Supports a major detail.

Is a secondary support for the thesis statement.

Offers the most specific details in the essay.

Conclusion
Reinforces the importance of the writer's overall point.

PHOTOGRAPHIC ORGANIZER: TITLES, INTRODUCTIONS, AND CONCLUSIONS

Study the following pictures of alternative forms of energy. Identify major details to support a point in an essay. Then, write captions that provide a title, an introduction, and a conclusion for the point you want to make.

WRITING
FROM LIFE

Title: ....

**First Alternative
Energy Source:**

What is this?

....

....

....

....

Introduction: ....

....

**Second Alternative
Energy Source:**

What is this?

....

....

....

....

What is the point? ....

....

**Third Alternative
Energy Source:**

What is this?

....

....

....

....

Conclusion: ....

....

**Fourth Alternative
Energy Source:**

What is this?

....

....

....

....

LO 3 Write an Essay Step by Step

To create an effective essay, use the complete writing process. Begin by prewriting; then, move on to drafting, revising, and editing. Writing rarely develops in a neat and orderly process. Some writers need to generate details before they can compose a working thesis statement. Others have to know exactly what their main point is before they can generate details. The following series of workshops encourages you to follow the prewriting steps in a certain order. Feel free to move between steps or to return to any step in the process as needed.

For an overview of the writing process, see pages 288–298 of Chapter 18.

For more on the prewriting stage of the writing process, see 290–302.

Prewriting

During the prewriting stage, you figure out what you want to say, why you want to say it, and to whom you want to say it.

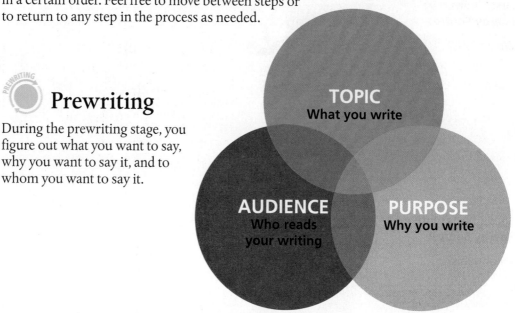

TOPIC
What you write

AUDIENCE
Who reads your writing

PURPOSE
Why you write

Practice 3

WRITING FROM LIFE

WRITING AN ESSAY STEP BY STEP

Select and Narrow Your Topic

Select a topic of your own, or choose one of the following topics. The photographs illustrate a narrowed focus of each topic. You may choose a different focus for any of these topics. Identify your audience and purpose.

- A popular musical artist: Rihanna

- An organization worthy of support: The Salvation Army

- A person who has overcome an obstacle: Bethany Hamilton (lost arm in a shark attack)

A popular musical artist: Rihanna ▶

▲ An organization worthy of support: The Salvation Army

▲ A person who has overcome an obstacle: Bethany Hamilton (lost arm in a shark attack)

Create a Tentative Thesis

Then, draft a tentative thesis statement.

TOPIC:

AUDIENCE:

PURPOSE:

THESIS STATEMENT:

Practice 3

Practice 4

WRITING FROM LIFE

Generate Supporting Details with a Writing Plan

Generate primary and secondary supporting details by listing, or use the concept map to create a writing plan. Use the reporter's questions *who? what? when? where? why?* and *how?* to produce details.

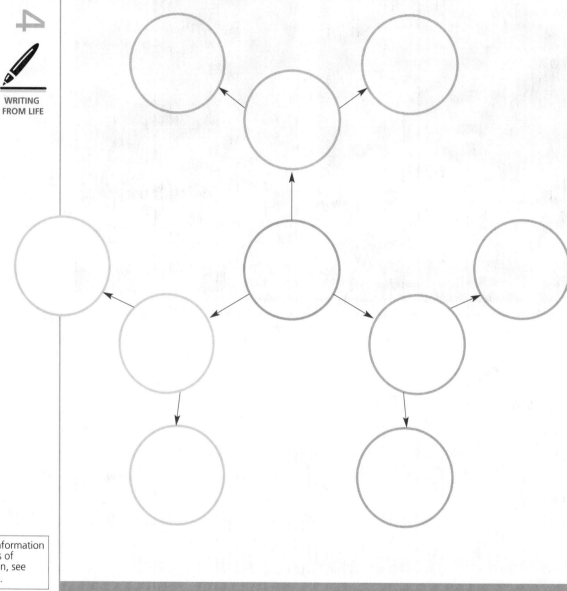

For more information on patterns of organization, see Chapter 20.

Now that you have generated some details to support your tentative thesis, you probably have a clearer sense of your controlling idea. The following thesis statement has been revised to focus the topic by including the writer's opinion and a pattern of organization.

TOPIC   WRITER'S POINT: CONTROLLING IDEA

Conflict in the Middle East remains controversial for several reasons.

OPINION   PATTERN OF ORGANIZATION (CAUSE AND EFFECT)

Revise Your Thesis Statement

Revise your thesis so that it includes the topic, your point about the topic, and, if appropriate, a pattern of organization.

WRITING
FROM LIFE

WRITING AN ESSAY STEP BY STEP

Evaluate Your Details

Use a writing plan to test your details. Complete the following outline with your revised thesis statement and details from your list or concept map. Make sure you have an adequate amount of details to convince your reader of your point. If you do not have the necessary major and minor details to support each topic sentence, brainstorm additional details. Delete details that are not related to your thesis statement or to the topic sentences (the primary supports for your thesis statement).

I. Introduction

REVISED THESIS STATEMENT: ....

....

II. ....

....

    A. ....

    B. ....

III. ....

....

    A. ....

    B. ....

IV. ....

....

    A. ....

    B. ....

V. Conclusion

....

....

Organize Supporting Details: Use Logical Order

In an effective essay, body paragraphs are arranged in a clear, logical order for a coherent flow of ideas. Likewise, effective writers link each paragraph to the next so that readers can follow their chain of thought. As you generate ideas, think about the way you will order them.

You can achieve a coherent flow of ideas in several logical ways.

1. *Follow the order of ideas as presented in the thesis statement.* Often the controlling idea of the thesis statement divides the topic into chunks of information.

2. *Follow space order.* At times, a writer describes how something is arranged in space to develop a main idea. Description moves from top to bottom, side to side, front to back, or the reverse of these.

3. *Follow time order.* A writer may record an event or a process as it unfolds in time.

4. *Present ideas in order of importance.* Often, a writer decides upon and arranges details according to his or her opinion about the importance of the details, known as **climactic order**. Usually, climactic order moves from the least important point in the first body paragraph and builds to the essay's climax, the most important point in the final body paragraph.

Practice 6

WRITING
FROM LIFE

USE LOGICAL ORDER

Study the following prewrite a student created for a college writing assignment. Use the blank outline to order the ideas in the logical order that makes the most sense to you. Explain the type of order you used in a discussion with your class or in a small group.

PREWRITES:

Topic: *Differences between men and women*

Audience: *A group of men and women in a support group for couples*

Purpose: *To discuss reasons based on research*

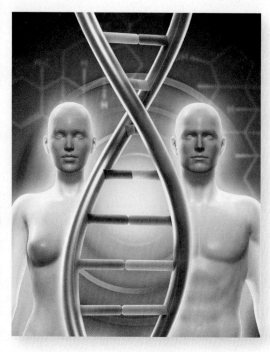

Reason: *Due to biology*

Examples: *Born with certain traits, i.e., aggressive, nurturing*

Reason: *Due to traditional gender roles*

Examples: *Social rules based on gender, i.e., parents, teachers, clergy*

Reason: *Due to sexism*

Examples: *Less social power, i.e., more polite, obedient*

I. THESIS STATEMENT: ....

II. TOPIC SENTENCE: ....

    A. ....

    B. ....

III. TOPIC SENTENCE: ....

    A. ....

    B. ....

IV. TOPIC SENTENCE: ....

    A. ....

    B. ....

Practice 6

Organize Supporting Details: Connect Paragraphs

In addition to ordering paragraphs coherently, writers clearly connect each paragraph to the next so that readers can follow their chain of thought. You can use several options to connect paragraphs to each other. The following chart lists and illustrates each option.

CONNECTING PARAGRAPHS

Echo or repeat important words or phrases from the thesis statement in body paragraphs.

Thesis statement:	*Grief* is a *process* that occurs in *several stages.*
Topic sentences:	The first *stages of grief* are shock and denial.
	The last *stage of grief* is acceptance.

Refer to the main idea of the previous paragraph in the topic sentence of the present paragraph.

Thesis statement:	Apple computers are better than typical personal computers.
Topic sentences:	*Apple computers are more reliable* than personal computers.
	Not only are Apple computers more reliable, they are also easier to use.

Use transitional words, phrases, or sentences.

Thesis sentence:	Two basic types of energy exist, and the sources of energy are classified into two groups.
Topic sentences:	*One type* of energy is kinetic (or active) energy.
	Another type of energy is potential energy.
Transition sentence:	*Kinetic and potential energy* are stored in the energy sources that we use every day. *These sources* are divided into *two groups,* which are *renewable* and *nonrenewable.*

Practice 7

WRITING
FROM LIFE

CONNECTING PARAGRAPHS

Read the following essay. Underline the connections between paragraphs. Circle the key ideas that are repeated throughout the essay. Discuss with your class or in a small group the different types of connections the writer used and evaluate their effectiveness.

Types of Volcanoes

(1) Throughout time, volcanoes have fascinated people because of their power. (2) Volcanoes are vents for hot magma beneath the surface of the earth, and when they erupt, they create new land on earth. (3) Geologists generally group volcanoes into four main types.

Cinder cone volcano

(4) One type is the cinder cone, the simplest type of volcano. (5) These volcanoes are built from bits and blobs of lava ejected from a single vent. (6) As the gas-charged lava is blown violently into the air, it breaks into small parts that fall around the vent to form a

circular or oval cone. (7) Most cinder cones have a bowl-shaped crater at the summit. (8) They rarely rise more than a thousand feet or so above their surroundings.

Lava dome volcano

(9) Another type of volcano is the lava dome. (10) They are formed by somewhat small, round masses of lava too gooey to flow any great distance; as a result, the lava piles over and around its vent. (11) A dome grows largely by spreading out from within. (12) As it grows, its outer surface cools, hardens, shatters, and spills down its sides. (13) Some domes form craggy knobs or spines over the volcanic vent.

Shield volcano

(14) Shield volcanoes, the third type of volcano, are built almost entirely of fluid lava flows. (15) Pouring out in all directions from a central summit vent, or group of vents, its flow builds a broad, flat dome that looks like a warrior's shield. (16) They are built up slowly by thousands of lava flows that spread widely over great distances, and then cool into thin, rolling sheets. (17) Some of the largest volcanoes in the world are shield volcanoes.

Strato volcano

(18) Each type of volcano poses a serious threat to human life when it erupts. (19) However, the strato volcano has caused more causalities than any of the others because it is the most common type of volcano. (20) Strato volcanoes are typically large, steep-sided, symmetrical cones, and they may reach as high as 8,000 feet above their bases. (21) The volcano Vesuvius in Italy has erupted over 13 times and killed thousands of people; in fact, its eruption in AD 79 destroyed the city of Pompeii. (22) More recently, in 1980, the eruption of volcano Mt. Saint Helens killed 57 people. (23) Ultimately, the power of volcanoes makes them worthy of our interest and concern.

Practice 7

For more on the drafting stage of the writing process, see pages 303–305.

 # Write a Draft of Your Essay

Using your writing plan, write a rough draft of the body of your essay. Don't worry about the introduction and conclusion for now. Have a dictionary and thesaurus nearby just in case you get stuck trying to think of a word.

For more on the revising stage of the writing process, see pages 306–307.

 # Revise Your Essay Draft

Reread your essay, and as you revise, mark up your rough draft with the changes you intend to make: (1) cross out irrelevant details and vague, weak, or trite expressions, and write stronger words directly above or near them; (2) draw arrows to show where you want to move information; (3) add more details in the margin and draw a line to indicate where you will put them. The following chart offers you some helpful questions to guide you through your revision.

Questions for Revising an Essay

☐ Does the essay have a clearly stated thesis statement?

☐ Are my topic sentences clearly stated?

☐ Have I provided relevant support?

☐ Is each body paragraph fully developed with major and minor details as needed?

☐ Which ideas need more support?

☐ Is each topic sentence directly related to my thesis statement?

☐ Is each detail in each body paragraph related to its topic sentence?

☐ Have I used logical order?

☐ Have I provided clear connections between paragraphs?

☐ Have I provided clear connections between sentences within paragraphs?

☐ Have I used effective expression?

☐ Do my sentences vary in type and length?

For more information about sentence variety, see pages 370–385, Chapter 21.

For more on the proofreading stage of the writing process, see pages 308–309.

 # Proofreading Your Essay

Proofread to correct spelling and grammar errors. Mark the corrections you need to make directly on the most recent draft of your essay. Create a neat, error-free draft of your essay.

Earlier, you read an essay by Heather Brady about sharks. Take a moment to reread her final draft on pages 494–495. Then, study her revisions of one draft of the essay's introduction and conclusion. Discuss with your class or a small group the reasons for and the effect of each revision.

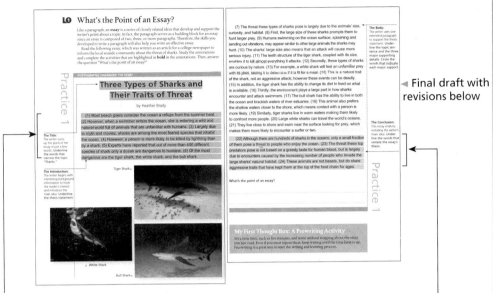

◀ Final draft with revisions below

WRITING FROM LIFE

(1) Most beach goers consider the ocean their playground and a refuge from the summer heat. (2) However, when a swimmer enters the ocean, they are entering a wild and natural world full of animals that are unfamiliar with humans. (3) Largely due to myth and movies, sharks are among the most feared species that inhabit the ocean. (4) However, a person is more likely to be killed by lightning than they are fatally attacked by a shark. (5) Experts have reported that out of more than 400 different species of shark only a dozen are dangerous to humans. (6) Of the most dangerous are the white shark, the tiger shark, and the bull shark.

(22) Although, their are hundreds of sharks in the oceans only a small fraction of them pose a threat to people who enjoy the ocean. (23) The threat these top predators pose is not based on a greedy taste for human blood, but is largely due to encounters caused by the increasing number of people who invade the large sharks' natural habitat. (24) These animals are not beast, but do share aggressive traits that have kept them at the top of the food chain for ages.

L❹ Use Effective Titles, Introductions, and Conclusions

For more on the parts of an essay, see pages 483–485.

Thoughtful titles, introductions, and conclusions enhance an essay.

Effective Titles

An **effective title** fulfills the following purposes:

- It hooks the reader's interest.

- It vividly describes the topic of your essay.

Your title should be brief, and you should not use italics, quotations, or underlining for emphasis. Instead, center the title on the page about an inch above the introductory paragraph. Capitalize the first word and other key words of the title, except for prepositions such as *in, on, for,* and *at* and articles such as *a, an,* and *the*. The following chart illustrates several types of effective titles.

For more on using description, see pages 334–337.

For more on using patterns of organization to develop paragraphs and essays, see. Chapter 20.

TYPES OF TITLES		
The question title: States the main point as a question.	EXAMPLES:	Is Sexism a Problem in America? Is Sexism a Myth in America?
The descriptive title: Uses key words to form the thesis statement.	EXAMPLES:	The Danger of Obesity The Power of Change
The recommendation title: Calls for action.	EXAMPLES:	Cloning Must Be Banned Clone On!
The general-specific title: States the general topic, followed by a controlling point.	EXAMPLES:	Cloning: An Unethical Procedure Cloning: The Scientific Method Working for Progress

Practice 9

USE EFFECTIVE TITLES

Read the following three-paragraph business memo and supply a title in the blank labeled RE (for the topic of the memo).

Memo

To: Maintenance Department

From: Tia Jones, Supervisor of Sales

RE: ....

It has come to our attention that the main sales office is not being properly cleaned. The lack of cleaning services is evident in two areas.

First, our trash and recycling bins are overflowing so that we cannot dispose of any more trash until they are emptied. According to company policy, trash containers are to be emptied on a daily basis. In our area, we are lucky if the trash is emptied on a weekly basis. Second, several overhead lights need new bulbs, and the carpet needs to be vacuumed.

These problems are not in compliance with company policies and detract from a professional appearance. Company rules require that you respond to this written request for service within 24 hours.

Effective Introductions

An effective introduction serves the following purposes:

- It introduces the essay topic.

- It explains the importance of the essay topic.

- It presents the essay's main idea in a thesis statement.

The following chart illustrates several types of introductions. The thesis statement in each introduction is italicized.

For more on thesis statements, see page 484.

For more on using narration to tell an anecdote, see pages 338–341.

TYPES OF INTRODUCTIONS

An interesting illustration or anecdote	EXAMPLE:	When Rachel Frederickson became a contestant on the 15th season of *The Biggest Loser,* she weighed in at 260 pounds. By the end of the season, she had lost 155 pounds. She won the title of Biggest Loser by proving change is possible. *Positive change occurs for three reasons.*
A surprising fact or statement	EXAMPLE:	Nearly two out of three American adults are obese, and nearly 400,000 deaths a year occur because of obesity. *The obesity epidemic is due to several factors.*
A direct quotation	EXAMPLE:	According to a Chinese proverb, "One does not become fat on one mouthful." For most of us, it isn't the type of food we eat that makes us too heavy, it's the volume of food we consume. *Portion control is the key to weight control.*
A definition	EXAMPLE:	The term "obesity" refers to a person's overall body weight and where the extra weight comes from. Obesity is having a high amount of extra body fat. *You can help prevent or treat obesity if you follow three simple steps.*

For more on using definition, see pages 358–361.

USE EFFECTIVE INTRODUCTIONS

Read the following three introductory paragraphs. Underline the thesis statement and identify the type of introduction used in each one. Discuss your answers with your class or in a small group.

a. An interesting illustration or anecdote
b. A surprising statement or fact

c. A direct quotation
d. A definition

.... **1.** The term "civil rights" refers to the personal rights of an individual to have the equal treatment and equal opportunities due a citizen of the United States. Cesar Chavez, a Latino farm worker, led a non-violent struggle for the rights of migrant farm workers.

.... **2.** Roughly 43 million people in the United States are physically or mentally disabled. Often, the civil rights of the disabled are denied, yet a just society must guarantee the civil rights of everyone. A concerned citizen can help the cause of disabled Americans in several ways.

.... **3.** The poet Maya Angelou has reminded us "How important it is for us to recognize and celebrate our heroes and she-roes!" Today, we honor a woman who changed the course of our nation. Rosa Parks, the mother of the Civil Rights Movement, was a brave woman of action.

Practice 10

Effective Conclusions

An **effective conclusion** fulfills the following purposes:

- It brings the essay to an end.

- It restates the essay's main idea and sums up the major points in the essay.

Just remember that a conclusion must stay on point, so don't introduce new information.

The following chart illustrates several types of conclusions.

TYPES OF CONCLUSIONS		
A question	EXAMPLE:	Doesn't everyone want to experience the joy of making a positive change in his or her life?
A call to action	EXAMPLE:	Do not delay! Join the National Organization for Women and fight against sexism in America.
A warning about consequences	EXAMPLE:	Obesity increases the risk of heart disease, cancer, and many other life-threatening conditions. The end result of obesity is death.

Practice 11

USE EFFECTIVE CONCLUSIONS

Read the following three conclusions. Identify the type of conclusion for each selection. Discuss your answers with your class or in a small group.

a. A question

b. A call to action

c. A warning about consequences

_____ **1.** The denial of civil rights sows the seeds of rebellion.

_____ **2.** Migrant farm workers labor to put food on the tables of millions, yet often face an empty cupboard in their own homes. Who would deny these hard workers their basic human rights?

_____ **3.** An offense to one is an offense to all. Each and every one of us should follow the example of Rosa Parks and Cesar Chavez in the fight for civil rights for all.

REVIEW: EFFECTIVE TITLES, INTRODUCTIONS, AND CONCLUSIONS

1. What are the basic parts of an essay? ....

....

2. Identify and define the types of supporting details in an essay. ....

....

3. What are the two levels of secondary details? ....

Complete the chart by filling in the blanks with information from the chapter:

Types of Titles

- The Question Title
- The Descriptive Title
- ....
- The General-Specific Title

Types of Conclusions

- A question
- A warning about consequences

Types of Introductions

- An interesting illustration or anecdote
- ....
- A surprising fact or statement
- ....

- ....

Writing Assignments for an Essay

Plan and illustrate your essay with one or more photographs of your own choosing. Write caption(s) for the photographs(s) that reflect your point(s).

Considering Audience and Purpose

Study the photographs of sharks at the beginning of the appendix. Assume you are the county's Supervisor of Safety for a seaside town. Write a letter to the editor warning the community about the dangers of sharks. Be sure to give your readers advice about what to do if they encounter a shark.

Writing for Everyday Life

Assume you have a remarkable family member or friend who deserves special recognition. Write a letter of tribute to this person.

Writing for College Life

Assume your history professor has handed out study questions for the final exam. A member of your study group has suggested that each member take one question to answer and share in a study session with the group. Write an essay that answers the study question: Which current public figure will be remembered in history? Why?

Writing for Working Life

Assume you are the supervisor of a worker who is up for promotion from a receptionist to an assistant to the manager. Write a report that recommends her for the promotion.

Academic Learning Log:
Appendix Review

PORTFOLIO

REVIEW: WRITING AN ESSAY

1. What are the four parts of an essay?

    a.

    b.

    c.

    d.

2. What are the levels of information in an essay?

    a.

    b.

    c.

    d.

    e.

    f.

3. What are the two types of details in an essay?

    a.

    b.

4. What are the two levels of secondary supports?

    a.

    b.

5. What are the four phases of the writing process for composing an essay?

    a.

    b.

    c.

    d.

6. An effective title fulfills the purpose of

7. An effective introduction fulfills the purpose of

8. An effective conclusion fulfills the purpose of

9. **How will I use what I have learned?**
    In your notebook, discuss how you will apply to your own writing what you have learned about writing an essay. When will you apply this knowledge?

10. **What do I still need to study about writing an essay?**
    In your notebook, describe your ongoing study needs by describing what, when, and how you will continue studying essay writing.

Text Credits

12: Henry, D.J.; Kindersley, Dorling; Brady, Heather, *The Effective Reader/Writer*, 1st Ed. © 2015. Reprinted and Electronically reproduced by permission of Pearson Education, Inc., New York, NY; 115: D.J. Henry and Dorling Kindersley, *Writing For Life: Sentences and Paragraphs*, 3e (Hoboken: Pearson Education, 2017); 173: Steve Jobs: Stanford commencement address, June 12, 2005; 211: Zack O'Malley "Greenburg, Country Fireball: Inside The Rise Of Florida Georgia Line," *Forbes*, January 5, 2015; 217, #1: Braudy, Susan. *New York Times*, Section 2: Arts and Leisure, "He's Woody Allen's Not-So-Silent Partner." 1977 August 21, Page 11 (ProQuest Page 83), New York. (ProQuest); 217

#2: Robert Andrews, Mary Biggs, Michael Seidel, editors, *The Columbia World of Quotations*, 1996., ISBN 0231102984he World of Quotations, 1996, CD published by Columbia University Press, NY; 217 #3: Pauline Kael, *Kiss Kiss Bang Bang* (Boston: Little Brown, 1968); 217 #4: Erica Jong, *How To Save Your Own Life* (New York: Signet, 1978); 217 #5: Poirier, Agnès. "Happy Birthday Brigitte Bardot." *The Guardian*. Monday 21 September 2009 19.05 EDT; 217 #7: J. K. Rowling, Harvard Commencement Address, June 5, 2008; 218 #9: Ayn Rand, *Atlas Shrugged* (New York: Random House, 1957); 319: Michaelle Gilson/Pearson Education, Inc.; 372: The Saint John Tragedy. The Boston Daily Bee, October 9, 1849.

Photo Credits

vi, 2: Rob Marmion/Shutterstock; 3 top: Thomas Perkins/Shutterstock; 3 upper middle: Galina Semenko/Fotolia; 3 lower middle: Iriana Shiyan/Shutterstock; 3 bottom: Andresr/Shutterstock; 20: Pictorial Press/Alamy; 21: Pictorial Press/Alamy; 24: Twentieth Century Fox/Album/SuperStock; 27: Bettmann/Corbis; 30: Clive Rose/Staff/Getty Images; 37: shock/Fotolia; 42, 43: Klaus-Dietmar Gabbert/epa/Corbis; 45: Dennis Mac Donald/Alamy; 57: Paul Warner/Contributor/Getty Images; 60: Deepspacedave/Shutterstock; 61: James Myles/Fotolia; 64: Ed Andrieski/AP Images; 69: Mario Anzuoni /Reuters/Corbis; 73: NASA; 75: Paul Goguen/Bloomberg/Getty Images; 77: Layne Kennedy/Corbis; 79: Rich Carey/Shutterstock; vii, 84: Imaginechina/Corbis; 85: Imaginechina/Corbis; 89: Luchschen/Shutterstock; 92: Andres Rodriguez/Fotolia; 93: Mike Segar/Corbis; xi, 100: JGA/Shutterstock; 101: JGA/Shutterstock; 118: Bikeriderlondon/Shutterstock; 119: Holbox/Shutterstock; 123 left and right: D. J. Henry; 125: Diego Cervo/Fotolia; 127: Italo/Shutterstock; 129: Clive Brunskill/Getty Images; 131: chas53/Fotolia; 134: Blend Images/Shutterstock; 135: Shawn Zhang/Shutterstock; 138: Luminaimages/Shutterstock; 141: Blend Images/Shutterstock; 142: Roy Pedersen/Fotolia; 148: Pixel Embargo/Fotolia; 150: Patricia Hofmeester/Shutterstock; 153: Lisa F. Young/Shutterstock; ix,156: Richard Cummins/Corbis; 157: Bill Varie/Corbis; 159: James Leynse/Corbis; 163 top: Lauren Orr/Shutterstock; 163 bottom: Ken Seet/Corbis; xiii, 166: Andrey Popov/Shutterstock; 167: Auremar/Shutterstock; 173: Peer Grimm/epa/Corbis; 174: Jeffrey Mayer/Contributor/WireImage/Getty Images; 177: Moodboard/Alamy; 178: Liu song/epa/Corbis; 180: Robert Galbraith/Reuters/Corbis; 186: Reprinted by permission of Charles Hannum; 187: Rita Kochmarjova/Shutterstock; 189: Eric Isselée/Shutterstock; 191: Kelly Marken/Shutterstock; 193: Ivan Polushkin/Fotolia; 194: Yan Ke/Shutterstock; 195: Corbis News/Corbis; 200: Richard Cummins/Corbis; 201: Jeff Gynane/Fotolia; 205: Minerva Studio/Shutterstock; 208: Douglas Kirkland/Corbis; 209: Barry Lewis/Corbis; 215: Blondie/King Features Syndicate; 222: Chris Buler/Idaho Statesman/Contributor/Tribune News Service/Getty Images; 228: Alamy; 230: Andrew Holbrooke/Corbis; 233: Belka G/Shutterstock; 236: James R. Martin/Shutterstock; 237: Anonymous/AP Image; 242: Creativa Images/Shutterstock; 244: Paul Whitfield/Dorling Kindersley, Ltd.; 257: Matej Kastelic/Shutterstock; 260: Edhar/Shutterstock; 273: Ace Stock Limited/Alamy; 278: Diego Cervo/Shutterstock; 279 top left: Monkey Business Images/Shutterstock; 279 top right: Andrey Popov/Shutterstock; 279 bottom left: White House Photography; 279 bottom right: Blend Images/Shutterstock; 282 top left: Ammentorp/Shutterstock; 282 top right: Junko Kimura/Getty Images; 282 bottom left: Ramin Talaie/Corbis; 282 bottom right: Brian Weed/Fotolia; 284 left: Monkey Business/Fotolia; 284 right: Andres Rodriguez/Fotolia; 285 left: Monkey Business Images/Shutterstock; 285 right: Saul Loeb/Getty Images; 286 left: Monkey Business/Fotolia; 286 left middle: Andres Rodriguez/Fotolia; 286 right middle: : Monkey Business Images/Shutterstock; 286 right: Saul Loeb/Getty Images; 290: Mike Baldwin/CartoonStock; 292: Monkey Business Images/Shutterstock; 294: Macrovector/Shutterstock; 300: Sandra Manske/Fotolia; 312: Jonathan Wilker/Shutterstock; 314 top: Twin Design/Shutterstock; 314 middle: O Driscoll Imaging/Shutterstock; 314 bottom: Wavebreakmedia/Shutterstock; 316 top: Ollyy/Shutterstock; 316 middle: Blend images/Alamy; 316 bottom: Wavebreakmedia/Shutterstock; 319 top: Ed Quinn/Corbis; 319 middle: AXL/Shutterstock; 319 bottom: Jamie Duplass/Shutterstock; 326 left: Boggy/Fotolia; 326 right: Education Images/UIG/Getty Images; 332: Jezper/Shutterstock; 333 top: Any keen/Shutterstock; 333 upper middle: Woe/Shutterstock; 333 lower middle: Auremar/Shutterstock; 333 bottom: Marekuliasz/Shutterstock; 334 top, middle, bottom: D.J. Henry; 338 top: Jaroslaw Janowski/Fotolia; 338 upper middle: Stefan Schurr/Shutterstock; 338 lower middle: Oksana.perkins/Shutterstock; 338 bottom: D.J. Henry; 342 top: Shebeko/Shutterstock; 342 second from top; martinsl73/Fotolia; 342 upper middle: Joseph C. Salonis/Shutterstock; 342 lower middle: sakura/Ftolia; 342 second from bottom: 3445128471/Shutterstock; 342 bottom: RoJo Images/Shutterstock; 346 top: Oleg Zabielin/

Index